THEOLOGIANS UNDER HITLER

THEOLOGIANS UNDER HITLER

Gerhard Kittel, Paul Althaus and Emanuel Hirsch

Robert P. Ericksen

YALE UNIVERSITY PRESS
NEW HAVEN & LONDON 1985

Filmset in VIP Times by Clavier Phototypesetting and printed in Great Britain at The Bath Press, Avon

Library of Congress Catalog Card Number 84-40731
ISBN 0–300–02926–8
ISBN 0–300–03889–5 (pbk)

Contents

List of Illustrations

List of Abbreviations

CF	*Christliche Freiheit und politische Bindung. Ein Brief an Dr. Stapel und anderes* (Hirsch)
DS	*Deutschlands Schicksal* (Hirsch)
GG	*Die gegenwärtige geistige Lage im Spiegel philosophischer und theologischer Besinnung* (Hirsch)
J	*Die Judenfrage* (Kittel)
KW	*Das kirchliche Wollen der Deutsche Christen* (Hirsch)
MV	*Meine Verteidigung* (Kittel)
OF	*Obrigkeit und Führertum* (Althaus)
PC	*Politisches Christentum. Ein Wort über die Thüringer 'Deutscher Christe'* (Althaus)
SG	*Die Sache mit Gott: Die protestantische Theologie im 20. Jahrhundert* (Heinz Zahrnt)
TG	*Theologische Gewissensethik und politische Wirklichkeit; Das Beispiel Eduard Geismars und Emanuel Hirschs* (Jens Holger Schjørring)
TK	'Die Theologie des Kairos und die gegenwärtige geistige Lage. Offener Brief an Emanuel Hirsch, Göttingen, von Paul Tillich, z Zt. New York', *Theologische Blätter* (Paul Tillich)
TO	*Theologie der Ordnungen* (Althaus)
VC	*Völker vor und nach Christus* (Althaus)
WC	*Das Wesen des Christentums* (Hirsch)

Acknowledgements

I began this study under the gentle and instructive guidance of James Joll at the London School of Economics and Political Science, London University. I am indebted to Professor Joll for his broad knowledge, wise counsel, friendly encouragement and extensive contacts among scholars in England, Germany and America. During preliminary stages I also received helpful advice from Professors Jonathan Wright (Oxford) and Fritz Fischer (Hamburg) and the Reverend R T C Gutteridge (Cambridge). I then contacted a number of people, especially in Germany, who helped me with personal memories and private collections relating to the main protagonists here: Gerhard Kittel, Paul Althaus and Emanuel Hirsch. For example, Pastor Gerhard Althaus graciously discussed his father's career and allowed me to work with the Althaus papers. In addition, he and his family welcomed me into their home for midday meals and stimulating conversation. Professor Herman Preus, Luther Seminary, St Paul, Minncsota, who studied at Tübigen University in the 1930s, generously shared his large file of correspondence with and about Kittel. This provided valuable information concerning Kittel's attempts to exonerate himself and reestablish his career after 1945. Professor Wolfgang Trillhaas, systematic theologian at Göttingen University in the postwar era, gave me insight into his close contact with Hirsch during those years and also access to correspondence between the two. In addition to these individuals, the following German professors of theology shared with me their memories and insights: Hermann Dörries, Götz Harbsmeier, Joachim Jeremias, Hans-Walter Krumwiede, Klaus Scholder and Walther Zimmerli. Finally, in the latter stages of this project I have profited from the advice and encouragement of Professor Eberhard Bethge, Dr Carsten Nicolaisen, Dr Leonore Siegele-Wenschkewitz, and, most of all, Professor John Conway, whose extensive knowledge of the German church and university under Hitler has been a great help to me.

Throughout the course of my research, I depended upon helpful staff and useful collections at several libraries and archives, including the Wiener

Library (then of London), the British Museum, the Göttingen University Library and Archive, the Tübingen University Library and Archive, the Regional Church Archive in Hanover, the Berlin Document Center, the British Library of Political and Economic Science at the London School of Economics, and the personal library of the Reverend R T C Gutteridge. Financial support came to me from the Leverhulme Foundation, the London University Central Travel Fund and the American Council of Learned Societies; moral support from students, colleagues, friends and family.

This book fits into the large category of projects which took longer than anticipated. During these years my wife, Melissa, has given me stimulation, encouragement, advice, three children and an occasional harried glance. I appreciate her patience and that of the children. I can now say about this book what I say about the children: I hoped they would be perfect. If impartial observers conclude they are not, as they no doubt will, I accept full responsibility.

All translations are my own unless otherwise indicated.

CHAPTER I

The Crisis

A. Introduction

IN A century of horrors, Adolf Hitler remains the chief symbol of evil in the twentieth century. As such, it is difficult to understand how the German people could have supported the Nazi Party with their votes or accepted the leadership of Hitler after he assumed power. This difficulty becomes even more acute when the German people are broken down into their constituent groups. Did doctors support Hitler? Did scientists support Hitler? Did university professors support Hitler? Did the clergy support Hitler?

None of these questions can be simply answered, partly because no simple answer will do. Some doctors did support Hitler and some did not. Part of the support was enthusiastic and part was coerced. Some individuals saw Hitler as the lesser of two evils, some as the perfect leader. Another reason why these questions cannot be simply answered is that the research has not been done.[1] The purpose of this study is to pursue two of the above groups. At first glance it might seem that university professors would be too intelligent to endorse Hitler, or that pastors might be too sensitive to spiritual values to give him support. But such was not the case. This study will deal with three men who were intelligent and respectable German university professors. Each was also a Protestant theologian. And each supported Hitler.

These men represent different universities — Tübingen, Erlangen, and Göttingen — and they represent different approaches to theology. Gerhard Kittel was an expert on Judaism, who studied the New Testament in light of its Jewish roots. This specialization took on a new significance, of course, in the Third Reich. Paul Althaus was also a New Testament specialist. His prominence grew out of his role as a Luther scholar and a representative of the German Lutheran tradition. Emanuel Hirsch was a systematic theologian whose goal was broader. He attempted to distill the philosophical heritage of the nineteenth century to produce for the contemporary world a philosophical-theological foundation for society. Each of these men was prominent and internationally respected. None was a Nazi prior to 1933, and none can be relegated to the radical fringe of Nazi fanaticism. However, one fact ties them together: they each supported Hitler openly, enthusiastically, and with little restraint.

Adolf Hitler was the political answer to a very difficult question. To understand his rise to power, it must be appreciated that the German people widely perceived the period of the Weimar Republic to be one of crisis. That was certainly true for the three men in this study. Because the crisis was perceived to be severe, a mood of panic underlay political attitudes, and radical, less than perfect solutions were more readily accepted. The first goal of this study, therefore, will be to describe that crisis. This chapter will outline what has been called the crisis of modernity, with special reference to its acute manifestation in Weimar Germany. And because the three men under study were theologians, it will also consider the impact of the crisis of modernity upon the discipline of Protestant theology.

The crisis of modernity, in which the crisis of Weimar Germany took place, is the result of several identifiable, interwoven, destabilizing elements which have combined to exercize a potent and pervasive impact upon Western society in the past century or so. One of those destabilizing elements is the industrial revolution, with its socio-economic consequences. The modern, industrial, technological world produces a rapidity of change in lifestyle and values which Alvin Toffler has labeled 'future shock.'[2] Change and mobility in occupation and migration to urban areas wreak havoc with family ties and traditional values, to the extent that vice, crime, prostitution and pornography are all rightly associated with the modern city. Pluralism, resulting from the mobility and inter mixture of people of disparate cultures and values, further adds to the breakdown of a shared set of traditional ideals.

A second element in the crisis of modernity is the democratic revolution. Coincidental with the massing of workers in the cities of the Western world, these masses have been given some of the political powers and legal protections of democracy. That can create a frightening prospect for the established classes of society, who no longer hold all of the political strings.[3] And it also gives legal sanction to pluralism. Democratic principle denies the right to impose one set of values or one set of religious beliefs on all citizens. To the extent that this principle is practiced, outsiders in society suddenly have the rights of citizenship and the protection of the state to believe as they choose. And in the midst of this movement towards personal freedom, modern culture has pushed against the barrier of middle-class tastes in its pursuit of artistic freedom of expression. This represents yet another challenge to traditional shared values.

A third element in the crisis of modernity is intellectual. By the turn of the last century, intellectuals in the Western tradition began to realize that reason cannot lead to truth. Since the Renaissance, Western philosophers had attempted to replace the diminishing body of traditional, largely religious truth with a knowledge built upon rationalism. Positivists in the nineteenth century believed that empirical analysis of the real world would produce reliable knowledge. For a brief period the prestige of scientific method was so great that virtually all human thought was pushed into the categories of science. Karl Marx labeled his socialism scientific; even theologians became scientists in their quest for the true message from God. But the search for truth proved elusive. Idealists countered the positivist school with their assertion that empirical knowledge can never rise above the trivial. Values cannot be empirically tested, for example, and yet virtually all of the human sciences ultimately concern themselves with what is good or bad for human society. Max Weber attempted to create an objective, social scientific method of analysis, but he could not eliminate subjective, relativistic premises as his starting point. H. Stuart Hughes argues that this problem of relativism perplexed the entire generation of 1890: Croce, Dilthey, Troeltsch and Durkheim as well as Weber.[4]

One perhaps unavoidable result of the crisis of relativism is the nihilistic view that no values are valid. This view is most widely associated, especially for the German audience, with the name of Friedrich Nietzsche. Searching for a philosophy to live by, Nietzsche went through a nearly endless process of negation. In his book, *Human, All-too-human,* he replaces all metaphysical value systems, whether based on religion, ethics or art, with naturalistic explanations. Human beings are indeed all-too-human. All their behaviour, ideals and modes of thought can ultimately be claimed only to have utility; they have no universal validation beyond themselves. Erich Heller has captured a central point in the title to his book, *The Disinherited Mind*. The lost inheritance of Nietzsche and his disciples was not only traditional Christian culture and values, which Nietzsche rejected altogether, but also any hope of finding a real world beyond the symbolic and relativistic world perceived by our senses. With no ultimate reality by which to judge our values, Nietzsche had to proclaim the death of God.[5] And he thereby captured much of the desperate mood of the generation which followed him.

The impact of Freud and Einstein must also be considered in reckoning the impact of an intellectual crisis in this century. Psychoanalysis recognizes that subconscious, irrational forces dominate human behavior; modern physics proves that even in the supposedly solid physical sciences the body of our truth is based upon ephemeral rather than concrete building blocks. As Werner Heisenberg has written, 'Quantum theory thus provides us with striking illustration of the fact that we can fully understand a connection though we can only speak of it in images and parables.'[6] This is a long way from the optimism of positivists before the intellectual revolution. And just as with the industrial and democratic revolutions, this intellectual change has proven a destabilizing force. As Nietzsche clearly showed, intellectuals now have to recognize an almost infinte number of possible questions and a similar number of possible answers. Certainty does not exist. Any common foundation of values or knowledge can be explained away as prejudice, conditioned by environment or inner, subjective needs.

In order to recognize the full import of the crisis of modernity for the individuals in this study, it is necessary to tie the crisis to Weimar Germany. Most of the elements in this equation are widely recognized. First of all, Germany had experienced a recent and rapid period of industrialization under the political auspices of Bismarck's unification. The subsequent dislocations, which had occurred earlier and at a slower pace in England and America, hit with full force in the Wilhelmine and Weimar periods.[7] Secondly, Germany moved only slowly to the rhythms of democratic principle, and did so fully only under the forced circumstances of a lost war and the Versailles peace. The sudden political ascendance of the Social Democratic Party and a few Jewish politicians, coupled with the legal defense of pluralism implicit in democratic theory, thus produced more than the normal amount of resentment. These elements of democracy have discomfited representatives of the establishment in all democratic nations, but in Germany the discomfort came quickly and could be blamed on outsiders, the Western powers, who forced an inappropriate system on the German people. The humiliation of a lost war, economic chaos and disaster, political and economic uncertainty, and resentment were all part of the mixture of public attitudes in Germany during the Weimar years. Their combination brought the discomforts of future shock to a high level of intensity.[8]

Alongside the sociological impact of modernity, Weimar Germany also experienced a cultural flowering which proved divisive. As noted by Peter Gay, the 1920s witnessed a perhaps unprecedented outpouring of artistic genius in Germany. However, the Nazis later labeled this art degenerate, probably with a good deal of public support.[9] The nature of modernism in the arts is at issue here. Western art has always valued innovation; copying old masters is defined as mere craftsmanship, rather than art. Ever since the Renaissance new artistic schools have experimented with spontaneity and change in their approach to creative expression. The logical culmination is an art in which form and representation give way to total spontaneity. By the 1920s many Germans considered modern art idiocy, and at least some of the artists responded derisively with the coarse satire of the Dada movement. Furthermore, a self-professed political and social statement frequently underlay the artistic expression of dramatists such as Brecht or painters such as Kollwitz. These statements typically endorsed freedom, backed the underprivileged, and attacked tradition, and thus they were resented and feared by traditional society. So the very flowering of genius in the 1920s added to the popular perception of polarization and crisis.[10]

The German intellectual tradition is another important factor in the crisis of Weimar, for it participated more fully in the intellectual crisis of modernity than that of any other nation. German academia in the nineteenth century was perhaps unparalleled. The physics revolution, for example, grew largely on the efforts of Germans. In the crisis of relativism in the social sciences, the work of Weber and Nietzsche stands out as representative of the

German contribution. The German idealist tradition made it difficult for German intellectuals to accept the facile conclusions of empiricism, and the thoroughness of the German tradition allowed scholars to work out the implications of relativism more quickly and completely than in other nations. Even Freud worked within the German language. This was the intellectual environment in which Gerhard Kittel, Paul Althaus and Emanuel Hirsch received their education in the years preceding the First World War.

Finally, the nature of the First World War itself cannot be ignored in describing the intellectual climate of Weimar Germany. Machine guns, mustard gas and trenches helped to destroy whatever belief remained in the progress of mankind. This war was unexpected, not in itself, but in its intensity. It was longer, bloodier, crueler, less human and more insane than anyone had expected. Therefore, intellectual pessimism of the pre-war era was more than substantiated. Technology had somehow gone astray and become hideous. Weapons of destruction gave the lie to material, technological progress. And the concept of rational man was shaken by the unreason of the war, both in its inception and its conduct. Centuries of progress were belied by four years of war. Men had acted like brute animals. For all participants and observers, this was a sobering experience. For the Germans, who also suffered the dislocations and humiliation of losing the war, it was a particularly destabilizing experience. The old world in which they had grown up and developed their basic attitudes towards life, seemed sadly and irretrievably lost.[11] Weimar Germany thus experienced the crisis of modernity in microcosm.

B. The Crisis in Theology

As described above, the former belief of Western society that reason and progress were dependable and beneficial was badly battered in the last century. On the most obvious level, at least at times of crisis, it has become apparent in our century that something has gone wrong with the dream of progress. And on the deepest level, the intellectual crisis has shown that reason rests only upon a leap of faith, whether modern man is aware of his leap or not. Reason can reach no bedrock of certainty on its own. Ultimately, then, the crisis of modernity is a crisis of faith, though in a secular age the word may sound anachronistic. Aspiring for something to believe in, Western man has filled that need in the past with religion, reason and science. But now each of these myths has been broken, or at least bruised, near to submission. And so the modern age is marked by an attempt to cope with this uncertainty, to live meaningfully when the term itself may be naive, to find something to believe in.

This recognition makes an evaluation of modern theology particularly intriguing. How has it responded to the crisis of modernity? Again, Germany is an unusually suitable place to begin the inquiry, for modern theology has been pursued most thoroughly by German Protestant theologians of the past two centuries. This inquiry will also help further to picture the environment in which the careers of Kittel, Althaus and Hirsch must be understood.

The increasing importance of reason and science in the eighteenth and nineteenth centuries was significant for all intellectuals, but for theologians it presented a challenge to their very existence. Voltaire's attacks may have been directed mainly aginst the evils of clericalism, but the implication that the Christian message itself was also unacceptable could hardly be ignored. Reason was contrasted to superstition during the Enlightenment, and theology was often relegated to the latter sphere. In the face of this challenge, modern theology employed the tools of reason to earn its place of intellectual respectability. For more than a century it pursued this rational agenda. Then, when reason collapsed at about the turn of the century, theologians turned from rationalism too. It is interesting to note the parallel. But it is also instructive to view the internal dynamic of theology which corresponded to the phases of rationalism and irrationalism. Such an analysis illustrates that theologians were not just following the winds of change; they had their own good reasons to abandon rationalism. And the deficiencies of reason as they appeared in the academic discipline of theology give insight into the crisis of reason as a whole.

One prominent goal of theologians of the late eighteenth and nineteenth centuries was to isolate the historical Jesus and identify the true nature of Christianity on that basis. The most obvious problem was that of miracles. Could those supernatural events possibly be accepted as true? Could they somehow be explained away? A close reading of the New Testament revealed a plethora of further problems. How could Jesus be accepted as unique when he drew upon a broad spectrum of religious ideas of his day and when the subsequent Christian faith was encrusted with ideas borrowed from the Greeks and others? How could the mild Jesus of the Sermon on the Mount be reconciled to the rigorous Christianity preached by Paul? Was the biblical picture of Jesus accurate? Why do the four gospels tell different stories? The order is different, the content varies, and there is outright contradiction. After the Englightenment, theologians could no longer assume that the biblical and traditional picture of Jesus was unquestionably true. Such an assumption was contrary to reason. The logical response was to search for the truth about Jesus through reason, especially using the tools of historical scholarship. This quest had an additional, important motivation, based on a further obstacle to the enlightened Christian. That obstacle was the obviously flawed history of Christian institutions. Perhaps if the true nature of Jesus' life could be rediscovered, Christianity in a pure and beautiful form could be given back to the world.

Albert Schweitzer has provided a useful summary of the nineteenth-century view of Jesus in his famous study, *The Quest for the Historical Jesus,* first published in 1906. His judgment is hardly neutral, for he was a participant in the fray and judges all other studies by the yardstick of his 'correct' theory of eschatology. Nonetheless, the relevant scholarship is presented as it developed over the years, and a good overview can be obtained.

Late eighteenth-century attitudes towards Jesus can be seen in two fictional works which appeared at that time. Karl Bahrdt rewrote Jesus' life, placing his actions and those of John the Baptist under the influence of the secret Jewish order, the Essenes. In Bahrdt's portrayal this order trained Jesus and John for their roles, with the hope of leading the Jews from temporal concerns toward a higher, religious, rational purpose. The angels who appeared were really Essenes in disguise, and other forms of trickery were derived from the medical and magical skills of this order. Even the death and resurrection of Jesus was a trick planned in advance. Because the Disciples were not aware of the Essene role, the New Testament record distorts the true picture of Jesus' ministry.[11]

The second fictional work, *Non-Supernatural History of the Great Prophet of Nazareth,* by Karl Venturini, presents a similar viewpoint. Venturini also emphsizes the Essenes and their rational-spiritual as opposed to physical-temporal concerns, and he asserts that magic and trickery were not basic to Jesus' message, but only necessary to capture the attention of his audience. Bahrdt and Venturini provided a wealth of ideas which have been borrowed frequently since. Schweitzer notes that Venturini's life of Jesus has been reissued virtually every year in some form, almost always unacknowledged.[12] Recent popular fictional accounts of Jesus, including *The Passover Plot* (1965) by Hugh J Schonfield, seem radical only insofar as Venturini and Bahrdt have been forgotten.

By the start of the nineteenth century, a direction had been set, but the search for the historical Jesus was far from over. Research remained to be done; perhaps most important of all, the question of miracles had to be resolved. Miracles were both obnoxious to post-Newtonian science and deeply set in the fabric of Christian belief. Eighteenth-century theologians had not been ready to let them go, but in the following century Heinrich Paulus set himself to that task.

Schweitzer provides an interesting picture of cause and effect in the life of Paulus. As a boy his father forced him to participate in feigned mystical practices, such as speaking with the dead. In reaction he became a convinced rationalist, resistant even to the allure of romanticism in post-1789 Germany. In a long career at Heidelberg University (1811-51), he developed natural explanations for the miracles of Jesus. Healings were the result of psychology and medicines known only to Jesus. Rising from the dead was really delivery from premature burial preceded by the lance wound as a phlebotomy, with recovery further enhanced by the ointments and the cool tomb. An earthquake moved the stone and allowed Jesus to walk out of the grave.[13]

Paulus' natural explanation of miracles met the requirements of science and its orderly view of the laws of nature, and it managed to retain the basic outline of the gospel narrative of Jesus. But its inordinate reliance on coincidence could not be considered a lasting solution. Evidence of the uneasiness of mid-century theologians can be seen in the work of Karl August von Hase, who taught at Jena from 1830 to 1890. Von Hase draws upon the natural explanations of Paulus in his treatment of miracles, but with less certainty and with some evasion. For example, he notes that the feeding of the five thousand seems incredible, but that the growth of grain every year from a few seeds is also a miracle. Could bread possibly have been increased as well? Perhaps uncomfortable with this line of thought himself, von Hase chose to change the subject, lightening the importance of miracles in his theology.[14]

The uneasiness which men like von Hase felt over the direction of rational theology reached full flower in two of the most radical and significant theologians of the last century, David Friedrich Strauss and Bruno Bauer. Schweitzer introduces the former with the comment, 'In order to understand Strauss one must love him.'[15] The radical disruptiveness of Strauss' work was indeed accompanied by an abrasive personality; it must have been difficult to love Strauss in the flesh. But a willingness to consider his work sympathetically, rather than with the defensiveness of a tottering faith, reveals the inexorable realism of his approach to theology. Strauss concluded that early Christianity was thoroughly distorted by later Greek philosophy. They cannot be mixed, he argued. As with oil and water, 'They separate when you quit shaking.'[16] Strauss' solution to get past the Greek philosophy was to seek the ideas of early Christianity in their pristine form by probing the meaning of the mythology in which those ideas are presented. In his *Life of Jesus* (2 vols., 1835-6). Strauss follows good Thomistic form. He presents the supernatural explanation of the gospel view of Jesus alongside the rational view. Then he destroys each. He concludes by presenting a picture of Jesus based on the three synoptic gospels, Matthew, Mark and Luke, consistently interpreted as mythology. Strauss provoked a flood of criticism in his own day, but elements in his work have proved durable. Mythology has been a focal point in theological controversy since he introduced it, and his unwillingness to reconcile early Christianity and Greek philosophy has been redeveloped with great impact in recent times.[17]

Bruno Bauer (1809-82) bears some similarity to Strauss. He also had a feuding relationship with other theologians in which his increasing bitterness and antagonism helped delay the impact of his work. He too developed a consistent approach to the gospels by which he reached a radical solution. Bauer's approach is literary analysis. His first premise is that the Gospel of John is art rather than eyewitness history. He then suggests that Matthew and Luke, and even their supposed common source, Mark, are also art, though less developed than that of John. Bauer's conclusion is that the Jesus known today was created by the gospel writers. They told a good story serving a specific propagandistic purpose. They had a religious view to express, and they created Jesus as a vehicle by which to express it.[18]

The combined impact of Strauss and Bauer was great, though not fully appreciated for decades. Theologians continued their search for the real Jesus, but in the latter half of the nineteenth century they should have felt a bit of anxiety. Strauss and Bauer had hinted that the real Jesus was forever lost, hidden behind the mystery of myth and the artfulness of literature.

In fact, life-of-Jesus research in the second half of the nineteenth century accomplished relatively little. A typical detour was the search for a psychological understanding of Jesus, the end product of which tended toward a Germanic ideal. Again theologians found in Jesus what they wanted to find; this ideal image became their key to analysis and they judged as unhistorical those elements in the gospels which did not fit. This illustrates what had become a debilitating problem, i.e. the subjective nature of 'keys' to Jesus research. Reason decreed that some elements in the gospels had to be rejected if the message were to be consistent and believable, but faith for the Christian and vocation for the theologian decreed that some parts of the story had to be retained. The means of accepting and rejecting in the nineteenth century were based on sophisticated and complex scholarship. Historical-critical analysis of the biblical documents is a marvel of modern research. But ultimately the choice of a connecting link could never rise above the arbitrary. The conclusions drawn by individual theologians could perhaps be explained as effectively by their own idiosyncrasies as by historical-critical reason.

Schweitzer concludes his analysis by indicating the two remaining alternatives for life-of-Jesus research: 'thoroughgoing scepticism' or 'thoroughgoing eschatology.' William Wrede (1859-1906) published a work in 1901 called, *Das Messiasgeheimnis in den Evangelien*, in which he takes the former position. The authenticity of the life of Jesus could not be proven, so Wrede opts for the idea that Mark created the entire story in order to buttress the developing Christian dogma. Schweitzer is impressed with the candor of this approach. But he naturally prefers the alternative suggested by himself, also in 1901, under the title, *Das Messianitäts- und Leidensgeheimnis*. Here he proposes eschatology as the key to unlock the door to Jesus' life. He argues that Jesus' ideas grew out of the eschatology of the Jewish faith, making his apparently mysterious and cryptic pronouncements on the Kingdom of God understandable to his audience. But his brand of eschatology was out of phase at the time. So when Jesus sent out the Disciples to usher in the Kingdom, they eventually had to return and acknowledge that the Kingdom was not yet in sight. Jesus was thus forced to realize his error, and it was only then that he decided he must take all pain on himself and die a martyr's death. This theory is impressive. Drawing heavily upon Mark and Matthew, Schweitzer accepts most of what they write at face value, though giving natural explanations for the miracles. He has a strong admiration for Jesus and a conviction that we must not remake him into our own image. Thus Jesus emerges as a rather strange figure, preaching repentance and a new Kingdom in a manner and in a world that are both foreign to us. But we must accept him as he was, not as we would like him to be.[19]

The Quest for the Historical Jesus tells an interesting story. Reason boggled at the picture of Jesus presented in the gospels, a picture flawed by contradiction, error and a naive acceptance of miracles. More than a century of careful research was applied to that picture of Jesus. The tools of science were employed by members of what was perhaps the strongest academic community in Europe or the world. Yet Schweitzer concludes that the quest led only to a scepticism in which the author of Mark was believed to have created the Jesus story or an eschatology by which the diverse elements could be reinvested with meaning.

In fact, Schweitzer has given a better illustration of the failure of the scientific search for a historical Jesus than he intended. He noted the failures which ultimately left only two alternatives, but his two alternatives are also inadequate. Wrede's 'thoroughgoing scepticism' was not thoroughgoing enough. For the view that Mark created the story of Jesus is no more convincing than the belief that he reported it at second or third hand. And the eschatological key to Jesus' life, while intriguing, is just another key among many, another arbitrary yardstick by which the elements in the gospels can be measured and then accepted or rejected. The real lesson is indeed one of scepticism. The real, historical Jesus, as Strauss and Bauer imply, is still beyond the ken of rational inquiry. Whether this impasse is absolute or limited depends partly upon the future, upon the discovery of new documents, for example. The Dead Sea Scrolls once gave hope of providing life-of-Jesus research with a fresh start, but that hope now seems to have been misplaced. Even if discoveries much greater than the Dead Sea Scrolls are made, however, the problem will still be complex, for the actual goal of life-of-Jesus research is to discover what Jesus was *really* like. Only a rather complete knowledge can give a rational guide for consideration of his religious significance and meaning. But such knowledge is difficult to obtain even for concrete and well-documented figures, such as Bismarck and Napoleon. Today it is widely accepted that Jesus was a historical person, but such knowledge is insubstantial in itself and hardly a satisfactory result of the search for a historical Jesus. The hope for substantial knowledge seems illusory.[20]

The above story sets the difficulties of rational-scientific theology in sharp relief; but the picture is not yet complete. There is another field, systematic theology, which must be considered. As the historical-critical theologians went out in search of new data, systematic theologians attempted to place the latest and best data into a coherent understanding of theology as a whole.

The former were concerned with a total rational theology by implication, the latter by definition. Therefore, as the problems of a scientific theology and the clash between reason and faith became prominent, systematic theologians were forced to wrestle with them head to head.

The father of modern systematic theology is Friedrich Schleiermacher (1768-1834), a monumental figure who represents uniquely within his person the tensions between faith and reason and the closely related tensions between romanticism and positivism.[21] This comes partly from his early education under the guidance of the Moravian Brethren, which left in him a 'pietistically colored religiosity.'[22] He was also influenced by the romanticism of the Schlegels, especially early in his career, an influence seen in his book of 1799, *Ueber die Religion. Reden an die Gebildeten unter ihren Verächtern.* Here he defends religion by reference to feeling, a feeling of the 'universal' and a religious feeling which, he maintains, all people experience. But the real purpose of the book is to give a rational, and therefore acceptable, foundation to Christianity for educated people. This insistence upon reason *and* faith marks Schleiermacher's career. His rationalism never excluded romantic and pietist insights. This allowed him to approach Christianity as religious feeling and experience rather than as a body of truth; it also corresponded nicely to Kant's dictum that the reality beyond our empirical world is beyond human knowledge.

Schleiermacher replaced this missing body of truth with a content that would engage the empirical efforts of theologians for most of the century, i.e. the historical *experience* of the Christian community. He suggested that a reality could be found in history and culture which, when sifted and tested, would provide a rational framework for Christian faith. Schleiermacher's influence was great. His romantic-pietist elements were not retained, but his signpost toward history was followed by the entire school of rational, liberal theologians. Some studied Christianity in terms of the broad spectrum of religious history, and some sought historical evidence of the real James and the primitive church. But the balance within Schleiermacher's solution was not maintained. Theologians who followed his lead towards historical-rationalism were unable to maintain his respect for religious experience. Some even became atheists. Reason, if carried to its logical conclusion, seemed inimical to faith.

Albrecht Ritschl (1822-89), professor of theology at Göttingen, was the most influential systematic theologian in the second half of the nineteenth century. Whereas Schleiermacher always bore the mark of romanticism, Ritschl was anxious to satisfy the god and religion of his day, positivism. In order to retain for theology a respectable niche within the academic world, Ritschl rejected such terms as 'feeling' and settled upon historical-critical research as the strongest weapon in the theological arsenal. Therefore, his emphasis was on Jesus more than on Christ. Knowledge of this Jesus secured through historical research should form the basis of the Christian message.

Ritschl also denied the importance of objective guilt, an objective Incarnation, etc.[23] That is, he readily gave up those supernatural elements in Christianity which defied reason. A final important element in Ritschl's theology was designed to resolve the Kantian problem of not being able to talk about God. Ritschl replaced 'being judgments' about God with 'value judgments,' so that one does not speak of what God is *to* him but rather what God is *for* him.[24]

Ritschl's impact on theology was such that turn-of-the-century theologians great in their own right, e.g. Adolf von Harnack, are still referred to as Ritschlians.[25] Ritschl developed the basic form of liberal theology, a theology which sought its place of equality in the liberal academic world. But with Ritschl the problems have obviously not vanished entirely. In retrospect it is apparent that he was somewhat too sanguine about the prospects of life-of-Jesus research. And lacking this solid foundation, the other leg of his synthesis, value judgments, becomes much more apparently weak. How and why are they formed? How do Christian value judgments about God differ from non-Christian? Intelligent analysis could quickly reveal this option as an evasion and not a solution. It should also be noted that Ritschl stirred up opposition in conservative theological and church circles. A resolution passed at the 1881 *Landessynode* of Hanover was directed against Ritschl's liberal influence on the Göttingen theological faculty.[26] Theology clearly had a flank to defend in addition to the rational, academic one.

A final representative of liberal theology is Ernst Troeltsch (1865-1923), a man perhaps as famous for his ventures into history and philosophy of history as for his theology. But it is possible to suggest, as an American theologian has done, that this very interest in history makes him the most important spokesman for liberal theology. In a book entitled, *Christian Faith and History: A Critical Comparison of Ernst Troeltsch and Karl Barth,* Thomas W. Ogletree suggests that since history is the basic rational approach to Christian belief, the most important questions are between Barth and Troeltsch.[27]

Troeltsch's approach to theology is almost completely rational. He observes the fact that religious practice is widespread throughout human history. Then he makes the *a priori* assumption that this is due to an inborn religious feeling. Finally, he adds the value judgment that Christianity forms the best foundation for values in Western society and therefore must be maintained. Given this mixed tripod on which to base his work, Troeltsch proceeds to describe a Christianity acceptable to reason. He sees science and history as the two overwhelming realities of modern life and he allies Christian theology to this twin force. The result is a general science of religious phenomena in history in which Christianity is given high marks for certain of its values which Troeltach found admirable. This theology is *almost* inoffensive to reasons. Only the assumptions of an *a priori* religious feeling and the judgment about Western Christian values might be thought subjective. But Troeltsch's rational Western audience shared his cultural environment and prejudices and might not have found his assumptions remarkable. Such ethnocentric assumptions lie deep in the human psyche, a source which natural law and natural theology have long tapped. But they are, nonetheless, extra-rational.

The second problem for Troeltsch is more apparent, the threat to that other flank of theology mentioned above. Can Christianity live with Troeltsch, or is his honesty to reason lethal? Christianity has always claimed a certain uniqueness and a certain authority, based on a unique and authoritative Bible and church. But this becomes untenable, or at least highly vulnerable, in the relativistic sociology and history of religion. With Troeltsch we can finally see that it is these claims to uniqueness which are most obnoxious to reason, for they are beyond reason; and it is also these claims which are most central to the Christian faith.

The work of historical-critical theologians and the work of systematic theologians thus led to the same impasse by the end of the nineteenth century. Both sought to strip away the inessential, supernatural trappings of Christian faith which it had acquired in naive, pre-scientific times. Both expected to find a purified and rational core at the end of their road. To their surprise, the super-rational permeated even the core of Christianity. Did Jesus have a special relationship with God? Does the Christian tradition harbor a unique message from God? None of this can be established by reason, yet Christianity is possibly not recognizable without these elements. The cleft between liberal theology and the man-in-the-pew, therefore, went beyond the obtuseness of the latter. The man-in-the-pew had recognized, perhaps inadvertently, crucial difficulties in an academic theology. Thus, the result of rational theology seemed to be both a loss of its constituency and a loss of its content. Is theology believable if not scientific? Is it valuable if scientific? The dilemma looked to be insoluble.

Given this dilemma, one workable solution would seem to be the abandonment of Christian theology. Decades earlier Ludwig Feuerbach (1804-72) had asserted that Christianity, in company with all other religions, is an attempt to project the best human virtues of strength and goodness onto an anthropomorphic God. Here is a solution susceptible to reason. Here is a solution which does not retreat at moments of danger into the safe arms of mystery. It may well be that this is the only final solution and that seeming paradox will dissolve once it is fully accepted. In that case twentieth-century theology becomes the preserve of pitiful delusionaries attempting to wrest faith from its coffin in the past for comfort in the present. Nonetheless, it must at least be admitted that the delusionaries have made a bold show. Twentieth-century theology is filled with brilliant and imaginative insight. The changed conditions of the twentieth-century intellectual world also make the self-satisfied rationalist a rarer creature. If Christianity cannot be proven true, it also cannot be proven wrong. Theologians today cherish the hope that they have something unique and useful to offer a chastened world.

Twentieth-century Protestant theology responded to the crisis of liberal theology by denying the efficacy of reason. This trend can be recognized by viewing the three most dominant figures in modern theology: Karl Barth (1886-1968), Rudolf Bultmann (1884-1976) and Paul Tillich (1886-1965). It is interesting to note that these men were born within three years of each other, and that each arrived on the theological scene in Germany during the prolific cultural period of the 1920s. The impact of each has come in sequence, with Barth the dominant figure in the twenties and thirties, Bultmann emerging to preeminence after 1945, and Tillich receiving acclaim more recently.[28] Their theology is highly disparate and they did not hesitate to criticize each other. But each is linked by one dominant fact, a rejection of liberal theology with its implied claim that man can discover and describe God. Barth, Bultmann and Tillich each rested on the irrational faith that God reveals himself to man and can only be known on that basis. Each inserted this irrational faith at some point in his system. The arguments between them center around the extent and the location of that irrational insertion. This overview will begin with Barth, the most significant of the three in terms of the timing and the impact of his ideas.

In 1918 Karl Barth published *Letter to the Romans*. In 1921 he published a thoroughly revised second edition of the book, and he began his academic career as a professor of Reformed theology at Göttingen University. These events introduce a revolution in modern theology. To use the term, revolution, is both as questionable and as legitimate as it is in most circumstances of change, i.e. it is a case of judgment and degree. Karl Barth's theology has been given a new name, or several new names (dialectical theology, crisis theology, neo-orthodoxy), to distinguish it from liberal theology. Karl Barth's theology commenced with a comprehensive attack on liberal theology and a rejection of its primary tenets. Modern theology has never been the same since Karl Barth, and that is due at least in part to insights which he first developed. In these ways he is a revolutionary figure. But it remains possible to detect aspects of his theology in nineteenth-century figures, indicating that some evolution is involved; and Barth also had contemporaries charting the same new seas.

Barth's theology begins with a triple rejection of the past. First, he rejects Schleiermacher's idea of religion as a starting point, asserting that Christianity is not one among many religions but a unique relationship with God. To consider Christianity as a religion immediately obscures the truth and presupposes an inadequate language. Secondly, Barth rejects the Jesus of history, or rather the theological concern with discovering that Jesus. Instead, he speaks of Christ as preached by the Christian church. This Christ is the 'living Word' of God, the message which is constantly made known to the faithful through revelation. Finally, Barth rejects Schleiermacher and

Ritschl's implication that secular man can approach the truth of the Christian faith in academic terms. Christianity can be fully understood only through faith. In this way Barth rejects the entire rational approach to theology as false and misleading. It is reductionist and it is relativist, not through any weakness of Christianity, but because reason alone provides a totally inadequate means of approaching the Christian faith.

This triple rejection of Barth's can be distilled to reveal a single discovery or assertion, that of the gap between God and man. This gap is absolute and unbridgable. Therefore, man cannot speak of God nor understand him. Man's reason and man's academic presumptions do not suffice. Religions are false, anthropological attempts to bridge the gap, and therefore not in the same category as Christianity. Christianity is acceptance of the fact that God has bridged the gap by sending the 'living word,' Christ. These few statements summarize Barth's theological position in the 1920s and also shed light on the terms used to describe that theology. 'Crisis theology' refers to the crisis precipitated by man's separation from God. Therefore, it denotes an existential, spiritual crisis and not the cultural or political crisis of the time.[29] 'Dialectical theology' refers to the dialectic formed by the gap between God and man.[30] It revels in antitheses, the absolute 'no' to man's hopes of reaching God versus the absolute 'yes' of God coming to man in Christ, the absolute divinity of God versus the absolute humanity of man, etc. As a method of speaking about God it asserts paradox, e.g. God is infinitely far removed from man and at the same time infinitely close. Since human logic falls entirely short, such paradox is the only way man can come closer to the truth about God. 'Neo-orthodoxy' signifies a basic retention of Christian dogma relative to the reductionism of the liberal school, but it is a 'new' orthodoxy in that it accepts the results of historical-critical research. Barth does not deny historical-criticism, but denies only that it can provide the crucial answers over and above the answers of faith and revelation.[31]

It is not entirely safe to speak of Barth's theology as if it is a unified whole. Two phases can be noted in his work, a destructive one dominated by his polemical attack on liberal theology, and a constructive one marked by his monumental, eight-thousand-page systematic theology, *Church Dogmatics*. In the first phase he is hard, sarcastic, and emphasizes the 'no' of God's separation from man; by the second he has mellowed somewhat, writes with greater humor, and concentrates upon the 'yes' of God's absolute grace.[32] In his dogmatics there is also the need to explain ideas he has only asserted before, which forces a more consistent wrestling with concepts in terms of reason. Barth even largely replaces the dialectical method with a method of analogy as his favourite means of speaking about God.[33]

But there remains a basic consistency in Barth's response to the problems of rationalism. His brilliance lies in seizing the difficulties and turning them around. If the study of religion leads to relativism, reject it. If the study of Jesus leads to scepticism, reject it. He claims the right to make these rejections in the faith that God does speak to man, and that is how man finds truth. The Bible, though its limitations are apparent, is God's word. It can be treated rationally by man, but its substance cannot be challenged. When people read the Bible, the mystery of revelation occurs again; when Christians preach the word, God speaks through them.[34] This is the central miracle for Barth, and it has the advantage of making him virtually unassailable. If there is a God, a fact which can only be accepted on faith; and if this is the way he has chosen to make himself known, another fact which can only be accepted by faith; then Barth is right and he has brilliantly rescued the Christian message from the well-meaning but awkward hands of reason. Barth isolates the problems of liberal theology, rewrites the ground rules, and sets out again. If one accepts his new ground rules, the result is beautifully and rationally coherent. But the ground rules *are* irrational.

It is natural that Barth's irrational premises would produce irrational, extreme implications. As an example, Barth's opinion of humanism was revealed in a lecture he gave at a conference on humanism in Geneva in 1949. He opened his remarks by acknowledging that his opinion might be embarrassing because of the totality of his view. He explained that Christian humanism is based on the Incarnation in which God became human in Jesus Christ. From that starting point he outlined the following sequence: 1. Man is created by God. 2. Man has a relationship to other men and is a human among humans. 3. Man wants to be God and thereby breaks the beautiful picture. 4. But through Jesus Christ a new complete human being is possible.[35] This is not the stuff of academic give-and-take. Barth told delegates to this world conference on humanism that only Christianity offers true humanism.

Barth's view of history is also radical. In order to refute the authority of life-of-Jesus research but maintain the fact that Jesus really lived, Barth resorts to mathematical imagery. For example, he says that God through Jesus did not act within history but intersected history at a unidimensional point not subject to normal historical treatment.[36] Having thus challenged reason, he further requires that all secular history be seen in Christological terms, for all of man's history is permeated by God's relationship to man. To treat history in any other way represents human pride, man trying to place himself on God's level.[37]

As revolutionary as Barth's ideas may seem, they do draw upon nineteenth-century sources. First of all, the Christological emphasis can even be traced back to Schleiermacher, at least in his preference for the term 'Christ' in place of 'Jesus.'[38] Martin Kähler (1835-1912) and Wilhelm Herrmann (1846-1922) carry Christocentrism much further. Though remaining within the liberal tradition, they recognize contradictions within life-of-Jesus research and respond by substituting the spiritual Christ for the historical Jesus in a thoroughgoing manner. In 1892 Herrmann wrote:

We . . . know our faith created not through a fact that could be historically proved. Of course that would be meaningless. We owe our faith to a fact that each of us experiences for himself in a particular way from the same tradition.[38]

Kähler's views are evident in the title of his major work, *The So-called Historical Jesus and the Historic, Biblical Christ*. He believes that 'the real Christ is the preached Christ.'[40] The implications of this Christocentrism are a denial of nineteenth-century rational theology, but it remained for Barth to say so. And he did that in comprehensive and coherent terms. The line of transmission of these ideas to twentieth-century theology is clear, for Herrmann was the teacher of both Barth and Bultmann, and Kähler was the teacher of Paul Tillich.[41]

A second nineteenth-century influence on Barth was the Dane whose impact has been widely felt in existentialism of the twentieth century, Søren Kierkegaard (1813-55). Kierkegaard's life task was to show that Christianity was irrational. He believed God was too far removed from man to make him approachable through mere human reason. That would not allow faith. An impressive illustration of the irrational character of faith is found in Kierkegaard's treatment of the sacrifice of Isaac in his book, *Fear and Trembling*.[42] According to all human reason, the act of Abraham of sacrificing his only son was insane. Isaac's birth had been long awaited, Abraham was old, and progeny was Abraham's greatest concern. But he heard the voice of God and acted in the insanity of faith; and then Isaac was spared. Christian faith does not often require the sort of sacrifice requested of Abraham, but in every case it is just as insane. For in every case it rests solely upon God speaking truth to the believer; the certainty of that message is in no way subject to rational analysis.

Kierkegaard's ideas were picked up by Franz Overbeck (1837-1905) and passed on to Barth to form his concept of the gap, or the 'infinite qualitative distinction,' between man and God.[43] This 'infinite qualitative distinction' is the root of Barth's irrationalism. Herein lies his radicalism, his rejection of secular, academic theology and his rejection of any modes of historical thought not based on Christocentric faith. Each of these is vanity; each tries to place man on God's level.

The difficulty which plagues the theology of Kierkegaard as well as that of Barth is that of distinguishing the insane from the believers, i.e. the problem of subjectivity. One example, not quite in the realm of insanity, will serve as illustration. Barth always felt that a political stance is incumbent for every Christian, and in the course of time he counseled opposition to Nazi Germany but advised cautious cooperation with communism in Eastern Europe. This seeming contradiction became noticeable in 1948 when Barth toured Hungary. Emil Brunner, a Swiss similar to Barth theologically but more conservative politically, attacked Barth in an open letter and asked for consistency in Barth's political activism against totalitarian states. Barth's rebuttal is convincing. First, he emphasizes that Hitler had been a tempting figure to Christians and therefore a threat to pervert Christianity. No Christians were in danger of being seduced by the Soviet Union, so the necessary negative reaction would take care of itself.[44] Barth further responds with a lucid description of the Cold War as a power struggle between America and the Soviet Union, an analysis which, written in 1949, anticipated much of the insight of recent revisionist history on the Cold War. Barth also suggests that the West is on thin ice complaining of the political injustice of the Soviet Union before it begins to handle economic justice more effectively within its own borders. He concludes that the issues between East and West are not clearcut, but that they are clearly political more than spiritual. Therefore, the church should work against open conflict, but should not work for either side.[45] This argument is incisive and reveals the scope of Barth's intelligence; but it is not decisive without the faith that Barth's interpretation of God's will is correct and Brunner's is not. Ultimate acceptance of Barth or Brunner is subjective.

Barth shares this weakness of subjectivity with many notable figures, including Martin Luther, who fully expected that his clear exposition of Scripture would correct error and yield a purified and still unified faith. Somehow God's will and message to man does not result in such uniformity. But Barth offsets this weakness with the great strength of having boldly challenged liberal theology. He changed the subject away from arguments about the existence of God and historical accuracy of the Christian message toward a consideration of the meaning of Christ's message for Christians today. Barth had the genius, and the cheek, to ignore two centuries of rational theology and return to the question of what God's message really is. Most twentieth-century theologians have followed his lead in that direction.

Rudolf Bultmann emerged as a dialectical theologian in the 1920s, fighting battles alongside Karl Barth. He recognizes the deficiencies of liberal theology and calls upon the separateness of God and uniqueness of Christian revelation to overcome them. He adds a specifically Lutheran touch to this irrational theology with his thoroughgoing *Rechtfertigungslehre*, i.e. the teaching of justification by faith alone. But to a greater extent than Barth, he retains respect for the tools of liberal, rational scholarship and a conviction that theology must correspond to the best of human reason rather than contradict it. In fact, Bultmann helped to pioneer a specific type of biblical analysis, the form-critical or form-historical *(formgeschichtlich)* method. And he borrowed a specific philosophical system, the existentialism of Martin Heidegger, to provide the foundation for his theology.[46] Barth and his followers accuse Bultmann of being liberal and anthropological, the two strongest epithets in their vocabulary. But there is no doubt that he is playing a variation on the Barthian melody.

Bultmann's systematic theology develops from his interpretation of the New Testament. His goal is to make the New Testament speak a language in which modern man can perceive the message of Christ, a language not obscured by the confusing myths and concepts of a former age. Bultmann takes seriously the famous passage in Paul that this message of Christ will be a 'stumbling block to Jews and folly to Gentiles.'[47] But he seeks to remove 'false stumbling blocks,' those rooted in the human limitations of the biblical sources and the encrustations of legend and myth, so that the real stumbling block of Christ's call to irrational faith can be clearly recognized. The method he employs is form-criticism, a technique of viewing the gospels in terms of units of oral tradition. These units can be identified and classified according to their form, e.g. isolated sayings, parables, etc. This classification allows an evaluation of the credibility of the units in terms of the 'place of life' in which they are found.[48] Bultmann denies that anything consequential concerning the life of Jesus can be learned by this or any other method, but he asserts that form-criticism allows a demythologization of the Bible through which an accurate picture of the preached Christ can be traced.

Bultmann brings two further presuppositions to the task of New Testament interpretation. One is that the 'justification doctrine' of Luther, the emphasis that man is justified by faith in Christ alone, is the crucial, central message of the Bible.[49] This determines Bultmann's Christocentrism and his assertion that the crucificion and resurrection, the foundation stones for justification through Christ, are the crucial historical and spiritual events around which the Bible revolves. The rest of Scripture must be understood in this light, and it can readily be demythologized with no harm — on the contrary, with clarification — to the central message.[50]

Bultmann's second presupposition is that the existential philosophy of Martin Heidegger creates a fortuitous, modern, secular, philosophical basis for the understanding of justification doctrine as found in Luther and in the New Testament. Heidegger describes the existential situation in which man chooses between authentic and inauthentic existence. Bultmann merely inserts Christian terms. Man's existential dilemma is separation from God, which can also be experienced as separation from other men, from the world and, finally, from himself. Man wants to know who he really is. He wants to discover his authenticity. But if he tries to do this on his own, if he tries to find God through religion or bridge the gulf of separation through science, sociology or introspection, he fails; and this is interpreted as inauthentic existence. Only when man comes up against Christ and responds in faith to the radical and irrational demand to follow him does he experience authentic existence, i.e. justification. He cannot earn it through good works, he cannot wrest the secret from God through reason; but if he waits in patience, God will reveal his authenticity to him.[51]

Heidegger's concept of history is also incorporated by Bultmann. In opposition to the positivist hope of assembling facts to create an accurate picture of the past, Heidegger maintains that the past is better understood if one tries to consider it as a possible mode of existence. The verb *begreifen* (to

understand) is replaced by *ergreifen* (to grasp); one must be seized by the past and
pulled into it. Bultmann could readily accept that the positivist approach of
assembling facts about Jesus' life is unsatisfactory, as well as the corollary that to
be seized by the reality of Christ as he appears in the historical moment is the
proper Christian mode of historical understanding. 'Historicity' replaces 'history' in his thought.[52] History is not known, it is experienced.

The chief concern of Bultmann throughout his career was intellectual
honesty. Dietrich Bonhoeffer wrote in 1942,

> Bultmann let the cat out of the bag . . . He ventured to say what many
> repress (I include myself), even though he did not vanquish the problem.
> But he provided a service to intellectual neatness and honesty.[53]

Through demythologization, row upon row of mythical and supernatural
concepts are dismissed as 'disposed of' or 'not understandable.'[54] But even in
the rational tools Bultmann chooses, there is a hint of the irrational lying not
far beneath the surface. Form-criticism is intriguing, but hardly different in
kind from those 'keys' to the Bible of which Schweitzer *almost* despaired.
This is witnessed by the strong role *Rechtfertigungslehre* and existential
philosophy play in the results of Bultmann's form-criticism. And existential
philosophy, the second pillar in Bultmann's rationalism, at least flirts with
the irrational. It can be argued that existentialism is impervious to rational
explanation and must be experienced to be understood at all. The final leg in
Bultmann's rationalism, honesty to history, is really honesty to a particular
view of historical moment. This history makes no claim to being verifiable.
Bultmann maintains that the Jesus event occurred, but he says this in faith
and judges historical scholarship irrelevant to the question. Even his pupils
have seized upon lack of historicity as Bultmann's weakest point. As Jürgen
Moltmann has noted, 'one is not only historical, one has also a history!'[55]
This leaves only justification doctrine in Bultmann's arsenal, and that is
admittedly an item of faith rather than reason.

It is ironic that in relation to Barth, Bultmann made a more rigorous use of
reason and the tools of reason only to reject reason more completely in the
end. Barth rejected reason quickly and antiseptically, allowing him to devote
all his energies to an interpretation of the Christian message from within the
faith. But the pull of reason is subtle and cannot be easily separated from
faith in the real world. So Barth gradually began to wrestle with some of the
rational enigmas in his dogmatics on more rational terms. Bultmann began
his work with a determination to be honest with his intellect. But, as is not
uncommon in the twentieth century, intellectual honesty led him to despair
of objective reason.

Neo-orthodox theologians criticize Bultmann for employing a man-made
philosophy in this theology and for casually dismissing elements of traditional dogma as unnecessary myth. This is significant in so far as it points to

the central question, which Bultmann illustrates quite clearly; how far can a theologian carry the protection of reason before abandoning it for his leap of faith. Regin Prenter notes that Bultmann's demythologization is selective, for he removes 'unnecessary' myth but retains a central myth about God in Christ.[56] That is a rational imbroglio. Roy A. Harrisville takes even better aim at the rational-irrational borderline with his analysis of the transition from inauthentic to authentic existence in Bultmann's theology.[57] Harrisville asserts that so much continuity is maintained in this transition that the uniqueness of Christian authenticity is lost. It cannot be distinguished from the authenticity envisioned by Heidegger. Bultmann admits that authentic faith is *intelligible* to secular man as an option; then he says man cannot seize this option on his own but must receive it through grace. Harrisville worries that this qualifying clause is not sufficient. If reason can discern the content of authentic faith, why can it not grasp that faith? Feuerbach might have been right in saying all of Christianity is a self-sufficient rational construct. Bultmann would reply that he does believe in a discontinuity, that the existential choice of faith is ultimately a gift from God. But he cannot demonstrate the discontinuity which he affirms.

A group of Bultmann's pupils are concerned that he cannot demonstrate the historicity of Jesus which he asserts is real. In a book on the historical Jesus, Bultmann writes, 'I am of the opinion we can learn virtually nothing more about the life and personality of Jesus.'[58] Led by Ernst Käsemann, a new life-of-Jesus research has developed in the past thirty-five years based on the assumption that Christianity and the Bible are meaningless if the historical transition from Jesus to Christ cannot be maintained.[59] This new direction will no doubt reduce the tension found in Bultmann's irrational faith; but there seems little hope it can avoid those tensions which occasioned Bultmann's faith.

Paul Tillich, the third great Weimar theologian, had a career which diverged both geographically and theologically from that of Barth and Bultmann. The geographic division came in 1933 as Tillich became one of the first German professors to lose his position. His ties to religious socialism and his sympathy for the Jews made him unacceptable to the Third Reich; but he received an invitation from Reinhold Niebuhr, a leading American theologian, to come to Union Theological Seminary in New York. He continued to teach at American universities, including Columbia, Harvard and Chicago, until his death in 1965.[60] In contrast, Bultmann retained his professorship at Marburg throughout the period of the Third Reich. Barth was forced out of Germany in 1935; but he crossed just one border, accepting a position at Basel. The theological difference between these men is a result of Tillich's closer ties to liberalism. To an even greater extent than Bultmann, he is unwilling to throw out reason. Along with Bultmann he believes that a human philosophical system can be employed in theology. And, contrary to the trend in this century, he does not reject religion out of hand. Tillich has the distinction of being thought liberal by the neo-orthodox and neo-orthodox by liberals. But in the crucial questions between faith and reason, he always sides with faith, placing him ultimately alongside Barth rather than opposed to him.[61]

Tillich begins with the faith that Christianity harbors significant truth. But he assumes that this truth must be reinterpreted by theologians to make it intelligible for modern man. His method is to pose existential questions, i.e. questions developed from the actual concerns of man in his present existence, and then to apply the answers of faith to these specific questions. Tillich's brilliance lies in the understanding he had of the existential questions of this age. He lived and thought through a volatile period of history. The result is that Tillich saw revolutionary change as the crucial fact of our era. This first became apparent to him in his duties as a chaplain in the First World War, as indicated by this memory of Verdun:

> As I awoke, I said to myself: 'That is the end of the idealistic side of my thought!' In that hour I grasped that idealism was broken.[62]

The Second World War added to his sense of crisis, which was further confirmed by his knowledge and interest in modern culture, e.g. psychoanalysis, art, literature and existentialism.

Tillich recognizes that this crisis is ultimately a crisis over the meaning of life, the 'question about the sense and essence of all historical reality whatsoever.'[63] Modern man has learned to doubt. His need is to retain his sense of 'being,' but that sense of being is constantly threatened by 'non-being' in three ways: 1. ontologically, the anxiety of non-being as seen in fear of death; 2. morally, the anxiety towards guilt and punishment; and 3. spiritually, anxiety over the senselessness and emptiness of life. Tillich associates the first of these fears primarily with antiquity, the second with the late Middle Ages, and the third with the present age.[64] Meaninglessness and the threat of non-being is man's problem today and God, understood as the 'Ground of all Being,' 'Being itself' or the 'Power of Being,' is the solution. Because God is the power and essence of being, he can provide man's escape from non-being.

This 'being' terminology forms the philosophical base for Tillich's theology; it is also significant as an attempt to rise above the subject-object or faith-reason dilemma in speaking about God. God is the ground of being but not *a* being, and therefore not understood in terms of being. By this usage Tillich intends to place the question of God beyond the scope of human logic. He also says that the word 'God' and every statement about God is symbolic, which is not to say that these statements are untrue, but that they are meaningful even though not accessible to exact, rational inquiry. It is worth noting that this explanation parallels almost exactly Heisenberg's observations on the terminology of modern physics quoted above (p.3).

In 1936 Tillich wrote a brief autobiography to introduce himself to his American audience. The title of this book, *On the Boundary,* provides a key to his life's work. Tillich roams the border areas between conflicting regions, e.g. philosophy and religion, Christianity and socialism, and attempts to mediate between them. In direct contradiction to Barth, who emphasizes the gap between God and the world, Tillich's goal is to close that gap.[66] The resulting mediation has been particularly useful in providing a critique of Christianity and suggesting directions which it should take. For example, Tillich leaped over the mutual animosity and distrust between Christianity and socialism and became one of the leading religious socialists in the 1920s. Two elements in his theology allowed him to do this. First, from Protestantism he picked up the idea of the priesthood of all believers, i.e. the idea that the profane can have holy qualities. He concluded that everything in the world is potentially holy. Secondly, Tillich asserted that the core of Protestantism, the 'Protestant Principle,' is the prophetic protest against considering any finite thing infinite.[67] A movement such as socialism, though profane, is potentially a better 'bearer of grace' through its inherent religious potential than the churches are in their tendency toward selfimportance.[68] The same logic applies to ecumenical and Christian-Communist dialogue today. At any given time Christians might be less in harmony with Christ's will for humanity than non-Christians; therefore, dialogue is not only possible but highly desirable.[69] Finally, Tillich's evaluation of religion rules out the exclusivism which Christianity in general and Barthian theology in particular maintain. Tillich writes that religion is 'the name for the reception of revelation.'[70] The revelation of God is the objective material of theology, but the reception of this revelation is always subjective. Some religions receive the revelation much better than others, perhaps; but pure truth is never known because the revelation of God is always colored somewhat by the religion which receives it.[71]

The critique of Tillich has taken several forms. It is possible, for example, that Tillich was wrong in his interpretation of the existential crisis of the twentieth century. Bonhoeffer, in one of his early letters from prison, writes of Tillich, 'He sought to understand the world better than it understood itself, but it felt entirely *mis*understood and rejected the imputation.'[72] Bonhoeffer criticizes not only Tillich, but existential philosophy and psychoanalysis as well, for trying to tell strong and healthy people that they are really sick. This leads to a Christianity or philosophy which seeks 'to attack and overcome a few unfortunates in their weakest moment.'[73] A second danger threatening Tillich is that his concern to bring God into the world and make him understandable through new symbols might lead to a generalized pantheism instead of a specific Christianity. In one of his sermons he writes:

The name of this infinite and inexhaustable depth and ground of all being is *God*. That depth is what the word *God* means, And if that word has not much meaning for you, translate it, and speak of the depths of your life, of the source of your being, of your ultimate concern, of what you take seriously without any reservation.[74]

Tillich speaks here of experience which men can recognize, but is he speaking about the Christian God?

A final danger is that faced by any systematic philosophy. Tillich made a bold attempt to build a coherent system which contains both his ontology of being and his theology of Christian faith. He has sometimes been criticized for remaining in the nineteenth century, and possibly his attempt to build such a system is one basis for that view.[75] The twentieth century has been unkind to such projects. But the content of Tillich's system, particularly his openness to change within the church and within theology, has led to the judgment by some that he was ahead of his time.[76] It is at least possible that a man who has been relegated both to the past and to the future may lay claim to have drawn upon the best of both worlds. In terms of the tension between reason and faith, Tillich balanced an intelligent reliance upon reason in the formation of his questions with the faith that the Christian answer to those questions is the answer of God. But the ultimate foundation to that stance is the irrational one of faith.

The connecting link between the broader intellectual crisis of the twentieth century and the circumstances of modern theology is that both secular and religious intellectuals in this age must ultimately rely upon an existential leap of faith. This was the fate of Croce, Durkheim and Weber as well as Barth, Bultmann and Tillich. In terms of value judgments, the problem with existentialism is that it is morally neutral. A leap of faith towards Hitler is no less valid than a leap of faith away from him. The relevance of this problem is illustrated by a glance at several additional theologians in Weimar Germany.

Dietrich Bonhoeffer (1906-45) is widely known for his participation in the plot to kill Hitler and his subsequent martyrdom in 1945. He was a theologian, but his participation in the church struggle during the Nazi years led him deeply into the political conflict.[77] Kittel, Althaus and Hirsch, as has already been mentioned, were theologians who took the opposite political stance and worked in support of Hitler. Is it possible to explain their differing stances on the basis of their intellectual position, i.e. their theology? If so, Bonhoeffer's intellectual position would be powerfully validated. However, that sort of validation does not seem possible.

Bonhoeffer was a dialectical theologian, much in the tradition of Barth. His goal was not to establish truth through some human, philosophical system, but to interpret and proclaim Scripture, always with the *a priori* assumption that it is the word of God. For example, in Christological lectures delivered in 1933, Bonhoeffer proclaimed the 'who' of Christ and denied that the 'how' and 'where' could even be considered.[78] In his uncompleted

Ethics, his last major project, Bonhoeffer's presumption of faith is just as great. He maintains that no ethical questions are really complex, for each is answered simply by listening for direction from Christ.[79] This is the same irrational assumption recognized by Kierkegaard as the crux of faith, the belief that God really does speak to man and can be understood. Unless God is capricious, however, it would seem that all Christians would ensorse similar values, and in Nazi Germany that clearly did not happen.

Some conclude from Barth and Bonhoeffer's example, that Christians who were dialectical and Christocentric in their emphasis were protected from the temptations of National Socialism. Christocentrism implies a unique set of timeless values, and dialecticism, the recognition of a gap between God and man, precludes thinking of any earthly political system as hallowed by God. Kittel, Althaus and Hirsch did, in fact, tend to see God's hand in the elevation of Hitler to power. And they also reinterpreted some Christian values to fit their contemporary need. However, the problems of this line of thought are great. First of all, some dialectical theologians, most notably Friedrich Gogarten, endorsed Hitler when he came to power.[80] Secondly, some theologians who opposed Hitler, including Tillich and the whole group of religious socialists, tended to agree with the position of Hirsch and Althaus that certain historical moments and political systems are more acceptable to God than others. And that message undeniably permeates the Old Testament as well. So the dialectical position that all human life is absolutely profane is controversial at best. Finally, the pro-Nazi theologians described here always carefully defended their Christocentric concern and their respect for the true Christian values.[81] The difference lies in emphasis and definition.

Several other clues to a 'Hitler-proof' theology might be noted. Karl Barth was a Reformed Protestant, and some see in the political activism of that Calvinist tradition a better protection against political totalitarianism than the teaching of Luther about the two kingdoms. Luther's separation of the kingdom of God and kingdom of this world may have reduced concern for the latter. However, many of the strongest opponents of Hitler were Lutherans, including both Bonhoeffer and Martin Niemöller. Another attractive conclusion is that theologians who stressed gospel, love and grace more than law, obedience and authority tended to be immune to Hitler's charms. Althaus and Hirsch did, in fact, develop a theology known as 'orders of creation theology,' in which the orders of creation in God's world assumed major importance. This theology was implicitly conservative and law-oriented, suggesting that one is born into a station in life and should uncomplainingly recognize that as God's will. It may well be that a law-and-order frame of mind was congenial to Nazism and a loving, gracious attitude inimical to it. However, Christian theologians have always wrestled with the law and gospel tension, and to attempt to place all opponents of Hitler in one camp and all supporters in the other would be arbitrary and unfair to the subtleties involved.

In the end arbitrary factors of background and environment may explain the political stance of these individuals more effectively than do their intellectual positions. For example, Barth was a Swiss, to whom the appeal of German nationalism would not have been heartfelt. Tillich developed ties to religious socialism in the 1920s which made the Nazi solutions anathema to him; and Bonhoeffer had both an English family tie and international living experiences to give him a cosmopolitan outlook on life. For example, he served a German-speaking parish in London during the mid-thirties and also lived for a period in New York.[82] Kittel, Althaus and Hirsch, by contrast, grew up in conservative, patriotic families in which ties to some broader perspective were minimal. Freud's suggestion that subconscious factors motivate human behavior must be recalled in this context. The irrational leap of faith basic to every political stance may find its source in background and environment.

C. Conclusion

THIS chapter has attempted to establish several premises to be employed in understanding the political attitudes of Gerhard Kittel, Paul Althaus and Emanuel Hirsch. One is that the crisis of modernity at the start of this century was real. It was particularly acute in Germany for the generation which experienced the First World War and its aftermath in Weimar; and its sociological, economic, political, intellectual and spiritual dimensions created anxiety, unease and real dislocation. Furthermore, the crisis was more acute for some groups than for others. Jews and political leftists, for example, might benefit from the rapid political changes of democratization; but academics and theologians were more likely to be hurt by rapid change, both in terms of their comforts and of their prestige and respectability. Therefore, Kittel, Althaus and Hirsch faced a crisis in Germany in the 1920s and 1930s in which they felt personally vulnerable and in which they believed the future of their nation might hang in the balance.

Within the context of this crisis, the following chapters will argue several points:

1. That Gerhard Kittel, Paul Althaus and Emanuel Hirsch were well-meaning, intelligent and respectable individuals who also happened to support Adolf Hitler.

2. That each of these men developed a rationale for his political stance which was intellectually defensible.

3. That each ultimately based his political judgments on an existential leap of faith, whether consciously or not.

4. And that since political judgments are ultimately existential, the differences between Barth, Tillich and Bonhoeffer on the one hand and Kittel, Althaus and Hirsch on the other cannot be explained on the basis of superior or inferior intelligence or insight. Stated another way, we cannot rely upon intelligence or rationalism to protect us from political error.

This chapter opened with an acknowledgement that Hitler was evil. Therefore, to support him was wrong. Before condemning his supporters, however, we must recognize the complexity of the crisis which faced Germans in the Weimar period. We must further acknowledge that neither rationalism, intellectual capacity nor Christian values protected Kittel, Althaus or Hirsch from supporting Hitler. This is a disturbing conclusion and one which requires careful consideration if we desire the Hitler phenomenon not to recur.

CHAPTER II

The Case of Gerhard Kittel

A. Introduction

IN the closing days of the Second World War, the comfortable old university town of Tübingen, nestled on the banks of the Neckar south of Stuttgart, fell under French control. This proved disruptive for all inhabitants, since the small town was turned into a busy administrative center. But it was especially disruptive for Gerhard Kittel, Professor of New Testament Theology. On 3 May 1945 French authorities knocked on his door and carried him off to prison. Thus began the last, sad years in an otherwise happy life. Kittel was imprisoned for seventeen months; he never returned to his position or his colleagues at the university; he was denied a pension; and he died on 11 July 1948, a disappointed man of 59 years.[1]

Kittel must have been taken by surprise, for he was a solid, respectable academic. His father was the famous Old Testament scholar, Rudolf Kittel, and Gerhard, born 23 Spetember 1888, had grown up in an atmosphere which represented the best of German, middle class, academic, Christian values. Rufolf Kittel was not only an established scholar, he was also a sensitive, moderate man who won praise for guiding the University of Leipzig through two tempestuous years as *Rektor* from 1917 to 1919.[2] The younger Kittel followed naturally in his father's footsteps. His field of interest was the Jewish world at the time of early Christianity, his father's had been the Jewish world in Old Testament times. His first publications were in *Beiträge zur Wissenschaft vom Alten Testament*, a series edited by his father.[3] At the age of 25 he became a lecturer at the University of Kiel. He joined his father at Leipzig in 1917, before being named Professor of New Testament at Greifswald in 1921 and at Tübingen in 1926.

Kittel was not a giant among German theologians. He does not rank with Barth, Bultmann or Tillich. But he was a solid and respected scholar in his field. Students came from Europe and America specifically to study under his guidance, and he traveled to Amsterdam, Cambridge, Copenhagen, Lund and Upsala to lecture, turning down invitations to the United States only on the grounds of ill health.[4] He also edited a reference work, the monumental *Theologisches Wörterbuch zum Neuen Testament*, which has

made his name a household word among New Testament scholars.[5] Kittel
was an intelligent man, counterpart to academics throughout the Western
world and rather more successful than most, with none of the eccentricities
or flaws that would mark him as a crank or a knave. Yet he was ultimately
thrown in prison, an unusual fate for an academic.

One clue to Kittel's demise is that he was a National Socialist, having
joined the Party in May of 1933.[6] More importantly, when Walter Frank
started his politicized *Reichsinstitut für Geschichte des neuen Deutschlands*
(National Institute for History of the New Germany), Kittel was a charter
member, and he gave his expertise and reputation to the *Forschungsabteilung Judenfrage* (Research Section on the Jewish Question) when it
opened in 1936.[7] It was this association with Frank and his Jewish studies
which provoked the French authorities and caused Kittel's arrest. He had no
other sins to hide. He was not even among that radical group of German
academics who abandoned all semblance of objectivity to push the Nazi
Party line. A British colleague wrote him in 1933:

> No one in England, Jew or Christian, troubles about the views of Nazi
> professors who have given themselves to Hitler and sinned against the
> light. It is just not worthwhile . . . But about you we are troubled and
> grieved because we reckoned you to be on the side of the angels.[8]

Kittel reckoned himself on the side of the angels as well, but the French
obviously disagreed. The question is, what went wrong?

The 'case' of Kittel cannot be resolved easily. Two scholars, for example,
have given very negative verdicts. Max Weinreich makes Kittel one of the
chief villains in his early post-war study, *Hitler's Professors*.[9] The
archaeologist and Christian humanist, William Foxwell Albright, also
attacks Kittel.[10] However, a November 1947 article by J. R. Porter in *Theology* praises Kittel's 'profound Biblical scholarship' with no reference at all to
his unseemly politics; and the obituary appearing in the *Neue Zürcher
Zeitung* also praises Kittel's work. The latter refers to a postwar attempt to
take editorship of the *Wörterbuch* away from Kittel, but it then takes Kittel's
side:

> That the constant disruptions and restraints of the war and postwar period
> hindered the advancement and completion of the fifth and last volume,
> and that in the storms of the postwar years an attempt was even made to
> snatch away from Gerhard Kittel the editorship of this work, against
> which even English scholars intervened, all this must be counted alongside
> physical suffering and privation as a chief spiritual sorrow of the excellent
> scholar.[11]

In Germany, church historians have shown surprisingly little interest in

Kittel. His editorship of the *Wörterbuch* plus his self-proclaimed role as theological expert on the 'Jewish question' make him an important figure, especially under a regime for whom the Jewish question was so uniquely and so tragically significant. However, Tübingen's Klaus Scholder, for example, has written a major history of the church struggle through 1934 without even mentioning Kittel's name.[12] This wall of silence was finally broken in 1978 when Leonore Siegele-Wenschkewitz, Scholder's assistant at that time, published an article on 'Gerhard Kittel and the Jewish Question.' She carefully stresses that we must judge him with the eyes of 1933, rather than with our own:

> I plead for this historical method: to evaluate in relation to our own questions and judgments the real possibilities which single individuals, corporations such as universities and faculties, and church institutions had on the basis of their tradition and historical position; and further to make visible their actual room for action, or rather their restrictedness with regard to possible action.[13]

This historical method is admirable; we should attempt to see Gerhard Kittel as a real human being and not as a caricature formed by our hindsight.[14] But Siegele-Wenschkewitz makes several mistakes in this early article which combine in a final analysis that is much too mild. First, she chooses to restrict herself to 1933 and Kittel's speech and publication of that year, *Die Judenfrage*. Historians can and must limit their subject area, but to discuss 'Gerhard Kittel and the Jewish Question' and ignore his increasingly harsh work after 1933 is at best misleading. Siegele-Wenschkewitz also ignores much of the harshness of *Die Judenfrage*, harshness which he himself acknowledged and justified, pleading with Christians not to become sentimental or soft.[15] The significance of these restrictions in her work are multiplied enormously by her careless statement near the end of the article: 'From a sympathizer of the presumably moderate *Führer*, he became an opponent of the National Socialist politics of destruction.'[16] Although Siegele-Wenschkewitz gives no timeframe, the implication seems clear that after a short time Kittel saw the error of his ways, presumably when the *Führer* was no longer 'moderate.' This implication is supported by Siegele-Wenschkewitz' conclusion that Kittel's chief error was to misunderstand Hitler and his real attitude towards Christianity. In fact, there is very little evidence that Kittel experienced a change of heart prior to 1945, despite abundant evidence to correct his misunderstanding. Should he really be compared to Paul Althaus, for example, who made a similar misjudgment, but who never prostituted his work so completely and who never took a positive stance towards National Socialist politics after 1937 or 1938? Contrary to the rather innocuous implication of Siegele-Wenschkewitz' conclusions, Gerhard Kittel produced a body of work between 1933 and

1944 filled with hatred and slander towards Jews and warmly supportive of National Socialist anti-Jewish policies (Siegele-Wenschkewitz has acknowledged this more fully in her most recent work on Kittel).[17] On the other hand, the political and theological questions facing Kittel in the 1930s were inordinately more difficult to answer then than now. And we have much evidence in support of his stature as a theologian and his warmth and humanity as an individual.[18]

This chapter will attempt to show that the problem of Kittel is more complicated than heretofore recognized. He was not an evil man, but he took an evil stance. It may or may not have been proper to try, convict and imprison Kittel in 1945. That judgment is lost in the very debatable questions of war crime trials in general and moral culpability in particular. But it is relatively easier to conclude that Kittel was wrong, whether or not he was criminally guilty. Perhaps historians should avoid moral judgments, as Siegele-Wenschkewitz suggests. But Adolf Hitler provides one of the few, clearcut moral quantities in history, and, unfortunately for himself, Kittel allied himself with Hitler. Furthermore, he was linked to the single most objectionable aspect of Hitler's reign, the Jewish policy. On both counts Kittel was singularly unlucky in his associations and distinctly wrong in the judgment of posterity. This chapter will attempt to determine what went wrong, why Kittel, respectable theologian and scholar, came to his indisputably tragic end.

B. Kittel's Defense

IN the first weeks of his incarceration, Kittel prepared a 42-page statement in his own defense. This document, together with a revised version, clarifies many of the issues surrounding the case of Kittel and provides the only comprehensive defense of his position available. From the first page it is clear that he was indicted because of his writings on the Jewish question, but it is also clear that he admitted no guilt and apparently had no second thoughts.[19] As he explains:

> The case of Kittel is a perfect example of the frightfulness which must arise if one equates every serious discussion of the problem of Jewry and the Jewish question with the vulgar antisemitism of Nazi propaganda, the 'Stürmer,' Rosenberg's office, etc.[20]

This distinction between 'vulgar' antisemitism and his own version of anti-Jewish thought is fundamental to Kittel's argument. He readily admits that much of his work may appear anti-Jewish, but he insists it was always Christian in motivation and scientific in method. Without doubt the question of Jewishness is significant for Christianity. For a start, Christian identity can only begin with a recognition of its Jewish roots. The Christian tradition also has a long record of antisemitism, including bans on social intercourse with Jews and creation of ghettoes during the Middle Ages. Finally, the significance of Jesus can and perhaps must be understood as opposition to certain Jewish traditions of his day. These facts make the study of early Judaism a legitimate, scientific concern of New Testament theology. Kittel claims to have studied these questions for over thirty years, consistently emphasizing the similarity as well as the dissimilarity of Christianity and Judaism. He saw the Jews as both the chosen people and the disobedient, cursed people. Long before 1933, he writes, he had pointed 'to the inexorable and irreconcilable opposition of the Christian and Jewish interpretation . . . specifically in the sense not of a historically accidental, but of a metaphysically necessary 'opposition.'[21] Kittel quotes several favorable reviews from Jewish publications as proof that his work was fair, but these reviews praise two books published in 1926.[22] Did Kittel's attitude remain impartial after 1933?

As if in anticipation of this question, Kittel devotes a long portion of his defense statement to *Die Judenfrage*, a speech he gave in Tübingen in 1933, which was subsequently published through three editions and 9,000 copies. He admits the obvious, i.e. that this book is political, but he claims it represents the only instance in which he strayed from strictly theological and historical questions. He also related his ideas to points in the Nazi program, but that was only to avoid giving 'vulgar antisemites' ammunition by which to attack him.[23] His real purpose was to raise discussion of the Jewish question above the level of slogans and vulgar racism and give it a moral, Christian basis. Judaism had not been true to its roots, he believed. It had become a secularized Jewry, 'to some extent overflowing into modern relativism and atheism.'[24] Even 2,000 years ago Jesus and the Apostles used words like 'refuse,' 'curse' and 'condemnation' in reference to Jews, and for over 1,000 years Christianity had insisted upon ghetto walls. But the Enlightenment perverted both Christianity and Judaism through secularization and Jewish emancipation. This was now the 'Jewish problem.'

Kittel opted for a solution of 'guest status' for Jews in Germany, a solution he traced to a Swiss converted Jew of the nineteenth century, Karl Friedrich Heman. Since this solution had not been applied when Heman suggested it, it would now be more painful, for the situation had gotten further out of hand. But Kittel believed that somehow the separation could assume a humane form. Then:

> if one works seriously from both sides on the basis of such principles, perhaps lifestyles would again be found which would allow a respectful and friendly coexistence of Germans and Jews.[25]

Kittel also believed that pious Jews would affirm his analysis of the situation and accept his solution.[26] In return, he insisted upon justice and respect for the religious practices of Jews, so that piety would be rewarded and assimilation discouraged. As proof that this stance was distinct from vulgar racism, Kittel notes that he was attacked in the Nazi press the day after his speech, and claims that only the intervention of friends prevented a catastrophe.[27]

This fear of retaliation seems to have been exaggerated. Kittel even claims to have warned his family that he might be sent to a concentration camp, a threat which appears highly unlikely in retrospect.[28] But his distance from rabid antisemites was real enough. They did not distinguish between pious and secular Jews, as he did, and they preferred racial to spiritual arguments. Nonetheless, in his defense statement, Kittel glosses over some of the difficulties in *Die Judenfrage*. His brief mention, for example, that guest status might create hardships, veils an endorsement of the thoroughgoing removal of Jews from the professions. Even Kittel's frank rejection of the Enlightenment and the entire liberal tradition, though not criminal, is slightly unnerving. People outside of Germany have also rejected the Enlightenment, and there are certainly Jews who oppose secularization, assimilation, and possibly even emancipation. But for Kittel to have taken this stance in the Third Reich was a portent of disaster.

Kittel picks up two further issues in his defense statement which illustrate his attempt to apply Christian principles to questions about Jews. On the question of baptized Jews, he once gave a written opinion for the Tübingen theological faculty in which he affirmed the New Testament words, 'Here is neither Jew nor Greek.'[29] Therefore, a genuine Jewish Christian should be accepted as a Christian brother; but that does not make him a German brother. Thus, state measures against Jews can be carried over into the church, so long as the Christianity of a Jewish Christian is not denied.[30] Kittel believes he put the lie to one-sided racial theories with this distinction, as well as separated himself from radical Nazi Christians, who tried to divorce Christianity from its Jewish roots.[31] This is true to a certain extent, but Kittel's position is still questionable. While he accepted the Jewish Christian as a spiritual brother, he apparently felt no need to defend him against the practical problems of job forfeiture, property confiscation and forced emigration, all of which pertained only to his 'Jewishness.'

On the basis of this same racial principle, i.e. denial that a Jew could ever be a real German, Kittel came down against mixed marriage. He compares his position to marriage restrictions found in Ezra and Nehemiah. Assuming these strictures to be *völkisch* as well as religious, Kittel argues that orthodox Jews and orthodox Christians should all agree with Nazi policy. Mixed marriage is wrong.[32] Early Christian practice further confirms this position, for various synods of the church raised similar prohibitions. Though Kittel admits that in those instances the ban was centered on baptism rather than race, he counters that the church is now guilty of weakening and abusing baptism. It has become a mere 'assimilating and civilizing baptism'; therefore, Kittel concludes, the marriage ban should now be racially based, even if it was not before. On the strength of these examples, Kittel claims to have shown that Jewish questions were for him, 'questions of biblical norms and the Christian ethic.'[33]

One of the most compromising factors in Kittel's predicament was his membership in the *Forschungsabteilung Judenfrage* of Walter Frank's *Reichsinstitute für Geschichte des neuen Deutschlands*.[34] In 1936 he became one of fifteen members of the 'council of experts' for this research department, and he published prolifically under its auspices.[35] Kittel begins to defend his relationship with this institute by denying the significance of his position. He refutes the 'misunderstanding' that he was a director by claiming he was only one of about fifty scholars on the council of experts. He adds that he joined this institute only because it offered a scientific platform from which he could spread his Christian views, and he rejected all ties to other antisemitic organizations. This defense is marginally inaccurate. First, Kittel was one of only fifteen original members of the council of experts, though the number may subsequently have grown.[36] Furthermore, Kittel did not reject all ties to other anti-Jewish organizations, for one of his most polemical articles was a contribution to *Archiv für Judenfragen*, a publication of Goebbel's *Anti-Jüdische Aktion*, which carried the subtitle, 'Journal for the intellectual Subjugation of Jewry.'[37] Finally, Kittel's praise of the 'scientific' nature of Frank's institute must stand alongside official statements, such as:

> It is the service of the *Reichinstitut* to have provided as a weapon in the fight against Jewry a national-socialistic science, i.e. a science which follows our *Weltanschauung* in point of view and attitude, which allows every possibility for truly free research.[38]

Numerous speeches and other evidence, including the attendance of Julius Streicher at two of the annual conferences of the *Forschungsabteilung Judenfrage*, attest to the political direction of the institute.[39] Compared to Rosenberg's *Institute zur Erforschung der Judenfrage*, founded in 1939, the work of Frank's institute was perhaps less radical and less racial in tone. For example, Frank's journal, *Forschungen zur Judenfrage*, was criticized by Rosenberg's *Nationalsozialistische Monatshefte* for 'theological reminiscences,' lack of a rigorous *Weltanschauung*, and too little racial emphasis.[40] But this represents the bitterness among rivals more than the innocence of Frank's position.

These 'theological reminiscences' justified in Kittel's mind the work he did for Walter Frank. His convictions as a Christian and a theologian were respected, he felt. Thus, without compromising himself he had gained an important forum in which to oppose the vulgar antisemitism threatening the church and undercutting the Old Testament. Kittel claims that everything he wrote was directly or indirectly related to this one overriding purpose:

To break through a path of historical truth over against the distortions of the time, and thereby to make possible a fair and appropriate valuation of the Bible and Christianity.[41]

His many publications for this organization, however, reveal a consistent attempt to characterize the Jewish people as 'refuse' (see below). To the extent that this was a common Christian viewpoint, Kittel's claim that all of his work was related to his Christian and theological stance may be valid. But this also shows his Christian, theological stance to have been uncomfortably close to the *Weltanschauung* of a good Nazi, whether Christian or not.

Indeed, Kittel admits that he was a good Nazi. He had not joined the Party under pressure or for pragmatic reasons; rather he thought, 'as did countless people in Germany,' that the Nazi phenomenon was 'a *völkisch* renewal movement on a Christian, moral foundation.'[42] So although he had never belonged to a political party before,[43] he joined this one and long retained the hope that in time the 'healthy forces' would prevail; and he felt bound 'to use the knowledge given to him to assist this convalescence and to overcome the abuses.'[44]

Kittel describes three attempts on his part to work for good within the Party. In the fall of 1938 he attended a local Party gathering in which the church and the name of Jesus Christ were insulted. Kittel complained to his district leader, who denied knowledge of the incident but promised to look into it and try to prevent a recurrence. In September of 1939, Kittel was called to the University of Vienna, so he went to his district leader to resign his refugee work. Upon being thanked for his helpfulness, Kittel responded, 'Please carry over your thanks to me to the other theologians and pastors and to my church —, and treat them accordingly!' Finally, upon his return from Vienna in 1943, Kittel looked up his Tübingen district leader only to tell him that growing attacks on theologians and the church forced him to refuse any further work for the Party. Kittel professes never to have spoken with his district leader except on these three occasions. He did write once to claim his exemption as a theologian from the *Volkssturm*, the German equivalent of the Home Guard. In this letter he complained of the insulting form which theologians were forced to use to claim their exemption.[45] In his revised defense statement Kittel even claims he tore up and threw away his Party insignia on a public street in protest against the exclusion of theologians from the *Volkssturm*.

The difficulty with these incidents related by Kittel is that they cannot be proven. They may have happened, but that cannot be established for certain. And the tone of the exchanges could easily have been adjusted in retrospect to fit Kittel's circumstances in 1945. Beyond these incidents, Kittel claims to have taken no active role in the Party, never having joined the SA nor any but the most innocuous auxiliary organizations. He adds that his wife and grown children did not join the Party. All of this is probably true, though it also lacks any documentation. The Nazi records which have been preserved at the Berlin Document Center contain only Kittel's membership card in the central catalogue and one letter from the National Socialist University Lecturers' Federation leader in Vienna, observing that Kittel had returned to Tübingen on 7 April 1943 and, therefore, his file card was being returned to the national leadership in Munich. There must have been further correspondence between Kittel and various branches of the Party, but it apparently has been lost.[47]

Kittel believes there was a concerted effort by people within the Party to 'deconfessionalize' him and thereby put his expertise to better use for the movement. He counts as evidence of this seduction, 1. three offers of a professorship within a philosophical faculty (Tübingen, Berlin and Vienna); 2. a confidential approach in 1939 by the National Students' Federation leader about the possibility of leading a new Jewish institute (which Kittel assumes was the Frankfurt institute established under Rosenberg in April, 1939); 3. invitations to write brochures for the Propaganda Ministry; and 4. an invitation to the National Party Day in 1938.[48] Some of these offers were attractive, especially the chance for a professorship outside of theology at a time when the future of theological faculties was in some doubt. But Kittel claims to have resisted all such blandishments.

Another incident of interest concerns a proposed trial of Herschel Grünspan, the Jew who had murdered von Rath in Paris in 1938. After the fall of France, Grünspan fell into German hands. Someone decided to hold a trial which would prove he was an agent of world Jewry and that his brief attendance at a Talmudic school in Frankfurt had taught him to hate and kill non-Jews. Kittel was to be an expert witness on the basis of his Talmudic knowledge. However, he refused to perform his function unless he could speak with Grünspan beforehand and examine both the German and French documents. Kittel became convinced that Grünspan's act was his own, prompted by bitterness that his parents had been forcefully moved from their home in Hanover back to Poland. The trial never took place. Without directly claiming responsibility for this result, Kittel strongly implies that his role was significant. He cites it as justification for working within the Party, for 'if he had refused to cooperate at all, [the trial of Grünspan] probably would have occurred.[49] In his second defense statement Kittel portrays his role even more grandly. He suggests in light of the subsequent extermination of Jews that the trial of Grünspan may have been intended to build a public justification. Although he does not want to 'exaggerate the significance' of his preliminary participation in the case, he suggests:

> It could be that he obstructed the path to Jewish murders at least at one point — the only point at which he was placed — in that he neutralized the plan to legitimate these murders by his refusal to give expression to anything but the objective truth [about Grünspan].[50]

As further proof that he resisted seduction, Kittel reports that between 1933 and 1945 he gave only nine lectures on the Jewish question at other than religious gatherings, a minimal number for an expert in his field.[51] Only two of these lectures were at Party functions, and on both occasions Kittel claims to have defended biblical religion and confessed his Christian faith. He notes his failure to be invited back as proof he had not compromised himself.[52] In this same vein Kittel observes that he received no decorations from Party or state, though he was 'the first authority in Germany in the scientific consideration of the Jewish question.'[53] Finally Kittel resisted numerous requests to contribute to Party newspapers, agreeing to do so on only three occasions. In two of those instances he claims his articles were badly distorted, which was reason enough not to comply with futher requests (though his third contribution actually came after the two which he says were distorted).[54]

Kittel had been aware that after 1933 Nazi Jewish policy was not following the direction he had hoped. He claims that prior to 1942 solid information was not available on the treatment of Jews; even with obvious instances, like the pogroms of 11 November 1938, no one knew where to place the blame. But Kittel does not deny that some response was necessary, even to the limited facts that were known. Indeed, he claims to have indulged in a certain amount of resistance. He describes several instances in which he expressed his warnings and opposition, e.g. in *Reichsinstitut* circles and among low level officials in the Reichs Ministry of the Interior. He soon realized, however, that he was not reaching high enough. Thus he tried in 1938, 1939 and in 1940 or 1941 to send a message to Rudolf Hess, using three different intermediaries. Kittel never got an interview with Hess, and he never knew whether his messages got through or not. But he felt it was important that he had tried. In 1937 or 1938 Dr Erwin Goldmann of Stuttgart had an interview with Winnifred Wagner, apparently to express his reservations on Nazi Jewish policy. Kittel knew of this meeting and associated himself with it, though he notes he did not arrange or take part in it. Finally, Kittel claims to have helped Gustav Entz, a professor of theology at Vienna, in his statements sent to *Reichsminister* Lammers and *Reichsleiter* von Schirach. He describes these as strong letters of warning and adds rather ostentatiously:

> Both Kittel and Entz may claim for themselves that they — though the public may have known nothing about it — belonged to the men in Germany who never ceased warning in those years, even to the highest authorities. Without personal fear they reminded that in all cases, whoever sows the wind reaps the whirlwind.[55]

This seems a very bold claim. It is not even certain from the context that Kittel signed his name to these letters of Entz. He performed all of these acts in greatest secrecy so as to give his enemies among the vulgar antisemites no ammunition. He believed he was being watched and that his enemies may even have included Bormann. 'He knew since that Tübingen attack of 2 June 1933 (the newspaper review of his speech from the previous day), that he constantly stood with one foot in a concentration camp.'[56] This led him to warn his family against his sudden disappearance and instruct his son what to do in that event. This is either highly melodramatic or else indicative of how pervasive fear of denunciation had become in Nazi Germany. But if Kittel was really as frightened as he indicates, must not this have convinced him of how unjust the German *Rechtsstaat* had become? And in that case, would he have continued to publish works in which no trace of opposition on the contrary, in which confirmation of Nazi policy is found?

Kittel claims in one instance to have voiced public opposition. At the beginning of 1943 he received from his son his first reports of Jewish murders in Russia and Poland. This news preceded his lecture in a 1,000 seat auditorium in Vienna in March 1943, so he closed his lecture with these words, 'all horrors are gathering and all demons raging.'[57] He believes that his meaning was clearly understood, so much so that a Roman Catholic theologian, Dr Karl Prümm, visited the next day to make sure that the Gestapo had not arrested him. Prümm called this speech 'an act.'[58] It is hard now to conceive of the Gestapo calling on the basis of such vague provocation. Indeed, all of Kittel's acts of opposition are described in such imprecise terms that it is very unclear what he protested. He probably opposed some combination of pagan elements in the Nazi *Weltanschauung* coupled with rough treatment of the Jews, and his mode of expression seems to have been cautiously ambiguous. Perhaps in the atmosphere of the Third Reich subtle hints and gestures would have been understood. On the other hand, Germany after 1945 is sarcastically said to have 'blossomed' with members of the resistance. Kittel's recital in 1945 of his acts of opposition, acts which by their nature cannot be verified, seems insufficient to establish his innocence of intent.

Another barometer of Kittel's actual position during the Nazi years was his behavior towards those groups which were out of favor at the time. Kittel recalls a whole catalogue of good deeds rendered towards opposition churchmen and Jews. For example, he supported Bishop Wurm (Württemberg) in 1934 when the bishop was removed from office and placed under house arrest. The appropriate Nazi minister, Mergenthaler, forbade all members of the Tübingen theological faculty from taking any action in the matter; but the faculty publicly supported Wurm anyway and thereby helped him to be reestablished. Kittel joined with his colleagues he claims, and also 'ostentatiously' visited Wurm during his house arrest, a gesture he repeated in a similar incident in 1943.[59] The outline of this incident is accurate, and Kittel probably played the role he describes, which would have been commendable.[60] But in the circumstances, it did not prove an especially hazardous act, for Bishop Wurm enjoyed overwhelming public support. Kittel goes on to list fourteen different instances in which he intervened or attempted to intervene on someone's behalf. Many of these incidents involved pastors or professors who were disciplined for their associations with the Confessing Church. Kittel also assisted the *Württembergische Bibelanstalt* in 1939-40 and again in 1942-3, defending their publications on the Old Testament. Finally, Kittel claims to have demonstratively walked out of two different Party gatherings in which the speaker defamed Christ or the church, and he adds rather vaguely, 'Both cases had a sequel.'[61]

Kittel also lists fourteen acts of kindness towards individual Jews. For example,

1. In 1926 he dedicated a book to his recently deceased Hebrew teacher, Issar Israel Kahan.
2. In 1933 the Tübingen Jew, Chaim Horowitz, upon emigrating to Holland told Kittel, 'You have a deep love for Israel and know the essence of this people better than many who are called Jews.'
3. On 1 April 1933, the first day of the Jewish boycott, Kittel assisted Hugo Löwenstein, a Jewish-Christian carpet merchant. He protected Löwenstein from sabotage and insults by walking with him in front of his store.
4. In 1933 a Tübingen philosophy professor, Konstantin Österreich, was released from his position for being married to a Jew. Kittel intervened with the Stuttgart culture ministry, but to no avail.
5. In Vienna Kittel and Bishop Eder personally intervened with the Gestapo to allow devotions to be conducted for Jewish Christians in the ghetto.
6. Kittel and his wife were close friends with a half-Jewish Roman Catholic, Elisabeth Ortner-Kellina, an actress at the Vienna *Burgtheater*. They helped her often and she wrote many letters of appreciation.[62]

Some of these references are footnoted with the names of people who could corroborate the story, and some are not. But in spite of this uncertainty of documentation, it seems probable that Kittel would not have risked fabricating these stories. He attaches special importance to these acts because of a Party order prohibiting association with Jews. Thus, he feels each instance was a 'spiritual good deed' and he requests that this be considered in assessing his overall character.[63]

One inadvertent conclusion to be drawn from Kittel's evidence is that he was quite aware of a good deal of injustice in Nazi Germany. His friends were being harassed, his colleagues dismissed. He witnessed illegal treatment of Jews and even admitted learning in 1943 about Jewish murders. In retrospect, one must ask why he confined himself to individual acts of benevolence and rather vague and secret initiatives. He was, after all, quite closely tied to the Third Reich through his Party membership and his work with Frank's *Reichsinstitut*. He admits having wrestled with the question of whether he should, if not protest, at least have gone silent. But he felt his participation in the crucial issues of his day was necessary. Many of his friends may have wondered at his behavior, he acknowledges, and some may even have been led astray. But good friends would now believe in his sincerity and selflessness, and recognize that he had been called by God to speak out:

> Kittel was in a special, wholly unique situation. His scientific considera-
> tion of the Jewish question meant at the same time a decisive support of
> the Christian church's position in the struggle over *Weltanschauung*. A
> completely unique opportunity was given to him to become accepted in
> circles outside the church and to build for them a path to the truth. This
> was an opportunity which in this form was available to Kittel and to no one
> else. So, if he had kept silence and made no use of this opportunity, an
> essential and irrecoverable positive element would have been omitted in
> the struggle over Bible and Christianity. On this basis Kittel felt himself
> bound to express himself within the scope of his Christian and scientific
> convictions wherever he could.[64]

Often he wanted to withdraw, but his position was like that of Moses:

> who, according to Exodus 3:11 and 4:1, 10 and 13, as God commissioned
> him to speak, resisted, 'Lord, send, I pray, some other person.' But God
> did not give him the freedom to withdraw.[65]

In 1943, Kittel claims, he began to pull back from the struggle and restrict himself more narrowly to historical and theological work.[66] But until then he believed that the words Ezekiel ascribed to God were directed at him:

> Son of man, I have made you a watchman . . . Whenever you hear a word
> of warning from my mouth, you shall give them warning from me. If I say
> to the wicked, 'You shall surely die,' and you give him no warning . . . his
> blood I will require at your hand. But if you warn the wicked, and he does
> not turn from his wickedness, or from his wicked way, he shall die in his
> iniquity; but you will have saved your life.[67]

To make the connection perfectly clear, Kittel goes on:

> Thereby Kittel stood at an almost completely solitary point, a position
> at which he could not only not give the burden over to another, but also to
> which no one could accompany him.[68]

Did Kittel's role in God's plan indirectly give aid to vulgar antisemitism? He acknowledges that individual statements he made about Jews might sound as harsh as those of any antisemite. But again he insists that his different goals and overall purpose made him a separate case. He also thought it unlikely that vulgar antisemites borrowed from his work, first because it was read only in academic circles and, secondly, because vulgar antisemites could quickly sense the gulf that separated Kittel's work from theirs.[69] Nonetheless, Kittel's contributions to Walter Frank's *Forschungen zur Judenfrage* must have crossed many an antisemitic desk. And Max Weinrich has noted an instance in which Kittel's research seems to have been quickly picked up. Kittel made reference in 1943 to an incident in the second century A.D. in which Jews were supposed to have murdered 250,000 people in Cyprus. In 1944 the same reference appeared in one of Goebbel's newspapers.[70] This may have been coincidence, but at the very least it shows that Kittel's work was of potential interest to antisemitic apologists.

Near the end of his defense, Kittel ventures a more specific plea. He has been accused of criminal, or at least morally objectionable conduct, he writes, and he would raise six questions in return:

1. Could the prosecution name an instance when Kittel persecuted a Jew, or could it detract from those good deeds enumerated by him?
2. Could it not be believed that Kittel's position towards the Jewish question was imposed upon him by God?
3. Were Kittel's assertions throughout this defense accepted as believable? He admits that evidence was often not possible, but he suggests that he be allowed character witnesses, including the *Rektor* and the theological faculty at Tübingen.
4. Did Kittel's work not represent the quality expected and the sense of responsibility assumed for a man in his position? Kittel suggests a number of witnesses, including several members of the Confessing Church, the Swiss theologian, Emil Brunner, and the Luther scholar, Paul Althaus. He does stipulate that these witnesses must not be under the influence of the Enlightenment or relativism, nor take an unclear or negative stance towards 'any of the basic facts of revelation testified to by the Old and New Testament and the confessions of the Reformation.'
5. Did Kittel's work on the Jewish question strengthen or weaken the church's defense against attacks on the Old Testament and on Christianity in general? Did it strengthen or weaken the church's position in the *Weltanschauungskampf?* Kittel suggests that church leaders, e.g. Bishop Wurm, should testify to this position.
6. The final question is 'whether in the Christian cultural world it counts as a crime which must be prevented through legal punishment, that one represents a position on the Jewish question based upon the instructions of Jesus and his Apostles?'[71]

Kittel closes with a statement affirming he has nothing to hide and will not disclaim responsibility. He hopes for a clear verdict so that his children, students and friends will know whether they must be ashamed or not, and whether:

his human and scientific reputation is pure or sullied . . .

This does not change the fact, however, that he believes he has the right to question, no matter what the final judgment of his contemporaries and posterity, whether his case is really of the type that he should be kept in dishonorable circumstances weeks, perhaps even months, as a criminal in prison.[72]

Despite his protest, Kittel then spent seventeen months in prison. This gave him time to reconsider his past. It was also the period in which the full horrors of Nazi Jewish policy were exposed to the German populace and to the world. It is instructive, therefore, to compare Kittel's revised defense statement of November/December 1946 to the first one analyzed above.

Kittel's second statement does include an expression of guilt:

Kittel is ready and willing to take upon himself and to carry as a part of the fate of his *Volk* all that has befallen: arrest and loss of his position, shame and poverty. He is deeply permeated with the solidarity of guilt by which he as a German man is surrounded and from which he, as little as any other responsible and conscientious German, cannot and will not separate himself. He is unreservedly prepared, as a member of his *Volk*, to share all consequences of the terrible events which have occurred.[73]

Kittel's sense of *völkisch* unity is obviously intact. But he goes on to stress that his sense of personal guilt is very limited:

This affirmation of solidarity in a monstrous collective guilt, however, under which he knows he stands, does not remove from him the right and the duty, in the interest of truth and justice, to question whether he bears in similar fashion a personal guilt, based upon his individual behavior, which requires a punishment as if he were unworthy of his position in life?[74]

Throughout his revised defense statement, Kittel attempts to establish the purity of his intensions and the innocence of his behavior. His main theme again is that he chose to work *within* the Nazi Party in hopes that a religiously-based anti-Jewish policy would prevail over radical and vulgar racism. He tries to establish the anti-Jewish credentials of Jesus:

Never has a more terrible judgment been spoken against the so-called world Jewry as a demand for power than in the 'woe' of Jesus Christ in Matthew 23:15; never a more negative characterization of the Jewish religion as a religion of privilege than that found in John 8:40-44![75]

and of Paul:

Certainly Kittel has exposed the presence of degeneration in modern as well as ancient Jewry as sharply as any antisemite . . . In these cases, however, Kittel can point to the fact that the words of Paul on the Jews of his day were often interchangeable with the anti-Judaism of contemporary heathens: yes, it even appears that Paul borrowed and used as his own — without any polemic, but also apparently without any differentiation — the catchwords of this vulgar anti-Judaism (for which 1st Thessalonians 2:15 offers irreproachable exegetical proof.)[76]

And he defends all of his work, including that for Frank's *Reichsinstitut*, as part of his God-given role as a theologian.[77] At one point he acknowledges a sense of guilt for not having developed more fully the harshness of his anti-Jewish views before 1933; he thus allowed the vulgar antisemites a headstart in their attempt to direct the Jewish policies of the Party.[78]

There is no evidence in Kittel's revised defense statement that he believed his personal political and theological views to have been in error. He does confess to one error, however, not in his views but in his judgment. He misjudged the true intentions of Hitler and the National Socialist movement:

I did not know to what extent the genuine national thoughts which reside in every *Volk* became falsified into a system of imperialistic and megalomaniacal politics of brutality, and the social and socialistic ideal misuscd as camouflage for lies and corruption. Today I know that my endeavor was based upon the most bitter deception of my life.[79]

Kittel had advocated National Socialism enthusiastically and honestly, but mistakenly:

Above all no one will be able to suggest at any point that the methods and results of his discussion were determined or even influenced in the slightest through compromise with the current of the times. If he occasionally, in a very few instances, attempted to interpret contemporary events through his scientific conclusions, this interpretation was based, as he knows today, upon an illusory hope.[80]

He even places himself in the innocent company of Karl Barth and Carl Gördeler (a leader of the resistance movement), as individuals misjudging Hitler.[81] And, finally, he places himself in the midst of an entire *Volk* betrayed:

I believe that I can and may compare my activities and my error with the activities and error of the honest and brave German soldier. He knows today that he sacrificed himself not only, as he thought, for the existence of his *Volk,* but for a cause in which he was deceived and betrayed and for which he must be ashamed as a staining of the German name. Exactly in this manner I know today that the cause with which my honest scientific work was associated was an infamous cause.[82]

In short, Kittel's self-interpretation is essentially that advanced by Siegele-Wenschkewitz in 1980, i.e. his chief (or only) error was a misassessment of Adolf Hitler and National Socialism. I would suggest that a deeper reading of Kittel betrays a deeper complicity on his part.

On the basis of his own defense statement, what can be determined about *what* Kittel did between 1933 and 1945 and *why* he did it? Although many of the details in his statement cannot be substantiated, it seems safe to assume they are largely true. This would indicate that Kittel was not malicious in his attitude towards individual Jews, nor was he otherwise malevolent. Rather, he felt a genuine concern for friends unfairly treated, and that included Jewish friends. His academic interest in Judaism was a legitimate subject of Christian theology, and even his understanding of the Jews as 'refuse' was not unique. It is also apparent that Kittel was very conservative, if not to say reactionary, in his political, social and intellectual attitudes. He rejected the Enlightenment, and with it those ideals of equality and justice admired in the Western world. He rather uncritically accepted *völkisch* and racial ideals as the appropriate German alternatives to Western liberalism. He emphasized the decadence of Jewry in his work, an emphasis which, at the very least, roughly corresponded to Nazi attitudes no matter what different premises Kittel may have nurtured.

One important premise for Kittel is indicated in this statement:

Also the Jewish question stood for him completely under a theological, Christian point of view; it was and became in increasing measure plainly a part of the question of church and Christianity within the modern *Weltanschauungskampf* [struggle over world view.][83]

Weltanschauungskampf is the significant word. It appears frequently in this defense statement, and it seems to be the one idea which ties the others together. Kittel's position was not merely Christian; many Christians did not share his bias. It was not merely antisemitic, for he did oppose those antisemitic strains which threatened Christianity. Finally, his position was not simply political. Rather, he was involved in a struggle to unite a certain type of Christianity, antisemitism and political-social conservatism into a single *Weltanschauung*, and to preserve that *Weltanschauung* against its enemies. He set German, Christian, social and *völkisch* unity against the Enlightenment, modern secularism and liberal democracy.

In the post-1945 world, Kittel's defense statement seems almost enough to condemn him, even if accepted at face value. But many questions remain.

Was his work really theologically motivated and scientifically conducted? Were there elements in his actions or his writings which, more than being an affront to liberal ideology, were morally unacceptable or even criminal? Did anything in the life of Kittel justify the harsh fate which befell him? Both his actions and words prior to June 1945 must be evaluated to provide answers to these questions.

C. Kittel's Actions

LITTLE in the daily life of Gerhard Kittel distinguished him from numerous colleagues. He followed a rather routine academic career, and his subsequent trial centered less on acts than on words. But a brief look at the biographical information available does put his life in some perspective. Kittel was nearly twenty-six years of age when the First World War began. His academic career had already begun: for after studying at Leipzig, Tübingen and Berlin he joined the theological faculty at Kiel in December 1913. But with the outbreak of war he volunteered to become a chaplain, and he served from November 1914 to December 1918 as a naval chaplain at Cuxhaven.[84] After the war Kittel entered into the neo-conservative reaction of his generation. For example, he was a member of the 'German Christian Student Movement,' and he edited a series of publications for that group in the 1920s intended to relate Christianity to *völkisch* questions.[85] His rejection of the Enlightenment and his readiness to think in racial as well as *völkisch* terms also place him toward the radical right in the context of the Weimar Republic.

The political orientation of the Kittel family, father and son, represents a pattern that is probably quite typical. The elder Kittel was certainly conservative and patriotic. As *Rektor* at the University of Leipzig, he gave several speeches at the close of the First World War in which he, 1. attacked Woodrow Wilson for his villainy in failing to push through the Fourteen Points; 2. advised that the Treaty of Versailles not be signed, so that at least German hands would not assist in the violation of Germany; and 3. mourned Germany's dead soldiers in romantic, patriotic language, exemplified by the oft-repeated phrase, 'the weeping Mother Germany.'[86] Rudolf Kittel also wrote, *Die Universität Leipzig im Jahr der Revolution 1918/19*, in which he showed no love for the revolutionaries or the Weimar Republic.[87] But there was no fanaticism, no reference to communists or Jews, no stab-in-the-back legend. The elder Kittel's feet were firmly planted in nineteenth-century liberal academia, so much so that even the traumatic events introduced in 1918 did not tear him loose from rationalism and tolerance.[88]

The younger Kittel shared his father's political conservatism as well as his roots in the pre-war era. But the roots were not nearly as deep, so his conservatism was more easily swept along with the prevailing wind, which after 1918 meant irrationalism, *völkisch* mysticism and antisemitism. The elder Kittel died in 1929, four years before the rise of Hitler. But the younger Kittel was only forty-four when Hitler came to power, and he was conditioned by his environment to appreicate much of what Hitler seemed to offer.[89]

After 1933 Kittel registered his approval of the Hitler phenomenon by joining the Nazi Party and working in Walter Frank's *Reichsinstitut*. Kittel admits in his defense statement that he joined the Party out of enthusiasm, not opportunism, and that he continued to feel responsible for the 'purity of the movement' for many years.[90] He adds the common, though in retrospect incredible, judgment that he took it for a Christian moral renewal. On the surface this judgment seems to have placed inordinate faith in Hitler's promise that the Party stood for 'Positive Christianity.' *Mein Kampf* was ignored. Alfred Rosenberg was ignored. The one explanation which clarifies this widespread misconception is that Christianity became confused with such a large package of cultural factors that it was no longer distinguishable on its own. Christianty was German culture. Christianity was middle-class morality. Christianity was respect for authority. Christianity was law and order. Christianity represented an established class in its opposition to turmoil from the left. It was on this basis that so many Christians mistook the Nazi movement for a religious renewal, and it was on this basis that Kittel joined the Nazi Party.[91]

Kittel's membership in Frank's *Reichsinstitut* must also have been based on a misunderstanding, or else he slightly misrepresented his membership in his defense statement. Frank's institute was clearly an avidly antisemitic organization. The opening ceremonies of the *Forschungsabteilung Judenfrage* in 1936 were attended by Rudolf Hess, among other dignitaries, and the institute was given full Party blessing. The *Völkische Beobachter* announced this opening ceremony in front-page headlines three inches high and underlined in red, with the full implication that this was to be the scientific weapon in the Nazi fight against Jews.[92] Frank himself described his intentions on many occasions, once with a paraphrase of von Schlieffen, 'Strengthen my anti-Jewish flank.'[93] The antisemitism was also not in any way 'refined.' For example, a speech at the first annual conference asserted that Jewish scientists obviously stole ideas from Aryans. The proof was that most German Nobel Prizes in physics had gone to Jews. This speech was ascribed to one of the few Aryan Nobel Prize winners, Philip Lenard, though it was actually delivered by another physicist.[94] Julius Streicher, the infamous editor of *Der Stürmer*, was also a featured speaker of the *Forschungsabteilung Judenfrage*. He honored the second and third annual conferences with three-hour lectures based on his firsthand experiences in the struggle against Jewry.[95] This was the 'scientific' institute through which Kittel hoped to combat vulgar antisemitism. It was perhaps less radical than the institute subsequently opened by Rosenberg in Frankfurt, but it was hardly a neutral and objective research organization for all that.[96] And Kittel seems to have been an enthusiastic member. Helmut Heiber describes him as a vocal participant in discussions and a prominent figure behind the scenes.[97]

Outside of his membership in the Party and the *Reichsinstitut*, there is no dramatic evidence of Kittel's support for the regime. Minor services were rendered, as he admits in his defense statement. He spoke on several occasions to the NS Lecturers' Confederation; he made three contributions to Party newspapers. But Kittel was probably justified in claiming these services represented limited cooperation for a man in his position. Max Weinreich suggests that Kittel's move from Tübingen to Vienna in 1939 was a reward for his faithfulness.[98] However, this fails to take into account, 1. that it was intended as a temporary appointment,[99] and 2. that for a German Lutheran theologian, the friendly confines of Tübingen, with its highly regarded theological faculty, may have been preferable to the Roman Catholic, Austrian city of Vienna.[100]

In the question of Kittel's relationship to the Nazi regime, it is important not just to ask what he did do, but also what he did not do. The two institutions to which Kittel was most closely tied, church and university, suffered interference and manipulation at the hands of the Nazis. And the issue most central to Kittel's life work, the Jewish question, was pushed in a direction which he later professed to have abhorred. What actions did he take?

In the spring of 1933 the church struggle began. It was precipitated when German church leaders sensed that, in the spirit of the times, they should bring about the long-deferred unification of the several regional churches into one Reichs church. Hitler assisted their decision by naming his old friend, Chaplain Ludwig Müller, special representative of the *Führer* to the churches. A great deal of backstage maneuvering took place as the various factions hoped to strengthen their position in the new church, with the crucial decision centering around the naming of a Reichs bishop. Moderate hopes rested on Fritz von Bodelschwingh, who was non-political and widely respected. Müller naturally thought the honor would fall to him. The first round in the rather confusing events which followed went to Bodelschwingh. In May he was announced by the regional church representatives as the new bishop. But Müller and his allies, the radically Nazi *Deutsche Christen*, were outraged. They brought in the SA to harass Bodelschwingh's offices, and in Prussia they convinced the cultural minister, Rust, to appoint a state commisar for the Prussian church. Bodelschwingh, recognizing his position was hopeless, resigned at the end of June. The election was then thrown open to a vote of the full church membership. On the evening of 22 July, Hitler made a surprise radio broadcast, requesting support for Müller; and in the elections of the next day, with Bodelschwingh out of the way and a number of unfamiliar faces filling the churches, Müller achieved over seventy per cent support.[101]

In September this new church administration attempted to apply the restrictive Aryan Paragraph to the church (approximately 35 of the 18,000 pastors and church officials were non-Aryan). Martin Niemöller responded by forming the Pastor's Emergency League *(Pfarrernotbund)*.[102] In November the *Deutsche Christen* held a rally at the Sports Palace in Berlin, during which a Dr Krauss delivered a speech denouncing the Jewish influence on Christianity and calling for the removal of the Old Testament from the Bible.[103] This further discredited the new church officials and gave impetus to the formation of an opposition church structure. In 1934, the Barmen Declaration *(Barmenerklärung)*, inspired by Karl Barth, was established as a confession of faith on which the new church structure, the Confessing Church *(Bekennende Kirche)*, could base its opposition to *Deutsche Christen* heresy.

Thus, in a very few months the lines were drawn between Nazi policy and the church. Church opposition was rarely thoroughgoing, it is true. Churchmen, accustomed to respecting the state and sharing much of the anti-bolshevic and anti-Jewish bias of the Nazis, opposed interference with church affairs but not National Socialist policy in general. Only a few, Karl Barth and Dietrich Bonhoeffer, for example, did that. But where did Kittel stand as his church was roughly treated? He supported Bishop Wurm against Nazi threats. He privately tried to assist individual members of the Confessing Church against reprisals. But he showed no public affection for the Confessing Church, and he attacked the Barmen Declaration on the basis that the church must respond to the 'historical hour' of the German people. In a letter to Karl Barth in 1934, Kittel spoke for 'some of us National Socialist theologians in Württemberg' who believed that agreement with state and *Führer* was obedience towards the law of God.[109] And, somewhat ironically, he cited that passage in I Corinthians, 'to the Jews I became a Jew, in order to win Jews,' as support for his belief that Christians in Germany must endorse the *Volk*.[105]

Kittel's instincts in 1933 were to side with the *Deutsche Christen*, who also believed in the 'historical hour,' but he realized before the year was out that he could not accept their exclusive politicization of the church and radicalization of the Jewish question.[106] In 1938, the *Deutsche Christen* established at Eisenach an anti-Jewish institute, the *Institut zur Erforschung des jüdischen Einflusses auf die Kirchen*. Again Kittel kept his distance.[107] Indeed, the existence of the *Deutsche Christen* is one of the most fortuitous circumstances in Kittel's favor. Their extremism makes Kittel seem to have been in the mainstream by comparison. These theologians rejected the Old Testament, proclaimed an Aryan rather than Jewish Jesus, and fused pagan and Christian elements into a peculiarly German mysticism.[108] On all of these counts Kittel was innocent. He remained true to basic orthodoxy. Kittel thus fell into that vast middle sector of German Protestantism which accepted neither the religious heresy of radical Nazism nor the political heresy of opposition to the state. He claimed in 1945 to have worked within the system to protect the church, but he never took a clear, public stand either against Nazi policy or for the one rival alternative, the Confessing Church.[109]

The second important institution in Kittel's life, the university, proved slightly more amenable to Nazi policy, which in itself might have troubled Kittel's academic conscience. He was certainly aware of a heavy hand applied to elements within the university that did not conform. E. Y. Hartshorne estimates that between 1933 and 1937, fifteen to twenty per cent of university faculty members were dismissed, largely on grounds of political unreliability or non-Aryan background.[110] In the field of theology, Kittel lost colleagues as prominent as Karl Barth, Paul Tillich and Martin Buber. For those who did remain, the sacrifices of objectivity to Nazi orthodoxy were often immense, as Kittel should have recognized in the *Reichsinstitut*.[111] But there is some evidence that Kittel did not reach that realization. He thoroughly respected his colleagues in racial science, apparently, and made forays into that suspect discipline himself.[112] Concerning faculty dismissals, Kittel claims to have intervened in individual cases to secure redress. But he also clearly states in his book, *Die Judenfrage*, that Jews were overrepresented in the professions and should be dismissed. Though this would cause personal hardships, that was a necessary price for past excesses.[113]

Some insight into what may have been Kittel's general attitude is suggested by Hartshorne, who studied in Germany in 1935-6. During that time he observed the university situation and he interviewed many people. He concluded that the typical apologetic for Hitler was based on the lost war, the resultant hardships and ignominy, and the breakdown of the cultured classes due to inflation and the depression. Extreme tendencies in Nazi Germany were accepted on the assumption they would disappear once the situation had returned to normal. The universities had been under radical and Jewish influence, it was thought, and they needed to be more true to their German roots. The supposed lack of scientific objectivity in Nazi Germany was a false issue, since valueless, presuppositionless science was known not to exist.[114] Concerning academic freedom, Germans accepted the Hegelian definition of freedom, not as irresponsibility but as obedience to law, morality and state.[115] Thus Kittel had a strong and widely supported basis on which to accept the German university in its Nazi form. Science was rooted in the depths of the *Volk* experience, not in the pseudo-freedom of enlightened, liberal, democratic irresponsibility.

What about Kittel's attitude towards Jewish policies? In his defense statement he admits that these policies went counter to his prescription for the situation. He claims to have always advocated a Christian answer to the Jewish question, and he suggests that his benevolence towards individual Jews proved his good intent. Fortunately, there is a body of evidence on which his intent can be measured. Kittel published books and articles relevant to the Jewish question throughout his thirty-year career.

D. Kittel's Writings

KITTEL'S publications prior to 1933 established him as a leading scholar in the field of Judaism and its relation to early Christianity. His work centered on a painstaking study and comparison of the literary sources of the two faiths, and this placed him in the middle of a controversy over the significance of Judaism in the origins of Christianity. Some scholars, e.g. the liberal theologian, Adolf von Harnack, had maintained that Christianity was totally unique from Judaism and that the Old Testament should be removed from the Bible.[116] He argued on the basis of internal inconsistency between Old and New Testament, but the conclusion he reached coincided with the antisemitic prejudice that Judaism was necessarily inferior and unworthy to be considered the source of Christianity. Kittel rejected both arguments. On the one hand, his research on the relation between Judaism and early Christianity would be drastically devalued if that very relationship were denied. So he defended the affinity between the two faiths out of self-interest. But his orthodoxy and opposition to liberalism also dictated this stance. Kittel was unwilling either to throw out the Old Testament or to deny Jesus' Jewish roots.

In 1914, Kittel produced a very short work, *Jesus und die Rabbiner*, which laid the groundwork for his position. His basic argument is that in both content and form, the Talmud and New Testament are very similar. New Testament passages such as, 'do not pray before men but in secret,' 'forgive our sins as we forgive others,' and 'do not store up treasures on earth' all have their counterpart in the Talmud.[117] Parables and miracle stories also find their place in both traditions. Therefore, study of the Talmud would surely yield a better understanding of Jesus and his world. The young Kittel was not totally unbiased. For example, he takes pains to show the superiority of Christianity to Judaism by noting the 'pair of pure, clear, brilliant sentences' with which Jesus resolved moral questions, as opposed to the 'exacting deliberations and considerations' and the 'puzzling out of all the filthy possibilities' on the Jewish side.[118] But the general stance of the book is favorable towards Judaism.

The year 1926 was an important one for Kittel. He was called to the University of Tübingen. He also published his entrance lecture and two additional books in that year.[119] The main work, *Die Probleme des paläs-tinischen Spätjudentums und das Urchristentum*, is a bibliographic study which raises Kittel's theme from 1914 of the close ties between Judaism and early Christianity. But in this book he supports his hypothesis with more evidence, affirms it more fully, and exercises more caution towards his earlier prejudices. For example, Kittel urges objectivity in comparing religious. Do not try to prove superiority or inferiority, he advises, but merely seek out what is unique.[120] He praises the Talmud more highly than ever:

The Talmud is in its essence like a giant sack into which was stuffed everything which Judaism had stored up in terms of memories and traditions, so that its contents are the most colorful and joyful confusion and juxtaposition that one can imagine.[121]

Judaism at its highest point united the ethical and the spiritual, he writes, which was unprecedented. Other religions were either pious-mystical or ethical, but not both. Judaism was able to unite the two because its ethic was rooted in belief in God: God commanded and the Jews obeyed.[122]

Jesus distilled the original essence of Old Testament piety, and thereby retained this unity of the ethical and spiritual.[123] In a remarkable passage, Kittel affirms the ties of Jesus to his Jewish roots:

One need only make these connections clear to know how absurd and historically false it is, without any exception, to attempt to separate Jesus and Christianity from the Old Testament and from the spiritual history of its people . . . The ethic of Jesus did not arrive unassisted, it did not grow *ex nihilo* . . . It is nothing less than the most concentrated development of that powerful movement of Israelitic-Jewish religious history which finds its condensation in the literary complex that we call the Old Testament. That means obviously, that Christianity, which prides itself on being the 'majesty and moral cultivation of Christendom,' of which old Goethe said to Eckermann, 'as it glitters and shines in the Gospels' — it [Christianity] may never forget that the Old Testament is not in its Bible by accident. All Christian culture and all Christian ethics have their roots in the moral consciousness of Old Testament piety. That can and may not be wiped away.[124]

Because late Judaism and early Christianity grew out of the same Old Testament roots, Kittel claims, there is no single word or ethical teaching of Jesus which does not have its counterpart in Jewish literature.[125] Kittel does not neglect to distinguish between Christianity and Judaism. He writes that the tragedy of Israel was not to have maintained a unity between ethical and spiritual emphasis. The ethic tended to become a moral philosophy (as in Lessing's *Nathan der Weise*) or a ritualism, and in each case the spiritual element was lost.[126] But he quickly returns to the defense of Judaism, criticizing those who would seize on one word either to attack or defend, for:

No one who knows the rabbinical literature and gives honor to the truth can deny that in the midst of the ritualism and dialectic, the quite genuine tone of pure, ethical actions and thought rings out again and again. This tone still carries the spirit of the prophets, and it is this spirit from which late Judaism also originated.[127]

This book represents the highpoint of Kittel's tolerance, admiration and respect for the Jews. It contains no ridicule or unfair criticism. Kittel does close with a statement that the two religions must remain distinct, but this statement has an honest, descriptive rather than polemical intent:

> If Judaism wants to remain Judaism, it cannot do otherwise than declare battle on the claims of Jesus. And wherever Jesus is recognized as reality and as truth, there Judaism has found its end.[128]

As a believing Christian, Kittel was unable to place the two faiths on an equal footing, but he retains a tone of respect for Judaism throughout.

Kittel's second book of 1926, *Jesus und die Juden*, is a restatement of one portion of *Die Probleme des palästinischen Spätjudentums und das Urchristentum* specially adapted for a specific audience. The audience in question was the German Christian Student Movement, and the intent of Kittel's study was to approach *völkisch* questions from a Christian standpoint. Kittel may have felt himself on dangerous ground with this audience, especially after having so warmly praised Jews in *Die Probleme*. His audience shared his Chrstian basis, of course, but they were also fully exposed to and no doubt influenced by prevailing racial attitudes and opposition to Judaism. In spite of this fact, Kittel changes his tune relatively little. He insists upon dealing with the Jewish question in religious terms, though he admits that racial considerations are also relevant; and he maintains his emphasis upon the importance of Jewish roots for an understanding of Jesus. He adds a reference to the non-religious Jew, representative of an 'average enlightenment,' who falls too easily into frivolity and lasciviousness.[129] But he observes that secularized Christians often follow a similar direction; and he cites the Jewish philosopher, Hermann Cohen, and pious Talmudic scholars as representing two types of modern Jewry, both of which are fully praiseworthy.[130]

Jesus und die Juden has been reprinted in a recent study of Jewish-Christian relations in the Weimar period. In the introduction Hans-Joachim Kraus praises Kittel for having approached the Jewish question from a religious rather than racial standpoint. But he takes issue with certain preconceptions that circumscribed Kittel's analysis. For example, Kittel approaches the question of Jesus' Jewishness with the words:

> It is conceivable that Jesus, if he was a Galilean, had a couple of drops of non-Jewish blood in his veins — I say, it is conceivable, it is not completely impossible. But it is absolutely certain that in any case he bore very many drops of genuine semitic blood.[131]

Kraus first objects to the uncritical use of the term 'semitic', a sloppy word borrowed from racists. He also thinks Kittel should have clearly stated, 'In

terms of his human origins the Lord was a member of the Jewish *Volk*.'
Taken in conjunction with his very strong statement in *Die Probleme*,
however, Kittel in this instance might well have been employing irony rather
than skirting the issue, as Kraus suggests. Kraus' further criticisms are more
to the point, e.g. that Kittel uncritically accepts the common view of Jewish
legalism and ritualism. He does, though to a lesser extent than he did in
1914. Finally, Kraus dislikes Kittel's strongly Lutheran interpretation of the
Sermon on the Mount, i.e. that it is an absolute and unfulfillable demand,
designed less for moral guidance than to point sinful man towards the saving
Messiah. This makes Jesus the sole criterion of religious truth and thereby
rules out Jewish-Christian dialogue except in conversion. Kraus thinks the
Sermon on the Mount should also be seen as a new and serious moral
direction. Jesus would then be less a stern judge against the Jews. Potential
for a loving openness towards Jews would be developed as Christians grap-
ple with the profound implications of Jesus' words.[132]

Kraus' critique is certainly justified if Kittel's work is to be held against the
goal of meaningful Jewish-Christian dialogue. Since 1945, Christians have
been struggling to define an understanding which does not immediately
condemn Jews for not accepting Jesus as the Christ. Some progress has been
made, nourished by a strong dose of guilt, no doubt, and that is the standard
by which Kraus' criticism must be understood.[133] Judged by the standards of
1926, however, Kittel's publications of that year seem remarkably warm
towards Judaism. In 1929 he published a short contribution, 'Judentum und
Christentum,' in a major reference work. Here he worked in conjunction
with Jewish scholars and he continued to stress the close relationship between the two faiths. For example, regarding Jesus' Jewish origins he writes:

> Jesus, the circle of his followers, as well as Paul, were Jews by race,
> nationality and religion. All attempts to prove the non-Jewish and non-
> semitic origins of Jesus belong in the realm of fantasy. Even if the blood of
> the Galilean should have had a couple of drops of non-Jewish blood, in
> any case it held very many drops of fully Jewish blood. And more impor-
> tantly, without any doubt Jesus understood and thought of himself as a
> member of his *Volk* . . . Also Paul, the apostle to the gentiles, belonged
> among those Christians who stemmed from and continued to feel con-
> nected to Judaism.[134]

If the case of Kittel revolved around his work prior to 1933, he would
certainly be cleared of any wrongdoing. Unfortunately for him, his pen was
active long after the advent of Hitler.

As early as 1921, Kittel gave a hint of what was to come. In that year he
delivered a speech in Sweden on 'The Religious and the Church Situation in
Germany.' Because it ranged outside his discipline, this speech gave Kittel a
freer rein and may now yield a more accurate insight into his basic political

instincts than his strictly academic work. Kittel describes a Germany which is
sick, not just because it has lost a war, but because it has sold out to the
Enlightenment. The result is rational secularism, materialism and socialistic
religion. Movies, the theater, prostitution, the spread of veneral disease,
divorce and crime all illustrate the decadence threatening Germany.[135] But
Kittel remains optimistic for several reasons, mainly centered around a
renewal he sees in the church and especially in the Christian student movement. Fortunately, rationalism is 'in the process of dying out . . . Our entire
intellectual life, from philosophy to poetry, stands under the sign of a return
from rationalism.'[136] Kittel does not want to throw out reason altogether:
'We want to be learned theologians.' But he clearly recognizes the limits of
reason: 'We also want to be pious theologians.'[137] He foresees fifty to one
hundred years of suffering for Germany, but, in a last burst of patriotic
fervor he asks, would he miss those years? Would he like to join a happier
Volk or trade places with anyone outside Germany's borders? 'Never!'[138]

This speech of Kittel's is not fanatical. He does not blame all Germany's
troubles on Jews, for example. There is a strong spiritual emphasis, and
those sentiments which touch on political, social, national and philosophical
issues might have been repeated by clergymen or theologians representing
any other Western country in 1921. Many pleasant and harmless English or
American Christians would have appreciated Kittel's words, and Swedish
Christians certainly did.[139] But in Kittel's case these sentiments represented
a line of thought which was eventually going to get him into trouble. The
potential for trouble suddenly became concrete in 1933.

In those exhilarating days of 1933, on the first of June, Kittel addressed
himself to the Jewish question in a public lecture in Tübingen. This speech,
Die Judenfrage, defended by Kittel in his defense statement, had an impact
suggested by a disappointed English admirer:

> It gives me great pain to find that so great an authority and leader of
> thought should give expression to such views. I have read your previous
> books with pleasure and profit, and I have learned much from them . . .
> Your present pronouncement is quite incompatible with your previous
> teaching, and it is as unjust to Christianity as it is to Judaism . . . It is a
> grievous disillusionment to find that one's idol has feet of clay.[140]

What prompted such an outburst? In *Die Judenfrage* Kittel addresses
himself to a completely different subject than he had ever considered before,
at least publicly: the political question of what should be done with Jews in
Germany. He acknowledges that so much confusion surrounds this subject
that some serious-minded people might have, 'one is almost inclined to say,
. . . a bad conscience' when they think about it.[141] Kittel proposes to
overcome this problem by establishing a solid Christian foundation for
opposition to Jews, so that the question can be approached 'simultaneously

as German and as Christian.'[142] Kittel warns against being sentimental. 'God does not require that we be sentimental, but that we see the facts and give them their due.[143] He also warns that the question must not be turned to the fate of individuals:

> It is not a question of whether individual Jews are respectable or disrespectable; also not whether individual Jews are unjustly ruined, or whether that occurs justly to individuals. The Jewish question is absolutely not a question of individual Jews but a question of Jewry, the Jewish *Volk*. And, therefore, whoever wants to get to the root of the question may not first ask what shall become of the individual Jew, but what shall become of Jewry.[144]

The present Jewish problem, according to Kittel, results from: 1. the diaspora, which means that Jews are always foreigners and never at home (their racial stock is also foreign), and 2. emancipation and assimilation, through which Jews inject their foreign blood and foreign spirit into the German *Volk*, resulting in decadence.[145] Only four solutions seem possible:
    1. Extermination. Kittel rejects this solution, but he rejects it, rather insensitively, solely on the grounds of expedience. It has not worked before and it will not work now.[146]
    2. Zionism. Kittel rejects this for a number of reasons, including its impracticability, the small percentage of Jews that Palestine could accommodate, and the hostility that would be aroused among displaced Arabs. He also observes that many Jews are socialists and communists, so it is not likely they would work hard enough to make a go of it.[147]
    3. Assimilation. This is clearly the chief evil in Kittel's view. It results in racial mixing and, more importantly, leads directly to decadence. 'This decadence, however, and nothing else, is in every respect the actual, basic problem of the contemporary Jewish question.'[148] Kittel describes the impact of assimilation quite graphically:

> It can be weary, delicate, and yet, because it weakens and infects, dangerous resignation, which eats away the marrow of a *Volk*; it can be a cold, calculating, perhaps a self-tormenting and lacerating relativism; it can be a wild agitation and demagoguery to which nothing is holy. It is always spiritual homelessness, and therefore poison and decomposition.[149]

Assimilation leads to a literature and journalism before which nothing is holy, a legal practice which does not serve the interests of the *Volk*, an irresponsible seeking after money, and even a medical practice interested in money more than the health of the *Volk*. Kittel admits that some Germans are like this and some Jews not. But he believes that assimilated Jewry is the 'native soil' for this decadence.[150]

Assimilation is thus the key for Kittel's entire thesis. Wilhelmine Germany, which he is old enough to have known, has disappeared. The Weimar Republic and everything it represents — defeat, shame, disrespect for religion, disrespect for the established classes, secularism, immorality, dangerous radicalism, i.e. all the effects of modern, urban life — all this has one simple cause, assimilated Jewry, Jews torn from their roots, Jews corrupted by the Enlightenment. Since assimilation is the cause of Germany's troubles, Kittel thoroughly rejects further assimilation as a possible solution. That leaves only one alternative.

4. 'Guest status,' or the separation of Jews from the peoples with whom they live. Kittel advocates this as the only possible solution, and he draws out its implications for the current situation in Germany.[151] This theoretical framework allows Kittel to support those National Socialist policies which might otherwise have seemed inhumane or illegal, and in practice it places him perilously close to the 'vulgar antisemites' whom he professed to oppose.

Prior to the advent of Hitler, Kittel declares, academics refused to deal with racial problems. They even laughed at racial science. As a result, the racial situation in Germany grew worse until the people instinctively broke out with acts of antisemitism. Kittel does not blame them: 'The youth and the *Volk* knew, however, that despite all these theories there was a moral right to refuse to tolerate such things, and, if necessary, to erect barricades and throw stinkbombs.'[152] The fault really lay with the liberal intellectuals who had let the situation get out of hand:

No one who took part in this confusion may today 'wash his hands in innocence.' He carries guilt on himself if today many harsh things do occur and must occur. He shares the guilt if it must come to explosions and if innocent are buried in the wreckage. This must be expressed openly and clearly, as a reminder to all those today who do not like to think about the sins of the past.[153]

These words became poignant and damning in 1945. Kittel then wanted to wash his hands of guilt, but his sins were certainly as great as those of the liberal intellectuals he condemns here.

Kittel clearly recognizes that hardships will occur if Jews are to be made 'guests' rather than citizens. For example, normal civil rights would be denied the Jew and a new set of rules worked out appropriate to his position as a 'foreigner.'[154] In the field of literature, Jewish writers should be free to write, but their works should be clearly designated as Jewish rather than German. Kittel laments that his friends in England and Scandinavia think Emil Ludwig and Leon Feuchtwanger represensive of German literature but have never heard of Paul Ernst or Erwin Guido Kolbenheyer:

It remains one of the most insane grotesqueries of recent intellectual history that the Berliner who for decades exercized the most influence in developing the literary taste of the German public, the publisher Samuel Fischer, was an east European Jew who at age twenty-one immigrated from Slovakia.[155]

The same hint of paranoia is evident in Kittel's assessment of the educational field. He finds it questionable that any foreigner should teach German youth; but one group of foreigners, Jews, now fill university faculties in great numbers:

It is part of the great superficiality of the intellectual period which lies just behind us, that a moderately clever and scientifically shrewd Jew appeared to have a special qualification to become a university professor, so that there could be universities in Germany in which more than half the professors were Jewish.[156]

These 'countless, mediocre Jewish intellectuals' represent such a distortion that Germans must 'reestablish the normal situation with inexorable severity and radical consequences.' Perhaps after the situation had been rectified, an occasional highly qualified Jew could be offered a teaching position, as would be the case with any outstanding foreign academic.[157]

At first glance other professions might not seem to endanger German spiritual and intellectual life as much as the teaching profession, but Kittel argues for controls there too. Jewish doctors popularize 'certain perceptions about sexual life'; and Jewish lawyers twist the law 'with the help of the casuistry that is part of their spirit, to achieve an administration of law which remains true to the letter of the law, but which produces for the German legal consciousness the opposite of justice.'[158] Jewish businessmen also manipulate within the letter of the law while destroying German peasants and craftsmen. And all of these problems are exacerbated because Jews shove themselves into these professions in disproportionate numbers.

Kittel recognizes the question of whether Jews might just be more intelligent and capable than Germans, but replies that the Jewish student succeeds, 'not because he is more capable, but because he is more nimble. The nature of the German, on the other hand, lies in the fact that he matures slowly.'[159] In the second and third editions Kittel further treats this concern that Jews might be superior. It may seem, he writes, 'as if antisemitism were the equivalent of envy towards the more capable, the equivalent of powerless hatred of the incapable towards his superior.' But he then skirts this problem to ask whether it is unfair to suggest that Jews be given places in the schools and professions only in proportion to their numbers in Germany.[160] This seems a weak response. It is also misleading, since Kittel has already denied this proportional idea in his suggestion that Jews be removed from the teaching field altogether.

A final condition of guest status would be a ban on mixed marriages, for Jews could not be allowed to continue corrupting the German race. If a German did marry a Jew, he should lose his rights as a German and fall under the laws for the foreigner.[161] Jews who were 'proper' in their respect for their position as guest would receive better treatment, and assimilated Jews would be treated worst of all. Kittel asserts that a pious, eastern European Jew would be much less a danger to Germany than an educated, assimilated Jew of several generations German citizenship.[162]

The full implications of guest status were clearly broad, and Kittel leaves no doubt that he recognized them. He admits that fine, honorable Jews would be forced out of their professions and would not know where to turn. Germans were sensitive and would not be unmoved by the hardships. They would give assistance where they could:

> But we may also not become soft. We may not through weakness let a development go further which has already shown itself a failure, both for the German and the Jewish *Volk*. It is hard if officials, teachers and professors, who have no guilt exept that they are Jewish, must move aside. It is hard if Germans, who with their fathers and grandfathers have conditioned themselves for hundreds of years to being equal citizens, must find themselves again in the role of the foreigner. But such considerations must never lead to a sentimental softening and paralysis.[163]

Kittel especially warns Christians against damaging the struggle through 'so-called' Christian sensitivity. 'If the battle is correct in its object, then the Christian also has his place at the front.'[164]

In addition to this harsh solution to the Jewish question, Kittel adds his expectation that genuine Jews would agree with him and accept this as the proper solution for their *Volk*. They should throw off liberal secularism and assimilation, return to the religion of their fathers, and accept the role of alien as God's judgment on the Jewish people for their disobedience, the 'God-willed tragedy' which they as pious Jews must affirm.[165] As Kittel expresses it:

> To come to the God of their fathers always means also for the Jews to come to the God of history. But the history of God with the Jewish *Volk* has meant for two thousand years: alien status among the peoples of the world.[166]

Die Judenfrage produced an uproar. Kittel later could honestly claim that some Jewish papers praised the book and the Nazi press attacked him.[167] Each of these reactions was possible. Kittel's Christian emphasis aroused the animosity of racial mystics, who were unwilling to distinguish between orthodox and secularized Jews in apportioning their hate; and conservative, anti-assimilationist, anti-secularist Jews would have recognized common ground with him. But among his colleagues Kittel ran into a good deal of criticism. The first edition of his book shows that he expected this and was not prepared to give in:

> We must not allow ourselves to be crippled because the whole world screams at us of barbarism and a reversion to the past . . . How the German *Volk* regulates its own cultural affairs does not concern anyone else in the world.[168]

This belligerent tone was not likely to dampen adverse response, and the response did come. Kittel's second and third editions provide evidence on how he reacted to it.

Kittel softened his position slightly in some instances where his wording seemed unduly harsh. For example, to his discussion of Jewish doctors and lawyers he adds the statement, 'Of course there are many respectable, honorable, truly sociable Jews among doctors and among lawyers.' Concerning businessmen, he prefaces his attack with the comment, 'It is unfair to deny that there were and are many honest Jewish businesspeople; but . . .'[169] Kittel's paragraph on extermination of the Jews also provoked a sharp response, which prompted Kittel to add a qualifying statement. Extermination was not only impractical, he admits, but also unchristian.[170]

Beyond these cosmetic alterations, however, Kittel changed nothing. His exchange with Martin Buber is a case in point. Buber published an open letter to Kittel in the August 1933 issue of *Theologische Blätter*. He does not dispute the views put forward by Kittel. 'They are the ruling ones,' he writes, though he does express surprise that Kittel would go along with them. But he concentrates his attack on Kittel's suggestion that Jews should support this 'defamation' and 'discrimination' as if it corresponded to Jewish faith. Buber cites passages from the Pentateuch to prove that God demands love towards the neighbor, and one law for guest and member of the *Volk* alike. Therefore, Jews need not accept Kittel's pronouncements as if they were the will of God. Perhaps if Germany really practiced the justice and love imposed by God in the Bible, one could properly speak of 'obedience in the role of alien.' But Buber argues that the whole concept is false anyway. The 'eternal, wandering Jew' is a Christian concept, he writes, not a Jewish article of faith. The only Jewish obligation is to prepare for the gathering of Israel, not endorse the diaspora or the discrimination associated with it.[171]

Kittel responded to Martin Buber in a fifteen-page letter printed in the second and third editions of *Die Judenfrage*. This response is slightly tart and certainly unrepentant. Kittel first expresses his disappointment, not over differences of opinion, but 'because I thought that we . . . could have a discussion, and because I see that this is also hardly the case.'[172] This rhetorical jab seems unfair. Buber's letter was not polemical or personal.

Kittel's real complaint seems to have been that Buber did not agree with him, not even partially. Kittel then goes on to argue point by point. Does Buber think one law for everyone means non-Jews would be allowed to become Jewish priests?[173] Is it defamation of Jews to say many Jewish intellectuals and literary figures are mediocre or bad? It would only be so if Kittel said they were bad because they were Jewish, he thinks. Instead of this 'inferiority' idea of vulgar antisemitism, Kittel claims to emphasize the 'differentness' of Jews.[174] Is it defamation to bar Jews from legal practice in Germany:

> if we first establish that in recent years Jewish judges and Jewish lawyers have attempted to distort German law and rape German legal consciousness; and, secondly, if we believe 'justice' is not an abstraction, but something which grows out of the blood and soil and history of a *Volk*.[175]

Kittel praises Buber's translation of the Hebrew Bible into German, but is it defamation if to him the German text is as foreign as the original Hebrew? Kittel cannot agree with those who compare Buber's translation with Luther's, not because both are not good, but because one is Jewish and one is German. It would be like comparing a bird and a fish.[176]

Herbert M. J. Loewe, Reader in Rabbinics at Cambridge, carried on a private correspondence with Kittel over *Die Judenfrage*. In a letter of 10 September 1933, Kittel admits that criticism of his book has been unsettling:

> Several experiences of these past weeks have forced upon me the painful realization that a mutal understanding between me and some of my colleagues and former friends is very difficult [to achieve].[177]

However, in response to Loewe's suggestion that he perhaps wrote under political pressure, Kittel reaffirms his stance and denies any pressure had been applied:

> I can answer you in no other way . . . except that I stand by my former opinion . . . It is also not true, as you suggest, that I wrote my book under political or any other kind of pressure. What I say today I have said for many years, only I always had hoped that insightful men would understand what was necessary before violence set in.[178]

These exchanges make it clear that criticism of *Die Judenfrage* prompted no second thoughts. Kittel was convinced that his book represented an appropriate Christian response to the pressing Jewish problem. In retrospect, his premise that there was a problem may have been his first mistake. Once this premise was accepted, and it was widely accepted in Kittel's environment, it easily led to unfortunate conclusions. One of Kittel's conclusions was that radical separation between German and Jew could be humane and just. Events in the next few years proved him wrong, but even in 1945 Kittel made no retraction. That is because he remained thoroughly convinced of the Jewish 'problem.' Though he affirmed humanity and justice, he really meant Germany should be as humane and just as circumstances would allow. Thus, his assessment of the circumstances was the crucial factor. Kittel's other post-1933 writings shed light on these circumstances as he saw them.[179]

Die Judenfrage is a political statement, Kittel's plan for resolution of the Jewish question. In his defense statement he claims that his other work after 1933 was purely academic and that it represented a continuation of the work he had begun in 1914. That is not entirely true. Before 1933 Kittel's publications argued the close ties between Christianity and Judaism. His work was rooted in literary analysis of Jewish and Christian sources. Though he evidenced some prejudice against Jews, an overall polemical tone was wholly lacking. After 1933 Kittel's work changed in content and in tone. His new topics included the racial composition of Jews 2,000 years ago and the spread of Jews in the Roman Empire. Anthropological evidence replaced the New Testament as a major source, and a polemical tone replaced the former objectivity. The difference was one of purpose. Before 1933 Kittel defended Judaism, afterwards he attacked it. It is true that Kittel still upheld the Old Testament and opposed those who would divorce it from Christianity. But he now took pains to distinguish Old Israel from post-exilic Judaism. Genuine, pious Jews were all right, but decadent, secular Jews were not. This was basic to the Jewish 'problem,' and Kittel's purpose after 1933 was to analyze that problem on the basis of his understanding of Christianity, his concept of the German *Volk*, and his analysis of history.

A good deal of Kittel's creative work after 1933 appeared in *Forschungen zur Judenfrage*, the journal of Walter Frank's *Reichsinstitut*. The first four volumes of this journal consist of speeches given at annual conferences of the *Forschungsabteilung Judenfrage* from 1936 through 1939, and Kittel is quite well represented. At the opening conference he spoke on the origins of Jewry and the Jewish question. This speech was clearly designed to dissociate the Old Testament, which Kittel valued, from the modern Jew. Kittel approaches his goal by arguing that a transition took place. In the period from about 500 B.C. to A.D. 500, the Jews of the Old Testament degenerated into the 'Jewry' of today.

Kittel first describes the diaspora. In 538 B.C. the Israelites were released from Babylonian exile, but many chose not to go home. At that point something 'wholly different' began to emerge. Earlier Israel had been a normal small state, with its own boundaries, soil and political structure. But as the political and physical bases broke down, Jewry became a religion and a race without a homeland.[180] In addition to homelessness, the diaspora produced two other problems: 1. widespread racial mixing, and 2. transition from the rural, rooted lifestyle of the farmer to the urban life of the merchant and trader.[181]

Despite the disintegrating effect of diaspora, Jews remained conscious of being Jewish. Kittel attributes this to the development of the Talmud at that time. Earlier the strength of Israel's religious development had been its prophetic tradition, which Christianity managed to retain. During the diaspora, however, the Talmud began to stress legalism. Although this resulted in a casuistic, hypocritical religious practice, it also formed a strong basis for Jewish cohesion.[182]

Finally, Kittel identifies a third element in the transition from Old Testament Judaism to Jewry: a drive for world power. Jews had always considered themselves a chosen people, but in the early stages this had to do with moral values and a God-relationship. As the actual political authority of Jews decreased, they began to see this relationship in a new, more political light. They now called on God to smash their enemies, for example, and they dreamed of world power.[183]

The end result of diaspora, Talmud and the drive for power was that Jews now became a problem for their neighbors. Kittel's conclusion, therefore, is that Jewry and the Jewish question developed at the same time, in the period from 500 B.C. to A.D. 500. He calls for more research on this critical period, but he also illustrates his belief that the most important lessons are already clear. First, Christianity is the most logical rival to Jewry; therefore, it has been the strongest anti-Jewish force in history.[184] Secondly, only 'bunglers' view the Jewish question as minor or harmless. Kittel affirms his own view:

> that it was not despotic brutality and barbarism but rather a genuine political transaction born of historical sobriety when the *Führer* of the new Germany acted. In his radical resolve he established the German *Volk* as the first *Volk* in modern times to place the Jewish problem on a wholly new foundation.[185]

Kittel also spoke at the second annual conference on a research topic consistent with his advice from the year previous. The question at issue is the extent of racial mixing among Jews in the thousand years before they were sealed off in the ghetto. Kittel notes a paradox: the decrees of Ezra and Nehemiah in the fifth century B.C. absolutely forbade marriage of Jews and non-Jews; but Kittel finds ample evidence that in the next centuries such intermarriage did occur. He explains that this paradox was only apparent, not real, for diaspora and proselytization overcame the decrees of Ezra and Nehemiah. The diaspora brought a natural pressure towards intermarriage because Jews became spread among so many peoples. To justify an unavoidable departure from the faith, Jewish dogma decreed that a proselyte became the equivalent of a Jew. Virtually unrestrained racial mixing resulted from this combination, Kittel concludes. He adds that this process also indicates the Jewish quest for power, with the marriage of Esther to the

Persian King, Xerxes, a prime example.[86] Kittel's conclusion leaves no doubt as to the purpose behind his study:

> Moreover, our historical consideration shows irrefutably that the radical suppression of connubium between Jews and non-Jews carried out by National Socialism is not, as almost the entire non-German world maintains, an unheard of cruelty against the Jews. In reality it is a healthy constraint upon assimilated Jewry to return to its own foundations and to its own laws.[187]

Kittel did not speak at the third meeting of the *Forschungsabteilung Judenfrage*, but his name still appears among the list of contributors to the corresponding volume of *Forschungen zur Judenfrage*. He published a two-page retraction concerning his *Konnubium* article. In citing examples of Jewish mixed marriages, Kittel had asserted that the early Christian, Origenes, was half-Jewish. He interpreted a passage from a letter of Hieronymous in the fourth century (over one century later) to indicate that Origenes learned Hebrew from his mother and sang psalms with her. On that basis Kittel wrote, 'It was exactly the same with Origenes, who was born in A.D. 202 as the son of a Jewess and a heathen, later a Christian father.'[188] But Kittel then discovered he had interpreted the passage incorrectly. It referred to Blaesilla, the daughter of Paula, rather than to Origenes. It read properly,

> While Origenes, over whom all Greece marvelled, learned Hebrew in a few months, she [Blaesilla] overcame the difficulties of the Hebrew language in just a few days, so that she could compete with her mother [Paula] in the learning and singing of Psalms.[189]

Kittel acknowledges that since the mother who taught Hebrew was not Origenes' mother, Origenes was not half-Jewish. But he fails to notice that Blaesilla was also apparently not half-Jewish, for Paula was a Christian. The point of the quote, in fact, is that Hebrew is a language which can be *learned*. This example throws a shadow of doubt on all of Kittel's research in this vein. Broad conclusions based on slim evidence are dangerous, especially if a person brings strong preconceptions to the work. Though insignificant in itself, this incident hints that Kittel's factual base may not always have been strong enough to support the conclusions he drew.

Kittel did not speak at the fourth and last annual conference of the *Forschungsabteilung Judenfrage* in 1939, but again he contributed to the journal representing that conference. He made two special studies, both concerned with the racial characteristics of early Jews. Kittel poses the question of whether any pictures might exist which would give evidence as to the physical appearance of ancient Jews. Although Jewish dogma opposed depiction of the human figure, a synogogue uncovered in 1932 at Dura contained walls covered with human representations. With this for a start, Kittel proposes that archaeologists, anthropologists, historians and theologians study these and other pictures for further evidence.[190]

Kittel also suggests that several terracotta figures discovered in Trier and dating from the third and fourth centuries represented Jewish caricatures. These figures were badly fragmented, few retained head and torso in one piece and none of the group figures retained the head of the female. Nevertheless, Kittel is able to draw rather broad conclusions. The male figures had large, hooked noses. This is a common caricaturist device, and Kittel admits it could imply any middle eastern type, but he assumes it signifies a Jew. On three of the phalli he found a faint line, evidence of circumcision, he thinks, which confirms his judgment. One 'obscene group' especially attracts Kittel's interest. It consists of a male, hook-nosed figure with two phalli, front and rear, together with a woman striking a 'shameless' pose. This woman has no head, but Kittel assumes her to be a non-Jew because the few female heads remaining in the collection do not have hooked noses. On this basis Kittel begins to draw conclusions. These carica-tures were directed against Jews, especially lusty Jews who committed racial sins with non-Jewish women.[191] The next question is where this racial opposition to Jews originated. Kittel had found a church edict in Spain as early as A.D. 300 forbidding mixed marriages, but the 'obscene group' dates from A.D. 275, long before the Spanish decree and also while Trier was still heathen. Roman civilization did have antisemitism, but due to its urban decadence, Roman society never maintained this attitude in a thoroughgo-ing manner or on racial grounds.[192] That left only one explanation: the pure, Germanic instincts of the people around Trier made them recognize the evil of racial mixing. As Kittel expresses it:

> Perhaps it is . . . no accident that these judgments show themselves to us —
> if in veiled form — just where the world of the old Empire, which had
> brought the Jews along with it, came up against a population of unbroken
> instinct and youthful power.[193]

After the appearance of this volume Kittel found his collaborator, for volume seven of *Forschungen zur Judenfrage* is devoted entirely to a joint effort by Kittel and a prominent racial scientist, Eugen Fischer. The book is nominally a study of Jewish portraits and the Trier caricatures; but in their introduction the authors reveal clearly their underlying goal. They hope to prove the Jewish problem existed even 2,000 years ago. They also argue that an apparent paradox of Jewry, the tendency towards assimilation on the one hand and proselytization and separation on the other, can best be under-stood as a conspiracy for world power. Assimilation represents an insidious push into the places of power; proselytization and separation represent an intended consolidation of that power:

> There is always one goal: power over the world . . . Always, at all times, whether in the first or the twentieth century, the dream of world Jewry is sole domination of the world, now and in the future.[194]

The first and largest section of this book, written by Kittel, attempts to substantiate this hypothesis. Kittel assembles evidence, much of it from his earlier work, to show that Jews were widespread in the Roman Empire, that they became racially mixed, that they assimilated with other cultures and religions, that they sought and attained positions of influence and special privilege, and that they represented both internationalism and Zionism. But this is a case where Kittel's conclusions exceed the data intended to sustain them. Individual instances could certainly be found to support some of his contentions, but there is no evidence presented by Kittel to suggest any one of these qualities was representative. In so far as the qualities were contradictory, e.g. assimilation versus separation, Kittel's theory that this contradiction is resolved in a cynical conspiracy for world power seems ridiculous. The best evidence he can muster is the Book of Esther coupled with a few harsh Talmudic passages, which, Kittel believes, prove that Jews are 'enemies of humanity.'[195] In 1926, Kittel wrote that virtually anything could be found in the Talmud, but that only a person of bad intentions would seize upon a few negative passages to condemn Jews.[196] By 1943 this warning had become self-diagnosis.

In the second and third portions of this book the authors finally take up the analysis of Jewish portraits and caricatures. Although Kittel writes an introduction to each section, here is where Fischer displays his scientific expertise. First he deals with eighty Egyptian mummy portraits dating from the second and third centuries A.D., hoping to classify them according to racial type. He explains:

> There is a something (perhaps better expressed, many such details) in the Jewish facial features, which is not measurable, which in individual instances may hardly be describable, but from which the reader or hearer can develop a clear picture.[197]

Many of these portraits were of Jews, he believes. Eight or nine were of the 'intellectual Jewish type,' and one even had that 'insolent' *(frech)* expression typical of the intellectual Jew.[198]

From today's perspective Fischer's scientific method seems questionable, but at least on the subject of the Trier terracotta figures his influence appears to have been salutary. In his introduction to this section Kittel backs down from many of the wreckless conclusions he had drawn previously. He now makes no mention of the female figures nor of racial mixing. His only comment on motivation behind the caricatures is that these figures might represent anti-Jewish feeling. Fischer then comments on the figures, noting that even pre-Columbian, Mexican caricatures often have large, hooked noses. But Fischer does accept that the evidence of circumcision in the Trier figures is convincing, so he assumes the figures do represent Jews.[199]

Kittel's only other contribution to *Forschungen zur Judenfrage* was in volume five. Here he published a study of the diaspora during the time of the Roman Empire, tracking down every fragment of archaeological and historical evidence on the spread of the Jews. Commissioned by the *Forschungsabteilung Judenfrage*, this work resulted in a map of Spain, France, Germany and the Danube and Black Sea area. An accompanying text lists grave markers, literary references, etc. which suggest that Jews once spread to a certain location.[200] Kittel hoped to publish a second installment in volume nine, covering Italy, Greece, the Mid-east, North Africa and Egypt, but volume nine was cut short by the end of the war.

Altogether Kittel contributed to six of eight volumes of *Forschungen zur Judenfrage*, claiming the dubious distinction of being its most frequent contributor. This forms a large segment of his published work after 1933. In his defense statement Kittel explains that his position in the *Reichsinstitut* was a rare and useful opportunity to raise a Christian voice in an otherwise secular institution. But there is some doubt that his voice remained as fully Christian as it was National Socialist. The body of work he produced was not very theological, but it was useful propaganda, It may be the supposed direction of influence reversed itself.[201]

Several other articles and speeches support the impression made by Kittel's *Forschungen zur Judenfrage* articles. In 1939 he gave a speech in Berlin, sponsored by the *Reichsinstitut*, on the historical background to the Jewish racial mixture. This is a recounting of this theory that the mixture developed in the thousand years between Exile and ghetto. But one new element probes the question of why the Jewish racial mixture would be worse than other European racial mixes:

> The fundamental difference is that it does not now involve a unified, organic, growing and becoming process of the *Volk*. Rather, it is a process which disintegrates into hundreds and thousands of individual instances recurring time and again in many different landscapes and nationalities and intermixtures, with constantly recurring variations on the underyling races of the Mediterranean area.[202]

Kittel closes this speech with a tribute to Hitler and National Socialist Germany, the saving force which stemmed the tide of Jewish infiltration.[203]

In 1943 Kittel published an article on the Jewish treatment of non-Jews as prescribed in the Talmud. The prospects for this article were all bad. It was published in *Archiv für Judenfragen*, journal of the Goebbels-sponsored *Anti-jüdische Aktion*, with the subtitle, 'Journal for the Spiritual Overcoming of Jewry.' And this article was published in 1943, long after genocide had become official policy within the Third Reich. Max Weinreich uses this time factor to suggest that Kittel knew what was going on and intended this article as a justification.[204] Kittel did learn in 1943 of Jewish murders in Russia, as he later admitted, but it is unclear whether the news came before or after he wrote this article.[205] At any rate, the article is one of the most ill-advised he ever produced — and he totally ignores it in his defense statement.

Kittel begins with the assertion that in the Talmud:

> a deep-seated hatred against the non-Jew comes to expression, out of which all consequences are drawn, right up to the full freedom to murder; for example, when it can read: You may kill even the best among the gentiles, just as you should smash the brains of even the best snake.[206]

To support this assertion Kittel quotes a Talmudic passage to the effect that anyone who accidentally killed a Jew while intending to kill an animal, an aborted foetus, or a non-Jew, would not be punished.[207] That is, killing a non-Jew was only equivalent to killing an animal in terms of moral culpability. Kittel also cites passages to show that common honesty need not apply towards non-Jews, nor need a Jew rescue a non-Jew who has fallen in a ditch. Kittel admits that animosity towards foreigners is common among all nations, even to the point of excusing murder, but he then describes Jews as a unique case. Because they live in diaspora spread among people with no political separation, this permission to kill the non-Jew means permission to kill the closest neighbor. Kittel recognizes that the Talmud also has mild passages, which endorse love and justice. These passages have been 'seized upon' by apologists for Judaism in recent centuries, but Kittel dismisses this as opportunism. Jews now make a show of restraint because they are still too vulnerable, too thinly dispersed; but the desire for world rule remains under the surface, with the freedom to murder as a secret weapon.[208] This seems an extremely eccentric interpretation of the Jewish faith, inconsistent with centuries of Jewish history and with the emphasis of Kittel's early work. On the other hand, it was quite favorable to the Nazi Party line and an implicit justification for the most anti-Jewish acts. In his defense statement Kittel claims to have had three articles distorted editorially. Unfortunately, this is not one of the articles about which he complains.[209]

In March 1943, Kittel delivered a public lecture at the University of Vienna, dealing with his familiar theme that the Jews of the Old Testament began degenerating after the Exile into the Jews we know today. Kittel emphasizes the racial degeneration. Although all peoples result from crossing of the races. Jews mixed so indiscriminately in the diaspora (even with blacks, Kittel notes), that their racial stock became decadent and depraved.[210] He also observes that the Old Testament agricultural society turned into an urban society during the diaspora, thus losing its roots in the soil and its healthy, organic character. Finally, Kittel asserts that the spiritual life of Jews degenerated into a rigid legalism. Many leaders, including Jesus, condemned this change, but the mass of the Jews failed to heed their warnings. The 'chosen people' theme, legitimate as long as Jews remained obedient, was perverted into an idea of superiority and world domination.[212] Judaism provoked animosity in the ancient world, but only Christianity was clear-sighted and forceful enough to seal off the Jewish threat behind ghetto walls. Centuries later enlightened liberalism opened the floodgate to a renewed Jewish threat, but National Socialism was now in the process of setting that right.[213]

This is the speech which Kittel described in 1945 as an act of courage in defense of his Christian faith. He further noted that, having just learned of Jewish murders on the eastern front, he closed with the words, 'all horrors are gathering and all demons raging!'[214] It is true he defended Old Testament Judaism and he defended the Jewish roots of Christianity in this lecture. In the context of 1943, and especially in front of a National Socialist audience, that might have been construed as an act of courage. But his defense of Christianity implied no defense of the modern Jew. On the contrary, Kittel argued that Christianity deserved a place of honor in the Third Reich because of its stance on the Jewish question. Christianity was not weak sentimentality; it was a strong, principled, anti-Jewish force.

This lecture was a farewell, since Kittel returned to Tübingen in April 1943, after four years in the Austrian capital. But he was invited back to Vienna in 1944 to deliver a second lecture, in which he refined the racial arguments set out earlier. He established his right to apply racial analysis with the observation that racial factors were important as long as 2,000 years ago, even if unrecognized at the time. He uses the fall of Rome as his example. Since Rome's strength had been built upon its strong army and strong citizenry, and since the army remained strong, Rome must have fallen due to racial decomposition of her citizenry. Kittel then cites Jews as one of those elements of decomposition. Indeed, Judaism with its claims of privilege and superiority coupled with its racial degeneration, threatened to take over the world in those waning years of Roman influence.[215] Only Christianity had the strength and determination to halt the Jewish threat. Kittel is careful to show that Christianity had no racial sins to hide. Jewish converts had been mostly proselytes to Judaism, and, therefore, not racially Jewish; and Christian missionaries had been very few in number, thus racially insignificant. Christianity is universal, Kittel acknowledges, but only on a spiritual level. It allows for full *völkisch* development among the peoples. On the question of Jesus' Jewish origins, Kittel is much less forthright than in 1926. He asserts that at least Jesus' ideas were anti-Jewish.[216]

The picture of Kittel which emerges above is not that of a devout Christian

1.   Gerhard Kittel in the winter of 1943-4, aged 55.

probing issues of salvation and the Christian life. But there is evidence that Kittel also had this side to his character. He continued to edit the *Theologisches Wörterbuch*, for example, and that remains an important reference work to this day. And Kittel produced a few articles of a strictly theological nature during this period after 1933. Two of these articles concern the revision of Luther's Bible, which became an issue among German Protestants in 1938 when an experimental New Testament was issued. Kittel's respect for Scripture, his concern for the value of Luther's work, and his recognition of the need for a translation suitable for daily use are wholly unobjectionable.[217] In 1938, Kittel wrote a tribute to his predecessor at Tübingen, Adolf Schlatter. He praises Schlatter as a believing Christian whose relation to Jesus and the Bible were never in doubt.[218] Kittel must have hoped that the same could be said of him.

E. Conclusion

HOW should Kittel be judged? In his book, *History, Archaeology and Christian Humanism*, William Foxwell Albright devotes a short chapter to an unrestrained attack upon Kittel. For example, he writes that the story of Kittel is 'even darker and more menacing than the more flamboyant stories of Goering and Goebbels, since Kittel was a trained scholar and a Christian theologian.'[219] He credits Kittel and Emanuel Hirsch with 'the grim distinction of making extermination of the Jews theologically respectable.'[220] But then he adds on another occasion:

> In view of the incredible viciousness of his attacks on Judaism and the Jews, which continued at least until 1943, Gerhard Kittel must bear the guilt of having contributed more, perhaps, than any other Christian theologian to the mass murder of millions of Jews by the Nazis; an *apologia pro vita sua* written by him about the beginning of 1946 [presumably Kittel's defense statement] . . . painted an utterly amazing picture of a diseased conscience.[221]

Albright is a prominent archaeologist and Semitic scholar whose goal in this book is to illustrate the value and sufficiency of Christian humanism as an approach to life. He argues that history revolves around the Bible, both Old and New Testament, and the 'drama of salvation,' and that the goal of Christian humanism is to demonstrate this truth.[222] This may partially explain his vehemence against Kittel; Kittel's work cannot be seen as anything but a satanic distortion of Christianity, or Christianity itself might be called into question. As much as I value the judgments of Albright against Kittel, I question this dogmatic assumption with which he begins, and also his failure to acknowledge the complexity of the problem of Gerhard Kittel.

His attack admits no defense; however, in the years after 1945 many credible individuals came to Kittel's defense.

In the immediate post-war period French authorities imprisoned Kittel, and his colleagues at the University of Tübingen were unable to support him, either with his old job or with a pension. But a denazification proceeding eventually rehabilitated him, and preparations for the trial produced a flood of support on his behalf. Concerning his academic role, note the testimony of Freiherr von Campenhausen, *Rektor* at the University of Heidelberg in 1946 and visiting professor at Vienna from 1939-1941. After Kittel was imprisoned, he wrote:

> Although I belonged to the Confessing Church and never was a member of the NSDAP, in all things concerning the faculty and the church we were in agreement. Professor Kittel understood his work at the University of Vienna fundamentally as a service to the church and he stood in close contact with the leading men of the protestant church in Austria.[223]

Walter Rey, a student in Kittel's seminar on 'The Race Question in the New Testament' at Tübingen in 1944-5, later reported:

> Thereby he [Kittel] not only conveyed the public-endangering Party ideology ad absurdum, but at the same time he put into the hands of us students the weapons for fighting this Nazi error. I visited this seminar as an anti-Nazi . . . in order to see the Jewish question illuminated objectively from the Word of God.[224]

Another student, Claus Schedl, attended Kittel's lectures on the Jewish question in Vienna in 1941-2 and subsequently reported:

> [We] had sufficient opportunity to learn to know and to examine the attitude of the professor. Here one heard not a single word of malice . . . but, rather, serious historical research was pursued and the only goal was truth . . . In all his work a conception was developed which — if one understands Kittel properly — totally overcomes National Socialism. It is one of the ironies of history that a man who overcame the race problem of Nazism in the Jewish question is now brought to trial because of that . . . Professor Kittel truly did not collaborate; on the contrary, he was one of the few who, in spite of the danger, had the courage to advocate an opinion on the Jewish question other than the existing official one.[225]

Professor Martin Dibelius of Heidelberg, a theologian persecuted by the Nazis, commented on Kittel's work:

> The works of Kittel under question [relating to ancient Judaism] are of

purely scientific character, do not serve the Party interpretation of Judaism, have a theological consciousness as their presupposition, and hopefully will not fall as sacrifice to some judgment of condemnation, but will further fructify science. Their author deserves — to whatever extent one may agree with him — the thanks of all who are interested in the scientific study of Judaism.[226]

And a church leader, Thomas Breit, wrote in Kittel's defense:

Professor Kittel has . . . provided the church with an irreplaceable service. That can only be held in doubt by those who know nothing of the determined attack of National Socialism on the fundamentals of the church's proclamation. The intention of the lecture [presumably *Die Judenfrage*] and the perceptions developed in it are to be understood as a theological resistance movement against National Socialism.[227]

Finally, a number of baptized Jews testified to the friendly assistance they received from Kittel. Wilhelm Dittman, who studied theology at Tübingen from 1937 to 1939, wrote:

As a crossbreed of the first degree [one-half Jewish] according to the Nuremberg Laws, I had the greatest difficulties in achieving the normal completion of my studies, and I was in a very exposed position among the students. But Professor Kittel helped and advised me through word and deed in his fatherly way, as only he could. When my admission to graduation stood in question because of my family background, and when I myself wanted to give up my plans to graduate, Professor Kittel moved me to submit my application; and his reference is responsible for the fact that I received permission.[228]

Annemarie Tugendhat described another instance in which Kittel's attitude seemed above reproach:

My father is Jewish. During an action against Jews in 1938, he was brought to the concentration camp Welzheim. I met Professor Kittel in 1938, shortly after this action, at an evening lecture in Stuttgart. I was still strongly under the impression of the events of those days and the imprisonment of my father. That evening I sought out Professor Kittel, who was known to me only through his book, *Die Judenfrage*, in order to ask him what he as a Christian had to say about these events.
    I would like now to testify clearly that he was ready at once to enter a conversation with me, in spite of his strenuous lecture . . . and the conversation lasted until two o'clock in the morning — even though in those days it was dangerous for anyone to acknowledge his acquaintance with a Jew

with so much as a greeting . . . Professor Kittel raised the sharpest objections against the actions which were being directed against Jews, and as a
Christian he protested against any justification of these dealings. During
our conversation it became quite clear that the basis for Professor Kittel's
considerations on the Jewish question was not built upon the racial
theories of National Socialsm but upon his theology. This showed itself
especially in that as a Christian he was unconditionally concerned to find a
human and loving solution to all of the difficult problems. By no means did
this conversation take the form — as occurred all too often in those days —
of the exalted aryan and professor over the despised crossbreed. Rather,
in a loving and sympathetic manner he sought to understand the need and
to help.

    Professor Kittel preserved this personal respect on a human level also in
the years of the greatest persecution of us Jews. If he came to Stuttgart, he
always inquired how my parents and I were faring and thus maintained his
ties with us. It was known among us Christian Jews that one could come to
him and find help and advice. I politely request that you will give attention
to this declaration of mine in judging the 'case of Kittel.'[229]

This testimony cannot be ignored. It also conforms to the emphasis in
Richard Gutteridge's work and to his personal statement, 'Gerhard Kittel,
as the present writer, who was one of his pupils and greatly valued his
friendship can testify, was a gentle and warm-hearted person.[230]

Siegele-Wenschkewitz, too, stresses the honesty and sincerity with which
Kittel approached the Jewish question from his theological perspective. In a
letter to this author she makes this valuable point:

I see that that which Kittel believed he could advocate as a Christian
theologian on the Jewish question after 1933 can still be advocated in
unbroken form in the exegetical and general theological scholarship of
today. In presenting Kittel as plausibly as possible, I wanted to hold a
mirror before the eyes of today's contemporaries so they can recognize:
We ourselves are exactly the same, we ourselves think exactly the same. I
too do not find Kittel in any way harmless . . . but he is much more typical
of his discipline, perhaps of all German protestant theologians of his time,
then one would like to think when one makes him an outsider and a
scapegoat.[231]

It is too easy to make Kittel the scapegoat or sacrificial lamb, as Albright
does. We must recognize that he considered himself and appeared to be a
genuine Christian with traditional Christian concerns. He was a sensitive
human being, he was academically respected, and he took a stance on the
Jewish question that was distinct from National Socialist policy. All this
cannot and should not be ignored. But the bulk of Kittel's research between

1933 and 1945 was devoted to a rigorous and harsh anti-Jewish stance. Although his work maintained Christian roots, it also corresponded to the worst of Nazi propaganda. The tragedy of Kittel is prefigured in the case with which his Christianity was distorted to this unholy purpose.

The time sequence is important. In 1914 Kittel was a young scholar of Judaism who showed some promise and some prejudice. In 1926 he was a more mature scholar, with the confidence to rigorously defend the value of Judaism and its relation to Christianity. He almost broke through to a position of real tolerance and understanding towards the Jewish faith, pointing in a direction that post-war theology has tentatively begun to take. Perhaps it is coincidence, but this high point in Kittel's attitude towards the Jews came during the best years of the Weimar Republic. In 1933 Kittel suddenly lost his tolerance towards the Jews. His defense turned into an attack. Perhaps the bad years from 1930 to 1933 helped build up bitterness within him; the rise of Hitler was certainly the decisive factor that released it. But the question remains: what went wrong? Although Kittel found colleagues to defend him as late as 1947, there is no doubt the thrust of his work changed after 1933 with unfortunate and longlasting results.

Perhaps Kittel's genuine feelings burst forth in 1933. His animosity towards Jews must have had some genuine foundation for him to have developed it in so thoroughgoing a manner; but it was certainly submerged in 1926. A better explanation is opportunism. It was very good for Kittel's career to be anti-Jewish after 1933. His field was well suited to Nazi Germany, and he stood to reap the benefits if he supported the Party line. He later claimed to have opposed the Party line, and colleagues supported him in this claim; but their argument rests on a distinction which, though recognizable in the atmosphere of the Third Reich, is unconvincing today. Some of Kittel's colleagues appreciated his support against the *Deutsche Christen* and their desire to throw out the Old Testament. Others still accepted the 'Jewish problem' thesis, which colored their evaluation of Kittel's research. His contribution was to make antisemitism spiritual rather than biological.[232] The fact remains that Kittel never opposed anti-Jewish policy as such, and he never opposed Nazism. He did dislike the aspects of anti-Jewish policy which evolved in Nazi hands, and he pushed his own point of view within the confines of the Party. This distinction was enough for Dr Karl Prümm to describe Kittel's Vienna speech of 1943 as 'an act.' It was enough so that Kittel could meet individual Jews with genuine human sympathy and words molded to their ears. But the words he published were less carefully measured. He believed in the Jewish menace, he proposed harsh measures to deal with it, and he directed his research to reveal Jewish degeneracy. In short, he swam in the Nazi stream, though he may have preferred a different stroke.

Ego involvement and peer pressure must have played a role in Kittel's career after 1933. His position in the *Reichsinstitut* was an important one and it would have given him satisfaction. Not many theologians hobnobbed with the Party semi-elite. Kittel seems to have been impressionable, his personality marked by a desire to please, to fit in and be acceptable.[233] These characteristics are not surprising, perhaps, in the ambitious son of a great father.[234] Like a politician speaking to different constituencies, Kittel was able to express personal compassion to Jewish-Christian friends, acceptable theology to seminar students,[235] and harsh antisemitism to *Reichinstitut* audiences.

Kittel's mind was nimble enough to draw connections between all these versions of himself. And, although Albright read Kittel's defence statement and saw a 'diseased' mind, it might also be seen as a flexible or clever mind, searching for a middle thread strong enough to hold the cloth together. But a flexible mind may be too easily influenced by its surroundings, and Kittel's surroundings, e.g. at the *Reichsinstitut*, were uniformly bad. Charlatans were treated as scholars and even the best scholars maintained mystical, racial ideas that failed to outlive the special atmosphere of the Third Reich.

Constant exposure to such ideas naturally influenced Kittel, especially since a broad ideological and intellectual framework in Germany supported them. Shallow empiricism was opposed by *völkisch* and organic modes of thought. The truth of German experience became the final arbiter of truth in an otherwise relativistic world. In this environment legitimate research could veer into dangerous and tragic paths with no signposts to give warning. Kittel rejected one such signpost, the Enlightenment, with its ideals of equality, basic human rights and tolerance. Christianity also failed him. It was his misfortune to seize upon the anti-Jewish thread within the Christian tradition to the virtual exclusion of compassion, love and grace. This was a tragic error, but one to which Christianity has been vulnerable.

If Kittel was malleable, does that also mean he was unprincipled? Can his indiscretions in the Third Reich be explained solely as opportunism or as submission to political pressure? This question of sincerity is an important and a difficult one, but I believe Kittel's stance under Hitler was sincere. He vehemently affirmed his sincerity, denying the influence of external pressures in his letter to Loewe in 1933, and stressing the continuity of his thought in both versions of his defense statement after the war. Siegele-Wenschkewitz also emphasizes the open honesty of Kittel along with his 'adaptability.'[236] In addition, there is one thread which helps hold the cloth of Kittel's life and thought together, so that in the midst of his opportunism and impressionability his ultimate sincerity can be acknowledged. This also has the advantage of being the thread stressed by Kittel himself: the *Weltanschauungskampf*.

Kittel believed the world out of joint, to his detriment personally and as a patriotic German. In 1933 he saw a weak, defeated and demoralized Germany. He saw uprootedness, immorality, rebelliousness, materialism, secularism, relativism; in short, he saw the breakdown of the 'good old days' into a modern, urban, cosmopolitan, pluralistic world. He did not like what he saw, and he blamed it on the Enlightenment and all its progeny. Then, in harmony with National Socialism, Kittel learned to blame the Enlightenment, rationalism, secularism, immorality and decadence on Jews, especially assimilated Jews.

Kittel later gave us his version of what went wrong: he misjudged Hitler and National Socialism. Siegele-Wenschkewitz accepts this self-analysis and makes it the cornerstone of her book. But both of them are wrong; the judgment is too self-serving, and it ignores the deeper complexity of the problem of Kittel. It is more accurate to say that Kittel viewed Hitler and National Socialism clearly and liked what he saw, because he thought himself on the same side of the *Weltanschauungskampf*. This interpretation explains why Kittel endorsed Hitler publicly and enthusiastically not only in 1933, but also in 1944. If 'misjudgment' were Kittel's mistake, plenty of evidence was in by 1944. But his writings *throughout* the period correspond to and support Nazi politics, including all of the policies on the Jewish question, with the possible exception of genocide.[237]

Of course, there were radical and moderate elements within the spectrum of National Socialism, a diversity which blurs the edges of the question. Kittel did oppose radical, pagan, anti-Christian elements within National Socialism, and he was opposed by them in return. But it was part of Hitler's political genius to encourage diversity and a blurring of edges, in order to cast his nets more widely. Clearly, Kittel was one of those caught in the net. Another point of confusion stems from the natural tendency to condemn Hitler and National Socialism most vigorously for the policy of extermination. Kittel never said, 'Gas the Jews.'

But Kittel fought his *Weltanschauungskampf* by attacking the Jews. He resurrected Christian antisemitism from the Middle Ages, refurbished it with a touch of contemporary racial mysticism, and raised it as a German, Christian bulwark against the Jewish menace. This never corresponded exactly to Nazi policy, but it was too close for comfort. It allowed Kittel to work for twelve years within rather than outside the Party, and this physical and spiritual cooperation, whatever the limited and qualified assumptions on which it was based, was Kittel's tragic mistake. He deserves ignominy, for his writings from 1933 to 1945 were harsh and cruel. But he also deserves understanding and close attention, for his ideas taken individually, as Siegele-Wenschkewitz notes, live on.

F. Epilogue

IN October 1945, a few months after Kittel's imprisonment, efforts began among friends in France, England and America on his behalf. A French theologian, Theo Preiss, initiated this effort after having visited Kittel in prison while observing the religious situation in Germany for the French government. He wrote to Professor C. H. Dodd of Cambridge, requesting that Dodd contact other friends of Kittel and enlist their support. The main issue concerned Kittel's continuing editorship of the *Theologisches Wörterbuch*. Preiss thought he had already secured Kittel's release from prison, the only stipulation being that Kittel report in weekly; but Preiss seems to have been too optimistic. A letter from Kittel's wife in June 1946 indicates he was still in prison; in fact he was not released until October.[238]

Professor Dodd wrote to Herman Preus in the United States and asked Preus to contact several Americans whom Kittel had named. Preus complied, and it is through his files that the subsequent network of correspondence can be pieced together. Preus contacted the four names on his list, all pastors, and each of them sent a letter to the French Military Government, endorsing Kittel's work on the *Theologisches Wörterbuch*.[239] In March 1947 Kittel reported to Preus that the French authorities had authorized his continued work on the *Wörterbuch*, and he credited these American letters with influencing the decision.[240] But he then faced a new problem. With the work to be published in Stuttgart, part of the American Zone, American permission was also necessary. Kittel sent a new list of individuals whom he hoped would provide assistance, and he asked if Preus would contact them. This effort resulted in three endorsements supporting Kittel's further work on the *Wörterbuch*. But two theologians declined on the grounds they were not in a position to judge Kittel's former stance, nor did they want to send a statement which might be construed as a blanket endorsement.[241] Kittel continued corresponding with Preus through February 1948, with no indication that American permission was ever granted. Rather, the issue was diverted by a denazification proceeding against Kittel, after which his German colleagues would eventually decide whether his work should continue. Kittel reported in November 1947 that he was awaiting rehabilitation and in February 1948 he confirmed he had received it.[242] But he added no news about the *Wörterbuch*.

Letters from Kittel to Preus indicate that Kittel was imprisoned, first in the Tübingen Castle prison and later in the Balingen internment camp, from May 1945 until October 1946. During fifteen months of that period he saw no member of his family.[243] Even after his release, life was hard. He secured a position at the Beuron monastery where he received a modest stipend in return for work in the library. He also served as pastor to a small group of Lutherans there, and he had some time for his own studies.[244] But he was under travel restrictions, especially prohibiting a return to Tübingen, and Frau Kittel was not allowed to stay with him at Beuron. She lived at their summer home on the Walchensee with their daughter and newborn granddaughter until the spring of 1947, when that home was turned over to a refugee family.[215] Then the three of them moved to a two-room flat in Mannheim. Several weeks later, Frau Kittel was allowed to return to their former home in Tübingen, but she was given only two rooms for herself and shared the house with twelve other people.[246] These letters of 1946 and 1947 also describe severe food shortages and express warm thanks to the Preuses for Care packages sent.

Kittel never returned to the University of Tübingen, and he also was denied the customary pension. He explained to Preus only that 'difficulties' stood in the way of his return, but a letter from Theo Preiss amplifies this explanation. Bishop Wurm and Kittel's colleagues on the faculty explained to Preiss in confidence that they did not feel they could ask for Kittel's return, nor did they think it desirable.[247] Wurm did intervene for Kittel's release from prison,[248] but he confided to Preiss his personal belief that Kittel should have quit writing on the Jewish question as soon as it became apparent 'that the Nazis were laughing at scientific, Christian and even human arguments.'[249]

Kittel sent his last letter to Preus in February 1948. It contained the good news of Kittel's rehabilitation, which he attributed to Preus' acts of kindness:

> Your attitude made a deep impression over against the denunciations of my German adversaries, and that is the most important factor in my rehabilitation.[250]

A second item of good news was that the French Military Government had restored Kittel's freedom of movement, 'also for Tübingen.' So he finally returned to his home in Tübingen to live with his wife.[251] There is no mention of the fate of the *Wörterbuch*; but a favorable decision would have made little difference, for Kittel's days were numbered. He died on 11 July 1948.[252]

CHAPTER III

Paul Althaus: Mediator

A. Introduction

PAUL Althaus (1888-1966) was a Lutheran theologian of great stature in twentieth-century Germany. He began his career at Göttingen in 1914 as *Privatdozent* (Instructor, an entry level position in university teaching). During the war he served as a pastor in Poland, and in 1919 he resumed his academic career at Rostock. In 1925 he was named Professor of Systematic Theology at Erlangen, and there he remained the rest of his life.[1] Althaus is perhaps best remembered as a Luther scholar. After Karl Holl died in 1926, Althaus succeeded this founder of the 'Luther Renaissance' as president of the Luther Society, and he served in that position for more than thirty years.[2] He also published prolifically and served as editor of several journals.[3] In addition to his scholarly achievements, Althaus was widely respected in the church. For example, in 1933 when the Confessing Church and the *Deutsche Christen* each proposed a candidate for Reichs bishop and fought bitterly over the outcome, Bishop Wurm of Württemberg named Althaus as one of three persons who would prove a widely acceptable compromise candidate.[4] This suggestion did not become public knowledge and it had no effect at the time, but it is a good measure of the respect which Althaus enjoyed.

Moreso than either Gerhard Kittel or Emanuel Hirsch, Althaus represents respectable Lutherans in Nazi Germany. He never exhibited the vanity nor opportunism sometimes credited to Kittel, nor did he irritate or intimidate in the manner of his acerbic, biting colleague, Hirsch. Althaus apparently had no character defects. He enjoyed his intellectual and professional stature in quiet confidence, exhibiting to the world a warm and humane personality. He was the perfect gentleman, friend and teacher.[5]

Althaus' theology fit his personality: it was solidly respectable. He represents Lutheran orthodoxy, but he was not rigidly orthodox.[6] He did not ignore the intellectual difficulties posed by liberal scholarship in the nineteeth century, even though he rejected the solutions of liberal theology. He also was very aware of the inroads which modern secularism had made into the ranks of believers in Germany. Because of this twofold concern,

2.   Paul Althaus in 1939, aged 51.

Althaus quite willingly cast a critical and imaginative eye on the theology passed down by Luther and the Lutheran confessions. He believed it could be adapted for the modern era without loss of substance. This, of course, has been the belief of all modern theologians, divergence resulting only from varying opinions as to what is substantial. Placed on this continuum, Althaus remains close to the bosom of Luther; but that is not to say the adaptations which he developed were inconsequential. For example, he modified Luther in the matter of church and state, the so-called *Zweireichlehre*, and the consequences of this modification were great indeed. But it is best to begin an assessment of Althaus with the traditional view, recognizing his conservatism and orthodoxy.

Althaus maintained a running debate with his friend and ally, Emanuel Hirsch, in which his basic theological stance emerges. In 1940, for example, Hirsch published a controversial book, charging the church with not preaching and teaching honestly according to its theological understanding. He argues that the teaching of Easter and the resurrection is especially hypocritical; therefore, he focuses on the resurrection story and attempts to outline how it should be taught. Hirsch believes the oldest accounts of the resurrection in the New Testament mention only a spiritual appearance of the risen Jesus, similar to the vision which Paul saw on the road to Damascus. In his view, later authors embroidered on this basic idea to add all of the physical elements in the story, building up to an insistence upon the 'empty tomb.' Hirsch argues that this distorts the true picture of a risen Jesus, a Jesus who comes to man in spiritual form. The physical elements are unnecessary and untruthful additions and, furthermore, they distort Christianity in a number of harmful ways. For example, they focus attention on the hereafter rather than the present and on the physical, institutional church rather than on individuals and their response to Jesus' call. Hirsch concludes this book with four sermons illustrating how he believes Easter and the Easter texts should be preached.[7]

Althaus responded almost immediately, publishing an attack on Hirsch's interpretation. Admitting that Hirsch has a right to present his views on this crucial and timely question of reinterpreting Scripture, Althaus believes a public response necessary:

> For he places such extensive demands for the demolition and reconstruction of Christian thought and the church's proclamation that the church has a right to hear from others of us what we think of the crucial theses of E. Hirsch, where we agree with his attempts to reformulate Christian teaching and where we recognize something other than reformulation, namely loss of substance.[8]

Althaus impugns neither Hirsch's methods nor his motives; he merely disagrees with Hirsch's use of the data available to him. Althaus admits that much of the New Testament Easter account is a later construction designed for theological and literary purposes, but his reassessment of the evidence opposes Hirsch on two fundamental issues. Concerning the nature of Jesus' appearances, Althaus argues a distinction between the Easter appearances and visions of Jesus which appeared to men subsequently. Because the New Testament terminology differs, he rejects Hirsch's equating of the two phenomena.[9] Secondly, he argues that the 'empty tomb,' which Hirsch views as a later construction, is a self-evident part of the earliest Easter story. For example, the Disciples soon returned to Jerusalem preaching the resurrection. Had the tomb not been empty, Althaus assumes they would not have been believed.[10] He goes on to admit the empty tomb has been over-emphasized. It is highly ambiguous evidence of resurrection in any case and, furthermore, resurrection in a 'new body' need not include removal of the old from a tomb. This is the realm of mystery. But while acknowledging the mystery, Althaus is too orthodox to accept Hirsch's version of it. He accuses Hirsch of rationalizing and 'psychologizing' away an important reality in the Easter story.[11] Althaus' conclusion is a more traditional one:

> The genuine Easter experience consists of this, that the Easter testimony of the New Testament with its fundamental content brings us to faith in association with the entire message of Jesus.[12]

A similar controversy erupted between Althaus and Rudolf Bultmann. Bultmann concluded from the nineteenth-century search for a historical Jesus that history is inadequate as a basis for Christian faith. He despaired of finding a historical Jesus, substituting instead the image of Christ as preached by the early church. This *Kerygma* became his basis for faith. From this premise Bultmann began a process of 'demythologizing' the New Testament, seeking the true image of Christ as understood by early Christians, but which has since become hidden in the myths and symbols of that era. The result is an existential faith: the distilled message of Christ confronts man in his existence and requires a decision.[13]

Althaus does not deny this is a useful approach to the New Testament. He recognizes the difference between Bultmann and nineteenth-century liberal theologians; he recognizes that Jesus remained for Bultmann a real person and not a symbol.[14] But he argues that Bultmann's view of history is too simplistic. Bultmann despaired of objective history and allowed only an existential version, a history which has meaning only as encountered by individuals. Althaus argues that historical understanding occurs on several levels, extending from the objective to the intuitive. On this basis he believes a more promising historical understanding of Jesus is available than Bultmann was willing to admit; and therefore Bultmann's approach to the New Testament is only one of several fruitful approaches.[15]

In both of these controversies, Althaus remains conservative without being obscurantist. He recognizes the value of historical, critical theology, aproaching the work of Bultmann and Hirsch as a colleague rather than an opponent, from within rather than outside their frame of reference. However, he is more anxious than they to find a moderate solution, to throw out as little as possible of traditional orthodoxy. As he assumed the editorship of the journal, *Beiträge zur Förderung christlicher Theologie*, Althaus described his theological approach. First, he maintained that the journal should be specifically Christian. Religious studies which dilute Christianity by considering it one among many religions would not be acceptable. But secondly, he warned that this concern for pure doctrine must not result in a new orthodoxy. Rather a breadth of view should be fostered.[16] These are the parameters in which Althaus conducted his own theological work, and they indicate one of the strongest elements in his character. Althaus absolutely refused to be radical. He had a strong sense of where middle ground lay, and that is where he longed to be, that is where he felt most comfortable. Both Hirsch and Bultmann followed the logic of their research to uncomfortable, disconcerting conclusions. This was not in Althaus' nature. He also refused the opposite expedient of radical rejection of biblical scholarship. He did not proclaim 'inerrant Scripture' or complain that rational tools had no place in spiritual matters. Instead, he found middle ground. He used his rational tools to find and defend a place in the middle.

B. Althaus' Political Stance

POLITICALLY Althaus also sought middle ground, though he defined the middle from the viewpoint of his own milieu, in which left-of-center hardly existed. A first indication of his political stance came while he served as a pastor in Lodz, Poland, during the First World War. In August 1916 he addressed a group of pastors gathered at Lodz with the challenge that the church should take a positive stand on *völkisch* issues. He described the German *völkisch* movement as a growing force among German colonists in Poland. He himself encouraged those schools, lectures and organizations which supported the movement; and since he believed this a holy 'matter of conscience,' he felt the church at large should take a stand. He did not believe former Germans could be 're-Germanized,' but he insisted that further 'de-Germanization' should be opposed.[17] In taking this stance, Althaus departed from traditional Lutheran disinterest in political matters.

Shortly after the end of the war, Althaus again commented on the relation between church and *völkisch* issues, as he later reported:

At Christmas in 1918 I wrote, barely home from Poland and disgusted by the shameless voluntary surrender of the Germans, the impeachment of the leader, and the undignified confession of German guilt for the war: 'In the days of victory it was the task of the church to dash to pieces all arrogance, all wantonness, and all phariseeism in our *Volk*. Today, however, after severe defeat and in a state of collapse, it is incumbent on the church to recall for our *Volk* the value of a good conscience and the defiance of confident faith.' Then came 28 June 1919, the extorted confession of guilt of the German *Volk*. Did the church at that time fulfil its pastoral duty, or has it since? Has it rebuked the crimes of Versailles, not only the crimes of our enemies, but the German crime of signature [of the document]?[18]

These words, recounted by Althaus in 1933, indicate he shared in the right-wing, stab-in-the-back interpretation of the war. He also believed the extremity of the circumstances required a rethinking of the traditional Lutheran disinterest in political matters. In Romans 13, Paul prescribed obedience to the state, and Luther subsequently underscored that doctrine. Weimar was certainly a governmental authority in Paul and Luther's sense, and as such it deserved obedience.

But were they [such governments] authority in the same sense and degree as, for example, Bismarck and his royal master? Were they equally sacred? . . . The answer speaks for itself.[19]

The Christian in Germany might accept the authority of Weimar as a 'temporary structure,' but he also viewed it as the 'expression and means of German degradation and atrophy . . . The yes carried all provisionalness and reservation with it.'[20]

In 1919 Althaus returned to his academic career with a position at the University of Rostock and he played no political role in opposition to Weimar. The *Deutsche Christen* later attacked him for this. Julius Leutheuser, a leader of the *Deutsche Christen* in Thuringia, claimed that in a series of radio broadcasts in the 1920s, Althaus promulgated the old Lutheran idea of resignation towards the kingdom of this world and hope for the kingdom to come.[21] But in spite of political inactivity, Althaus cultivated an ideology which expressed his low opinion of Weimar. For example, in 1927 he addressed the Second Evangelical Church Conference in a gathering at Königsberg on the subject of *Volkstum*. The year 1927 was one of the more hopeful periods in the short history of Weimar, but Althaus assumed in his remarks that the German people were in a period of great tribulation. He described the *völkisch* vision of rebirth, emphasizing the organic, anti-modern, anti-urban, and with some qualifications, the antisemitic elements in that vision. He proclaimed this the spirit of the new age, and he appealed to the church not to be left behind.[22] This speech should not be confused with the most radical *völkisch* ideology, that of Alfred Rosenberg or even that of the *Deutsche Christen*. Althaus blended his Christian and *völkisch* principles in such a way that *v*ölkisch elements were constantly qualified. For example, Althaus repeated occasional anti-Jewish statements, but he also defended the Old Testament Jew and argued that the German *Volk* could identify with and learn from the experience of the Jewish *Volk* in their relationship to God. Posing the question of why an individual should love his *Volk*, Althaus answered, not 'because it is grander than others,' but only 'because it is my Volk'.[23] This sentiment is far removed from radical *völkisch* ideology. It illustrates Althaus' insistence upon honesty and moderation.

In spite of his honesty and moderation, however, Althaus warmly greeted the rise of Hitler in 1933. Some colleagues blame this initial enthusiasm on his commitment to a *volksmissionarische* concern as expressed in his speech of 1927.[24] He argued that the *völkisch* spirit was the spirit of the times and the church must enthusiastically ensorse the *Volk* if it were to regain any of its lost impact. Having expressed this concern so clearly, Althaus perhaps felt constrained to support Hitler when he emerged as the leader of the *Volk*. But there is ample evidence that endorsement of the *Volk* came easily to Althaus, for it coincided with his own political beliefs. The tone as well as the content of his pronouncements in 1933 and after make this abundantly clear.

In October 1933 Althaus published *Die deutsche Stunde der Kirche*, a book which went through three editions over the next year. His opening sentence is unambiguous: 'Our Protestant churches have greeted the turning point of 1933 as a gift and miracle of God.'[25] As proof of this claim he notes the statements of several church organizations. For example, the group of men assigned to write a new church constitution in April 1933 expressed 'a thankful yes!' to the political transition, and the Bavarian church synod proclaimed an Easter message which read in part:

A state which begins again to rule according to God's law may be sure that this activity will receive not only the applause but also the joyful and active collaboration of the church.[26]

Althaus even ascribes religious significance to the events of 1933. Just as in August 1914, the people now experience a sense of unity, of calling, of obedience and of profound meaning in life, all of which are religious in nature. Rather than reject this religious significance, Althaus believes the church should make use of the words of Paul, 'What therefore you worship as unknown, this I proclaim to you.'[27] This is an example of God teaching through history. Althaus concludes,

So we take the turning point of this year as grace from God's hand. He has saved us from the abyss and out of hopelessness. He has given us — or so we hope — a new day of life.[29]

In 1935 Althaus returned to a consideration of the 'hour' of the German people, explaining his preference for the Third Reich over the Weimar Republic in terms of God's will:

> According to the measure of this will, genuine and broken national existence distinguish themselves, as do genuine dominion and the degradation and depletion of the state to the service of dynastic arbitrariness or the will of the majority. As a Christian church we bestow no political report card. But in knowledge of the mandate of the state, we may express our thanks to God and our joyful preparedness when we see a state which after a time of depletion and paralysis has broken through to a new knowledge of sovereign authority, of service to the life of the *Volk*, of responsibility for the freedom, legitimacy, and justice of *völkisch* existence. We may express our thankfulness and joyful readiness for that which manifests a will for the genuine brotherhood of blood brothers in our new order of the *Volk*. . . . We Christians know ourselves bound by God's will to the promotion of National Socialism, so that all members and ranks of the *Volk* will be ready for service and sacrifice to one another.[29]

Within this one passage Althaus moves from the statement that the church should not pass out political judgments to the declaration that Christians are bound to National Socialism. This apparent contradiction is overcome in his mind for two reasons. First, he accepts the National Socialist myth that it is not a political party among others, but a movement which rises above politics. Therefore, Althaus considers support of the 'turning point' in 1933 an affirmation of the self-evident rather than a controversial political decision. Secondly, Althaus views the transition from Weimar to the Third Reich in conservative moral terms. He recognized in Weimar only secularism, permissiveness and a breakdown of all moral values. Because National Socialism promised to reintroduce discipline, reverence for institutions and respect for the churches, he would have thought it absurd not to welcome the National Socialist state.

One of these supposed Nazi attributes, respect for the churches, soon seemed to many a cruel joke. In 1934 Karl Barth and others, soon to be known as the Confessing Church, created the Barmen Declaration as an expression of their opposition to Nazi interference in the church. This statement expressed objections to the view of the *Deutsche Christen* that God was now speaking a new message to man through German history: Barmen affirms that God speaks to men only through Christ. It argues that any message not rooted in the New Testament representation of Christ is false, and any attempt to equate German history with holy revelation or to see in the events of 1933 God's call to the church is a dangerous heresy. Barmen was an explicit no to those who based their religion on the events of 1933, and it was an implicit no to those events.[30] Althaus could not accept

Barmen; it ran counter both to his politics and his theology. He had long insisted the church must say yes rather than no to the aspirations of the German *Volk*. Barmen appeared to him too negative. He also espoused a broader view of revelation.

Althaus first responded to Barmen by signing the *Ansbacher Ratschlag*, a statement written by his Erlangen colleague, Werner Elert, and signed by a group of eight pastors and theologians.[31] Althaus recognized the significance of his signature: this document was clearly an attack on the Barmen Declaration, and he and Elert, the most prominent of its signators, tied it to the Erlangen faculty. He cautiously requested two different rewritings of the document before granting his signature.[32] This caution proved well-founded but inadequate; the *Deutsche Christen* picked up on the *Ansbacher Ratschlag* with glee, reprinting it in one of their newspapers under the heading, 'Leading Theologians refute Barmen.' The paper enthused that these theologians of 'world reputation' had undercut Barmen for all time.[33]

The *Ansbacher Ratschlag*, printed less than two weeks after the Barmen Synod, addresses itself towards members of the 'National Socialist Protestant Pastors' League' as an attempt to present 'finally the genuine Lutheran voice.'[34] It consists of eight points directed implicitly against Barmen, although Barmen is never actually mentioned. The theological theme is that God's word may be interpreted with more freedom than that allowed in Barmen. In terms of politics and Romans 13, the *Ansbacher Ratschlag* states firmly that God intends for governments to be obeyed: 'As Christians we honor with thanks towards God every order, therefore also every authority, even if deformed, as a tool of divine preservation.'[35] But Christians also distinguish between 'benevolent and wayward masters, healthy and deformed orders.' Therefore,

> In this knowledge we as believing Christians thank God our father that he has given to our *Volk* in its time of need the *Führer* as a 'pious and faithful sovereign,' and that he wants to prepare for us in the National Socialist system of government 'good rule,' a government with 'discipline and honor.'
>
> Accordingly, we know that we are responsible before God to assist the work of the *Führer* in our calling and in our station in life.[36]

The rest of the document outlines the relationship between church and the natural orders, noting the church may even need to change its own institutional arrangements in accordance with the historical period.[37]

Public criticism of the *Ansbacher Rastschlag* came quickly. For example, *Junge Kirche* published an article entitled 'The Genuine Lutheran Voice?' with heavy emphasis on the question mark.[38] Hans Asmussen, a leader in the Confessing Church, also prepared a rebuttal.[39] Private criticism must have bothered Althaus even more. On 12 June a church official from Munich, an honorary doctor of the Erlangen theological faculty, vociferously responded to the rumor that the faculty intended to take a stance in opposition to Barmen. He describes this as a stab-in-the-back to Bishop Meiser and the Confessing Church in Bavaria.[40] Another correspondent complains about finding the *Ansbacher Ratschlag* reprinted in a *Deutsche Christen* publication, suggesting Althaus should now demand that the paper print a clarification of his position and a warning against misuse of the original document.[41] The most bitter letter came from Heinrich Benckert, a former student, who expresses his desire to 'scream' in Althaus' ear. He too uses stab-in-the-back terminology, and he describes the publication of the *Ansbacher Ratschlag* on the front page of a *Deutsche Christen* newspaper as more damaging than 'ten Reich bishops of the type of Müller.'[42]

It is difficult to fully identify Althaus' complicity in and support for the *Ansbacher Ratschlag*. Asmussen, for example, reports that Althaus distributed among a circle of theologians a 'Declaration' withdrawing his signature.[43] If true, this is not widely known and Althaus' name remains tied to his original signature. Letters addressed to Althaus in early July refer to his 'misgivings' about the *Ansbacher Ratschlag*, evidence that he did circulate a clarification of his position, and one which mollified his critics somewhat.[44] It remains difficult to know whether this clarification included an actual withdrawal of support. In 1964 Althaus turned down an invitation to write an article on the *Ansbacher Ratschlag*. He protests he was not one of the 'fathers' of the document, having joined the circle only in its last session. He signed it because he wanted to give public expression to his theological opposition to Barmen and the 'threatened canonization' of the Barmen thesis. But he admits not having read the theological statements carefully enough, and he asserts that the situation at the time has to be considered. The Röhm purge of 30 June had not yet occurred and President Hindenburg still lived, giving Althaus his basis for hope in 'good government.' 'Just a few months later I would not have been able to sign.'[45]

In early July 1934 Althaus published an article in a Bavarian church newspaper which probably gives a more accurate measure of his response to the Barmen Declaration and also to the criticism he had received for his role in the Ansbacher circle. First of all, he describes his interest in the issues of Barmen as theological, and he rejects use of his ideas in political in-fighting in the church. He also sides with the Barmen Synod idea that many *Deutsche Christen* are patently heretical.[46]

But he criticizes Barmen on two counts. First, it makes no attempt to address the questions to which the *Deutsche Christen* answers are given. Althaus reiterates that the aspirations of the *Volk* must elicit a response from the church. Secondly, Althaus criticizes the narrow view of revelation found in Barmen. He believes that Barmen emphasizes gospel to the exclusion of law, and excluding law it excludes the *revelatio generalis* in which God's law is amplified for man's understanding. Althaus believes in Christocentrism.

He agrees that the message of salvation *(Heilsoffenbarung)* centered on Christ is the primary revelation. But Althaus insists there is a general revelation *(Ur-Offenbarung)* which people can recognize if they first understand the primary revelation in Christ. Although the *Deutsche Christen* misuse this concept, giving too much weight to the secondary form of revelation, Althaus argues the proper response is not to give up the concept of *Ur-Offenbarung*, but to more rigorously define it.[47]

This is a more carefully reasoned and much less abrasive statement than the *Ansbacher Ratschlag*. Ernst Wolf, author of a history of Barmen from the Confessing Church point of view, describes Althaus' critique of Barmen as one of the most thoughtful.[48] But Althaus does reject the politics of Barmen, and he reaffirms his concern with the *Volk*.[49] This statement remains similar to the *Ansbacher Ratschlag* in substance, even though Althaus' mediating and compromising style make it less abrasive.

In addition to opposing Barmen, Althaus opposed the other extreme, the *Deutsche Christen* movement. He did so only with reluctance, for he shared the concerns and goals of the *Deutsche Christen*. But Althaus fell into opposition when he could no longer accept their fuzziness of thought. The *Glaubensbewegung Deutsche Christen* (Faith Movement of German Christians) published a ten-point program which reveals the basic elements in this movement. In the spirit of national unity the *Deutsche Christen* appealed for a united *Volks* church to replace the divided churches of the past. Point four suggests a rather general confessional basis for the union:

> We profess an affirmative, true to type *(artgemäss)* faith in Christ as it corresponds to the German spirit of Luther and heroic piety.[50]

An analysis of the historical failure of the church appears in point five:

> In the fateful struggle over German freedom and the German future, the church in its leadership has proven itself too weak. Up until now the church has summoned up nothing in the decisive battle against atheistic Marxism and the spiritually foreign Center Party [a Roman Catholic political party during Weimar]. On the contrary, it sealed a church treaty with the political parties of these powers.[51]

The document affirms that the proposed *Volks* church will fight against 'Marxism and the Christian socialists hanging onto its coattails, both of which groups are enemies of religion and the *Volk*.' It appeals for purity of the race and 'protection of the *Volk* from the incompetent and the inferior.' Finally, it opposes the Jewish mission, mixed marriages, and 'Christian cosmopolitanism.'[52]

In 1933 Julius Leutheuser, one of the leading *Deutsche Christen* in Thuringia, gave a speech which further describes the *Deutsche Christen* position. He begins with a comparison of Jesus and Hitler: the National Socialist state grew out of one and evangelical Christianity out of the other.[53] Then Leutheuser winds his way through history showing how the German state idea, the evangelical chuch and God's purpose in history are all bound together. For example, even prior to the Reformation the German church was in constant conflict with the Roman church, which Leutheuser describes as being of Roman body and Jewish spirit. Rome produced the monk, but Germany produced the 'holy worker.' When Frederick the Great described himself as first servant of the state, that corresponded to Jesus' injunction that he who would be first should serve others. Leutheuser believes that after Luther Germany enjoyed a unity centered on the gospel, the German state and the German soldier. Weimar destroyed this unity, but Hitler had now restored it.[54]

A second pamphlet by Leutheuser illustrates his manner of theological argument. In this instance he is responding to the criticism of Ernst Otto, a pastor in the Confessing Church in Thuringia. Otto accused him of throwing the Old Testament out of the Bible; but Leutheuser responds with the question, must a German become Jewish before he can become a Christian? He views the Old Testament as useful only in so far as it leads to a better understanding of Jesus. Otherwise, the New Testament brings it to an end. Otto says that Leutheuser de-emphasizes sin, but the latter responds that faith can move mountains, including sin and guilt. Jesus overcomes sin. Otto then charges that National Socialism is made into a religion. Leutheuser believes the Holy Spirit moves where it chooses. More 'spirit of religion' has come to Germans through Hitler, he writes, than through many of the churches. Otto cannot understand this because he has not had the National Socialist experience. Leutheuser adds that if he had lived during the Reformation, he would also probably have opposed Luther.[55]

In 1935 a colleague of Leutheuser, Siegfried Leffler, produced a book which attempts a systematic explanation of the *Deutsche Christen* position. He begins by describing the crisis which Germans face, a crisis he calls loss of 'homeland' *(Heimat)*. It is the crisis of modernity, the crisis of lost roots. Through the nineteenth century no one could recreate homeland for the people, Leffler writes. Instead, it was replaced by the empty values of mammonism.[56] Leffler then describes the *volkisch* ideology of the twentieth century as a 'homeward way' *(Heimweg)*. He employs religious terminology and asserts that through this message Germany has been given a mission from God.[57] The 'leader and prophet' is Adolf Hitler. Leffler describes him in glorified terms as a soldier and worker who experienced himself the travail of the German people as a whole.[58] Hitler also stands in a direct line with Martin Luther, according to Leffler. Luther first destroyed the Jewish, Oriental nature of Christianity with his realization that Germans need no priests or theologians between them and God. 'So we cannot think of Adolf Hitler without Martin Luther.'[59]

Leffler sees the modern religious debate as a contest between the law of Jewish religion and the creativity of German Christianity.[60] But he does insist the German religion remain Christian, emphasizing that the new German paganism must be opposed.[61] He describes the Bible and the Confessions as the two foundation stones of the *Deutsche Christen* faith.[62] With this emphasis Leffler retains a foothold within the Christian camp and an apparent common ground with Althaus. But Althaus reacted against the doctrine which Leffler and Leutheuser developed.

Althaus did indeed sympathize with much of the *Deutsche Christen* position. He shared with them a political enthusiasm for the Third Reich and an intellectual and emotional affirmation of the *völkisch* idea. He also shared a common enemy in the new German paganism.But Althaus was repelled by two elements which offended his conservative orthodoxy. First, the *Deutsche Christen* partook too much of nineteenth-century liberal theology. Liberal theology reduced for them the substantive content of the Bible, it taught them a scepticism towards traditional theology, and it allowed them the freedom to reinterpret Jesus' life in terms of an idea. The resulting theology was not sufficiently Christian for Althaus. It raised German history to too high a level of significance in relation to *Heilsgeschichte* (salvationary history, or the history of God's people, the Israelites, and God's son, Jesus). Althaus' second objection centered on the *Volks* church idea. The *Deutsche Christen* desired a unified German church to correspond to the unified *Reich*. Because of their liberal position theologically, doctrinal objections appeared to them insignificant. Althaus also wanted a unified church, but not at the expense of his principles. For this reason he opposed the call for union.

As early as 1933 Althaus hinted at his opposition to the *Deutsche Christen*. In *Die deutsche Stunde der Kirche* he notes their claim to see in the National Socialist experience the virtues of 'faith, hope, love, spirit of sacrifice, and obedience,' i.e. the Christian virtues but spread more effectively by National Socialism than by the church.[63] He describes this as very offensive to a theologian; but, on the other hand, he does agree that the spiritual element in events such as the *Wende* of 1933 must be recognized by theologians.

In a speech given in 1934, 'Christ and the German soul,' Althaus sides with the *Deutsche Christen* in attacking the idea of a Germanic religion. Commenting on those who believe that *Deutschtum* rules out Christianity, Althaus asserts that the examples of Luther, Arndt, Freiherr vom Stein and Bismarck show this to be absurd.[64] Except for the 'Saxon incident,' he argues, the early Germans freely accepted Christianity because it was suitable for them. As revised by Luther, Christianity fits the German character.[65] On the other hand, Althaus maintains that mysticism is not particularly German. Meister Eckhard's roots are Arabic and Jewish, not Indogermanic, he argues, and mysticism is found among all peoples.[66] Also, mysticism and its close relative, the heroic ideal, are out of touch with reality. They are too pretty to be true. Althaus says it is silly to question whether they are Semitic or Indogermanic, only whether they reflect reality. He believes they do not, but that they represent a false attempt by man to create his own glory.[67]

Neither Leffler nor Leutheuser would disagree with Althaus so far, but in this same speech of 1934 he begins to part company with them. He accuses the *Deutsche Christen* of accepting too uncritically the heroic, manly ideal of the German pantheists. As a result they preach Jesus as hero rather than Jesus as Savior; they emphasize his life more than his death. Althaus criticizes this as a return to the Enlightenment with its liberal view of Jesus as the teacher and example.[68] It is a departure from Luther's gospel, and it is close to the Germanic pagan position of Wilhelm Hauer, which rules out concepts such as sin and repentance as insufficiently 'true to type' *(artgemäss)* for the strong and courageous German.[69] Althaus argues that Luther's gospel can be preached in such a way that its strength, manliness and Germanness will be apparent.[70]

In 1935 Althaus directed his attention specifically to Leutheuser and Leffler in a pamphlet on 'political Christianity.' He first notes his appreciation of their concern for the relationship of the *Volks* movement to Christianity: 'This theme is also mine and has been ever since 1915 when I experienced and was involved in the German *Volks* movement in Poland.'[71] But he then turns to the attack. First he accuses the *Deutsche Christen* of interpreting German history as *Heilsgeschichte*. They see Germans as chosen people, a new Israel. Althaus quotes from Leutheuser: 'Whoever gives up hope for Germany, gives up hope for meaning in the world. Whoever does not believe in Germany's resurrection, does not believe in the resurrection of God.'[72] He attributes the origin of this idea to Fichte and considers it a ridiculous elevation of political events to messianic pretensions. He credits von Ranke with teaching man enough about history to be cautious in seeing mission in a *Volk*.[73] He adds that the *Deutsche Christen* are out of touch with Germany's leaders on this matter:

> What would the *Führer* of our state be inclined to say to the delirious words of the Thuringian *Deutsche Christen?* The national movement is concerned with the life of Germany and nothing else. We are not saviors of the world, we do not dream that our fate holds messianic significance for the entire world.[74]

Althaus agrees that National Socialism may be an example to nations facing crises similar to that of Germany, and he acknowledges that Germany does have a role in the world, as does every 'capable' *Volk*.[75] But why turn this into messianic pretensions? Althaus notes that the Anglo-Saxons made this mistake in the First World War.[76] But, he concludes, no *Volk* offers salvation. Only the Christian church does that.[77]

Althaus also criticizes the *Deutsche Christen* for viewing the Third Reich as a parable of God's Reich. He acknowledges there is a similarity but he says the *Deutsche Christen* neglect to notice the elements of dissimilarity which remain.[78] He also attacks the *Deutsche Christen* use of the phrase, 'Christ is our strength.' He describes this as a false claim on the power of Christ in fulfilling the German task. A task may be given to the German people by God, but he promises to no people that they will succeed: 'Belief in the success of the German task has nothing to do with belief in the victory of the kingdom of God.'[79] Furthermore, this view of Christ says nothing about Christ as Savior and Lord. He is simply part of an idealist view of history, as guarantor that it will all work out, that victory will be attained.[80] Finally, Althaus criticizes the *Deutsche Christen* call for a *Volks* church, arguing that the really burning issues do not concern German church unity but the struggle between Christians and the new Germanic religion. He calls on the *Deutsche Christen* to join in this struggle rather than argue over secondary matters.[81]

Leutheuser responded to Althaus in a pamphlet he co-authored with Erich Fascher, another *Deutsche Christen* theologian. Leutheuser rebuts Althaus' points one by one, refusing to compromise with him and defining Christianity for a specifically German context. For example, on the question of *Heilsgeschichte* Leutheuser argues that all history is made by God. It only becomes *Heilsgeschichte* for those who are able to see it as such, but he had not thought Althaus would be one of those blind to the religious importance of German history. He accuses Althaus of being too much the professor, sitting above the battles in neutral observation, refusing to join in. Therefore, Althaus does not experience the significance of what is happening.[82] He also denies Althaus' apparent belief that there can be any certainty of biblical interpretation. Barthians say, 'The Bible explains itself.' But if that is true, why are there so many Protestant sects? Leutheuser argues that in cases of differing interpretation, which are bound to occur, political leaders may step in as they did with the early church councils.[83]

Leutheuser also takes up the Jewish issue. He argues that the Jewish sense of God is opposite to that of the German. The Jew strikes bargains with God; the German trusts him. The Jew also lives off the sweat of others, endlessly quibbles, and manipulates in argument; his behavior in each case contrary to that of a German.[84] Another area in which Althaus offended Leutheuser was in his criticism of Fichte and the German idealists. Leutheuser views this as heresy. He lauds Fichte and Arndt and states that their dreams have finally been realized in Hitler.[85]

Fascher wrote the second half of this response to Althaus. His main point is that Althaus is untrue to himself. He points to Althaus' lectures and publications dating back to 1915 and argues that they express the same ideas as the *Deutsche Christen*. He repeats Leutheuser's accusation that Althaus is merely unwilling to enter into the fray.[86] And he challenges Althaus to attend a *Deutsche Christen* gathering the next time he is invited. Then he believes they will find more common ground than Athaus expects, and this discussion will have borne fruit.[87]

There is much logic in Fascher's position, but his hopes were frustrated, for Althaus never reconciled with the *Deutsche Christen*. He was unwilling to share their theological ground. As noted above, however, he was enthusiastically willing to share political ground with National Socialism. Was he fooled by the carefully nurtured image of National Socialism in the early days of the Third Reich? Did he change his stance in subsequent years? Perhaps so, but certainly not in an open or clearcut manner.

As late as 1937 Althaus released a number of publications which reinforced his earlier stand. This year is significant for it included one of the dramatic events in the *Kirchenkampf*, the arrest and imprisonment of Martin Niemöller. Eberhard Bethge, who with Dietrich Bonheoffer coincidentally visited Niemöller on the day of his arrest, reports he was detained for ten hours while the Gestapo searched the house. Niemöller was tried and acquitted, but the Gestapo immediately rearrested and took him to a concentration camp, where he became a symbol of the repression of the Nazi government. Bethge notes the Gestapo learned more subtle tactics after this debacle: speaking bans, banishment to small parishes, confiscation of duplicating machines. Finkenwald, the underground seminary of the Confessing Church run by Bonhoeffer, was also closed in this year. All in all, 1937 was a year in which differences between church and state were intense and intensely public.[88]

During 1937 Althaus wrote an article on church and state in which he describes totalitarianism as a perfectly satisfactory form of government. His premise is that the authority of a state is sanctioned by God because the state administers God's law. Without specifically denouncing democracy, he notes it is not the best form of government for every nation, and he places heavy emphasis on the need for sufficient authority for a state to govern effectively.[89] Chaos is a greater danger in his eyes than tyranny. A second premise in this article is that the desires of the *Volk* are the pre-eminent guideline. So long as the state recognizes this pre-eminence, it may use as much force as necessary to achieve its ends. Totalitarianism may then even be a necessity to guard against 'the disconnectedness of individuals . . . in the liberal state.'[90] Althaus acknowledges that totalitarianism may degenerate into an absolutism which destroys the 'free devotion' individuals and organizations feel towards their nation:

> But a state which knows itself as servant to the life of its *Volk* will not rob the other associations and orders in the *Volk* . . . of their self-reliant, spontaneous life. It will embody totalitarianism — not as an inflexible system, but it will call forth the free spirit of totality, i.e. the spirit of responsibility for all forms and spheres of life in the presence of the duty to be *Volk*.[91]

In this same article Althaus develops themes which may have been subtly critical of the Third Reich. He warns that church and state each have a distinct role to play and must not interfere with each other.[92] Government interference in chuch affairs and harassment of pastors may have crossed his mind as he wrote these words, making them something of a warning to the state. (At the same time he is telling churchmen they cannot interfere in writing the state's laws). Althaus also insists that neither a fanatical anti-semitism nor a new Germanic religion is acceptable. He even develops a theory which ties political survival to the maintenance of Christianity in Germany. He argues that when a society becomes Christian it achieves a fuller knowledge of the truth than it had under its primitive religion. Primitive religion through its partial truth provides some of the glue which holds a society together, but a post-Christian society cannot return to primitivism. It is too sophisticated. Therefore, without Christianity no truth remains for it, and the resulting lack of bonds will be mortal. 'For a *Volk* after Christ [that has known Christ], Christianity has become a question of its political existence.'[93] This is certainly a warning to the state that it must treat the church with respect.

Althaus wrote a second article in 1937 in which the same hint of ambivalence towards the Third Reich appears. The subject is 'Christianity, War and Peace,' and Althaus begins with an apparent defense of the militaristic German state. He describes war as an unfortunate but necessary means for nations to resolve their differences.[94] This analysis is not surprising; it is rooted in Althaus' belief in a fallen world and in the imperfectability of man. However, Althaus then adds a plea for peace. He argues that the destructiveness of modern war coupled with the constant threat that any small conflict will escalate into world war combine to make the preservation of peace a law of political reason. Althaus adds only one qualification to this nearly pacifist stance: he insists it is a political rather than a theological argument. He opposes those who see in peace a higher order of human life or something resembling the 'peace of God.'[95] Althaus added this last section to his article after it had been published elsewhere without the appeal for peace. It is possible that by 1937 he had begun to question the warlike nature of the new German state. But this is rather tenuous evidence of opposition. Hitler also talked peace. Althaus need not have believed he was distancing himself from the *Führer* with his arguments on this issue.

In a speech presented in 1937 Althaus followed his pattern of introducing a subtle hint of ambiguity or caution regarding National Socialism. He directs this speech towards the German church, warning that it must learn from its present divisions and difficulties. Althaus argues that the primary concern of the church must be to bring the Christian message to the German people. It must retain its distinctiveness and not become an adjunct of the state or a national political religion.[96]. This shows his awareness that

National Socialism was possibly a threat. However, his continuing affirmation of the *Volk* suggests a less critical stance. He asserts that church and
state must work together for the *Volk*. The role of the church is not to fight
Bolshevism in the streets: 'That was the privilege and splendid work of the
political movement, which we cannot thank enough.'[97] But the church had
helped during the Weimar years by fighting the 'spirit of dissolution of all
bonds.' Further:

> The church knows that her God-given responsibility today as yesterday
> points her into the fight against Bolshevism, against the horrible poison of
> destruction of all worthy order, all humanity. She belongs on the side of all
> who conduct this fight with earnestness.[98]

This statement leaves no doubt which side Althaus is on. He then expresses
the hope that the church will recognize its responsibility anew, and that
politicians will, 'despite all disappointments and misunderstandings, gain a
new recognition of the political significance of the church of Jesus Christ
within our *Volk*!'[99]

If Althaus hinted at an ambivalence towards National Socialism in 1937, it
may have been partly a tactic of conciliation directed towards the church.
With Niemöller under attack from the state and the church torn apart,
Althaus hoped to assist in pulling the factions back together, as he acknowledged in the lecture mentioned above.[100] But his ambivalence was more
than a tactic. He denounced the radicalism of the *Deutsche Christen* and the
German pantheists because he found their views offensive to his Christian
faith, and not just because this would reassure those elements in the church
which opposed National Socialism. And he endorsed totalitarianism not just
because such a stance would appeal to the *Deutsche Christen*. Althaus need
not have endorsed totalitarianism had he been disillusioned by Hitler's use
of it. And he need not have been so enthusiastic in his opposition to
Bolshevism had he not still approved of the National Socialist repression of
the left. By 1937 Althaus seems to have retained his support of National
Socialism, if not his unqualified enthusiasm. After 1937 his publications
were no longer political. Readers may have detected in the ambiguity of his
work in 1937 and the less political themes thereafter a disaffiliation from the
direction of the Third Reich. But the public evidence was subtle and
ambiguous. He never openly or clearly renounced his former views.

Is there private evidence to suggest Althaus' disillusionment with
National Socialism? Indirect evidence can be found in the archives of the
Hannoverian *Landeskirche*, where Althaus' correspondence with Bishop
Marahrens indicates a sharper and earlier rejection of the *Deutsche Christen*
than Althaus' public posture would imply. For example, during the summer
of 1933 Marahens reported on the large number of *Deutsche Christen*
elected to his synod and asked Althaus for his opinion on how to react. The

latter expresses surprise and shock at the large number. He advises working in common with the *Deutsche Christeb* but not joining them:

> In the meantime we have had the orgies of the general synod and the scandal of the takeover of the bishop's seat. It is totally impossible to indicate approval by joining them. The protection of the formula 'creation and fall' [*Schöpfung und Sünde*] does not go that far with me. It is impossible to speak with Hirsch and Beyer. I wrote a long letter with the question: how can you stand what occurred on the 2nd and 23rd of July — but one gets either no answer or an evasive answer. Hirsch is subject to such an absolutism it is no longer possible to have a true discussion with him. He sees in me a man who 'reasons against fate.'[101]

Althaus goes on to admit sumpathy with many *Deutsche Christen* goals, sympathy he knows is shared by Marahrens, and he suggests their theology is not so bad. But the takeover of the bishop's seat indicates an 'unchurchly will to power.' 'The worst thing is the dynamic of the "movement".'[102]

Despite his sympathy for the *Deutsche Christen* goals, Althaus was appalled by their tactics in the summer of 1933, and he gave his support to Bodelschwingh rather than Müller in the contest for Reichs bishop.[103] This situation captures the differences between Hirsch and Althaus very effectively. Hirsch was ever willing to take an extreme position consistent with his convictions and ever able to find a rational justification (in this case, 'creation and fall,' or the existence of evil in even the best of human developments). Althaus, on the other hand, instinctively opted for moderation, thereby rejecting the extreme behavior of the *Deutsche Christen*. But he also was too much the mediator to tangle openly with Hirsch or fight the *Deutsche Christen*. He did not want to interrupt the enthusiasm in Germany for the National Socialist rebirth by precipitating open quarrels. As a result he hid his true feelings from public view.

Another hint at Althaus' true feelings during the 1930s can be found in the testimony of his son and youngest child, Pastor Gerhard Althaus. The younger Althaus, born in 1935, cannot personally remember his father's attitude or behavior during that decade. But the two were close as Gerhard undertook his theological studies in the 1950s, and he reports on what his parents later said about those early days. For example, he notes that Paul Althaus, despite a conservative, monarchical aversion to *any* political party, saw in the rise of Hitler in 1933 a 'virtual pointing finger from God.'[104] But with the suspicious *Reichstag* fire in February came the first shock, the realization that 'something was not right.' Then in July 1933 Althaus gave a speech on 'Unworthy Life in the Light of Christian Belief,' which caused him trouble with the ministry of the interior in Bavaria. Rabid Nazis wanted to distinguish between worthy and unworthy life.[105] Ten years later this question reemerged under cicumstances Gerhard can remember personally. In

August 1943, on holiday at Tegernsee, Paul Althaus preached to a Sunday morning congregation which included troops on leave from the Soviet front. After the service an officer came home with Althaus to unburden his soul. In his confession he constantly repeated the word 'camp' (*Lager*, a word which baffled young Gerhard because he associated it with the Indian camps of his youthful reading). Civilians were shot; women and children were shot; unarmed Soviet prisioners were shot. After this incident Paul Althaus no longer spoke with his son about winning the war, but about 'our bloodguilt' towards the Jews. Gerhard also remembers that when his father now mentioned the term, 'bloodguilt', at the dinner table, or when he said, 'What has Hitler done with this war?'; his mother would caution, 'Paulus, not so loud.' She feared the maid would eavesdrop and denounce them.[106]

This testimony from Gerhard Althaus is mostly verbal and partially second-hand. It cannot establish that Paul Althaus became an opponent rather than a supporter of National Socialism; there is, moreover, no claim he ever openly or publicly expressed his internal disillusionment. Moderation was the cornerstone of his opposition as well as support of the Third Reich.

For this theme of moderation to make sense, it must be remembered that Althaus remained moderate *within his milieu*. He positioned himself among those who generally approved of National Socialism, and he studiously avoided what to him were the extremes of either fanatical support or any form of opposition to the Third Reich. In retrospect, this stance may not appear moderate. It was tied to National Socialism, and National Socialism is now viewed as the antithesis of moderation. But in Althaus' world National Socialism represented the popular idea. Within that world Althaus believed he stood on middle ground, and that is the mark of his political stance.

C. Theological Issues

ONE of the primary theological issues on which Althaus separated himself from Barthians on one side and the *Deutsche Christen* on the other is that of revelation. The narrow, Christocentric view of revelation is that God speaks to man only through the life of Christ as revealed in the Bible. This is the underlying premise of Barth, Barmen and the Confessing Church. This view of revelation is designed to weed out eccentric versions of the Christian faith, but it does not necessarily do so. The message of the Bible is susceptible to many varying interpretations. Another problem with this view is the danger of a static faith which does not relate to men in their present situation. The broader view of revelation is that God speaks to man through nature and history. During the nineteenth century *Kulturprotestantismus*, a phenomenon of liberal theology, espoused this view; and in the twentieth century it became the creed of the *Deutsche Christen*. The main problem with this approach is that history can be read indiscriminately as the new message of God.

Althaus, true to his basic instincts, struggled to find a middle ground between these two divergent views. He agreed with Barth that the central message from God, the message of salvation, is rooted in Christ. This is the *Heilsoffenbarung*; it is God's principal word to man and it comes to man through the Bible. However, Althaus accuses Barth of too narrow a 'Christo-monism' in his view of revelation.[107] He feels some room has to be found for the message of God through his creation. He specifically denies that he means a natural theology; natural revelation cannot be sufficient by itself, for it will not lead to Christianity.[108] Althaus is also unwilling to espouse a natural theology because of its ties to Roman Catholicism. However, the compromise which he develops does accept a revelation in nature. He qualifies this by insisting the revelation of God in nature can only be properly understood if one knows the message of God in Christ. With this qualifica-tion, nature (and natural events, i.e. history) can point the unbeliever to-wards Christ and it can enlighten the believer as to the will of God. Althaus labels this new concept of natural revelation *Ur-Offenbarung*.[109]

It is difficult to assess the significance of *Ur-Offenbarung* as a theological proposition. Althaus never gave up the concept.[110] He also has many allies, even if they fail to use his terminology or refuse to acknowledge the associa-tion. Hans Grass points out correctly that Tillich, for example, recognizes a 'universal revelation' in which God reveals himself through history and nature.[111] Both Althaus and Tillich reject the Barthian view of the 'infinite qualitative distinction' between Christianity and other religions; each takes the more moderate view that non-Christian religions are lesser versions of God's truth. Barth seems to them 'Christomonistic' in his extreme rejection of *all* truth outside Christ.

Despite this theoretical connection to Tillich and other 'acceptable' theologians, *Ur-Offenbarung* has had few acknowledged adherents since 1945. The main reason is it carries such heavy political baggage. Althaus may have disagreed, considering his position in essence theological. Grass agrees with Althaus, asserting that he opposed Barmen because of his *theological* commitment to *Ur-Offenbarung*.[112] Furthermore, the reference to Tillich, who was politically opposed to and exiled from the Third Reich, seems to imply the political neutrality of the concept. But there is an overwhelming sense in which *Ur-Offenbarung* conformed to Althaus' poli-tics. Many of the theological arguments between Althaus and Barth come close to resolution. Barth, if pressed, would probably admit to seeing God's hand in nature, and then he would argue that such recognition could not be regarded as instructive or authoritative. Althaus would agree it is of secon-dary importance to him as well. But the political differences between Althaus and Barth added an insurmountable barrier to any potential recon-ciliation on this issue.

The fundamental, though unexpressed, premise of *Ur-Offenbarung* as developed by Althaus is that God created and approves the political status quo. Barth opposed this concept of revelation in 1934 because he opposed the political situation. Althaus developed this concept because he approved it. This becomes clear in the *Ansbacher Ratschlag* as it describes the law of God:

> It binds each in the position to which he has been called by God and commits us to the natural orders under which we are subjugated, such as family, *Volk*, race (i.e. blood relationship) . . . In that the will of God also meets us continually in our here and now, it binds us also to a specific historical moment of family, *Volk* and race, i.e. to a specific moment of their history.'[113]

According to this theory, God's will equals the situation at any given moment, except, of course, for aberrations such as the Weimar years. Obedience towards God consists of accepting one's allotted position in life as handed down by years of tradition.

As noted above, Althaus was not totally committed to the *Ansbacher Ratschlag* even though he signed his name to it. In his own critique of Barmen he admits the concept of *Ur-Offenbarung* could be misused, as it was by the *Deutsche Christen*, to sanction the untenable.[114] At the same time he criticizes the narrowness of Barmen for ruling out the concept, rather than just the misuse of it. Misuse would include the de-Judaizing of Christianity or placing the German experience on the same level as God's message in Christ. But Althaus believes Barmen should affirm that *Ordnungen*, e.g. the German *Volk*, are a part of God's creation and therefore, a part of God's law.[115] This is essentially the position of the *Ansbacher Ratschlag*, although it is qualified and refined.

In a separate pamphlet, *Theologie der Ordnungen*, Althaus develops a broader and more systematic explanation of the given orders of creation, the *Schöpfungsordnungen*, and their Christian interpretation. In this pamphlet it is clear he is not naive. First, he defines *Ordnungen* as 'the forms of social life of people, which are the indispensable conditions for the historical life of humanity.'[116] He recognizes that these orders are imperfect, a part of the sinful world. He even quotes Burckhardt and Meinecke to the effect that the state is essentially power, which is evil, and that it has a dynamic of its own which is demonic.[117] Because of this, man cannot serve the natural order without serving evil. This realization might lead to scepticism or nihilism. Althaus avoids either by insisting that the natural order should also be understood as holy. It is created by God to serve his purpose of binding society together and creating stability.[118] This order never conforms exactly to God's order; there is no natural law. But it must be accepted as a human representation of God's order in an imperfect world.

Althaus argues that this is not a conservative theory, for the natural order is dynamic and ever-changing. Therefore, to oppose change may be to oppose God's will.[119] Althaus even develops a theory of revolution. He first cautions that since the natural order is human and imperfect, man must not expect perfection. He should be obedient to God's order even if it is implemented by evil men. But opposition is possible on two bases. First, God may call a person into opposition. As an example, Althaus cites the instance in which Jesus directed his followers to leave family and marriage to follow him, even though he otherwise supported the institutions of marriage and family.[120] Because God created the *Ordnungen*, he stands above them. Unfortunately, this is a very subjective basis for opposing the existing order. Barth no doubt believed he opposed the *völkisch* idea because directed by God to do so, and Althaus supported it on the same basis. The second ground for opposition to the status quo is no less subjective. Althaus asserts that the existing order may not be judged by any universal or natural law, but it may be measured by each person's 'implicit sense' of what an order should be. For example,

> There is no implicit state constitution, but there is an implicit function and sense of the state — and against this every constitution should be critically measured.[121]

Althaus reiterates that this 'implicit sense' is not a natural law but an idea. It is not objective or universal, but subjective and specific to a given setting.

Does Althaus' standard for opposition mean anything? Perhaps not. At least it is not the sort of standard which can be measured in any objective way. If Althaus did not oppose the *Ordnungen* as they developed in the Third Reich, it was because he did not believe they contradicted his 'implicit sense' of what the *Ordnungen* should be. Another person might oppose these *Ordnungen* on the same basis. Perhaps 'implicit sense' means nothing more than prejudice. Althaus' political, intellectual, emotional and socioeconomic prejudices favored the *Ordnungen* of the Third Reich.

At least Althaus was aware of the possibility that he might be mistaken in his 'implicit sense.' This awareness was incorporated in his recognition of sin and imperfection in the human order. He understood creation and fall to mean that the holy and demonic are inextricably bound together. But he still insisted that man must distinguish between good and evil, *Schöpfung und Sünde*, in spite of the possibility of error. Some people try to ignore the evil in the world; others see only the evil. Althaus thinks it necessary to recognize the close intermixture of both good and evil if man is to deal with reality.[122] The tension which results from this recognition can only be resolved, in his view, by the leap of faith which accepts forgiveness and redemption in Christ. This saves the Christian from nihilism, scepticism or hypocrisy.[123]

In spite of his claiming the contrary, there is a conservatism in Althaus'

Theologie der Ordnungen, and that conservatism is rooted in a fear of change and instability. But on a theoretical level his position is apolitical. He does not rule out change altogether; the institutions by which a society lives must themselves be living and dynamic. They must adjust to each new era, but within that era they must possess sufficient stability and validity to give order and meaning to life. Though Althaus was not an admitted existentialist, this position is existential. He recognizes both good and evil in human institutions; he despairs of perfectly distinguishing between the good and evil; and he advises bold action. This existentialism is conservative because he so strongly affirms existing institutions. He allows opposition only under the most compelling circumstances.

Within Althaus' theology of the *Ordnungen* is a more specific emphasis, that of *Volk*. This emphasis is vitally important. It is the root of Althaus' political concern, and therefore, the root of his insistence upon *Ur-Offenbarung* altogether. Along with many of his generation, Althaus was trained in German Romantic Idealism, with its *völkisch* emphasis. During the First World War, especially in the enthusiasm of the first month, Althaus believed he had experienced a mysterious confirmation of the romantic idea of *Volk*. He interpreted this as a religious experience, but he recognized that it was not wholly religious:

> The discovery of the *Volk* in the cultural history of Germany did not occur through theologians as such, but through poets, scholars and thinkers, through Herder, the Romantics, the idealistic philosophers. During the war, the experience of being a *Volk* (not just a state or an empire) came to us not as Christians, but simply as German men.[124]

It became Althaus' foremost concern to co-opt this wonderful experience of *Volk* for the Christian church. To do this he made *Volk* the primary *Ordnung*, the law of God as newly revealed for the modern German era. In another reference to 1914 he wrote:

> The splendor of that great historical moment remains unforgettable: there law became spirit, it no longer confronted a person with its demands, but moved him as a part of his own life.[125]

In a lecture of 1937 Althaus presented a theology of the *Volk*. First he explained why neither the Bible nor the Confessions mention the word. That is because they spoke to the situation in their own time, which did not include consciousness of *Volk*. But now theologians must speak to men in their present reality, of which *Volk* is a vital part. Althaus admits that *Volk* is not the 'final measure,' but he goes on to argue its place as part of God's creation. Beginning with the words of Luther's Catechism. 'I believe that God has created me', Althaus adds:

The belief that God has created me includes also my *Volk*. Whatever I am and have, God has given me out of the wellspring of my *Volk*: the inheritance of blood, the corporeality, the soul, the spirit. God has determined my life from its outermost to its innermost elements through my *Volk*, through its blood, through its spiritual style, which above all endows and stamps me in the language, and through its history. My *Volk* is my outer and my inner destiny. This womb of my being is God's means, his *Ordnung*, by which to create and to endow me . . . The special style of a *Volk* is his creation, and as such it is for us holy.[126]

Objective factors help to create a *Volk*, factors such as a common language and history, but Althaus believes these factors do not suffice by themselves. Only a mysterious process finally blends the necessary elements into an actual *Volk*. Althaus labels this mysterious process 'God's call.'[127]

After God calls a *Volk* into being, Althaus believes God's law and the law of the *Volk* are closely related, if not identical:

As a creation of God, the *Volk* is a law of our life . . . We are responsible for the inheritance, the blood inheritance and the spiritual inheritance, for *Bios* and *Nomos*, that it be preserved in its distinctive style and authenticity. We are unconditionally bound to faithfulness, to responsibility, so that the life of the *Volk* as it has come down to us not be contaminated or weakened through our fault. We are bound to stand up for the life of our *Volk*, even to the point of risking our own life.[128]

Althaus does distinguish between the human and the divine. A *Volk* is never the same as the kingdom of God; also, the various *Völker* come and go according to God's schedule. Devotion to the *Volk* is not because of any particular value in a specific *Volk*, but because the *Volk* is God's creation for man.[129] Despite these qualifications, Althaus goes on to show the *Volk* occupies a very high place in his system of values:

Our life in our *Volk* is not our eternal life; but we have no eternal life if we do not live for our *Volk*. This is not a question of the absolute value of the *Volk*, but of our absolute obligation to the *Volk*.[130]

Although this lecture was given in 1937, Althaus still refers to the *Volk* as holy, and he speaks of the 'absolute obligation' of individuals to the *Volk*. He develops this as a theology, but the political implications are unmistakable. Althaus is preaching the same virtues of unity and obedience which National Socialism expressed in political terms. If he had any reservations about the direction of National Socialism by 1937, he need not have allied himself so closely to the National Socialist ideology of *Volk*. In fact, it is clear he did have some reservations. Part of this speech defended the Jewish people of the Old Testament as a unique, once-and-for-all chosen people, and a major purpose of the lecture was to preserve a Christian interpretation of *Volk* in the face of anti-Christian threats.[131] These qualifications do appear, but they do not dominate the lecture. In 1937 Althaus apparently still hoped that National Socialism and Christianity would unite so that what he saw as the virtues of each would benefit the German people. This hope was the underlying basis of Althaus' opposition to Barmen and the major reason for his development of a broad *Ur-Offenbarung* to place alongside the specific revelation in Christ.

A second important issue in the theology of Althaus is that of church and state, the celebrated *Zweireichlehre* (doctrine of two kingdoms) of the Lutheran church. Luther attempted to reconcile the apparent difference between the gentle, loving behavior expected of the Christian, as indicated in the Sermon on the Mount, and the sometimes harsh behavior expected of the state, as indicated by use of the death penalty or war-making powers. Luther suggested that God rules the world through two kingdoms, the kingdom of God in which the rule is love, and the kingdom of man ruled by the sword. The latter may not seem Christian, but it serves God by maintaining order. It creates the conditions under which human life may prosper and the Word of God be preached.[132]

Luther's view of the two kingdoms defends against the enthusiastic notion that the kingdom of man might be turned into the kingdom of God through human action, through human reform. Luther's view of evil precludes that possibility. But this cleavage between the kingdom of God and the kingdom of man implies a devaluation and despair directed towards the kingdom of man. It represents man after the fall. Because it is rooted in sin, the kingdom of man cannot hope to see very much progress. Within the church this view of the human situation can be used to sanction conservatism and breed quietism, an unwillingness to meddle in the affirs of this world. Human hopes and aspirations are directed towards the kingdom of God. These hopes give a vicarious joy, or at least an expectation of joy, which is thought to be satisfaction enough for the Christian.

Traditional *Zweireichlehre* is cool to politics. It does not criticize any form of government which maintains a semblance of order, but it also allows no real enthusiasm for any form of government. Althaus found this view too stifling in those years after the First World War when bad government (the Weimar Republic) and the hope of good government (a nationalist revival) seemed so unalterably opposed. After 1933 he was even less able to restrain himself; the German 'turning point' had arrived, and he could not resist affirming this turning point theologically. Althaus' explicit reason was *volksmissionarisch*. He believed that the church could only witness to the German people if it showed enthusiasm and sensitivity towards the *völkisch* movement which now stirred the people so deeply.[133] This was especially true since the *völkisch* movement carried such heavy religious overtones. If

Christianity did not reach it, it might develop a religion of its own. A second, implicit reason why Althaus amended traditional *Zweireichlehre* is that he personally believed in the *völkisch* movement and desired to support it with his theology.

In the crucial New Testament passage on church and state in Romans 13, Paul begins with the words, 'Let every person be subject to the governing authorities'; and he goes on to declare that authorities are appointed by God to maintain order. To disobey is to disobey God. Luther interpreted this passage straightforwardly, requiring obedience to the state and forbidding revolution. In addition to opposing active resistance to the state, he opposed active support. That is, he believed political matters were generally irrelevant to the real concerns of the church. As noted above, Althaus began to question this teaching of Paul and Luther during the years of the Weimar Republic. He later wrote, 'We perceived at that time: with Romans 13 and the traditional Lutheran teaching alone, we could not sincerely master the difficult situation.'[134] The extremity of this circumstance required some reinterpretation of Paul's words.

In 1933 Althaus began developing arguments why the church should voice its approval of the transition from Weimar Republic to Third Reich. His main point was an ethical one:

> The dissolution of criminal law into social therapy and pedagogy, which was already far along in development, has reached an end: punishment shall again be taken seriously as retribution . . . It [the new state] has destroyed the terrible irresponsibility of the parliament and allows us again to see what responsibility means. It sweeps away the filth of corruption. It restrains the powers of decomposition in literature and the theater. It calls and educates our *Volk* to a strong new will for community, to a 'socialism of the deed,' which means the strong carry the burdens of the weak.[135]

Weimar led to disintegration of morality and National Socialism reimposed discipline. For this simple reason, Althaus believed 1933 comparable to 1813, i.e. a national rebirth so far removed from controversy that the church could support it without restraint.

Later Althaus realized that even the political stance of 1813 had to be explained, for it too was a departure from Luther. Here he introduced the concept of the *Volk* as a justification. Both Paul and Luther spoke to their time, and in neither case was *Volk* a part of their world. Both viewed the state as a *Rechtsstaat*, allowing it only a minimal role, that of maintaining order. Althaus argues that the concept of *Volk* brings with it a new and larger role for the state, and he adds that theologians should create a new view of church and state to fit this new reality.[136] Althaus' view is that the *Volks* state serves the 'creative will of God,' and he insists this is no romantic idealism, but a mere description of reality, just as Paul described the reality of his situation.[137]

In terms of authority, the goal must now be to recognize the 'characteristics of genuine authority,' rather than just obey any authority which exists.[138] The men of 1813 showed this. Whereas Luther allowed disobedience only if a government persecuted the word of God, the men of 1813 extended this to allow disobedience if a government destroyed national life. Napoleon's government was a good one, Althaus admits, not a tyranny, but Stein, Arndt and others believed the higher call of 'fatherland' justified disobedience to it. Althaus thinks this a legitimate extension of Luther; the Reformer showed national feeling, but this is simply a situation he did not face.[139] The events of 1933 present another situation in which Luther's view must be extended. According to Althaus, theologians now have to recognize *Volk* as an important new reality, a created order in its own right. He quotes the following passage approvingly, 'What once was a struggle about faith today is correctly considered [a struggle] about the *Volk* as a divine creation.'[140]

The implications of this new idea of *Volk* stand traditional Lutheran views of the state on their head. For example, on the question of revolution Althaus explains that Luther opposed revolution which was egocentric. In such a revolution people rebel because they feel oppressed by authority and hope to personally gain by their revolutionary act. But *völkisch* revolution is no longer an individualistic, private concern. It becomes acceptable as 'something mandated to us by our *Volk*.'[141]

Luther also believed in a limited state. Althaus agrees that an absolutist state is evil; it wants to be an end in itself. But a totalitarian state, on the other hand, is perfectly suitable if it serves the needs of the *Volk:*

> A total state can only mean for us: Laying claim to all individuals, all areas of life and all powers of life through the state for the necessities of life of the *Volk*, to be a nation in community and freedom of life.[142]

This total claim by the state is not only satisfactory but desirable so long as the state embodies the needs and desires of the *Volk*.

How can a totalitarian state determine the needs and desires of the *Volk*? Althaus solves this problem with the *Führerprinzip* (leadership principle). The *Führer* embodies 'authority,' as understood by Luther, but his authority is more extensive. Not only does he implement political order, he also leads the *Volk* in its social, economic and spiritual growth. The *Führer* is responsible to the will of the *Volk* in some sense. But he must not be subject to any sort of majority rule, for his responsibility is to the past and future of the *Volk* as well as the present: 'Therefore, he must be able to make decisions in freedom and independence from the will of the now living.'[143] Concern for authority, 'actual control' and 'a division between rulers and the ruled,' is very important for Althaus. The only restraint he places upon the *Führer* is a rather vague one: a *Führer* cannot lead forever without trust. But he may do so for a limited period. As an example Althaus cites Bismarck, who ruled for four years without support before the people swung behind him.[144]

The position of the church in this political image which Althaus develops is twofold. First, there is a function which is strictly religious in nature: the church should spread the message of Christianity. Here Althaus differs from Luther only in that he believes a more enthusiastic affirmation of the state, since it is a *Volks* state, will facilitate the spread of the gospel. Germans will more readily listen to a church which shares in the spirit of the movement. Although this concern is religious, it implies a political stance. Secondly, Althaus believes that church and state share a mutual responsibility for the *Volk*. The *Volk* needs leadership, organization, education and a spiritual consciousness. In all of these areas the roles of church and state overlap, especially when each assumes its proper responsibility. For the church this involves much more than empathizing with the *völkisch* movement as a tactic to get on the good side of the people. It requires an active affirmation of the state and cooperation with it, in a much more direct sense than Luther would have allowed.

Perhaps Althaus' reinterpretation of *Zweireichlehre* was not so significant as it first appears. The traditional, non-political stance of the church always supported the status quo, which is a political stance in reality, and it always opposed leftists as a threat to morality and order. Althaus fits into this pattern. But his reinterpretation provided a rationale for the distaste which many churchmen felt towards the Weimar Republic, and a justification for their enthusiasm towards the Third Reich. Weimar was the first period in centuries in which the church found it difficult to support the German state, so Althaus met a real need. Furthermore, he met this need without succumbing to fanaticism. He continued to maintain his distance from the *Deutsche Christen* by defending the Old Testament, the uniqueness of the Jewish people, and the ultimate supremacy of Christian over *völkisch* concerns. Even in his advocacy of the *Führer* principle, he added an important qualification: 'Only when both, *Führer* and *Volk*, stand consciously in the presence of the living God do they find the correct relationship to each other, both bound and free.'[145] The question is whether his moderating qualifications and disclaimers stuck in the minds of his readers as much as his overall support of the *völkisch* idea, the totalitatian state and the *Führerprinzip*.

A final significant issue in Althaus' theology is that of the Jewish question. On occasion he made use of National Socialist rhetoric rather indiscriminately, accepting, for example, racial, blood-oriented terminology. In 1937 he wrote:

Among the factors which determine and make up a *Volk*, the community of blood or race has become decisively important for us Germans . . . It has to do with a specific, closed blood relationship. Race is not already

Volk, the biological unity is not already historical unity. But the unity of race in a significant sense and its protection is an essential condition for the formation and preservation of the *Volk*.[146]

But even these words contain the hint that biological considerations were not crucial for Althaus. The above quote leads up to his assertion that *Volkstum* only grows out of its natural constituent parts when a mysterious process, the development of a 'we-consciousness,' occurs, and he describes this process as a creative act of God.[147] Another quote is more typical of Althaus, for it describes his essential view of the Jewish problem:

It does not have to do with Jewish hatred — one can reach an agreement directly with serious Jews on this point — , it does not have to do with blood, also not with the religious beliefs of Judaism. But it does involve the threat of a quite specific disintegrated and demoralizing urban spirituality, whose representative now is primarily the Jewish *Volk*.[148]

Althaus' position, similar to that of Kittel, was anti-secular, anti-urban and anti-modern. Although he accepted some racial theory, his own spiritual theory was more important to him. But on its basis he accepted the fundamental National Socialist policy of discrimination against Jews.

Since Althaus did not fully accept racial theory, he had no trouble accepting the Jewish contribution to Christianity. He frequently described the Old Testament Jews as a 'chosen people' whose relationship with God was unique. No other *Volk*, not even the German *Volk*, would ever experience God's *Heilsgeschichte* as they had done.[149] Their past was a 'unique, incomparable and unrepeatable history.'[150] Other *völkisch* theologians devalued Jewish law. For example, Wilhelm Stapel described it as a *Nomos* with no meaning outside the Jewish *Volk*. According to his view, each *Volk* has a *Nomos* of its own. Althaus refused to accept this relativism. He admitted that each *Volk* has its own law, but this is an addition rather than a replacement for the *heilsgeschichtliche* part of Old Testament law.[151]

The 'Aryan paragraph' issue which erupted in the church in 1933 provides a practical test of Althaus' views on the Jewish question. In October 1933 the Marburg theological faculty published a written opinion which proclaims the Aryan paragraph inconsistent with Christian teaching.[152] The same journal printed a statement on the New Testament and 'racial questions,' which argues that all racial questions are irrelevant for Christianity. This statement is signed by Rudolf Bultmann and twenty other theologians.[153] The theological faculty at Erlangen reacted by directing Althaus and Werner Elert to draft a reply. The result is an apology for the Aryan paragraph. Although there is 'unity in Christ,' Althaus and Elert argue that the church has always recognized restrictions based upon age, gender and physical ability in admitting persons to the ministry. If race is now added, they do not consider that objectionable. For example, when a mission church becomes a *Volks* church, it quite naturally draws its clergy from its own people.[154] Since the German *Volk* is now threatened by an emancipated Jewry, the state is restricting Jews, and 'the church must therefore demand of its Jewish Christians that they hold themselves back from official positions.'[155]

After developing this argument, the two authors immediately add that this rule should allow for exceptions, just as the state 'Law for the Restoration of the Professional Civil Service' does. A Jew ready to sacrifice his life for Germany might become part of the *Volk*, as might a Jew who is truly converted to Christianity. On this basis Althaus and Elert recommend that all Jews and half-Jews already in offices in the church be retained unless the weight of evidence dictates otherwise in individual cases. And the church should work out guidelines of its own to govern future situations, with the bishops designated as the most suitable persons to make decisions.[155]

This compromise is very representative of Althaus. His concern to affirm the 'movement' plus his own belief in *völkisch* ideology determined his theoretical approval of National Socialist policy. He also shared a personal aversion towards Jews and Jewish culture with most of his German Protestant contemporaries. He later commented to his son, 'you have not experienced the Jews.'[157] But Althaus' Christian sensitivity and intellectual honesty forced him to hestitate in application of these racial attitudes and theories. He believed at least some National Socialist Jewish policies were unjust, and he wanted to avoid the injustice. This illustrates that he was incapable of being a fanatic. But it does not prove his ultimate stance acceptable.

D. 1945 and after

ALTHAUS' position in the closing years of the Third Reich must have been uncomfortable. His hopes for the German 'rebirth' had long since dissipated, and by 1943 he knew of massive killing and recognized German guilt. As the war fronts pushed inexorably back towards German borders, enthusiasm and optimism disappeared generally. Although listening to foreign radio broadcasts was condemned as defeatist, Werner Elert, for example, opened a faculty meeting (when he knew no Party members were present) with the question, 'Have any of you heard inner voices?'[158] On a personal level, Althaus lost the eldest of two sons on a battlefield in France in 1940, and the second of three daughters had to be institutionalized in 1942.[159] He was not physically threatened or inconvenienced by the war. Erlangen remained outside the scope of fighting until a brief flurry of activity on 15 and 16 April 1945, when American troops occupied the city. The most frightening moment occurred on Monday afternoon, the sixteenth, when 120 rabid SS troops resisted the city commandant's order to surrender. They murdered him and Erlangen residents, frightened by such fanaticism, fled to the nearby hills. Even hospital patients were transported and bedded under the trees. By evening, American troops prevailed and the people gratefully poured back into town.[160] Althaus was able to preach the following Sunday in thankfulness for the little damage suffered by his university city.[161]

Two questions arise regarding Althaus during this era. First, did he experience any repercussions for his role in support of National Socialism? Secondly, did he rethink his political stance or express either repentance or guilt for his earlier position? Althaus' fortunes after the war at first seemed secure. He even became one of a three-member commission charged by the Americans with denazification of the university. But this commission moved slowly and gradually lost the confidence of American authorities. Erlangen developed a reputation for dealing leniently with faculty and even for hiring individuals removed elsewhere.[162] By 12 August 1946, Dr Hans Meinzolt of the Bavarian cultural ministry wrote Althaus suggesting he lower his profile:

> The reproaches against your position during the National Socialist period are known to you . . . I ask myself whether in the interest of the undisturbed continuation of your teaching activity and other academic work it would be wise for you to step somewhat into the background. Since you hold no other high office, in practical terms this would mean that you decline to serve as assistant dean of your faculty. I believe you could base and justify such a step, apart from all other considerations, solely on your health. May I give you the friendly advice to think this question over?[163]

Meinzolt goes on to note the delicacy of his role in this matter:

> If you want to discuss this with your *Rektor*, I have nothing against that; but the impression must be avoided under all circumstances that the ministry wants to exercise any sort of pressure on you. If you yourself were to have that impression from this letter of mine, then I would ask you to regard this letter as if it had not been written.[164]

The espionage-like tone of this letter represents the care of the Bavarian ministry to resist or at least temper denazification. It also indicates Meinzolt's concern that he later be accused of manipulating Althaus in violation of the principles of academic freedom.

Despite Meinzolt's advice, Althaus found his name on the list of seventy-six released faculty published on 3 February 1947.[165] According to a newspaper account of that day, charges against Althaus included reference to his books, *Die deutsche Stunde der Kirche* (1933) and *Obrigkeit und Führertum* (1936), in which he 'greeted the events of the year 1933,' justified 'the betrayal of the Weimar Republic,' and made democracy look 'laughable.' He was also accused of using his position on the Erlangen University's denazification committee to advocate 'the reinstatement of anti-democratic professors.'[166]

Althaus had already received many letters of support in response to rumors he was in trouble. Helmut Thielicke, for example, who had studied under Althaus, wrote in November:

> This matter moves me very much, and I want to use the opportunity of this difficult time for you to greet you and assure you of my heartfelt and faithful support. Where are we going when every theological direction which contains this or that objective error is simply liquidated? If one takes away the possibility of error, one takes away the possibility of any research whatsoever.[167]

Another former student wrote several weeks later that he had lost faith in any justice:

> You cannot judge what you, especially you, gave to us in strength, power and support in the years of the church struggle, in our underground struggle against the violent authority of the Nazis.[168]

A few days after Althaus' removal, Dr Künneth, dean of the Erlangen synod, circulated a secret statement expressing the church's opposition to the policy of denazification undertaken at the university. He notes the church agrees that cleansing must occur, but it doubts the denazification process will accomplish that. The church, therefore, had addressed a statement to the American military government on this general problem.[169] But such generalized advice did not help Althaus. He was left with the task of gathering more testimonials in his defense, which he describes as a 'repulsive business.'[170]

Thielicke wrote one of these statements, beginning by listing his credentials as a member of the Confessing Church, who had lost his position at Heidelberg in 1940 and had then lived under a travel and speaking restriction through 1945. Thielicke admits Althaus showed enthusiasm for National Socialism in 1933, but he argues it was really nationalism more than National Socialism which moved him. Althaus always opposed absolutist pretensions. And when the true picture of National Socialism became apparent, he became an opponent.[171] This latter claim is given without substantiation and seems to be an exaggeration.

Karl Heine took on the task early in 1947 of gathering statements from former students in support of Althaus. He had been removed from Marburg University in 1937 for Confessing Church activities. He then came to Erlangen, which he claims had a reputation as haven for Confessing Church theological students. Heine credits Althaus with helping to create this atmosphere generally, as well as personally helping him with bureaucratic and financial assistance. Heine continued his Confessing Church activities and thus came under Gestapo surveillance, but Althaus ignored the danger.[172]

Althaus' denazification board finally handed down a positive decision on 30 December 1947.[173] In February the military government concurred and Althaus was free to begin teaching again.[174] After this unpleasant interlude, Althaus continued to live and work at Erlangen, held in high esteem and actively teaching until his retirement and preaching and publishing until his death in 1966.

During these war years and after the defeat of Germany, did Althaus reconsider his earlier political stance? As indicated above, his enthusiasm for National Socialism finds no expression after 1937, and it no doubt dissipated into disillusionment, at least during the war years. A book of his sermons from that period helps give some clues to this progression. In November 1941 he notes 'how sweet the word peace now sounds in our ears;' but he sternly warns against becoming 'sorry for oneself' or 'soft'. 'In world history it often gets very hard, and that is not without God's will.' Jesus says, 'Be brave;' our God is the God 'who demands our sons of us.'[175] On Good Friday 1942 he says, 'We are no longer masters of this war,' but adds that light follows the darkest hour.[176]

In January 1943 Althaus preached on Romans 13, Paul's statement on obeying state authority. This sermon no longer retains the tone of the 1930s. Althaus stresses obeying authorities, but only if they honor God's law:

> Therein consists the deepest value of a state, that it holds itself to these commandments. Every authority which despises and neglects these basic commandments, degrades and dishonors its office. The state which does not in all seriousness hold the life of the individual person and the institution of marriage holy has betrayed its call from God, it no longer deserves the honorable name, authority. But so long as the state takes God's laws seriously, it is sacred and is itself a law which we are bound to obey.[177]

Althaus does not then drive this point home in the rest of the sermon, but perhaps he does not need to. Though it retains some of the ambiguity of his earlier writings, the disillusionment seems more palpable.

In his Christmas sermon for 1943, Althaus' references to the pain of war are more pronounced, and he also appears to direct a warning against Nazi conduct of the war. Although war has always been bad, since 'the first Christmas' it has been given its boundaries. You are not only enemy, you are also brother to your enemy: 'that sets an inner boundary on total war and reminds us of . . . humanity.'[178] On Good Friday 1944 Althaus reminds his listeners, Jesus disturbs the comfortable and tells states and people they are not the 'highest and last.'[179]

The many hints of opposition running through these sermons and the

3.   Paul Althaus lecturing in 1948, aged 60.

refusal to speak bravely or triumphantly about the war arouse great expectation for what Althaus will say after the Nazis have been toppled. His first
sermon after the arrival of American troops in Erlangen begins by speaking
of hard times and also the relatively good fortune of Erlangen residents, for
which they must thank God. Althaus then asks, was all the sacrifice in vain?
And he answers, comfortingly, that no sacrifice to God is in vain, although its
meaning might be hidden. Then Althaus indulges in phrases that imply guilt
and evil behavior: 'This [God's] hand — we cannot conceal it — is today also
the hand of a judge.'[180] In the last months of the war more and more people
recognized:

> that a defeat such as this cannot be understood or explained only in
> political or military terms. Here one must look deeper. We have felt it for a
> long time: *the blessing of God no longer lay on our path* . . . Why? Many of
> us have brooded over that for a long time. I believe there is no other
> answer than this: our public life no longer knew a *fear of God*, which is the
> beginning of wisdom.[181]

Althaus goes on to suggest the church should not try to sidestep its guilt; it
should have warned more loudly. He then suggests an evil reckoning to
come, for much is not yet known. Noting that Germany had been gaining the
world but losing its soul, he hopes that now churches will rebuild the
spirituality of the German people.[182]

In subsequent sermons Althaus returns to these themes of guilt and the
horror of Germany's crimes. In May, for example, after Germany's surrender, Althaus speaks of the meaning of the phrase, 'a multitude of sins.'
'Today sin has become sinful as never before . . . What a measure of lies and
brutality and vulgarity.'[183] What punishment is harsh enough? Althaus then
quotes his text, 'Love covers a multitude of sins,' and he suggests Germans
must learn as never before to practice brotherly love.[184] In the following
week Althaus comments on the:

> evil spirit which ruled the last twelve years — whatever was evil in that
> spirit should now be driven out, out of our entire public life, out of the
> judicial system, out of the press, out of the schools and education. The
> victors want it so; we ourselves want it so; and we are certain: God wants it
> so.[185]

By December Althaus raises the question of mercy. If the Germans now ask
for mercy, they will be asked in return, 'Were you Germans merciful, with
the Poles, with the Jews, and so forth?'[186] He also describes the German
government of the past twelve years as:

> resisting God's commandments and stepping on them in insolent wanton-

ness, one after another: you shall not murder, you shall honor the institution of marriage, you shall not steal and rob, you shall not lie.[187]

These sermons are an impressive statement of guilt. They express Althaus' condemnation of the Nazi years, and the condemnation seems genuine and comprehensive. The only problem with this confession of guilt is that it is plural and general rather than singular and specific. Althaus nowhere states openly and straightforwardly that he personally made a mistake. In response to his denazification trial, he prepared several pages of testimony defending his writings from the 1930s. These pages do not betray the self-righteous defensiveness of a Kittel; neither do they betray notable repentance. He expresses regret about the timing of the *Ansbacher Ratschlag* and that it was picked up enthusiastically by the *Deutsche Christen*, when he intended it to be merely anti-Barthian. He also notes that much in *Die deutsche Stunde der Kirche* was 'all too closely bound to the moment and therefore proved premature and mistaken. But in spite of that I am not ashamed of it even today.'[188]

In 1957 Althaus published a review of the controversy surrounding Luther's teaching of the two kingdoms.[189] He acknowledges the criticism that Lutheran teachings might have contributed to the rise of Hitler. In so far as he admits the connection, he blames it on Luther's followers rather than on Luther.[190] But he adds that Catholics were just as ready to support Hitler as were Lutherans,[191] and he passes up the opportunity to reflect upon this question from the point of view of his own experience.

E. Conclusion

WHAT were the determining elements in Paul Althaus' character? First, he was a Christian. He never sacrificed fundamental elements in his faith to the enthusiasm of National Socialist ideology. This is shown in his opposition to the *Deutsche Christen*, his defense of the Old Testament, and his unwillingness even to consider such questions as whether Jesus might have been non-Jewish. It is also clear that his response to 1933 was due at least in part to his desire to make Christianity relevant and attractive to the German people by tying it to *völkisch* images and issues.

However, an important second element in Althaus' character was his patriotic, romantic conservatism. Ever since his experience in Poland during the First World War, the plight of the German *Volk* was a cause very near to his heart. His subsequent diagnosis of the political situation combined a Christian, moralistic aversion to urban secularism and leftwing politics with an affinity for neo-conservative images: a mysterious, organic *Volk;* a limited antisemitism; and a belief in the rebirth of community through discipline, obedience to authority, national pride and unity. These elements went into Althaus' theology of the *Ordnungen*. He tried to place God's imprimatur on the sense of order and the form of German life which he desired.

The common denominator in Althaus' thought is opposition to modernity. He saw in the modern world 'a quite specific disintegrated and demoralizing urban spirituality.'[192] This form of spirituality revolted his sense of Christian morality, his sense of orderliness, and, due to the simultaneous humiliation of Germany after the war, his German pride. The political alternative which Althaus espoused took form in opposition to the disorder and instability he so feared. He longed for a Germany in which the people were strong and united, the state powerful, the church respected, and in which everyone accepted his station in life as the law of God. With such a political view, Althaus was unable to see any value in the Weimar Republic, and he fancied himself in basic agreement with Hitler.

It is obvious in restrospect that Althaus was not in basic agreement with Hitler. His virtues saved him from that. He was intelligent and intellectually honest, and he was a born mediator. Because of these qualities, he saw through the most outrageous of Nazi and *Deutsche Christen* theories and rejected them; and as a compromiser he always tried to stay within sight of the Confessing Church group and maintain a stance which would not alienate them. Nonetheless, it has been suggested that Althaus was the most culpable of German Protestant theologians in his relationship with the Third Reich.[193] This theory holds that the popular impact of his support for Hitler was greater just because of his moderation. The *Deutsche Christen* carried little weight in the Protestant church; they could be dismissed because they often said the most extreme things. But Althaus was widely esteemed in the first place, and he never made an unguarded statement. Every qualification, every caution added a note of reassurance to his overall support of the National Socialist state. And the fact of his support was unambiguous. Throughout his writings from 1933 to 1937, Althaus defended the totalitarian state, the *Führer* principle, *völkisch* ideals in general and the 'good government' of Hitler in particular. After 1937 Althaus' politically-oriented publications did cease. Almost certainly this implies a disillusionment with the Nazi state. But Althaus never openly recanted. The public which had read his praise of National Socialism never received a correction notice, never had cause to realize he had changed his mind. For all these reasons, Althaus' responsibility for the lack of widespread Protestant opposition to the National Socialist state is very great.

Where did Althaus go wrong? This is more difficult to establish. He advocated that the church become more active in the world and that it rephrase its message in terms more meaningful to the concerns which move modern man. This cannot be faulted in itself. It is also the message of a very different individual, Dietrich Bonhoeffer, in his *Letters and Papers from Prison*; and since the war this has been a dominant theme of progressive theology. A contemporary of Althaus, Paul Tillich, also shared this concern, but he directed it towards an affirmation of socialism, the working class and modern culture. This theme of relevance towards the world is neutral. It stands or falls with the political world or political ideal to which it is applied.

Althaus' intelligence and intellectual honesty are also above reproach. He does not appear to have been either hypocritical or self-serving. He also was not irrational, except in so far as both Christianity and Romantic Idealism are beyond reason. He believed in the mysterious reality of God and of *Volk*, both of which are extrasensory, non-objective premises. But he did apply reason after establishing these premises. He was not a fanatic. On the contrary, Althaus was a cautious and moderate man who envisioned himself a mediator.

Moderation is not usually judged a fault. Was it so in Althaus' case? Gerhard Niemöller has accused Althaus of trying to compromise with the devil. The result can only be a partial affirmation of evil.[194] But this is the critique of a partisan who believes in the absolute truth or falsehood of specific theological positions. Except by an act of faith, it is impossible to judge *Deutsche Christen* theology as wholly demonic. Rather, it was one of many competitors in the marketplace of ideas, and as such an apparently legitimate object of Althaus' mediation. Another flaw in this analysis is the assumption that Althaus conceded certain points to the *Deutsche Christen* as a compromise of his own beliefs. On the contrary, the political and theological ground which he shared with the *Deutsche Christen*, he occupied from personal belief. Niemöller cannot say he compromised with evil; he must charge that Althaus espoused evil.

A secular variation on Niemöller's critique might be that Althaus mistook the boundaries of the political spectrum when he sought his place in the middle. He certainly neglected the left, acknowledging in his analysis only those persons and groups who generally accepted National Socialist rule in Germany. This at least partially discredits his self-image as a moderate. But it must be admitted that people form their idea of moderation within their own milieu. Moderation can only be defined in terms of a norm, and norms for most people are nationally determined. Perhaps Althaus should then be accused of parochialism, of a narrow, German vision. This has the advantage of agreeing with Althaus' image of himself, for he gloried in the fact that his ideas, aspirations, and even his Christian beliefs were determined by his relationship to his *Volk*. He consciously rejected certain norms of Western civilization and the norms of traditional *Zweireichlehre*, arguing that the new concept of *Volk* outweighs other considerations. So it is only within this concept of *Volk* as understood in Germany in the 1930s that Althaus can be classified as a moderate. *Völkisch* ideology was a major blindspot for him.

The theology which Althaus developed contains no single unacceptable element, but in retrospect it is apparent that one of his emphases proved very suitable for National Socialism. In his 'orders of creation' theology, he

4. Paul Althaus in 1958, aged 70.

concerned himself with law more than gospel. This focused his attention on morality, order and stability and allowed him to view the Weimar Republic as a breakdown of God's intended order. By equating the traditional, pre-Weimar order of society with God's will, Althaus opposed progressive and revolutionary ideologies of the left which hoped to remake society in a new and better form, and he affirmed the authoritarian and paternalistic emphases of National Socialism.

In the end neither Althaus' theology, his intelligence, his personal qualities, nor his role as mediator was crucial in his support of a movement which he recognized too late as an evil phenomenon. The crucial element was the crisis of modernity, which produced in him fear of an unstable, modern, secular world. He erected a theology and a political-intellectual position in opposition to this instability, relying upon *völkisch* ideas as the foundation for both. He did not bend his professional values in support of Nazism, as did Gerhard Kittel; nor did he commit himself as radically to the movement as Emanuel Hirsch. But his *völkisch* stance tied him to the Third Reich more firmly and for a longer period than he should have allowed.

CHAPTER IV

Emanuel Hirsch: Nazi Intellectual

A. Introduction

EMANUEL Hirsch (1888-1972) was a close friend of Paul Althaus and a contemporary of both Althaus and Gerhard Kittel. He too supported National Socialism. But he is distinct from Althaus and Kittel in several ways. His support was less moderate than that of Althaus; in fact, radicalism denotes his character as much as moderation denotes Althaus'. He also was more clearly an intellectual than was either Althaus or Kittel, at least in the sense that he drew much more fully and consciously upon the intellectual heritage of the nineteenth century and made it an important part of his thought. Kittel seems to have reacted more instinctively to his fears and his concerns; he then put his special skills and knowledge at the service of conservative German nationalism and National Socialist ideology, with a superficial and defensive critique of enlightened modernism. Paul Althaus defended a similar conservative nationalist position. He did so intelligently and reasonably from his footing in traditional Lutheranism, applying his knowledge and principles to the political stance he chose to take. He thereby kept a greater distance from National Socialism, especially after the mid-1930s, and he was less directly implicated in the Nazi barbarities than was Kittel. In comparison to these two men, Hirsch was more intellectually facile, more historically and philosophically minded, more familiar with the full range of intellectual developments in the nineteenth and early twentieth centuries, more aware of the intellectual crisis of the twentieth century, and more rooted in the existentialism that marked the best theologians of his generation. And Emanuel Hirsch built upon this broad foundation a firmer commitment to the National Socialist ideal.

Hirsch thus brings this study to its culmination. The question surrounding intellectuals and theologians in the Third Reich is whether or not their intellectual and spiritual heritage was helpful to their political decision making. Actually, the question is even broader. In the light of the crisis of reason in this century, can the Western, Christian heritage be expected to lead an intelligent person to an acceptable political stance? In the case of Althaus and Kittel it did not. They were intelligent and respectable, but they each took a political stance which is not historically respected. Hirsch was also intelligent and respectable, and he devoted himself more fully to seeking an understanding of the Western intellectual and spiritual heritage. He also peered more deeply into the crisis of the age. Instead of protecting him from error, this effort made him a more committed supporter of Hitler and Nazism. This study of his career will attempt to explain such a result.

Emanuel Hirsch was born on 14 June 1888 in Brandenburg Prussia, the son of a Lutheran pastor. He turned naturally towards a theological career, and in 1906, shortly after his family moved to Berlin, he began his theological studies at the university there. This was the era of Harnack and Seeberg, but Hirsch chose to study under the Luther-renaissance scholar, Karl Holl, and he later expressed his admiration for Holl in glowing terms.[1] Throughout his career he pursued Holl's lead in reinterpreting Luther for the modern era, with a strong thread of German pride and nationalism interwoven.[2]

As a student Hirsch joined the Wingolf *Bund*. This student group echoed and reinforced the conservative nationalism he had learned at home. It also brought him his first important friendship based on common theological interests, for Paul Tillich was a fellow member. This friendship bore much, the first fruits being Tillich's suggestion that Hirsch study Fichte.[3] That philosopher quickly became an important part of Hirsch's intellectual equipment for several reasons. First, Fichte's theory of knowledge, based upon idealism, retains a high regard for moral and spiritual values. Fichte also stresses the importance of political responsibility and action, as exemplified in his writings during the Napoleonic period. Hirsch prepared his *Habilitationsschrift* on Fichte, and it was published in shortened form in 1914.[4]

After his encounter with Luther and Fichte, the third important person in Hirsch's development was Søren Kierkegaard. Hirsch began reading Kierkegaard seriously in 1920, apparently on his own initiative.[5] In 1922 he traveled to Copenhagen and met Eduard Geismar, a leading Kierkegaard scholar in Denmark. Then Hirsch, exhibiting his prodigious aptitude and intensity, quickly learned Danish so he could read both primary and secondary materials in the original.[6] By 1923 he was able to translate one of Geismar's articles for a German journal and add his own substantive introduction to the work. Throughout the 1920s, Geismar and Hirsch pursued their Kierkegaard studies as colleagues, and Hirsch produced a major Kierkegaard work in 1933 which remains a frequently cited classic.[7]

Hirsch began his academic career as supervisor of the theological seminaru at Göttingen University in 1912. In 1914 he moved to a similar position at Bonn University. The next year he became *Privatdozent* in church history at Bonn, where he remained until 1917, when he took leave to work in a parish in Baden. Then in 1921 he was called back to Göttingen to assume the chair in church history. He moved over to systematic theology in 1936, and he remained a professor at the University of Göttingen until 1945.[8]

5.   Emanuel Hirsch as a young man.

At the close of the war in 1945, Hirsch was relieved of his position at Göttingen. He was only fifty-seven years old and obviously not ready to retire, for he continued to research and write for another quarter of a century. The official reason for his release was failing eyesight. However, he had been nearly blind since at least 1931. The best interpretation of these events is that Hirsch was graciously let go before his prominent position attracted legal repercussions in the form of a denazification proceeding. His colleagues knew his politics were unacceptable, and they eased him out of the way.[9] This created financial hardships for Hirsch, but he never was brought to legal account for the role he played in the Third Reich.[10]

Hirsch must be seen as a major figure in twentieth-century German theology. He was certainly the leading Kierkegaard expert of his generation in Germany. He also contributed significantly to Luther studies and to systematic theology. He wrote prodigiously, edited several journals, and was a leading participant in political discussions and church politics in the 1920s and 1930s. Wolfgang Trillhaas, stressing the breadth and depth of Hirsch's knowledge, writes, 'One would be inclined to say: Hirsch was the last prince . . . of Protestent theology.'[11] His fame outside of Germany and after 1945 has not been as great as that of the major figures, Barth, Bultmann and Tillich. One reason, no doubt, is that much of his work was so very German in emphasis and intent. He intentially spoke only to the German people in much of what he wrote. A more important factor, certainly, is that he was politically *persona non grata* after 1945. His endorsement of National Socialism could not be ignored.

It has often been suggested that National Socialism, as an outbreak of irrationalism, had no intellectual foundation and could attract no genuinely intellectual support.[12] Without question National Socialism had no Karl Marx, and, undeniably, some intellectuals were driven out of Germany because of their opposition (in addition to those who were driven out because they were Jewish). However, that does not prove that all intellectuals found Nazism unattractive, nor that scholars demurred from giving the National Socialist idea of society an intellectual justification. In fact, Emanuel Hirsch, as theologian, philosopher and historian, saw his role in just that light.

This chapter will attempt to show that Hirsch, whose active career spanned the years from 1914 to 1945, developed a consistent, intellectually tenable political ethic and historical-theological philosophy which welcomed and then supported the National Socialist recipe for German society. His concerns were three, and each was of crisis proportions. Spiritually, Hirsch was a committed Christian. He fully recognized the impact of secularism, science and materialism on religious and moral beliefs, and he deplored this development. He called it decadent and destructive, and he hoped to contribute towards a turnabout. A primary goal was to make Luther relevant to the modern German. Intellectually, Hirsch was a committed rationalist. He was unwilling to reject the contributions and worth of science and reason. He insisted upon intellectual honesty and rigor and exemplified those qualities in his work. But he also recognized the crisis of relativism and appreciated its impact on the intellectual world. Therefore, he sought out two pillars, Fichte's idealism and Kierkegaard's existentialism, and hoped to build upon them a satisfactory theory of truth. Politically, Hirsch was a committed nationalist. His world, therefore, crumbled after the defeat of 1918. He saw the German people in a losing struggle for survival, and he hoped to contribute towards the rebirth of German greatness. Hirsch combined his spiritual, intellectual and political concerns throughout his life. His main theological goal was to build a political ethic rooted in Christianity. He hoped to do this with intellectual rigor and honesty, and he assumed the result would be the best possible prescription for German greatness and happiness.

It is suggested above that Hirsch's position was intellectually tenable. This is perhaps the crucial issue in this entire study. Can Hirsch's political stance be rejected on purely intellectual grounds? I would suggest that it cannot. It is easy to reject it in historical retrospect, since we regret the Nazi episode in German history. Hirsch's stance can also be rejected on the basis of certain premises vis-à-vis democracy, human rights, etc. But are these premises and values intellectually more sound than those of Hirsch? That is the intriguing question in this study.

B. Hirsch's Political Stance before 1933

1. The Ideological Base

AUGUST 1914 and January 1933 were the two most important months in Emanuel Hirsch's life. His political philosophy can certainly be focussed on the events of those two periods, and, since a political ethic was so integral a part of his theology and philosophy, his entire lifework can best be highlighted in this way. August 1914 gave Hirsch an inspired vision of the beauty and religious significance of a nation united and dedicated. This became his ideal for society. The defeat of Germany and the years of the Weimar Republic were, of course, a terrible disappointment for him; but the rise of Hitler in 1933 seemed to him an opportunity for rebirth.

November 1918 and May 1945 were months of nearly equal importance in the life of Hirsch. They brought the force of reality and defeat against his hopes and dreams. But they too served a creative function. In November 1918, he was only thirty years old and at the beginning of his career. He was able to give form to the enemy in his view of the world and developed a passion which was to fuel him throughout his life. The role of 1945 in

Hirsch's thought is more difficult to ascertain. In that year, the outer circumstances of his life changed for the worse yet he does not appear to have rethought nor to have changed drastically his world view.[13]

Hirsch's world view began to take concrete form in the earliest days of the First World War. He assumed Germany was forced into the war, particularly by the pressure of imperialistic England, and the only honorable course for Germany was to respond with the sword.[14] In a sermon delivered 13 September 1914 on the text of Jacob wrestling with God (Gen. 32:22-32), Hirsch proclaimed, 'All sacrifices of possessions and blood are nothing but the attempt to force from God a decision in our favor: we do not leave him alone, then he will bless us.'[15] War was seen as a natural, unavoidable occurrence in human history, the mechanism for meeting God's testing and working out his will:

> But where great things are at stake, where it involves what role a *Volk* shall play in world history in the future, where the question is even whether it shall play any kind of a role at all, whether it shall continue to exist as an independent *Volk* — there it would be immoral, unfaithful, and cowardly to give in.[16]

And Hirsch again emphasized:

> War is a judgment of God, but a *Volk* has the right to demand this judgment of God only if it is ready, if necessary, to bleed to death in this war.[17]

The enthusiasm of August 1914 did not outlive the trenches in any of the belligerent nations. When peace movements developed in Germany, however, Hirsch opposed them. He fully backed unrestricted U-boat warfare and maximal annexation.[18] In the spring of 1918 he still hoped for victory if Germany would only overcome its faintheartedness:

> Despite our timidity and indecision, despite our innumerable follies, we are standing now within sight of a brilliant victory. But God has not yet given us the decisive answer to our bold venture.[19]

On 21 October 1918, not yet giving up hope, he called for a last great exertion under the leadership of the Kaiser.[20]

Of course, Hirsch's hopes for the kiss of victory were to no avail. As for so many other Germans, however, the defeat was made even more bitter by the complete collapse of the Hohenzollern dynasty and the Bismarckian state system. He had no use for Social Democrats.[21] He also opposed democracy and blamed it for the tears in the German social and political fabric. Therefore, he began working almost immediately to write an interpretation of

6. Emanuel Hirsch as a young man with a book.

Germany's failure and a prescription for her success.

Before investigating Hirsch's work in the 1920s, it is important to note his own lack of physical participation in the First World War. On 3 August 1914 he volunteered for service, but was rejected as physically unfit. Hirsch was small and sickly all his life and possessed very bad eyesight. He could not even serve as a pastor in the field, as did Tillich and Barth. On the night of his rejection, as he noted in a journal, Hirsch heard the sound of excited troops marching to the station, and he lamented his sad fate.[22] Helmut Heiber cites the disproportionate number of individuals in the Third Reich who parlayed their own personal exemption from military service, based upon physical infirmities, into rousing militarism and chauvinistic war-mongering on paper: 'They take up their heroic ecstasy exclusively at the typewriter; in contrast, where it involves their own life, they handle themselves completely rationally.'[23] This may not be a fair estimate of Hirsch's role. I think it impossible to judge how he would have reacted to military service had he been physically able. However, his physical weaknesses probably influenced the development of his ideas. He often referred to himself as 'fighting the battle by other means,' and he even compared the staccato notes of his typewriter to those of a machinegun.[24] Among the interpretations which must be marshaled to understand Hirsch's career, this psychological one cannot be ignored.

In 1920 Hirsch produced his first major assessment of the German situation, *Deutschlands Schicksal*, a book which went through three editions in the next three years. This book opens a window on Hirsch's political-philosophical outlook, revealing those feelings born in 1914 and predicting his position for the rest of his life. He perfected this creation over the years, and brought out many new models in the thirties, but the invention was essentially complete.

Deutschlands Schicksal began as a speech delivered to students in the summer of 1920. Hirsch proposed to take the puzzle of human history, recently rendered so complex and confusing, and make it coherent for them.[25] He also proposed to these students an appropriate approach to the work: recognize that history presents questions of conscience which can only be resolved through decisions of conscience. Then he encouraged them to think through these problems with him, maintain open and calm minds, and make their own decisions.[26] Hirsch took this speech as a starting point and quickly developed it into a book.

In his introduction to the published work, Hirsch defends his emphasis upon history. After defeat and revolution, the only point of unity in Germany, 'for the more noble among us,' is concern for Germany's fate.[27] All proposed solutions are controversial. But Hirsch is sure of one thing: Germany's new leaders will have to have clear knowledge of 'the law of all historical human association,' and that will only occur if the new generation of students are taught history properly.[28] Hirsch then makes a final point about this historical assignment. He intends to approach it, not through a history rooted in data, but through 'historical-philosophical reflection.' Not that the former is improper, but his interest and his training point him towards the scientific study of this 'sense' of history.[29]

It is immediately clear that part of Hirsch's sense of history includes a dim view of the heritage of nineteenth-century thought. It had produced good physical science but bad philosophy:

> What we are missing today is contemplation of the ultimate bases of all our political as well as social historical judgments. The thought of our century has a remarkable capacity to grasp sharply and clearly technically accessible goals of limited character. But this capacity stands in strange contrast to the lack of clarity and shallowness of all our attempts to place this limited knowledge into patterns of a higher sort, to find from contemplation of the spirit itself guidelines for the life of the individual and the society as a whole. Even when we have honestly struggled to be both broad and profound, in the end we have produced nothing but a rather arbitrary and somewhat pretentious technical program. In almost everything said about the sense of our present historical moment, this deficiency reveals itself in its shocking nakedness. We can only work against it through serious attention to the most general questions of our being.[30]

In addition to the inadequacy of scientific thought in itself, it had also led to all-pervasive scepticism, especially towards any concept of God. Nietzsche's view of history, for example, represents this sceptical approach. Nietzsche, as described by Hirsch, sees man as an insignificant animal living in a corner of the universe with no purpose, goal or broader significance. Hirsch views this 'natural history' argument of Nietzsche as the kernel of his thought. He argues that neither Einstein's theory of relativity nor Spengler's history push scepticism beyond this end point reached in Nietzsche.[31]

Hirsch criticizes Nietzsche's position as removing seriousness and responsibility from human life. He also argues that scepticism is self-contradictory: e.g. when Nietzsche describes man as an intelligent animal *within* the universe (i.e. limited), he himself must stand above the universe and above all history to look down upon it. Is he not also a man, and thereby equally unable to recognize higher truth? Hirsch sees this flaw in all scepticism. The denial of truth is itself a claim to truth, and thus a testimony to the possibility of truth. It is also unwittingly a testimony to God, for God is the real 'overviewer,' which both Nietzsche and Spengler call the 'Free Spirit'. Nietzsche and Spengler argue that certain 'Free Spirits' can reach a vision of truth. Hirsch counters that mere humans cannot participate in the Godhead in that way, and he labels their philosophy an idealistic romanticism.[32]

Hirsch's own view is that:

Human history can . . . only be understood by those who see its metaphysical core and its religious connection. Human history and notions about God belong necessarily together.[33]

His proof is not empirical, of course. He proposes only that he will set forth his interpretation of historical knowledge alongside the interpretations of the sceptics. If his view is convincing, that will be its proof for an individual. Hirsch then underscores two of his major premises:

1. He argues that creativity does occur in history (listing Amos, Socrates, Luther, Leibniz and Kant as examples). Since such 'beginnings' cannot be explained by the physical environment (i.e. Nietzsche's 'natural history'), they are genuine 'creations' and they give testimony to the creative human spirit, behind which stands the God of creation. Of Nietzsche Hirsch then says, 'He saw the crucible, but not the chemist.'[34]

2. Hirsch also asserts that universal values and knowledge exist and can be discovered. He believes men have an internal certainty about eternal values which testifies to the universal: 'Out of the certainty of its connection to the eternal, an individual soul unites itself with the eternal through affirmation of a specific duty.'[35]

Hirsch then observes that even physical science speaks about symbols of reality rather than reality itself. Hirsch sees human knowledge as pointing towards symbols about God. These symbols too can create an inner coherence which can convince about the reality behind.[36] Hirsch adds in conclusion, 'It is simply not true, that human history is purely a human affair.'[37]

After dealing with Nietzsche's scepticism, Hirsch confronts the absolutist view of history posited by Hegel. Hirsch argues that Hegel fails to distinguish between God and man. This has its attractions:

An absolute philosophy of history produces a fascination against which it is difficult to defend oneself. I experienced that in my developmental years. But it is built upon a deceptive foundation.[38]

Hirsch cites Dilthey as having placed Hegel's concept of 'pure reason and truth,' upon which history is built, in its proper position.[39] Hegel's philosophy is beautiful, according to Hirsch, but it does not allow for imperfect reality. And it also accepts whatever happens in history as proper; it does not allow for criticism: 'What is, that is rational.' Almost certainly Hirsch's disappointment with Weimar sharpened his unwillingness to accept this affirmation of the status quo:

It [Hirsch's view] challenges us more to a moral judgment of history . . . In this way the present can only be understood when, instead of gazing at it in astonishment as a turning point in world history, one questions it in terms of its sense of duty, its sense of obedience, and its sense of guilt.[40]

As an additional element in his philosophy of history, Hirsch pursues the question of reason in a chapter entitled 'Idee und Leben.' He argues that the goal of the Enlightenment had been to bring all areas of life under the rule of reason, to overcome all problems through the use of reason. Did this succeed? 'A dark feeling within us says no.'[41] Hirsch complains that rationalism rules out mystery, greatness, the profundity of life. He finds Lessing's *Nathan the Wise* disappointing because of its sole stress on the rational idea. Reason is a necessary element, but greatness lies in individuality and creative intuition: 'All higher culture is based completely upon the inexplicable permeation of rational ideas with the vital functions of the individual.'[42]

In the tension between intellectualism and individual feelings, Hirsch feels that a nation must not forget to recognize that second element. It should seek out its own 'feeling for life.' In Germany, where the very possibility of a future is endangered, the necessity is even greater:

> What we Germans must now do in order to have a future can certainly not be told to us by the makers of ideas, who most of all want to achieve the realization of this or that set of principles. It can only be told to us by those who feel in their heart the perishing life of the German *Volk* as their own life, and who therefore set all of their thought and willpower on the goal of preserving that life in its power and uniqueness or creating it anew. They are poorer in words than the others, but they see more deeply and more truly.[43]

Intellectuals should not rule Germany's future, but rather those simpler people, less gifted with words, who feel inside themselves the death throes of the German *Volk* and recognize more immediately and accurately 'true' values and 'true' meaning. Hirsch admits there is danger in this path. It allows no intellectually acceptable proof; the proof lies only in the certainty of the individual of the rightness of his cause. To act on that basis requires the courage of faith:

> Is history really an unfathomable individual life process? Then it remains an impossible undertaking to lighten the mysterious darkness which lies over its present and future.[44]

This statement is ominous, especially in light of the next two decades. Hirsch admits that actions and results do not always follow plan: 'What we intend with our actions, and that which comes to life through them, these are in no way always one and the same.'[45] At this point we can only fall back on faith, act boldly in the best way we can, and recognize that God is still there: 'The history of humanity is not a work of humanity alone.'[46]

In this analysis of 'idea' and 'life', Hirsch argues that the two must be balanced, but his preference seems tilted towards the latter. This is partly as compensation for the rule of idea which he perceives to be the heritage of the nineteenth century. It also is relevant to a belief in the life cycle of civilizations which he borrows from Spengler. According to this view, each culture begins in 'living' enthusiasm and matures to 'sober' understanding. All creativity is lost by the latter stage and — here he cites Jacob Burckhardt — only a crisis can shake it up and restore youthfulness and creativity. The one saving grace in Germany's present travail is that it might allow this very rebirth. It is painful when, 'the plowshare goes over the already harvested and hardened field;' however:

> Nothing brings the human spirit so completely to consciousness of the finiteness and poverty of its rationality as the understanding that history must degenerate into deadly monotony, unless life from time to time turns against itself in hostile and destructive fashion.

And:

> Perhaps a new hope for the German *Volk* springs forth from this consideration. Crises make us young . . . It would be a hard path, but yet a path which has a destination.[47]

In a further analysis of history Hirsch takes on the idea of progress. He readily dismisses progress *(Fortschritt)* as false, because it simply has not occurred, at least in uninterrupted fashion. He is happier with the term development *(Entwicklung)*, which allows a movement towards 'becoming' that can include tensions, contradictions and crises. However, he faults those nineteenth-century historians, the best of whom he says is Wilhelm Wundt, who believes they can discover in *Entwicklung* the sense of history. Wundt, for example, sees in history the interplay of free individuals and their individual acts all leading ultimately to the 'Idea of Humanity,' the highest and best stage of history which lies just ahead.

The first problem Hirsch identifies in this theory is that particularly disruptive events, such as those of the First World War and its aftermath, might destroy it. He admits that some variation which employs spiral development or a wavy line might even incorporate that war; but Hirsch is even more concerned with the implication that individual nations and epochs can only be seen as passageways to an end goal. And although certain elements in history, e.g. technology, might be accurately portrayed by the concept of development, can poetry or morality be said to have improved over the centuries or from one culture to another? And what about the end goal? Can it be understood or recognized? Or is it simply *our* understanding of the tendency of *our* age, as in Wundt's 'Idea of Humanity'? Another problem: if life provides the parallel, will history really reach its peak at the end, or will society suffer a decline before death? And finally, is there any room for free choice in a developmental theory of history?[48]

Hirsch's answer to all of these questions is theistic and existential. Yes there is an end goal of history and it has been determined by God. And there is a sense of history which is known by God. As human beings we do not see the 'Idea of Humanity,' but we see the strivings of many individuals and many individual *Völker*. This very multiplicity denies a single human conception of history; we can only grasp something of the way the various groups and periods of history fit together. But Hirsch thinks this in itself points to the eternal:

> If history has any sort of a heart and a sense, one must seek it not in the multiplicity of developments and destinies, but in what is common to each place and time in historical life. That is the direct relationship of the human spirit in each of its movements to that which is beyond history, to the eternal.[49]

The imperfection of human history also points to the eternal. Since humanity is bound by the eternal, developmental history always will seem contradictory and filled with illusions. It substitutes the human spirit as the 'substantial spirit of historical existence . . . and that is, as things now lie, an empty pretension far removed from reality.'[50]

Another problem Hirsch sees in most historians is that while looking for the end goal of history, they pay no attention to the individual and forget that dead people were once living. Fichte, for example, describes an historical process ending in a perfect state he labels a 'moral community of reason.' But this ultimate perfection of society has little relevance for the perfection of individuals, since most will be dead before that state is reached. Lessing, exhibiting the Enlightenment concern for the individual, tries to overcome this problem with the concept of reincarnation. All individuals will reach perfection at last. But Hirsch objects that, since an individual cannot remember his earlier existence, the ultimate perfection will mean little to that earlier manifestation of himself. The problem, he feels, begins with the separation of history and ethics. That makes irresolvable the problem of a perfect 'final community' not allowing for the perfection of the individual.

Here Hirsch begins to introduce a particularly strong religious or theological element. The problem is one of developing a historical concept in which the perfecting of individuals within a society will not wait upon some perfect end time. Again Hegel is used as a foil. Hegel concerns himself with the morality of the individual, but only within the overriding concept of the state. The state's role is all-embracing; hence, morality and patriotism are the same thing and no scope is left for a personality with eternal or supra-state definition. Put another way, the state's authority allows no possibility of the free act, which Hirsch sees as the 'prerequisite of all higher morality.' Furthermore, Hegel's morality is only based on duty and makes no allowance for love.[51]

An opposite ideal of human society is the French and English concept. This liberal society allows development of individual morality and the subjective act; in fact, too much so. Hirsch objects that this loose individualism creates no concept of duty to bind society together. The bonds are all external, through business, contracts, etc., so the true development of individual morality (and, therefore, of the good life or the best society) cannot occur in either Hegel's state or the French and English society:

> The ultimate experience of conscience and the free personal act remain outside the grasp of a philosophy of history which has as its subject the appearance and disappearance of large human social organizations.

So:

> It is clear that the higher unity which is sought can only be found in an ethical-religious intuition.[52]

The proper relationship of individual and society has to allow for a. individual freedom, the prerequisite for morality, and b. unity, which will prevent chaos. Hirsch believes such balance can only be achieved if the bonds are spiritual, especially in a Lutheran sense. Even the unity of Catholicism, which approaches the ideal, is too much based on rules and external bonds. Morality has become 'churchianity' *(Kirchlichkeit)*.[53] So Hirsch describes the ideal society as a 'community of conscience' rooted in Luther's view of the religious community. It will be an invisible community with internal bonds. Such bonds will both allow more freedom and give more unity than external, legal ones. And this 'community of conscience' crosses all history and peoples, according to Hirsch, so it will give a meaning to history which nothing else can. Both the living and the dead, the present and the future are accommodated by this concept of history. And finally, if individual members of the 'community of conscience' will play their proper role in state and society, morality will blossom through the society as a whole.[54]

After having presented this ethical, theistic philosophy of history, Hirsch begins to consider elements within his theory of society. First, he discusses the role of law and state. He believes in the need for both, in spite of their limitations, based upon a concept of paradox. Law implies compulsion, but all freedom depends upon it, for example. The state may give power over the weak to the strong, but the weak cannot be protected without it. Law and state are imperfect, but necessary: 'The just state is the native soil of higher culture and of history.'[55]

Hirsch credits Kant with the realization that law and morality can never coincide. Hegel tries to break down the contradiction by making law equal reason, but Hirsch does not accept that.[56] He contrasts justice and love. The legal order of the state and the loving order of God will always be different; but the legal order of the state can be seen as an education towards morality. The second half of the Ten Commandments are now almost taken for granted, Hirsch notes, because of longstanding enforcement by the state. Tolstoy fails to appreciate this when he attacks the state as being all bad.[57] In spite of their imperfections, Hirsch concludes that law and state are absolutely necessary. Christians should enter in and assist the state, always applying the Christian concept of love to improve upon the justice being dispensed. Hirsch also quickly adds that this concept of love need not be simple or naive. In complex questions it can be strong and serious.[58]

In his next chapter on 'State, Volk and Humanity' Hirsch reaches the penultimate goal of his book. Based upon his view of history and society, he now grapples with the place of Volk. He believes state and Volk should be inseparable. The Volk will give to the state its community of life, its spirit, its character and its creative energy. It will replace the compulsory power of the state with the freely affirmed bonds of the Volk, thus becoming the secular basis for a 'community of conscience.'

Many implications radiate from this concept of Volk, according to Hirsch. For example, it reaches into both the past and future, so no state can think it governs for the present generation alone. Also, a democracy which places all governing power in the hands of a majority would be a perversion of the concept of Volk, in which the interests of all should be served. Hirsch notes that democracy is in fact limited in England, by custom and tradition, and in America, by the strength and roots of the two political parties. These safeguards are sufficient to guard against a tyranny of the majority. But a pure democracy in which citizens claim, 'We are the state' would be as bad as the 'I am the state' of Louis XIV.[59]

The proper understanding of Volk and Staat also rules out pacifism in Hirsch's eyes. Nineteenth-century thinkers decided war should be replaced by national self-determination and cooperation among states. This is rational, but it would require international law to be enforced. And that would mean an international state. Given England's position of dominance, Hirsch believes internationalism to be merely a code word for the hegemony of England; that is why England could say she fought for 'world peace' in the First World War.[60] And even if a balanced world government could be achieved at some point, no one could love it as they can their own nation. Finally, Hirsch quotes von Ranke to show that creativity arises from national diversity. So, Hirsch concludes, 'There is therefore no doubt where the deeper and richer form of life is to be found.'[61] Only a Volks state can make morality possible; only a Volks state allows true creativity. If that means the possibility of war must be retained, so be it; for a world order would create only a 'more superficial and impoverished spiritual and moral life.'[62]

Despite his rejection of internationalism, Hirsch believes a form of unity is possible in the world within the secret of 'superhuman, eternal necessity.' First, each state should be responsible to develop itself to the fullest, because each state adds to the whole of humanity with its contribution (e.g. Athens). Secondly, every nation has an obligation to operate within a framework of international justice. Power might be used, but only if a real necessity for it exists. A nation shames itself if it uses force and offers the world nothing in return. Finally, every nation may have its day but will someday have to step aside. Although no nation likes to think of itself as less than eternal, the world process pushes aside burned out nations so that new ones can blossom. These three factors, according to Hirsch, give unity and meaning to human history in the midst of its diversity.[63]

After developing his view of the importance of *Volk* in history, Hirsch then steps back to consider at some length three issues already touched upon. The first of these is war. Hirsch admits that war is awful, that talk of 'brisk, cheerful war' is absurd. But he affirms that in a world of nation states, the most desirable world, it must always be recognized as a possibility. The war-making power to protect the integrity of the state is comparable to the police power to protect the integrity of the law.[64] Does this mean wars can be just? That is more problematic. Hirsch thinks the concept of defensive war unclear because of the difficulty of defining the first 'act,' yet defensive war has been one of the historical criteria in defining a just war. Furthermore, just wars require some concept of natural law to identify just motivations, but Hirsch is sceptical of natural law. In the end he feels wars are won by the powerful, whether or not just, so they should simply be seen as tests of strength. War thus is a tool of history as complex and unpredictable as history itself.[65]

If it seems unjust for a *Volk* to secure land by war, Hirsch points to landholders who protect by law today what they earned by force yesterday. There are no equal economic rights for all individuals, nor should there be equal rights for all *Völker*. Nations which deserve strength and honor will win it through war because of their inner strength. If they pursue war as meaningless 'greed for power,' that is unjustified, according to Hirsch; but he also opposes the utilitarian idea that life is more important than freedom or duty. Pacifism would have to be the doctrine of utilitarians, he thinks, for that philosophy is by definition self-centered and unappreciative of eternal values, such as self-sacrifice.[66] A philosophy which recognizes the role of God in history, however, realizes that war is a 'question to God':

He remains the God of history and blesses only those . . . who set all their power and will on their freedom and their life goals. He does not listen to a *Volk* which questions only half-heartedly, which does not struggle for its life seriously and to the ultimate degree.[67]

And Hirsch adds for emphasis:

> If war truly is a question to God, yes, a struggle with God, which strikes investigatively at the main pillars of the national being, then it is an inconceivably hazardous undertaking. One can only justify it if one carries it through to the end, if one does not leave God alone until he gives his blessing. Fighting a lukewarm war, without the will to do and sacrifice everything, seems to me to be also a religious crime.[68]

Germans had taken the last war too frivolously, in contrast to the English. Now they must give up each separate will and devote their entire effort to the national duty. Hirsch speaks here of a peacetime effort, but it is obvious from the force of his remarks that he sees a future war as a likely and probably desirable opportunity for Germany once again to prove herself.

The second special subject to which Hirsch addresses himself is socialism. Hirsch charges that Social Democrats in Germany (in his view about half the population) fail to accept the important presupposition that citizens should freely give of themselves to the state for their own good. Rather, they see the state as a tool of oppression.[69] He disagrees, of course, and he also disapproves of their alternative, 'the rule of the proletariat.' Such an organization of society could not free and ennoble humanity, but could only lead to tyranny. Hirsch argues that Bolshevism is no accident, but the only possible form socialism can take. He calls it a mechanistic, arithmetic theory, which would destroy the soul of life. The worker does not create an article, as posited in 'surplus value theory,' he maintains, any more than a printer writes the book.[70] Life is more complex than that, and the complexity and even the disparities give it creativity and vigor.

Hirsch proposes an alternative to the socialist ideal: the national state which exists as a community of purpose and which looks after all its citizens. Only such a state will allow freedom for the individual while protecting the whole group. Fate will place some people in good positions and some in bad, but that fate is better than any construct reason could put in its place. The freedom for individuals will continue to inspire the vitality that produced England's empire and Germany's steel mills; the inequalities will continue to lead to such richness as the work Dostoievski produced in poverty and the work Tolstoy produced in wealth. Morality will also be served by 'the meekness and faithfulness of those who serve and the responsibility and nobility of those who rule.'[71] If property ownership brings injustice, then it is the duty of the state to regulate. Hirsch does not insist upon laissez-faire capitalism; but he advocates state regulation rather than socialism as the answer to economic injustices, for it corresponds so much better to the rest of his world view.

The final subject addressed by Hirsch in this book is Tolstoy. The Russian author made a great impact in Germany just after the First World War.

Hirsch traces this to two important qualities. First, Tolstoy is extremely sensitive to suffering and sorrow, and this makes him very sympathetic to Germans in the post-war era. Secondly, in his mystical idea of brotherhood and love, based upon the Sermon on the Mount, he promises that a community of love will come without effort or striving. He advocates passivity rather than force or organization. Do not oppose evil, love your enemy, etc. This too is attractive to Germans, who are both tired and despairing.[72] Hirsch sees the attractions in Tolstoy, but he rejects their basis both theologically and politically. He argues that Tolstoy's interpretation of the Sermon on the Mount, in which state, law and nation are denounced, is foreign to the New Testament. Jesus' love was not so delicate as Tolstoy suggests, nor did he reject the role of the state in enforcing justice.[73] Politically, Hirsch argues that every nation is lost which sits back and waits for fate. Nietzsche was right to criticize Tolstoy on this basis, but Hirsch complains that Nietzsche's 'will to power' lacks a 'where to' or a 'what for.' The best possible answer combines 'self-reliance' with 'selfless service,' i.e. some Nietzsche and some Tolstoy. Germans should be careful not to accept Tolstoy whole, however, just because he now appeals to their weakest point. It is not a time to dissolve into love, but rather a time for strong and bold, courageous and aggressive action.[74]

The conclusion of *Deutschlands Schicksal* comes in a chapter of the same name. Hirsch hopes to set out an interpretation of Germany's situation in light of his theistic view of history. First of all, this means recognizing just how low Germany has sunk. Although Hirsch approves the authority of the state as endorsed by God, present-day Germany can hardly be considered a sovereign state:

One describes Germany today most correctly as a colony of the Entente with sharply restricted self-government . . . We were a world *Volk*, a noble *Volk*, perhaps the most flourishing and best of all. We now stand in danger of being humiliated or even destroyed as a *Volk*, so that only a formless mass of workers in the service of foreign interests remains.[75]

It is apparent that the 'formless mass' of workers in Germany is not his favorite element of the population. He warns the workers, in fact, that they will soon learn no social gains can be achieved until Germany has regained her national power.[76]

Hirsch also subscribes to the 'stab-in-the-back' legend. He explains this with two-souls-in-the-breast imagery. The Germany of August 1914 was admirable. Had that spirit prevailed, Germany might even have won the war. But a second spirit developed which believed in the 'humanity' and the justice of Germany's enemies:

This soul lived in the German *Reichstag* [parliament] and in the great parties. It hated the strong men in army and government and supported the weak and incapable. With every year it led the fight more resolutely against the first soul. It degenerated more and more and finally, grasping all power to itself, presented itself naked in the revolution of 1918.[77]

It is perhaps confusing to find the leaders of this second Germany so idealistic, but that should not obscure the danger and harm they cause. Hirsch finds a quote in Fichte, addressed to a prince, which he now redirects towards these 'idealists':

> It is absolutely not allowed him to deviate arbitrarily from the eternal norms which give sense and reason to the administration of the state . . . [and then] to step back and say: I believed in humanity, I believed in faithfulness and honesty . . . He may believe in humanity if he wishes in his private affairs. Then, if he errs, the damage is his. But he may not risk the nation on this belief, for it is not right that the nation, and with it perhaps the most precious possessions which the people in a thousand years of struggle have acquired, will pass over into misery, just so that it can be said of him: he believed in human beings.[78]

This statement, of course, and the entire position taken by both Fichte and Hirsch, requires that they be correct in their perception of those 'eternal norms.' Otherwise, the tables are turned.

If Germany has been stabbed in the back and endangered in her very existence, what now is the solution? Hirsch proposes a simple answer: restore itself to what it had been before the war, whether that takes generations or centuries. Hirsch believes that will rather than fate rules history. For that reason Spengler's influence is damaging to Germany and should be rejected.[79] The most important element in Germany's rebirth will be her own will, her unity, her sense of discipline, purpose and sacrifice. Practical measures will also help, of course. Hirsch proposes that young people, both men and women, give one or two years of economic service to the state in lieu of military service. Rivers should be harnessed to electricity and wasteland brought under cultivation. New forms of justice should be insured through land reform, and industries in danger of falling under foreign control should be nationalized. This is not an ideological nor a dogmatic plan. It proposes to meet the practical needs of the German people on a practical level, but Hirsch reaffirms that *Geist* (spirit) is the most important ingredient.[80] He also is willing to accept the demise of the Hohenzollerns. Instead of restoring the monarchy, he proposes adding strength to the institutions of Weimar: strengthen the constitution, strengthen the presidency, strengthen the bureaucracy.[81]

It will be hard for Germans to discipline themselves and make sacrifices which will not bear fruit for them, but only for their children or grand-

children. German pride will therefore have to be retained, through education and through continuing German contributions to humanity. German
scholarship should continue to strive for excellence, for example, so that
German will remain a world language despite the loss of colonies. But Hirsch
turns to religious faith as the most important element in reinvigorating the
German spirit:

> We Germans must become a pious *Volk*, a *Volk* in which the gospel has
> power over conscience. Otherwise we will not be masters of our fate . . .
> Faith in God gives two things which are important for the preservation of
> our *Volk*. The one is that which I have tried to unfold in these hours. It is a
> clear view of humanity and history, of *Volk* and state, which sharpens in
> our conscience the law and the duty to do and to suffer everything for our
> own *Volk* and our own state, without regard for our own person. And only
> in relation to the perception of God as found in the gospel will these
> serious and mature truths prevail against the many modern dreams. The
> other thing is something personal. Belief in God awakens exactly the
> qualities of character and soul which we Germans now require so very
> much. As Ernst Moritz Arndt expressed it: belief in God creates men, men
> of unshakable desire for freedom and genuine faithfulness, whose will no
> person can break in two. And men with warm hearts, who are capable of a
> complete and strong love for their *Volk*, even when they gain nothing
> personally from this love, even when this *Volk* behaves ever so wildly and
> foolishly.[82]

Hirsch hopes God will now create such men in Germany. God is, of course,
the 'hammer' of history, under which glass or stone will break. But Hirsch
hopes Germany will prove to be ore, soon to be hammered into iron.[83]

Two years after *Deutschlands Schicksal* appeared, Hirsch prepared a
second edition. This gave him an opportunity to assess the developments
during that period in light of his analysis. His modifications of the text are
negligible, but he does add an 'afterword' to reveal his reaction to events.
First, he greets the failure of the socialist/pacifist dream with pleasure. This
shows Germans, especially the youth, the impossibility of human perfection
and points them towards God.[84]

Hirsch devotes the rest of this statement to explaining his disagreements
with the dialectical theologians, especially Barth and Tillich, although he
does not make it personal nor even name the latter. Rather, he criticizes
elements in contemporary philosophy, such as that which tries to separate
Christianity from the concepts of religion and culture (Barth). Hirsch feels
this is simply a desire to leave a sinking ship, and, changing the metaphor,
comments, 'With some one has the feeling that they relinquish with a heroic
gesture an apple, which they consider to be worm-eaten in any case.'[85] Such a
rejection of culture not only is politically significant, but also removes, in

Hirsch's view, an important support for the Christian ethic. In fact, he charges dialectical theology with ignoring ethics altogether with its complete no to the value of the human world:

> A natural human being does not cease being a natural human being just because he has peeked into the abyss of divine secrets beyond the borders of his life. He will actually make use also of this secret according to his natural disposition.[86]

Hirsch criticizes another characteristic of contemporary philosophy, the theology of revolution (Tillich). That theology is built upon a no to this world, particularly in a complete denial of the value of the existing social and political system. Hirsch, who does value state, law and order, is accused by them of regarding the imperfect human world as divine. He responds that, 'Life and order in nature and society are his [God's] gifts, not his manifestations.'[87] He too recognizes the imperfection of the human world, but the religious socialist's denial of that world is too complete.

Finally, Hirsch criticizes a third dialectical theologian, Friedrich Gogarten, for expecting people to believe in an 'unknown' God. This issue hinges upon the idea of revelation. Gorgarten, stressing the 'infinite qualitative distinction' between God and man, speaks of the 'concealment' of God, and adds, 'The final word allowed in religion is the question.'[88] Hirsch insists that his theology and his concept of ethics and conscience are based upon *knowledge*, 'For without a certain knowledge of the good we cannot think of the conscience . . . History, according to these presuppositions [Gogarten's], cannot be understood otherwise than as a region abandoned by God.'[89] Gogarten's position can hardly fail to lead to confusion and quickly fall into relativism and scepticism:

> So I also find among many contemporary messengers of the unknown God features which make me perplexed, yes, which leave me asking to what extent there remains here a religious proclamation at all. The no which they speak in the name of God to the traditional content of faith borders far too closely on the relativism and scepticism of recent worldly thought. The doubts which they direct in the name of God against the pious life run too much toward the disintegration of the praying and obedient faith and into the dumbstruck silence before the secret of a very worldly mysticism. One perceives much too much in their religious proclamation the echo of confusing contemporary events, which bring to the consciousness of all of us the enigmatic quality of the kingdom of God and the uncertainty of all earthly circumstances of life.[90]

Hirsch wants to avoid relativism and scepticism. His entire goal in this book has been to build a foundation for a positive view of state and nation through a theistic and ethical philosophy of history. Not paradox and speculation, but faith and obedience are his desire. As he concludes:

> The speculation which forgets itself in the paradoxes of infinity will not find it worth the effort to give fundamental reflection and total faithfulness to the realities of earthly life. But where the invisible is grasped by conscience, there grows an obedience which is ready courageously and unselfishly to wander the long, toilsome path of suffering resistance, which alone can lead our Volk again up to the heights.[91]

Deutschlands Schicksal presents Hirsch as an intelligent, conservative German theologian attempting to deal with the aftermath of the First World War. He recognizes the failures of nineteenth-century rationalism, and he can cite Hegel, Burckhardt, Nietzsche, Spengler and Einstein appropriately and with authority. He is not unaware of the problems of the poor and the working classes in Germany nor unwilling to help, but only within cautious, non-revolutionary limits. His main loves are Germany and Christianity, and the intellectual edifice he erects is designed to save these two entities from the intellectual-cultural crisis of the twentieth century and the political-material crisis of the First World War and its aftermath.

No one can deny that a crisis existed in Germany in the early 1920s. The issue is whether Hirsch's response to it was more or less appropriate than others, and whether or not he misused reason to reach his position. He disliked pluralism and change, the centrifugal forces of modern life. His ideal, therefore, was a society in which a self-aware and unified *Volk* worked together under the authority of a just state. His philosophy of history and theory of knowledge were existential. That is, he believed truth was not empirically verifiable; rather, it had to be individually grasped and then acted upon with courage. It required a leap of faith. He distilled this position from Fichte and from his own reading of the times, and then he turned to Kierkegaard in the twenties to substantiate it.

It is difficult to argue with any single point that Hirsch made. His premises were existentially based, and his thought was both coherent and internally consistent. Would empiricism have given a better theory of knowledge than existentialism? Was a socialist state a better ideal than a *Volksstaat* for Germany at that time? A capitalist democracy? It is hard to provide answers which are objective and which do not rely upon hindsight for their verification.

2. Political Actions

Just as Hirsch substituted his typewriter for a soldier's machine-gun during the war, he substituted his typewriter for a politician's rostrum during the peace. That is, he never became a politician himself. But he believed in the political relevance of Christian ethics, so he continued to make his ideas widely and forcefully known. For example, in his developing correspondence with Eduard Geismar in Copenhagen, he worked hard to convince his colleague of Germany's innocence and unjust treatment during and after the First World War.[92] He also developed a friendship with Paul Althaus which was at least partly based upon their very similar political views. The content of his politics during that time was always conservative nationalism, with strong emphasis on the injustice of the Versailles peace. His polemic was one-sided, and in the light of Fritz Fischer's work, questionable; yet it held a core of truth. Of course England was a world power, ambitious and protective of its best interests. Of course it had achieved power over the years through war and the threat of war. Obviously the Fourteen Points had been tendered to Germans as an inducement towards peace, and obviously Versailles had substantially ignored them.[93]

Jens Schjørring argues that during the mid and latter 1920s Hirsch disengaged himself from political concerns and even took some positions vis-à-vis Weimar which could be labeled liberal, e.g. wanting to limit the role of government in religious instruction.[94] Schjørring rightly concludes that continuity persisted in the thought of Hirsch into the 1930s, despite this disengagement; but I question whether the point about disengagement and 'liberalism' need be made at all. Hirsch recognized the long odds against diverting the direction of Weimar during its best years, and he did not shrilly protest its every move. But there is also no evidence that he changed any single element in his diagnosis and prognosis for Germany. He simply waited patiently, and when hard times stepped onto the stage in the 1930's, he was ready to give direction.

The first politically-oriented issue to catch Hirsch's attention in the 1930s was that of the international ecumenical movement. Already in 1925, before the Stockholm Conference, he raised questions about German participation in ecumenism. He charges that church unity has underlying political motives in which Germany and German interests will play a subservient role. Furthermore, he believes the ideal boundaries of a church should correpond to those of a *Volk* and that any broader organization can only be a forced ecclesiastical system.[95]

In 1931 Hirsch again had a chance to take a stand. In June of that year the German leadership of the *Weltbund für internationale Freundschaftsarbeit der Kirchen* met in Hamburg with the international executive committee of the organization. Hirsch and Paul Althaus used the occasion to publish a statement in which they urged German church leaders not to participate in any such ecumenical organizations. Their protest is really directed against the Treaty of Versailles. They disapprove the original treaty, of course, but they now argue it has been violated to the further disadvantage of Germany and that it reinforces the disastrous reparations payments which are destroying the German people:

Germany's enemies from the world war under cover of peace are carrying on the war against the German *Volk*, and this misrepresentation so poisons the politics of the world situation that sincerity and trust become impossible.[96]

The German church leadership will disappoint and confuse the German people if they participate in ecumenism with representatives of nations that attack Germany in this way. Hirsch and Althaus conclude,

that a Christian and ecclesiastical understanding and cooperation in the questions of the coming together of the peoples is impossible so long as the others push against us a politics which is murderous for our Volk.[97]

This statement immediately drew a response. Martin Rade and Friedrich Niebergall, for example, identify a spirit of hate instead of love in this supposedly Christian statement. They add, 'Here speaks a *völkisch* self-righteousness no different than in any nationalistic party paper.'[98] The negative response was great, and Hirsch acknowledges as much in a letter to Geismar. He defends himself, but asks, 'Or have I become a wicked animal in Danish eyes through the declaration with Althaus?'[99] 'Wicked animal' or not, Hirsch is ready for the fight. He enumerates a long list of injustices experienced by Germany since 1918. Then he says the only German mistake was its internal breakdown which allowed the disastrous signing of the Versailles peace, and he concludes:

The military hegemony of France, the maritime hegemony of England, the exclusion of the populous Germany from colonies, high German tribute payments, the fate of the east, all that should be borne by us as God-ordained destiny, all for the sake of understanding and world peace.[100]

And to Rade, Hirsch can only respond in bitterness: 'There is only one thing for me: fight.'[101]

Hirsch was not the only German ready to fight on this issue. Despite the opposition of theologians such as Rade, Hirsch and Althaus struck a responsive chord with their declaration. Already in March 1931, President Wolf of the Rhineland synod blamed German unemployment on the continuing reparation payments exacted from Germany and suggested:

It is to be questioned whether or not here the German churches in the interest of their God-directed call to the soul of the German *Volk* must reevaluate their relationships abroad.[102]

After Hirsch and Althaus published their statement, President Kapler of the

Prussian Union pointedly stayed away from the Life and Work executive committee meeting of August 1931. In October, this time against Kapler's wishes, the Prussian Church Commission issued a statement which picked up on the themes of German hardship and called on Christians outside Germany to fight the 'spirit of hate and falsehood.'[103] By August 1932 Kapler felt it necessary to warn Life and Work that 'responsible circles' in the German Protestant church were turning against the ecumenical movement on this issue.[104] So although Hirsch and Althaus may have been more strident than some, they expressed a view on the politics of ecumenism which was common to many church leaders in Germany.

Another issue in 1931 further highlights the political views of Hirsch. This is the case of a pastor and theologian, Günther Dehn (1882-1970).[105] In 1928 Dehn delivered a speech in Magdeburg in which he expressed vaguely pacifist views. He questioned, for example, whether 'heroic death' in war should be compared to the Christian concept of 'sacrificial death,' or whether war dead should have monuments in churches.[106] This earned him a mild reproof from church authorities, but did not block his appointment as professor of practical theology at Heidelberg nor his subsequent appointment to the University of Halle in 1931. However, at Heidelberg Gottfried Traub published an attack on Dehn which rightwing student groups then seized upon at the University of Halle. These students made his appointment a *cause célèbre*. The *Rektor* backed him and Dehn began to teach in the fall of 1931; but many faculty had already decided to switch to the student side of the issue when Dehn exacerbated the conflict in December by publishing an account of these events from his point of view. His parting comment in this book is an attack on conservative nationalism in the church:

> It could be that the church of today stands on the threshold of a most difficult struggle with modern nationalism, in which her very existence will be endangered. Should I give a gloomy indication of this coming conflict by cowardly yielding and withdrawing from the attack in the interest of my personal equanimity? Here resistance must be given. One cultivates the youth in their current struggles mostly by conceding to and praising their idealism, even if it is leading in the wrong direction. I must express serious reservations about that. Distorted idealism is demonic. It is simply not true that this fanatical love of fatherland, which in my view is colored by religion but actually dissociated from God, really helps the fatherland. On the contrary, it will lead the fatherland into destruction.[107]

Hirsch could not resist responding to this attack upon the most central values for which he stood, so he soon became a central figure in the 'Dehn case.' Together with Hermann Dörries, a younger colleague on the theological faculty at Göttingen, he published a statement on 27 January 1932 on the conflict at Halle. They profess their belief in academic freedom, even for persons of antipathetic views; but in this case they draw the line. The one, minimal qualification they feel necessary for any teacher of German youth is:

> the recognition that the nation and its freedom, despite all the question-ableness of human existence, remains for the Christian a good thing hallowed by God. It demands a complete devotion of the heart and the life. And from this recognition follows an endorsement of the passionate will to freedom of our *Volk*, which is being enslaved and violated by enemies hungry for power and possessions.[108]

This 'minimal qualification' demanded by Hirsch and Dörries is highly controversial, of course, for it contradicts both dialectical theology and leftwing politics. Dialectical theologians were not willing to accept earthly circumstances as 'a good thing hallowed by God,' nor were liberals and socialists all willing to accept the freedom of the German *Volk* as a major concern. Therefore, Barth immediately led the attack on Hirsch, and the conflict soon took the form of a discussion between the two. Barth tries to identify the issues as theological, but Hirsch concludes that, as a Swiss, Barth is simple unable to understand the issue:

> Whoever is not in the position with us to bring tremblingly before God the fate of Germany and to stake his own and his children's existence on that fate, whoever is not called through his very existence to stand with us in our inner self-determination, that person also cannot stand in judgment on whether our will is bound on God or not.[109]

Barth in his turn concludes that Hirsch is a nationalistic fanatic who cannot rise above the level of political slogans.

Barth and Hirsch carried on this conflict through several exchanges, and then never addressed each other personally again. This break was almost pre-determined by the gulf separating them both theologically and politically. The position of Barth insisted that theology stress the gap between God and man and the once-and-for-all nature of revelation. Incidentally, this made it impossible to value highly any earthly, national order. Hirsch insisted that God works in history, intersects human life, and can be recognized by man though a proper appreciation of history and a properly sensitive conscience. This made it possible to recognize the hand of God acting in the history of the German people. The conflicts of the 1930s are isolated in this dichotomy.[110]

Both the ecumenical issue and the case of Dehn were clearly of political significance in the mind of Hirsch. His anticipation of a change in government for Germany and his efforts towards that end are hinted at in other incidents at about the same time. His correspondence with Geismar, for example, took on a renewed polemical and political tone. In 1931 he expressed his concern about the impact of economic distress in Germany:

> You do not know how great the despair is among us simply because we have no food and no work for one quarter of the *Volk*. And this winter it will become one third of the *Volk*. You do not know how Bolshevism is fomenting among us. And Versailles carries the responsibility for all of this.[111]

Until April 1932, Hirsch supported Alfred Hugenberg and the rightwing German National Peoples Party, rather than Hitler and the more radically rightwing National Socialists. But on the eve of the presidential election in that month, he publicly threw his support to Hitler in a letter to the local Party newspaper:

> You know that I am not a National Socialist and that I have more than mild doubts about the NSDAP. You also know that I consider Hugenberg to be the right statesman for the present difficult times, although he is not recognized as such by the *Volk* . . . But I cannot get around the fact that a situation has developed without my assistance. And Hitler now is the only representative of a will to break with the mistakes of the twelve years from 1919 to 1931, the only candidate on 10 April to offer a new German beginning.[112]

Although he questioned the paganism and the racial teachings of Nazism, it is not surprising that Hirsch greeted the rise of Hitler with enthusiasm and a burst of activity. The enthusiasm was a direct outgrowth of the hopes expressed in *Deutschlands Schicksal*. But he had expected to wait at least a generation or more, and now he was pleasantly surprised, as he stated in 1933:

> All of us who stand in the present moment of our *Volk* experience it as a sunrise of divine goodness after endless dark years of wrath and misery. We experience it with a shiver of responsibility that our *Volk* not squander this moment, that it take this given opportunity to begin anew and bring it about in the correct way. We all thought we were captured in the destiny of an old culture, in which public life restricts itself to ordering external things and the common spirit becomes a religiously and morally neutral characterlessness. We all thought we must bear it that the taking seriously of simple faith in God and the keeping holy of moral values and discipline would restrict itself to the private sphere of small circles, that the large masses of our *Volk* would fall into godlessness and indiscipline, separated from the Christian proclamation as by a wall. Now new hope has been given to us. And should our hearts not burn with enthusiasm that the

Protestant church now say yes to this moment, that it seize the opportunity to cooperate with redeveloping the order and style of the German *Volk*?[113]

One way for the church to say yes to the moment would be to create a unified German Protestant church. Particularism among German Protestants had been largely unaffected by Bismarck's work of unification, and supporters of Nazism in the church, especially the *Deutsche Christen*, hoped to quickly rectify that error. On 15 April 1933 Hirsch wrote to his bishop, August Marahrens of Hanover, on the subject. On the one hand, a true Reichs church would be impossible because of the theological differences involved, he maintains. On the other hand, a unified German Protestant church has become a historical necessity. Hirsch fears the strength of the Old Prussian Union will prevail over Lutherans in the formation of a new church if the Lutherans do not immediately make preparations. So he proposes the appointment of a Protestant 'nuncio' with power to negotiate for the church; and he can only suggest Althaus, Heinrich Rendtorff or himself as theologians who are 'irreproachable as measured on the most passionate scale of Germanness.'[114] Before Marahrens could act, however, on 25 April 1933, Hitler named Chaplain Ludwig Müller (1883-1945) as his special 'Plenipotentiary for questions on the Protestant Churches.' Hirsch immediately became a major backer and advisor to Müller and remained so through the struggles of the months ahead.

Hirsch's reaction to and participation in the events of spring and summer 1933 are revealed in his publication, *Das kirchliche Wollen der deutsche Christen*, in which he reprints a number of statements and articles he had written during those months. It is clear Hirsch sees the problem in terms of his goal of an effective church. The church will be damaged if it remains aloof to the turning point of 1933, for the bulk of the German people will interpret such a stance as at least irrelevant, and possibly hostile, to the excitement and meaning they find in the German revolution. Instead, the church leadership should actively strengthen its ties to the German *Volk*, and this will require: a. a Reichs church in keeping with the unity of the *Volk*, and b. acceptance of the *Führer* principle in accordance with the new political values.[115]

Hirsch justifies these two changes for the church on several grounds. Although the message of the gospel reaches an individual through the mystery of the Holy Spirit, the message-bearer can get in the way if he appears strange, foreign or offensive in some way to the hearer. So the best foundation for an effective proclamation of the gospel is a common blood, nationality and culture.[116] The church should build upon this advantage rather than deny it. The church should also accept the principle of leadership presented by National Socialism. Hirsch notes that he as a pastor had felt a lack of direction from the church leadership, and he argues that without direction and discipline a completely appropriate idea or goal of the church leadership can die of inertia among the pastorate. Furthermore, the church has always borrowed political forms from the state (witness the Roman pontificate). There is nothing intrinsically wrong in continuing to adapt in such a way, and it has the advantage of allowing the church to strike deeper roots among the present German *Volk*.[117]

Hirsch stresses that the church is holy and that the message of the church is a holy matter which brooks no interference. But he also argues that the earthly side of the church's existence intersects the state in several important ways. For example, both church and state are concerned with education, moral values and a sense of duty. The church provides the moral underpinnings for an orderly state and the state insures the order and stability in which the gospel can be successfully proclaimed. Therefore, the church should cooperate with the state as much as possible, short of endangering the holy core of its message. Although the church always stands in danger of becoming too human, it must act boldly and rely on God's grace. True freedom for the church requires only 'that the church be free to bring God and the gospel to the German *Volk* without state command or state interference.'[118] And the happy result might be a true *Volks* church, in which the German people enthusiastically accept the message of Christianity as the appropriate culmination of the German rebirth. He feels a similar enthusiasm briefly surfaced in the Schmalkaldic wars and again in the War of Liberation. He hopes that this time the church will respond in such a way that the impact will be lasting.[119]

The clinching assurance for Hirsch in his encouragement of a *Volks* church was his conviction that Hitler was a heaven-sent Christian leader. As he wrote in the early summer of 1933:

> No other *Volk* in the world has a leading statesman such as ours, who takes Christianity so seriously. On 1 May when Adolf Hitler closed his great speech with a prayer, the whole world could sense the wonderful sincerity in that.[120]

He also believed that the emphasis of the Party on faith and values gave it a positive relationship to Christianity. Therefore, in the conflicts of the church struggle of 1933, Hirsch played a leading role in support of Ludwig Müller, the plenipotentiary of the *Führer*.

In May 1933 President Kapler of the Prussian Union, Bishop Marahrens representing Lutherans, and Pastor Hesse of Elberfeld respresenting the Reformed churches, gathered at Loccum to discuss the creation of a unified German church. Their meeting unleashed a flurry of positioning by various factions and a stampede of events. No one was quite sure what their agenda included or whether they would deal only with constitutional forms or with personalities. However, filling the position of the Reichs bishop quickly assumed major importance. On 18 May a small East Prussian group of *Deutsche Christen* publicly nominated Ludwig Müller. The 'Young Reformation Movement' quickly followed with the recommendation of Friedrich von Bodelschwingh, a candidate acceptable to moderates. Then the broader *Deutsche Christen* organization, led by Hossenfelder, protested against the presumption of the Young Reformers and insisted that Müller, since he had the support of the *Führer*, was the only acceptable candidate. Amidst a good deal of confusion and a split vote, the leaders of the existing church groups selected Boldelschwing on 27 May. He served for just a month, during which time political harassment made his position untenable. Finally, the *Deutsche Christen* successfully demanded a new election, this time by the church membership at large.[121]

During this conflict Hirsch stood at Müller's side. He was with him on the night of 16-17 May, just before the Loccum meeting, and during that night he composed a statement justifying the development of a *Volks* church and endorsing Müller for the position of bishop. This was printed in *Evangelisches Deutschland* on 4 June. On 7 June he wrote an appeal in the same publication for a plebiscite, both on the proposed constitution of the new church and on the person of the new Reichs bishop.[123] He also contributed an article to the *Völkischer Beobachter,* the official National Socialist newspaper, endorsing the election of Müller.[134] And on 9 July, shortly after Müller took office. he published in *Evangelisches Deutschland* his final defense of his role and that of the *Deutsche Christen* in these events.[125] Throughout these weeks and despite the clumsy show of force by Nazi enthusiasts, Hirsch opposed Barth and the Young Reformers and insisted upon the theological rectitude of a *Volks* church which could endorse the political turn-of-events in Germany.

The one other politically divisive issue which made an impact on the church in 1933 was that of the Aryan paragraph. Hirsch sent his personal written opinion on this question to the leaders of the Reichs church on 7 October 1933, and when the issue refused to die down, published it in *Deutsche Theologie* in May of the following year. This written opinion shows Hirsch taking pains to side with the government, but with qualifications that preserve the oneness in Christ of Christian theology and the Christian love ethic. He agrees with the Nazi concept of 'guest status' for Jews, asserting that Jews are more foreign by race and history than most of Germany's neighbors. Christians should accept that reality, but they can also perform several positive functions. For example, Hirsch feels Christians should insist this is not an issue of 'inferiority,' but only one of 'foreignness.' Individual Christians can keep their friendships with Jews, ameliorate the plight of 'in-betweens' when possible, and be happy if the time comes when exceptions can be made.[126]

The church leadership, however, has a relationship with and a duty towards the state, as implied by *Volks* church, and this has to be balanced with the demands of Christian unity. Hirsch resolves this problem, some-what ironically, by stressing the Lutheran concept of the pristhood of all believers. All Christians are equal before God and every Christian can perform the functions of the priest. Jewish converts should not be excluded. Pastors, however, perform an external, human role in the church, and they are chosen by human means, which may be imperfect. Many are kept from this role by mental or physical disabilities. If a *Volks* church should now decide that being a member of the *Volk* is also a reasonable qualification for office, that should be accepted as within the parameters of Christian one-ness.[127]

C. Hirsch's Political Philosophy in 1933

DURING the period 1930 to 1933, while actively engaged in these church-political controversies, Hirsch was also writing his major work on Kier-kegaard. As that effort came to a close he wrote his best and most com-prehensive explanation of his political stance, *Die gegenwärtige geistige Lage im Spiegel philosophischer und theologischer Besinnung*. He signed the introduction to this book on 30 January 1934, probably as an intentional celebration of the first anniversary of Hitler's rise to power.

The theme of this book is found in two quotations which Hirsch uses by way of introduction. First from Goethe: 'No one can judge history as he who has experienced history.'[129] Hirsch underlines the significance of this quote for him with a brief autobiographical assessment of the history he has lived:

It has been decisive for my entire intellectual position that my work and creativity have occurred almost entirely, at least from an age when I was still young enough to be adaptable, in a time of convulsion, of transforma-tion, of constant revolutionary change, and finally now in a time of new beginning for the history of my *Volk*.[129]

Hirsch's second quotation comes from Søren Kierkegaard, the subject of his intense study for the previous twelve years:

If one wants to attempt in all sincerity, then he will truly receive strength enough in the decision . . . It is certain: the conviction with which one ventures gives superhuman powers. But it is also certain (it is curious how exactly this applies): whoever does not have conviction, he also cannot understand it. See, the great warship first learns its destination on the high sea, the barge knows everything in advance.[130]

Hirsch recognizes the tumult of the times, the inadequacy of objective knowledge, and the fallibility of human actions. But he stresses, with

Kierkegaard, that 'an intellectually active person' must overstep the boundaries of objective knowledge and take a stand.[131]

Hirsch then explains — in his first and most important chapter on the general 'intellectual crisis' — why the content of objective knowledge is not very broad or useful. Looking back several centuries, he sees the breakdown of Catholic orthodoxy during the Reformation leading to the domination of a rational, humanistic world view from the Thirty Years War until the first World War. The focal point uniting diverse strands within this world view was the belief that human, rational inquiry produces the highest form of truth available to man.[132] Hirsch admits the valuable contributions of rationalism during the period, but he also argues that it undercut Christianity and all other 'law, morality, order and custom.' This was because of the counterpart to reason, freedom. The autonomous, rational human being has to be free to question and to choose his own values. Individualism and liberalism grow naturally in the soil of rationalism, as evidenced by the German Reformation of the sixteenth century, the Dutch war for independence of the early seventeenth century, and the English Revolution of the late seventeenth century.[133]

Hirsch then introduces a phrase from Kierkegaard which assumes enormous importance in his argument: reason and freedom lead ultimately to 'the all-encompassing debate about everything.'[134] This explains why rationalism is such an unsettling force, leading always to crisis and revolution, and this is why it has no unifying, creative power. Instead of being creative, rationalism is ultimately nihilistic, as Nietzsche correctly saw. He recognized every truth as a self-deceit. In his view freedom and reason destroyed all freedom and reason and revealed only the will to power as the final reality. This was true because for reason there could be no secret places in which truth could reside. Rationalism had to seek them out, remove all mystery, and thereby destroy the bases of truth. Idealistic philosophy, for example, trying to retain hold on an eternal ideal, fell prey to this attack.[135]

Hirsch sees in historicism another example of the failure of reason. Historicists emphasize the time and space boundaries of life. Each people and epoch has to be understood on its own terms in order to avoid unfair, subjective, anachronistic judgments towards another culture. The result, in Hirsch's words, is a 'freefloating lack of cohesiveness.' Reason loses its claim to truth, corresponding to the political judgment of the Weimar years that truth is a 'party matter.'[136]

Hirsch's conclusion is that modern philosophy, because of internal contradictions in rationalism, has committed suicide. Therefore, modern intellectual history presents a paradox:

It appears on the one hand as growing always richer in objective knowledge, and on the other hand as growing always poorer in the ultimate, inner, binding, living power of truth.

Without a revolution Hirsch predicts man will dissolve into relativistic nihilism.[137]

Fortunately, so Hirsch thinks, a revolution has now taken place in Germany. Perhaps Germans will be able to break through to the secret of life, to a new sense of community. Perhaps the hardships and 'the unfaithfulness in its own house' will ultimately seem a blessing in disguise. It is only a 'perhaps' because Hirsch admits no one can know for sure:

> But we have ventured on this possibility, on this perhaps, without reserve, we have cut ourselves off from the road back. We will realize it or else, but when we look into the eyes of our youth, there is no or else for us.[138]

The pain of transition will admittedly appear in Germany, causing protests and criticism; but Hirsch compares this to the pain of childbirth: necessary, even if unpleasant.[139]

Since Hirsch sees 'the all-encompassing debate about everything' as the destructive element within rationalism, his task is to find an intellectually acceptable protection against that debate. He does this by introducing three Greek terms: Horos, Nomos and Logos. Horos he defines as 'uncrossable boundary.' This boundary cannot be traversed by individuals or groups without destructive consequences. Nomos he defines as the 'conditions of order, life and thought.' This corresponds to law and order within a society. Logos, finally is seen as 'self-expressive, living spirit,' a living and dynamic form of reason.[140]

Hirsch believes the German turning point introduced by National Socialism represents a proper reintroduction of Horos, Nomos and Logos to German life. The Nazis do not allow 'the all-encompassing debate about everything,' but rather insist upon a 'consciousness of boundaries.'[141] And these boundaries do not need to be forced upon the *Volk*, nor are they an artificial creation of reason:

> The new will itself . . . is not artificially made by us; it is a *holy storm* that has come over us and grasped us . . . Of course, only a German can understand that internally.[142]

National Socialists not only recognize the importance of Horos, but they recognize it in the God-given 'secret of the bloodbond,' i.e. they see Horos as both God-given and individualized for each *Volk*. Hirsch argues that peoples which ignore these boundaries (no doubt thinking of Weimar Germany) lose their roots and will soon be destroyed.[143] Cosmopolitanism is a violation of God's boundaries of life.

The expression of Horos for each *Volk* is to be found in its Nomos, the rules, values and mores which regulate human behavior. The Nazi emphasis upon law and order, upon family and tradition, reveals its proper understanding of Nomos. This renewal of Nomos is seen by some as a step backwards into barbarism, especially in its emphasis upon blood and race. Hirsch argues that the concepts of blood and race are not a shallow, biological materialism. Rather, biology is used as a steppingstone towards appreciation of the deeper, spiritual, God-given significance of blood ties for each *Volk:* 'The recollection of blood and race is the way in which the whole great secret of boundaries most powerfully seized us.'[144]

Logos is interpreted by Hirsch as a form of rationalism which employs a new and more satisfactory understanding of reason and freedom, as exemplified in the German turning point. Reason can no longer have all-embracing pretensions. Science will continue to perform its useful service, but when it approaches border areas, it cannot claim to give solid, certain answers:

> Reason is human-historical life itself, which understands itself intellectually as Logos and develops a specific Nomos. Science is nothing but the cultivation and reckoning of this Logos for itself, determined by reality and based upon its own specific reality.[145]

Freedom, too, has to be reined in. Instead of creating a power in and of itself, it will now be rooted in responsibility to the Nomos of *Volk* and state. Any freedom which supersedes Nomos would really be demonic rather than true freedom. Hirsch even suggests that freedom might best be exemplified by military officers: 'Whoever does not hear the call to colors also does not know what freedom is.' For most others, 'Freedom, in an astonishing aberration, becomes actually equivalent to irresponsibility.'[146]

Hirsch recognizes the mystery in this concept of freedom and the possibility of error. Horos, he believes, is determined both by history and by God. Danger lies in mistakenly emphasizing one over the other. The only solution is to act boldly, but with religious seriousness and a strong hold on reality: Reason should be 'responsibility bound to reality.' And Hirsch concludes,

> Boundaries become genuine boundaries in their inseparability from responsibility . . . All tensions within our new restrictions upon freedom are tensions of an encounter with God . . . Is it then true that such an encounter with God is the ultimate secret of the German turning point?[147]

Hirsch believes that God stands with Hitler in this moment of German history, but he admits the final answer is not yet in: 'It lies in that which comes.'[148]

Hirsch's analysis of the crisis of reason in the early twentieth century is intelligent and clear. It could find a respectable niche in an anthology of intellectual history today. His attempt to divert 'the all-encompassing debate about everything' is rooted in an existential affirmation of eternal values, Horos and Nomos, and thereby an unexceptionable interpretation of Kierkegaard for the twentieth century. His work appears odd, however, because of the content of his 'eternal values.' He made judgments about Hitler and National Socialism which have not stood the test of time.

An example of Hirsch's judgment which seems anachronistic today is his analysis of the Jewish question. He accepts the antisemitic prejudice that Jews are a destructive force in Germany. But he then fits this premise into his system of thought in a coherent and consistent manner. Nineteenth-century rationalism emphasized the oneness of humanity. Jews benefited from this concealment of ethnic differences, for it led to their legal emancipation. So it was natural that Jews did everything in their power to break down all historical boundaries, so that only a neutral humanity would remain. But this is exactly the destructive force which Hirsch fears will result in 'freefloating lack of cohesiveness,' so Hirsch sees Jewish emancipation as part of the general crisis.[149] Furthermore, Hirsch ties Bolshevism into his argument. He sees it as the culmination of scientific materialism in which human beings become mere objects, and he argues that it has close and natural ties to the Jewish people:

> When later the human history of the nineteenth century is remembered, one will understand Marxism as the product of a German-Jewish mixed marriage and as an example of the inner impossibility of Jewish emancipation on the soil of a Christian *Volk*. Perhaps Bolshevism will even be designated an unbelieving aberration of the Jewish religion.[150]

This assessment ignores many gentile Marxists and mistakes the 'impossibility' of Jewish emancipation. But Hirsch is not alone in discerning Judaic thought patterns in Marx nor in recognizing an apparent affinity between leftwing politics and Jewish emancipation. Furthermore, Hirsch admits that Judaism is an auxiliary to the crisis in Germany, rather than a main cause. He says the roots of the crisis in Christian culture lie in the Christian culture itself.[151]

The rest of *Die gegenwärtige geistige Lage* is devoted to Hirsch's assessment of how philosophy and theology should deal with the reality of the German turning point. He says philosophy now has a new assignment, to create within the university and for the *Volk* as a whole the philosophical basis for a new Germany. In introducing this subject he defines three critical elements in philosophy. First, philosophy must have a theory of knowledge. This theory can either be based upon science, which Hirsch regards as ultimately unworkable, or it can be based upon an 'understanding intellectuality', a 'being grasped' by history. This latter, existential position is traced by Hirsch to Socrates:

> It is known that the philosophy of Socrates possessed an unprecedented

weight of historical, existential meaning, because its originator was grasped by the historical twists and turns of the hellenic Nomos of that time.[152]

The second important element in philosophy is an understanding of history. Hirsch believes a proper understanding of history will point towards the secret of community. Earlier philosophy tried to understand the 'pure humanity' of an individual, but an emphasis on 'understanding onself in historical existence' will correct that error. Again Hirsch points towards Socrates as an example, maintaining that he understood the importance of community. Finally, philosophy should have an understanding of religion. Hirsch regards this as the crucial point. German philosophy was prepared for 1933 in that it was already rooted in existentialism. However, existentialism can either lead to an atheism, in which the boundary is seen as 'nothingness,' or Christianity, in which the boundary is seen as God. Hirsch believes that if German philosophy will choose the proper theory of knowledge, 'understanding intellectuality,' and the proper philosophy of history, with its emphasis upon the community, a religious philosophy which accepts the Christian roots in Germany will result.[153]

The job for philosophy, then, will be to rebuild the German universities. Hirsch argues that idealistic philosophy was the foundation upon which the greatness of the German universities in the nineteenth century was built. However, idealistic philosophy ultimately failed, so the strength of the universities is in jeopardy. Hirsch also points to over-specialization and a general lowering of standards as contributing to the decline of the university. The solution is to rise above specialization and devote research and teaching to a common education for the new German. Although this will require 'relearning and new learning' for the faculty, it will produce a new comradeship between faculty and students; a 'community of questions,' an 'intellectuality of Volk and state,' and a common 'intellectual-ethical foundation.'[154] Hirsch's complete acceptance of the Nazi turn of events can be seen in his endorsement of the SA and SS students' role in shaking the universities. He predicts, 'When the transition is complete . . . then teachers and students will all together wear the same brown coat.'[155]

Philosophy also should have the task of clarifying the relationship between Volk and state in the new Germany. Because Hirsch has written on this subject during the Weimar years, and because of his understanding of Volk and state through Fichte and Treitschke, he claims the right to make some suggestions. His premise is that, although political sovereignty resides in the state, true sovereignty is rooted in the Volk. Therefore, democracy is neither necessary nor desirable for Germany. Former political philosophy knew only two options, autocracy or democracy. But Germany can now create a new form of authoritarianism in which people freely give their obedience to the state so long as the state properly represents the Volk. Hirsch also insists that egalitarianism is a sham, with a deleterious effect on excellence. He advocates instead an acceptance of inequality and a 'selection of the capable.' Finally, the German people have accepted the *Führer* principle out of 'primordial inclination.' Although Hirsch occasionally admits the possibility that this new formula for statehood might be corrupted, he feels that at the moment it is 'beyond discussion, self-evident.' 'The intellectual struggle is closed,' he writes. The role of philosophy is to clarify and build upon that base.[156]

Hirsch's major concern, of course, is not philosophy but theology, and he argues that the latter's roots in the German *Volk* are even deeper and its importance in the German turning point greater than that of philosophy. For example, he believes that theological education, by making use of all disciplines, has avoided some of the hazards of specialization which have afflicted philosophy. This has yielded a closer attachment to *Volk* and state among theological students, as revealed by their participation in the First World War: '[Theological students] offered . . .by far the greatest blood sacrifice of all Germans.'[157] Christian roots in Germany can also be seen in the fact that every great German in history has been a Christian. And although the origins of Christianity lie outside of Germany, the German church has realized it can most effectively spread its message by sinking into the human reality around it. It then points to the eternal from its place inside *Volk* and state.[158] On the basis of this defense of the importance of Christianity to the German *Volk*, Hirsch maintains that a proper renewal of Protestant theology can become a 'source of life for both, for Protestant Christianity . . . and for our *Volk* and our state.'[159]

Hirsch then presents his interpretation of recent theological developments in Germany. Before the First World War, Christian theologians thought they could unite with the spirit of the age, i.e. with reason and science. Positivism was dominant when Hirsch studied in the early years of this century; but among his generation, and especially among theologians, he believes, problems became apparent. Nietzsche was popular, and he pointed towards a questioning of the limits of natural science. Students then turned to Kant and Schleiermacher and to a historical consciousness in which at least the *historical* importance of Christianity could be established. But despite the contributions of Nietzsche, Kant and Schleiermacher, Hirsch admits that neither he nor his friends were satisfied. None felt they could have defeated Feuerbach in a debate.[160] There was also an 'inner strife' in which preaching and theology were seen to be far apart. Hirsch and his generation sought answers in idealism and in Søren Kierkegaard, he writes, but they achieved no breakthrough at that time.[161]

Theological study in those years was almost entirely historical. It produced refined research, but Hirsch feels it led theologians directly into the crisis of the age. Historical study led to Feuerbach, i.e. the conclusion that religion was the creation of human genius. God was no longer beyond the boundary, and faith in the Son-of-God dogma was no longer meaningful. So dogma and faith stood opposed to reason and science. Historical study also suggested that Christianity was not unique, but simply the religion of Western Civilization, which had borrowed, in fact, a good deal of the heritage of Eastern religions. The answer to this crisis, perceived by Hirsch and his generation but not yet fully developed, was twofold: 1. insist upon faith in the 'truth of the absoluteness' of the Christian God, and 2. be ready to recognize historical study as not fully, humanly understandable. In other words, this answer was existential and dialectical.

Along with the theological crisis facing Hirsch as a student, Germany also faced a social crisis. Hirsch blames this crisis on the late unification of Germany and the rapid, socially disruptive industrialization which followed. Since about half the German population lost their roots in this process, Hirsch feels they were ready-made for the crisis of the age.[162] Some well-meaning theologians and pastors, strongly affected by the social distress, turned to Marxism as a solution to the crisis. Hirsch understands their concern, but rejects their choice. He believes Marxism both a godless religion, and, therefore, antipathetic to Christianity, and also international and materialistic, thereby breaking down the *völkisch* values to which Hirsch is committed.[163] The second alternative is to attempt to improve the situation of the working masses within the established order, eventually restoring their basis in *Volk*, state and Christianity. Although Hirsch clearly favors this path, it too did not work before the war because the forces of destruction had been so great. In an autobiographical vein, Hirsch notes this social question taught him that the church is bound to earthly as well as spiritual concerns. He also learned to see God's hand in *Volk*, state and history.[164]

Hirsch next deals with theology in the period from 1914 to 1932, in which his generation actually began dealing with the theological questions that had arisen. He believes that war and the resulting period of instability proved fertile, especially for theology, because it was a time of decision. The questions of life and death in wartime were also the questions of encounter with God, and the need for decision in a volatile time was parallel to the decision required when meeting up with God. Hirsch believes the new generation of German theologians responded with remarkable unity to this challenge. They went back to re-read the New Testament, especially Paul, and they went back to re-study the Reformation, especially Luther. This led them to the question of 'belief and unbelief' and away from the theological questions which had begun to hide the message of the gospel.[165] They also were led to paradox and dialecticism. The war had made paradox more readily acceptable as an intellectual tool; then a common discovery of Kierkegaard and a recognition of paradox in the teaching of justification by faith *(Rechtfertigungslehre)* of Luther solidified its place of importance.[166] Hirsch believes the courage to accept paradox in proclaiming God's revelation separates this generation of theologians from that of the pre-war period, and he credits Kierkegaard with having exerted the greatest influence in this direction:

> From another time he was able through clear foresight to see the complete situation of the age of crisis. He sought to express a new understanding of genuine Christianity in a body of Christian thought which carried all essential questions of the time in itself. He thereby really awakened New Testament and original Lutheranism in a young form pregnant with the future, which can only now be properly grasped.[167]

Despite the unity on basic theological positions, Hirsch admits his generation split into two groups on the question of society and its place in theology. Both groups rejected the cultural Protestantism of the nineteenth century, with its hope that culture and Christianity could blend together. But the 'crisis theologians' (Barth et al., though Hirsch does not name them) carried this to a rejection of any ties to this world. Their eschatological view saw this world standing under sin and death, and they looked towards a new time, the coming of the Kingdom of God. In opposition 'The young national Lutheranism,' to which Hirsch belonged, saw a need to take a stance on the real ethical and political problems of the world:

> In the inner German struggle, it placed itself with passionate determination on the side of those who could not inwardly accept the conditions brought about by the defeat and revolution of 1918. In struggle against the ideas of 1918, against the dream of an international world culture of democratic or Marxist orientation and pacifist ideology, the dream of a levelling of peoples, they wanted to protect the will of the German *Volk* to itself, to a German rebuilding.[168]

Sharpened by the challenge of crisis theology, these Young Lutherans worked through Luther's *Zweireichlehre* anew. How could one distinguish between an order of society willed by God and a sinful one?

> One stood no longer as in former times with a self-evident world of norms, one stood ethically exactly in a chaos falling into disintegration, in which the judgments good and bad were thrown back and forth like balls by the squabbling positions. Even in opposition to the existing conditions one was drawn into this.[169]

Opposition to the 'existing conditions,' here referring clearly to Weimar, was not a position lightly assumed by a theologian trained in Luther. The Young Lutherans solved this problem by developing a theology of 'orders of creation' in which the concrete 'life in community' was found in the *Volk*, rather than the state. They 'thereby achieved legitimacy for the national struggle despite its expressed or unexpressed revolutionary goals.'[170] Even this position was not taken without recognition that they might have mistaken sinful reality for the reality of God's creation, placing inappropriate value on the former. So ultimately a stand could only be taken in the confidence of God's love and grace:

> Only in the depths of belief in justification by faith was it possible to allow the ethical involvement of the Christian in the historical community. This is not built on the basis of a law, but out of merciful responsibility based on the general self-testimony and rule of God in nature and history.[171]

When Crisis Theologians objected that this position did not recognize the gap between temporal and eternal, the Young Lutherans responded that the former position ruled out taking any stand on the pressing 'questions of conscience' in Germany, which in itself would be a position on the side of the 'November revolution,' an acceptance of the era of disintegration. It would also be a capitulation to sceptical nihilism.[172] Despite these harsh words, Hirsch expresses his admiration for both Crisis Theology and the Young Lutherans. They learned from each other, they both contributed towards a new German theology, and they both testified to the God of the gospel. Thus, this division did not add to the party spirit within church politics, but actually increased unity during the years of Weimar.

Neither group was very concerned with church administration, but rather with preaching the gospel. Here, however, another point of difference emerged. The Crisis Theologians argued that human error was removed from the proclamation of the gospel through a 'specific teaching and a specific power of office,' i.e. if a preacher conscientiously studied the Bible and church teachings, when he stepped into the pulpit God's truth would come through despite human weakness. This view stresses the distinction between the human and the divine, but it allows a point of intersection, that mysterious point at which God speaks in human voice.[173] The Young Lutherans, however, were more ready to accept the impact of human arbitrariness in the act of preaching. They acknowledged a difference between reality and the picture of reality presented in the pulpit; but God could be made known through human speech, under the cover of grace.[174] The significance of this difference is twofold. First, the Young Lutherans placed less stress on the absolute accuracy of a confession; that too was a human statement, effective only through grace. Secondly, the human role of the preacher corresponded to his position within the human community. He filled a role in the human order as well as the divine:

> A preaching and a church which recognizes the reality around it has no possibility of seeing itself as separated from the scope of *völkisch*, historical life.[175]

Again the difference between the Young Lutherans and the Crisis Theologians emerges as political.

Next Hirsch deals with German theology after the turning point of 1933. Somewhat surprisingly he praises the church struggle as an example of the 'honesty' of the Protestant church, its willingness to work through significant issues in depth. In fact, he seems quite charitable to his opponents in the church struggle, the Crisis Theologians, acknowledging a broad band of unity between them and a give-and-take profitable to both sides. But it becomes apparent that his friendly stance, though perhaps genuine, comes at least partly from the comfortable position of being on the winning side. He sees the Young Lutheran position vindicated in the events of 1933, and he describes the task for German theology as now falling within the confines of the German moment: 'Whoever lays his hand on the plow and draws it back, he is not sent to the kingdom of God.'[176] Theologians will have to stop getting lost in nitpicking and side issues and work creatively on the main issue of how Christianity can best spread its message within the German *Volk* and serve it in the *Stunde* of the present. Despite individual variations, this will require broad unity on questions of church, *Volk* and state.

Karl Barth thought the church's message spiritual, so that it could continue to teach 'as if nothing had happened.' Hirsch thinks this absurd. 'God does not speak to my heart today as if nothing has happened . . . He carries the danger that lies therein: He is the Lord and does not need to fear for his truth.'[177] The issue once again is that of how God speaks to man and whether that message is seen in, or should be renewed in any way to meet, changing historical circumstances. Hirsch believes that Christianity will die if it refuses to rethink its message in order to apply it to new times. He believes the various Christian confessions should be seen in this historical light, as expressions for their time, rather than as expressions of pure truth:

> Confession . . . is a common account of teachers, gathered in response to decisive contemporary questions. These teachers have been called to speak for their church on the theological precepts which they have developed as content and direction of contemporary Christian proclamation, based on their questions and answers bowing to the gospel.[178]

Furthermore, Hirsch thinks National Socialism is particularly susceptible to fruitful theological cooperative work, because it too recognizes the 'holy boundaries' in life.[179] Therefore, on the basis of his theory of revelation, his theory of proclamation, and his assessment of National Socialism, it is self-evident that the appropriate theological task of the moment is to build a new understanding of church, *Volk* and state within the context of the German turning point of 1933.

Finally, Hirsch turns his attention towards the significance of all this for church organization. He notes that during the nineteenth century, the church gradually took over a broad social role, working in orphanages, hospitals, etc. This was appropriate to the burgeoning social needs of the industrial revolution period, and to the failure of the state to fill the gap. But now that a proper *Volks* state has been reinstated, the church should quite happily go back to its main role of proclaiming the gospel. Where some charge the Nazi state with interfering in church business, Hirsch sees those areas as neither historically nor inherently the proper business of the church.[180] In addition to accepting this reduced role, the church should also adopt a new organizational structure, embodying 'leadership as passionate will':

If that is not easily understood nor understood by all today, that is because it has not yet gone into everyone's blood that National Socialism, based on the right of historical change, is becoming the self-evident and binding form of life for all Germans.[181]

Another issue worries Hirsch more. Why had the New Testament church assumed that, 'To be a Christian meant to immediately accomplish a break with all orders and assumptions of normal life?'[182] Hirsch can understand the circumstances in which that would be necessary, e.g. in the years of Weimar. But German Christians under the influence of Luther should recognize the difference between the inner and the outer church, and accept it as God's will that in normal times the outer church will work with the state to create a Godly order. Such a constructive role should now be the goal of the church:

Perhaps our external [church] will still go through much shame and misery of conscience. But we all believe and trust that God in his power can allow the misery to become a mercy, which crowns the misery with the victory of overcoming.[183]

In a supplement addressed to Karl Heim of Tübingen University, Hirsch makes one last attempt to explain his understanding of the paradox between the human and the divine which underlies his entire stance. Heim had attempted to identify two possible attitudes towards the German moment: 1. an acceptance of the rich depth of human life as *Ordnung*, in which God is seen as creator, but does not remain very close, and 2. an acceptance of God as 'the single basis for all life's reality,' which yields less respect for earthly duties.[184] Hirsh rejects these two alternatives and asserts that the second is the only possible position for a Christian. However, he points towards his paradoxical understanding of time and eternity as giving a better understanding of the complexity of that position. Two possible problems exist for Christians. First, they can view 'the eternal as justification and glorification of the earthly.' Or they can turn entirely to inwardness and reject any feeling for life or 'sense of being spoken to.' Hirsch accuses some (obviously the

Barthians) of fighting the first position so energetically they slip into the second. And others fight the second position to the point of slipping into the first, e.g. proclaiming an Aryan religion. Hirsch insists on a tension between the two in which 'a faith rising up from the eternal and desiring the eternal' acts within reality and points towards the eternal. This position is both religious and ethical:

> It is the eccentricity of the ethics which understands itself as religious decision, that it ties time and eternity together, and it does so not only through the command, but also through the inflamed movement of the heart.[185]

Hirsch points towards Luther, whose concept of vocation designates the daily tasks of even the most lowly individual as holy if done for the glory of God. One cooks soup for the glory of God, just as Bach composed music for the glory of God. These human tasks, therefore, partake of the divine. He also gives credit to German nationalists:

> Everything that a Fichte, a Kleist, a Henrich von Treitschke expresses concretely about the relationship of *Volk* to fatherland is as if it were burned into my heart. I know along with them, that God meets me through *Volk* and fatherland. God encloses me with a binding and consecrating and exciting reality, sustaining my life from the primordial depths and shattering my self-sufficiency.[186]

There exists a paradox in the free man tied to the eternal but living fully in the present. But since the paradox is backed by God — he entered the present, though he is eternal — we can live and grow within it. Again Hirsch points towards the war as a final contribution toward his understanding of his paradox:

> Then the conviction was born afresh every day that the entire direct experience of life is bound and should be bound in uncertainty.[187]

D. Hirsch's Stance after 1933

DIE gegenwärtige geistige Lage appeared early in 1934. It states Hirsch's position at that time and points towards his stance in the continuing church struggle. The next important question is whether his position changed during the next few years as the true story of National Socialism unfolded. His statements in 1933 appear to contain at least the possibility that he would later change his mind. He frequently noted the possibility of error in steps boldly taken in the heat of the historical moment. He naively (in retrospect)

attributed to Hitler and National Socialism a respect for the 'holy boundaries' and for Christian faith, attributions which should have changed over
time. The evidence, however, does not suggest any significant change in
Hirsch's position. The qualifications which he expressed in 1933 never grew
to larger proportions.

In 1937 Hirsch published a collection of articles that had appeared in
various places in the previous two years. This book allows him to react to the
ideas expressed in *Die gegenwärtige geistige Lage*. First, Hirsch admits that
his assessment of the theological crisis had been too optimistic. Whereas he
had expressed hope for a resolution of the crisis, the tensions had torn the
church apart. He now suggests that theologians lower their voices and their
profiles and begin to conduct their rebuilding work quietly.[188] Then he
clearly underlines his earlier stance in support of the National Socialist
turning point in Germany. He credits the Nazis with ending what theologians
and philosophers could not: 'the all-encompassing debate about everything.'
So he encourages theologians to serve the National Socialist world view, which
has given an acceptable homeland *(Heimat)* to the German people.[189]

In 1939 Hirsch published a book of lectures on the 'essence' of Christianity. Beginning with a slightly weary and defensive tone, he asserts that this
work is, like all his others, the expression of one individual intended to
represent no particular group within the church:

> I direct myself to German people who desire a truthful account of the
> essence of Christianity. What consequences they draw from this account
> does not concern me.[190]

He may have been wounded, and certainly was disappointed by the harsh
conflicts of the 1930s. In this book, the old struggles of the church do not
take center stage; it is an attempt to assess the essence of Christianity, not a
prescription for the German *Volks* church. But two threads run through it
which seem to confirm that his presuppositions are unchanged, now taken
for granted rather than strident.

First, Hirsch gives an ultimately negative assessment of Judaism, based on
the common Christian view that Judaism is legalistic and lacking in the grace
of the Christian gospel. Hirsch values the Old Testament for its ethical,
monotheistic view of history and does not want it removed from the Bible,
but he believes that Jesus created a new and unique religion.[191] For example,
he describes the Lord's Prayer as a simple, short summary of Jesus' religious
view, as opposed to the comparable Jewish prayer *(Achtzehngebet)*, about
forty times as long, which becomes a compulsive daily ritual for the Jew.
Jesus' prayer sees God as the God of humanity, so his is a universal, eternal
religion, while the Jewish prayer refers only to the Jewish people. And
Hirsch sees Christianity as the only religion based upon a free, personal,
individual relationship to God.[192]

None of the above is unorthodox, but Hirsch then makes a judgment about Jesus' racial origins which certainly is. He observes, as did Kittel, that Jesus' teachings were not Jewish. He describes them as of a 'wholly un-Jewish style.'[193] But Hirsch also maintains, on the basis of German theological scholarship, that Jesus stemmed from non-Jewish blood. His presupposition is that Galilee was heathen from the fall of the Northern kingdom in the eighth century B.C. until the area was reconquered about 100 B.C. He then argues that Jesus' origins in Nazareth in Galilee were so offensive to the early Jewish Christians that they covered them up with elaborate, but inconsistent, falsifications. First, they claimed that Jesus was born in Bethlehem (which also would tie him to Old Testament prophecy). But Matthew then had to invent a story (fleeing from the wrath of Herod) to explain his presence in Galilee one year later. Luke used Quirenius' tax registration as his explanation, but that occurred in A.D. 6–7, long after the birth of Jesus. Next, Hirsch argues that the two family trees which show a connection to David are falsified, for they never once put the same name in the same place. Also, Jesus himself denied the messiah would be the son of David in Mark 12:35–37, and John 7:42 corroborates that denial.[194]

Hirsch admits that Jewish colonists would have lived in Galilee after 100 B.C., but he estimates the number to be only about ten per cent of the population. Therefore, 'according to all the rules of scientific probability, Jesus was of non-Jewish blood.' But Hirsch feels he can go even farther and rule out the one chance in ten of an exception. In the first century Jews referred to Jesus as the 'Son of Panther,' and in the next century one of the derogatory legends about Jesus held that Mary had committed adultery with a soldier named Panther. Hirsch concludes that Jesus' grandfather had that Greek name, and that the gospel writers had tried to hide the fact in order to preserve the son-of-David legend and the Jewish roots. Jesus' cousin, Simeon, was a leader of the Jerusalem church for many years. Since he and Jesus had the same grandfather, he should have been able to give accuracy to the family tree, which was already being circulated before A.D. 70. But Matthew called Joseph's father Jacob, and Luke named him Eli. The early church fathers explained that one must have been the adoptive father of Joseph, but Hirsch argues that the real name was suppressed because it was not Jewish. A second-century historian, Hegasipp, wrote a history of Jerusalem in which he said Joseph's father Jacob had the surname Panther. Hirsch concludes that Joseph must have been known as *'Panthersohn'* and, furthermore, that the Jewish concern for ethnic purity would have ruled out either the casual adoption of a Greek name or the chance that Greeks would have intermarried with Jews. Finally, the great-grandfather of Jesus was the one name on which Matthew and Luke nearly agreed. Hirsch thinks the two names, Matthau and Matthat, are both Hebraicized versions of Matthew, and he thinks this proves that the great-grandfather's name actually was known. Therefore, it seems incongruous that the grandfather's would not have been.[195]

This issue illustrates the difficulty of judging Hirsch's work. First, his interpretations obviously fit in with Nazi propaganda and his interest in the subject was certainly occasioned by the unacceptability of the Jew in Nazi Germany. But were his conclusions wrong? Wrongheaded, yes, for Jesus was clearly rooted in the Jewish tradition no matter what his genetic background. Secondly, Hirsch believed in a relation between personality traits and blood which has not stood the test of time. But Hirsch too admits that Jesus' racial origins, though of interest, are not a conclusive determinant of his character. Although experts would have to judge each step in the case Hirsch builds, the steps appear logical and could possibly be the simplest explanation of the various enigmas in the story of Jesus' family tree.

The second element in *Das Wesen des Christentums* which confirms Hirsch's consistency of political view is his reference to *Volk*. In the first three-quarters of the book, there is only an occasional reference, but in each instance it is positive and consistent with his earlier views. For example:

> We set our entire power of life and spirit on this, to bring our *Volk* and Reich into a healthy, life-protecting order, and to create for them a durable and honorable existence in the circle of the white ruling peoples, to which God has entrusted the responsibility for the history of humanity.[196]

The theme of God's special relationship to the 'white ruling peoples,' and especially to the Germans, constantly recurs. When Hirsch describes the conversion of Germans to Christianity, he emphasizes it was never due to force from non-Germans (though Germans sometimes forced it on other Germans, e.g. the Saxons), but that Christianity was freely accepted as consistent with German character. It fitted into the German concept of leader and follower, which made it natural for religion to be based on nation or *Volk* and determined by the prince. And the Christian ethic allows freedom in diversity and the responsibility of the ruler and the ruled to their respective tasks, both of which Hirsch considers continuing German traits.[197]

Finally, as Hirsch reviews church history of the nineteenth and twentieth centuries, he builds up to a culmination in which 'German *Volkstum* and Christian faith' are seen as the ideal. The Anglican church, for example, reacted to the intellectual challenges of the nineteenth century with the Oxford Movement, a stress upon the sacramental, official importance of the church. This Roman Catholic emphasis within the Anglican church allowed it to overcome the 'questions of truth,' but only with an assent to dogma that grew increasingly formal and less honest or personal. Hirsch protests that this departs from the Protestant emphasis on the human-historical, offering magic and ritual in place of a personal God acting in the real world.[198]

German theology, on the other hand, opened itself to a thorough working out of the intellectual and theological problems of the nineteenth century. This yielded less unity and more argumentation, but Hirsch feels that is the only way to be true to the Christianity of the Reformation. The only alternative to walking courageously in the 'new country' is slipping back into a 'religion of law.'[199] Hirsch admits, in 1939, that church leaders have not yet worked out a position which can meet the challenge of the twentieth century. But he is certain of two things about this crisis of reformulation: 1. that Western Civilization will be in grave danger if Christianity cannot renew its meaning for the people, and 2. that the German concept of the Christian's relationship to a *Volks* state is the best probable basis for a solution. Some Christians emphasize freedom and love, i.e. the Sermon on the Mount, to the point where liberal individualism and pacifism are seen as the only Christian positions. But Hirsch insists that freedom can only be understood within the scope of responsibility, and that chaos can only be averted if responsibility is bound with a human community, such as that of the *Volks* state:

> There exists between German *Volkstum* and Christian belief absolutely no division or contradiction to make it difficult as a German to be a Christian, or as a Christian a German. Faith and love are created to be the deepest sustaining basis for a life in freedom and honor, as is appropriate to our community ethos. Whoever says differently, of him it means: either he misuses Christianity to anti-German purposes, or he has come to an incorrect judgment about Christianity through some other such misuse.[200]

From this conclusion it is clear that Hirsch's position, as developed through 1933 to 1934, had not changed by 1939.

Aside from his writings in the 1930s, is there other evidence to clarify Hirsch's political stance? The Berlin Document Center contains a Party form which Hirsch filled out on 1 July 1939. This form indicates he entered the Party on 1 May 1937, membership no.5,076,856, and that his activities included participation in the National Socialist German Students' League, the National Socialist *Volks* Welfare, the Reichs Air Defense League, and the Red Cross. He was also a supporting member of the SS, no.216,529.[201] Another file indicates he joined the National Socialist Teachers' League on 1 July 1934, as member no.294,388.[202] None of this information is very startling, though it confirms the sentiments already described. His entrance into Party membership in 1937 would seem to indicate that the first four years of Nazi rule failed to disillusion him. Finally, Hirsch's compatibility with the National Socialist regime is underlined by the fact that throughout those years of *Führer* principle, when university administrators were no longer elected annually by their peers, Hirsch was dean of the theological faculty at Göttingen.

At first glance, controversy might not have been anticipated in Hirsch's tenure as dean. For example, no member of the faculty was removed for political opposition to the regime, as was Paul Tillich at Frankfurt or Karl Barth at Bonn. Furthermore, the Hanoverian bishop, August Marahrens, was a friend of Hirsch and shared much of his enthusiasm for Hitler and the National Socialist renewal in Germany.[203] Almost all of the faculty supported the *Deutsche Christen* position in 1933. When new appointments were made, Hirsch was usually able to maintain this tendency; and even the one faculty member adhering to the Confessing Church, Hermann Dörries, shared Hirsch's conservative nationalism, as indicated by his role in the Günther Dehn affair.[204] Finally, Hirsch's stature as a theologian and teacher made him an obvious choice for dean; it was not solely a political appointment.

However, Hirsch's role as dean sparked an enormous amount of conflict and bitterness. His warm relationship with Bishop Marahrens cooled already in the summer of 1933. As Hirsch enthusiastically supported Müller and the *Deutsche Christen*, Marahens held back due to his Lutheran confessional scruples. Already in May he wrote to Hirsch's friend, Paul Althaus, despairingly, requesting help in diverting Hirsch from the disastrous course he had taken.[205] The request was to no avail. A gulf soon developed between Hirsch and Marahrens which marked the next years. During the church struggle, Hanover remained one of the three so-called 'intact' Lutheran churches, unwilling to accept either Müller and the *Deutsche Christen* or Barth and the radical wing of the Confessing Church.

Gulfs also developed between Hirsch and his faculty. Hirsch's commitment to National Socialism and the *Deutsche Christen* was stronger than most of his colleagues', and in his powerful position as dean his direct and sometimes caustic personality created an atmosphere of fear and bitterness. Herman Dörries, for example, later recounted his belief that he had been denounced by Hirsch and would have been sent to a concentration camp except for the friendly interference of the *Rektor*, Friedrich Neumann.[206] The Old Testament scholar, Friedrich Baumgärtel, accepted a call elsewhere despite his desire to remain in Göttingen, to escape the tension and bitterness there.[207] The suspicion that Hirsch indulged in secret denunciations is furthered by his role as representative from the theological faculty to the National Socialist University Lecturers' Federation, beginning in 1937.[308] Finally, the student pastor in Göttingen in the latter 1930s, Adolf Wischmann, has testified directly to a case of denunciation by Hirsch. In 1939 Wischmann's salary was cut off by the state. Hirsch denied instigating this action. However, when Wischmann was finally confronted with evidence it was a letter signed by Hirsch.[209]

The aggressive, intimidating, unsettling role of Hirsch within the theological faculty is substantiated in the archives of the faculty. For example, on 10 December 1934 the Confessing Church requested a written opinion from the Göttingen theological faculty on the question of oaths to the *Führer*.

Hirsch immediately recognized this as an attempt to assist Karl Barth, who was trying to avoid just such an oath at Bonn University, so he sent the letter on to a church official named Mattiat in the ministry of education in Berlin, with an explanatory cover note and a request for advice.[210] Almost immediately the minister sent a directive to all *Rektoren:*

> It has come to my attention that an invitation has gone out to deans of Protestant theological faculties from the so-called 'Provisional Leadership of the German Evangelical Church' . . . for an advisory position on the civil service oath.
>
> I request . . . that no response be given to this invitation.[211]

This incident suggests a pattern which persisted for several years. Hirsch maintained a flow of correspondence with Berlin, interspersed with personal visits, and he and the ministry put up a united and reasonably effective front against all Confessing Church-oriented activities touching upon the theological faculty.

During 1935 one conflict followed another. The Minister for Church Affairs, Bernhard Rust, sent a decree on 28 February 1935 protesting that theological faculty members had been mixing in the church struggle, behavior unsuitable to their role as civil servants. This decree prohibited such behavior and also encouraged professors to advise their students to keep minds on theology rather than church politics.[212] Six members of the faculty (Stange, Meyer, Bauer, Dörries, von Campenhausen and Hoffmann) signed a protest to Rust, affirming their loyalty to the National Socialist state, but also arguing for academic freedom and asserting their right and duty to participate actively in church affairs. This letter went through the dean's office, giving Hirsch a chance to add a cover letter. He recommended that his colleagues' objections be ignored, and they were.[213]

A more important issue erupted a month later in the controversial appointment, at first provisional, of Walter Birnbaum to the chair of practical theology. This appointment proved controversial for several reasons. Birnbaum's academic credentials were suspect, and he had worked closely with Ludwig Müller and even the notorious August Jäger in the battles of the church struggle, and the chair at Göttingen was seen as a reward for political services. From the beginning Confessing Church students boycotted Birnbaum's classes and protested his presence on their examination committees, and in the end he proved a particularly obstreperous member of the 'removed' faculty after 1945. Besides controversy, Birnbaum probably never contributed a great deal to the faculty. Even Hirsch, his strongest defender, was reported to have alluded to the boring quality of Birnbaum's lectures with the comment, 'If the Garden of Eden had contained a *Birnbaum* [pear tree] instead of an *Apfelbaum* [apple tree] the Fall never would have occurred.'[214]

Birnbaum had taken a batchelor's degree in theology, but he later failed his oral examination for the licentiate degree (a theological degree between M.A. and Ph.D.) at Leipzig in 1926 (though his written work, *Die katholische Liturgische Bewegung. Darstellung und Kritik*, was published that year). Instead of pursuing an academic career or taking a pastorate, Birnbaum became administrator of the Wichern Association at 'The Rough House' (*Das Rauhe Haus*, a famous Christian mission) in Hamburg. In his autobiography he stresses the concern with 'inner mission' which he developed from this work. He also describes wild, potentially violent evenings in debate with freethinkers and communists in the working class districts of Hamburg. Although Birnbaum never joined the National Socialists, his *völkisch*, nationalistic, anti-leftist stance was congenial to them and he quickly joined the *Deutsche Christen* in 1933. He later justified this move by stressing the large increases in church membership at that time and his conviction that the turning point of 1933 represented a great opportunity for *Volks* mission in the Wichern mold.[215]

Birnbaum joined the national leadership of the *Deutsche Christen* in late 1933 and he entered the national church government in April 1934, working closely with Müller and directly under August Jäger.[216] Birnbaum was on holiday by his own account in the latter part of 1934 when Jäger attempted a forced takeover of the Bavarian and Württemberg churches and arrested their bishops.[217] Jäger was soon fired for this debacle, and Birnbaum admits to difficulties with Jäger's successor, Dr Werner, who finally charged him with unexplained 'irregularities.'[218] On 20 March 1935 the cultural ministry offered Birnbaum temporary appointment to the chair in practical theology at Göttingen, thus easing him out of an uncomfortable situation.

Birnbaum's arrival at Göttingen in April 1935 provoked a flood of complaints from Confessing Church students to the regional church office in Hanover. For example, Wolfgang Schroeder, a student of theology, wrote to Pastor Eberhard Klügel in the church office in Hanover in July 1935, describing both his private conversations with Birnbaum and the content of public lectures. Schroeder complains on theological grounds, that Birnbaum regrets 'that Luther remained stuck at the doctrine of justification by faith.'[219] And when students protested or questioned him, Birnbaum sometimes responded insensitively, 'But children, you are too sensitive!' Schroeder finally complains of a 'mismash of opinions' and 'an unholy confusion and mixing of concepts and an incapacity to think theologically.' And he accuses Birnbaum of nearly deifying the Nazis with statements such as, 'National Socialism is the revolution of life against death,' and, 'National Socialism has now been entrusted with the assignment of saving the church.'[220]

While students were complaining to the church in Hanover, Hirsch was keeping an eye on students for the ministry in Berlin. In June 1935 Rust wrote to theological deans, 'strictly confidentially,' reporting that the

Confessing Church hoped to organize student groups at each university. He requested that deans report on this both to the Gestapo and to himself.[221] Hirsch responded quickly, estimating that about three-quarters of theology students were influenced by the Confessing Church. Despite occasional rumors, however, no boycotts of classes had yet occurred. Hirsch was concerned that Confessing Church student activities would interfere with student activities under faculty sponsorship, but he recommended non-intervention on the grounds that the faculty could deal with the problem more effectively on its own. Hirsch then suggested that one lever might be to tighten the process of faculty examination of theological students.[222] Two weeks later, on 4 July 1935, Rust wrote to theological faculties about 'rumors' of *Ersatz* lectures and examinations under auspices of the Confessing Church. He deemed this in violation of the church treaty of 1931, and he now decreed that only three years study at a German university followed by examination under auspices of the official church and the university faculty working cooperatively would be acceptable for future pastors.[223] This was not exactly what Hirsch had recommended, but a consistency of purpose between the ministry and Hirsch is obvious.

By the fall of 1935 Hirsch knew of student protests about Birnbaum to the church in Hanover. He then ordered the supervisor of the theological seminary (a living quarters for theological students at the university) to ban 'discussions on church-political questions in the public rooms of the seminary.'[224] He also insisted that the Hanoverian church was satisfied with Birnbaum's appointment. When an official of the church responded, telling him of continuing opposition to Birnbaum and welcoming student opinions on the subject, Hirsch replied in a very typical, intimidating fashion:

> I have the feeling that the letter you propose to send from the church office to the students passes out of my domain and into that of the Herr Minister.[225]

He promised to pass the letter on to Berlin and await advice.

At the same time Hirsch asked Birnbaum to report on student reactions to his courses, particularly with respect to evidence of a boycott. Birnbaum replied that his courses were much less well attended than in the previous semester. Birnbaum also reported hearsay evidence that Confessing Church students Bode and Reich had met on 4 November with an official from the church in Hanover named Mahrenholz, who had encouraged the students in their opposition to Birnbaum.[226] On the day Hirsch received Birnbaum's report he sent it off to Mattiat in Berlin, with a personal cover letter and an official report. Again he discouraged intervention, and he predicted Birnbaum would survive.[227] Hirsch also bragged of his own role, claiming that through numerous discreet conversations with students and assistants he had prevented an 'explosion'. He also had inquired with university counsel about the possibility of legal action against the Hanoverian church interference. For lack of concrete evidence Hirsch had been advised against action. He now passed that advice on to Mattiat, requesting that at least no action be taken until he could report in person at the end of the month.[228]

In December 1935 the minister for education wrote to university curators, again requesting reports on Confessing Church students.[229] In this report Hirsch named Bode as student leader and Professor Dörries and Lecturer Hoffmann as close associates of an active Confessing Church group in Göttingen. Hirsch added an accusation against Hoffmann for holding an *Ersatz* seminar in violation of the earlier ministerial decree.[230] Hirsch also wrote Hoffmann directly, attempting to intimidate him into giving up this activity:

> Your special exercises in homiletics are known to me. On the basis of the enclosed decree, I request you to express whether or not you are ready to give these up at once.[231]

Hoffmann responded that he had indeed since the start of the term been leading a private discussion group outside his normal lecture activity. This had been at the request of students who had formed a free 'working community,' and he did not believe it fell under the ministerial decree.[232] With Hoffmann holding his ground, Hirsch was stymied. He disagreed with Hoffmann's interpretation, and he again reported to Berlin with details of Confessing Church activity and names (Bode, Marahrens, Mahrenholz, Dörries and Hoffmann are all mentioned). But in view of the 'doubtfulness' and 'limited importance' of the situation, he recommended ignoring it.[233] Possibly in response to Hirsch's counsel of moderation, the minister wrote to university curators a few days later, expressing hopes for the development of peace in the church and his promise that punishments would now be minimized towards that end. But the decree proscribing theological faculty members from participating in the church struggle was not lifted.[234]

The year 1935 was an important turning point in the theological faculty. It was a year of conflict, and the sides were now drawn. Confessing Church students, the church office in Hanover, and a very small group of faculty formed one side; Hirsch, a majority of the faculty, and the ministry in Berlin formed the other. The atmosphere was poisoned by this conflict. Furthermore, the power and allegiance of Hirsch were now clearly established. Although he could not control students as fully as he would have liked, and although he eschewed violence, he employed intimidation and a hand-in-glove relationship with the government in his attempt to thwart the Confessing Church at every turn.

In 1936 this pattern continued. Initially, Hirsch attempted to squash Confessing Church student activities. For example, in February he recommended that the university curator not give financial support to a semester-ending retreat proposed by the student leader Bode, with support from Dörries. Hirsch accused Bode of sabotaging the retreat sponsored earlier by the faculty, and he described Bode's present suggestion as an act of 'opposition' which should not receive government or university support.[235] Then, Hirsch wrote to the seminary supervisor, von Campenhausen, warning against any further support of Bode's activities. Hirsch was willing to forget von Campenhausen's assistance to Bode in the past, but:

> I would like to make you aware that student activities are an official part of the political university and no group which influences students against participation in official student activities can be supported, either through advice or cooperation, from someone in the position of seminary supervisor.[236]

Von Campenhausen's response was similar to that of Hoffmann earlier. He denied activity opposing the official student activities, either intentional or inadvertent. He felt it his Christian duty to respond to student requests for advice and assistance, and, he added, 'I request to be allowed as before the freedom of my personal theological and church convictions.'[237] Hirsch then responded with sarcasm and tenacity. Von Campenhausen was free to advise and help 'all the dear students' as much as he wanted. However:

> It concerns this: the *special group work* of the students Bode and Harms may not be supported by you in any way so long as you are seminary supervisor and under my official command.[238]

It was not for von Campenhausen but for Hirsch to decide whether the activities were harmful.

The next phase of conflict in the Birnbaum appointment also came in the spring of 1936. Hirsch, *Deutsche Christen* members of the faculty, and the cultural ministry all wanted to make his appointment permanent, despite objections from Confessing Church students and the church in Hanover. Assistant dean Johannes Hempel visited Hanover in an attempt to diffuse objections, but to no avail. When the church office learned Birnbaum would be appointed in any case, it formally notified the ministry in Berlin of its 'doubts' about him, a significant but futile gesture.[39]

The permanent appointment of Birnbaum, the most controversial and perhaps least credible *Deutsche Christen* member of the faculty, led inexorably to the final stages of conflict over *Ersatz* courses and examinations. In the fall of 1936 Hirsch discovered three letters circulating among Confessing Church students. He immediately sent copies to Berlin, with a cover letter attributing the materials to the 'radical Berlin-Dahlem Confessing Church group' of Martin Niemöller, and adding:

It is remarkable that a representative of the church office in Hanover, Pastor Klügel, works together with this Göttingen branch of the Berlin-Dahlem circle ... It is even more remarkable that the bishop himself stands in close relation and feeling to this circle of Confessing Church students in Göttingen ... By my observation both things have given theological students the impression that the regional church requires a specific church and church-political stance from the students.[240]

Four days later, on 17 November, the minister of education employed his strongest weapon yet in the struggle against Confessing Church *Ersatz* education, the power to ban students from their studies. In a letter to deans of theological faculties he decreed:

It is forbidden for any student of Protestant theology to attend any *Ersatz* or similar contrivance in place of university lectures and to participate in a boycott against university instructors. If offenses occur, *Rektoren* must on the basis of the law for students of 1 April 1935 ban offending students permanently from any further study at any German university.[241]

In the next weeks a flurry of responses to this ministerial decree emerged. Hirsch published the decree to students and attempted to use it to intimidate leaders of the *Ersatz* courses. For example, Hirsch wrote to Pastor Lueder, stressing the danger of *Ersatz* courses and the harsh punishment faced by students. Lueder complained to the church in Hanover, which then complained to the Minister of Education about Hirsch's bullying tactics. But in the competition for influence which followed, Hirsch's superior leverage became obvious. He explained to the minister that his letter was 'nothing but a friendly information regarding the recent ministerial decree.' His purpose was to help theological students avoid 'conflicts of conscience' by making it clear they had no alternative but to give up the Confessing Church courses. It was logical to send the message via Lueder, since he had established one of the *Ersatz* circles and knew of the others. Hirsch then accused the church of indirectly attacking the ministerial decree with its attack on Hirsch.[242] The final ministerial response to this conflict was penned by Hirsch's friend in the ministry, Mattiat. It accepted all of Hirsch's arguments; in fact it nearly reads like a revised draft of Hirsch's letter.[243]

Students also protested the ministerial decree. In February 1937 Heinz Rettberg protested to the Reichs minister in the name of forty Göttingen students (who remained anonymous) that the decree of November placed them in 'great distress of conscience.' In view of their future church duties, theological students could only get a proper eduction from teachers whose ties to Scripture and confessions corresponded to the ordination vow. Therefore, they pleaded for 'learning freedom' to choose their study options.[244] Rettberg sent this letter by way of Hirsch's office, who forwarded it to the minister with several comments. First, Hirsch described Rettberg as a leader of the Confessing Church group which caused the trouble over Birnbaum's courses in the first place. Secondly, Martin Niemöller had recently spoken in Göttingen, attacking the minister's faculty politics and presumably inspiring this letter. Hirsch, therefore, recommended the student protest be ignored and the decree left in force, a stance soon confirmed by the minister.[245]

The whole question of *Ersatz* courses and theological examinations placed the Hanoverian church in a difficult position. It did not want to pick a fight with the cultural ministry, especially in circumstances not conducive to winning. However, the theological examination was the point of entry for clergy into the service of the church, and the church felt it must exercise control. Student opposition was also intense, not only to examination by Birnbaum but also now by Hirsch. In 1936 Hirsch published two works deemed beyond the pale of the Lutheran confessions.[246] Under strong pressure both internally and from students, the church finally decided to take a stand. In the spring of 1937 theological examinations were held on its own terms, i.e. only with examiners acceptable on confessional grounds.[247] In May Hirsch responded with a memorandum to all members of the theological faculty, forbidding their cooperation with the church on its examination committees and requesting reports on any contact initiated by the church.[248]

By August Hirsch was reporting to the university curator that no *Ersatz* courses appeared to be operating in Göttingen.[249] In October he informed the *Rektor* that disciplinary measures had not been necessary; the ministerial decree of 17 November 1936 had achieved its desired goal of suppressing illegal activities among theological students.[250] But in retrospect it is clear that a true peace could not be built upon this foundation; for while he felt himself in control of his faculty and students, neither he nor the state was controlling the examination process of the church.

On 16 May 1938 the state made its last and strongest effort to achieve complete success on this question of theological examinations. The office of church affairs closed the purse strings (future employment in state-supported churches) to any student who, from the fall of 1938, took theological exams under church auspices without the full participation of university faculty members.[251] Hanoverian students from the universities of Erlangen, Tübingen, Halle, Rostock and Greifswald, as well as Göttingen, immediately flooded the church with petitions opposed to this decree. Each of these students, about sixty in all, would normally sit their examinations in Hanover, but each rejected the possibility of examining under either Birnbaum or Hirsch.[252] A draft document in the church archive indicates the concern aroused by this issue. It seemed clear that examiners had to be in agreement with the confessions of the church to be acceptable:

In consequence, it is simply not acceptable now that professors, who are appointed to office by the state — even if also 'theology' professors — therefore oversee the examination process, which is so essential to the confessionally correct development of the church.[253]

And with regard to consequences for future clergy within the church:

It can already be seen that the ecclesiastically and confessionally clear and stable youth avoid testing in Hanover and, for the most part, will be lost to the Hanoverian church. And that is the group most valuable to the church. On the other hand, the *Deutsche Christen* . . . who used to avoid Hanover, will now feel very encouraged.[254]

The document goes on to suggest the church must either plan to replace the financial support students would lose from the state, or else recommend that Hanoverian students take their examinations in the Bavarian church (allowed by reciprocal agreement). But the fear is expressed that the state might also soon take over the Bavarian examination process for the *Deutsche Christen.*[255]

This conflict pushed Bishop Marahrens much closer than he wanted to outright opposition to the state. His instincts were for compromise, and he proposed such a path in June 1938.[256] But the minister for church affairs responded in August with another aggressive decree:

According to the church law on education of clargy of 31 October 1928, every first theological examination must include the participation of a full professor from the Protestant theological faculty of the university.
1. This provision has not been followed since spring 1937.
2. All first theological examinations since then (beginning in March 1937) have been illegal.[257]

The minister goes on to offer leniency to affected students, but only on the condition that future examinations strictly conform to the appropriate decrees and show full cooperation between the regional church and the faculty.[258]

The next day Hirsch addressed a letter to Göttingen theology students and posted it on the bulletin board:

I warn students of theology against taking part in first theological examinations under the auspices of the regional church office in fall 1938 without participation of the theological faculty. The examination is worthless for you, since it contravenes the decree of the church minister of 31 May 1938.[259]

He goes on to stress they will not be allowed to receive state funds or salaries, and then he offers them the alternative of taking their examination under the auspices of the theological faculty. He claims special ministerial approval for such an exam and assures that it will be accepted by 'a long list of regional churches,' and possibly even the Hanoverian church.

In August 1938, as the crisis reached its hottest point, a resolution finally emerged. Against all expectation, the solution was proposed by Hirsch when visited by a representative of the Hanoverian church on the 26th of the month. This individual first visited Confessing Church professors Dörries and Joachim Jeremias, and they were not optimistic about the chances for settlement. Then, his first moments with Hirsch grew so heated he feared the interview would end abruptly. But as they talked on, Hirsch finally suggested a compromise. He would voluntarily stop participating in examinations himself, and he would see that Birnbaum did not personally examine any student unalterably opposed to him. Otherwise, Birnbaum would participate and the legal requirements of the ministry would be met.[260] An internal document establishes that Marahrens was not fully happy with this compromise. He did not want to give up the legal claim that the church possessed final authority over the participation of faculty members on the basis of their confessional acceptability.[261] However, this compromise would resolve the immediate crisis of the fall examinations, it would probably assure the acceptability of examinations since 1937 (though this was not guaranteed), and it appeared a solution acceptable to most students. Therefore, it was approved by the church and the crisis was resolved.[262]

After six turbulent years in office, Hirsch resigned the deanship of his faculty, handing it over to Otto Weber, another loyal party member. Conflict now decreased. The examination question had been resolved, and that had been the major focus of contention. Furthermore, the outbreak of war turned the attention of individuals away from the church struggle and increasingly deprived the university of its students. And finally, as demands on the faculty decreased, Birnbaum's actual role in the faculty diminished considerably. In 1941 he answered Goering's call for academics to lecture *Luftwaffe* personnel on the Russian front. Speaking on the evils of Bolshevism, Birnbaum traveled extensively, giving numerous lectures and also enjoying rest and recreation in Holland, Belgium and France.[263] Hirsch played no significant political role after stepping down as dean of his faculty. He mourned one son who died in the war, but he also enjoyed a reputation as perhaps the greatest theologian in Germany during those years.

After 1945, in forced retirement, Hirsch continued to research and write. He also had students over to his home and talked with them about Kierkegaard and about theology.[264] Though he was now politically passive, there is no indication he changed any of his earlier views. Colleagues remember it was impossible to talk politics with him in those years, and at least some theologians spread the rumor that he kept a picture of Hitler in his basement until his death.[265] Whether true or not, this rumor supports the near certainty that Hirsch went through life with relatively unchanged political views. Compared to Althaus and Kittel, he had thought through his political position more clearly, with a greater attention to history, philosophy and the crisis of the modern world. It therefore seems appropriate that, despite the historical failure of the German turning point, Hirsch did not concede that his political, intellectual, theological position had been wrong.

E. Analysis

Is it possible today to confirm that Hirsch's political stance was wrong? That is problematic. He enthusiastically and persistently supported the German renewal under Nazi auspices, and as dean of his faculty he backed his philosophical position aggressively and sometimes harshly. In the terminology of the Nixon White House, he played 'hardball.' But Hirsch himself would want to be judged on the basis of his world view. He recognized the crisis of reason, which was very real at the turn of the century, and the impact of that crisis cannot be ignored. He also perceived the problem of centrifugal forces in modern, pluralist society — forces which can easily lead to a social breakdown. The 1960s and 1970s in America, Britain, Europe and elsewhere have born testimony to the crisis of modern puralism with which he dealt.[266] Furthermore, Hirsch employed existentialism, a popular twentieth-century philosophy, in developing his stance. He has been accused by his critics of misusing Kierkegaardian existentialism to arrive at his position. However, Hirsch acted boldly, based only on faith that his existential perception of God's truth was accurate, and that seems perfectly consistent with Kierkegaard's leap of faith. It might be helpful at this point to compare Hirsch's position with that of several theologians in Germany who came up historically on the correct side.

The relationship between Hirsch and Karl Barth has already been mentioned. They were colleagues at Göttingen in the early 1920s; they were friends for a number of years; they respected each other's views despite differences of opinion; and, in the early 1930s, they became bitter antagonists, assuming leading positions in the two opposing camps of the church struggle. Barth opposed Hirsch on the issue of Günther Dehn in 1931. Then he played a leading role in the creation of the Barmen Declaration and the Confessing Church. In 1935 he was removed from his position at the University of Bonn because of his open opposition to Nazism, and he moved to his native Switzerland. From his position of safety at the University of Basel, he called upon Christians everywhere to oppose Hitler as the epitome of evil.[267]

The major theological point of difference between Barth and Hirsch lies in their interpretation of God's role in history. Barth insists on the 'infinite qualitative distinction' between God and man. No human effort can ever be seen as holy, for holiness resides with God. Hirsch complains that Barth ignores God's connection with real, historical events.[268]

Two questions must be directed towards Barth's position. First, did God speak to the German people through Luther? Hirsch emphasizes that Luther was important because he redeveloped the Christian message to make it meaningful for Germans of his time. Without doubt Luther's translation of the Bible into German relied heavily upon his 'Germanness', i.e. his use of German concepts and experiences to make God's message meaningful. Hirsch proposes that the same work needs to be accomplished for twentieth-century Germans. Secondly, does Barth deny that a political stance can ever be taken vis-à-vis a human political order? In fact, his political views were liberal, democratic and socialist in orientation. In 1948 he even advised Christians in the communist nations of eastern Europe to support their governments.[269] How did Barth's political position-taking differs from Hirsch's? Barth would argue that Hirsch gave holy, normative qualities to political circumstances, whereas Barth took positions with the constant recognition that this world is never holy. But this clarification is at best one of degree. Hirsch too is careful to deny that the state can be holy. He too insists on the difference between the divine and the human. But he argues — as did Luther, certainly — that God can work through human, political institutions to make the world safe for the proclamation of the gospel and the living of a Christian life. And he asserts that Christians should affirm such work.

The relationship between Hirsch and Paul Tillich is even more significant, for they share a greater similarity theologically than do Hirsch and Barth. Both Hirsch and Tillich accept more of the heritage of nineteenth-century liberal scholarship than does Barth. They are also both more emphatically existential in their theology and more decisively political and ethical in their concerns. The difference is that Tillich was active in the creation of religious socialism on the left, Hirsch in the creation of Christian nationalism on the right. Therefore, Tillich was driven out of Germany in 1933, and Hirsch found a comfortable home in the Third Reich.

It has been mentioned above that Tillich and Hirsch met as theological students in the Wingolf *Bund* at the University of Berlin. Tillich pointed Hirsch toward his *Habilitations* topic on Fichte, and the two shared a friendship and mutual respect which only broke down in the crisis of the 1930s. In those early years, from 1908 to 1912, they were extremely close personally and intellectually. According to Tillich's biographers: 'Friends who accompanied them on long walks in Berlin said it was almost impossible to tell their thinking apart, it was so nearly identical.'[270] Hirsch nurtured a secret love for Tillich's closest sister, Johanna. She surprised everyone in 1912 by marrying Alfred Fritz after a secret engagement of four years. Again from the Tillich biography:

For Emanuel Hirsch the surprise was a painful one. He too had fallen in love with Johanna, and had determined to ask for her hand, but waited too long and suffered despair at the knowledge.[271]

But Hirsch graciously overcame his disappointment and joined Tillich in writing and presenting a humorous skit in honor of the bride and groom.[272]

Throughout the period of Weimar this friendship suffered from the huge political differences between the two. But it was not until Hirsch published *Die gegenwärtige geistige Lage* in '1934 that the break became bitter and complete. Tillich, already in America, responded to the book almost immediately in an open letter published in *Theologische Blätter*. He wrote,

> Dear Emanuel!
> The tension-filled unity of our personal friendship and theological antagonism has never come more strongly to my consciouness than with reading your new book: 'Die gegenwärtige geistige Lage im Spiegel philosophischer und theologischer Besinnung.' I agree with Karl Barth's judgment of its significance, and beyond that I believe I can feel what your concerns are.[273]

He adds that this letter 'has become more difficult for me than any other.' Tillich is astonished by Hirsch's use of concepts which Tillich feels are his own. He complains, 'The use and misuse through your book of the *Kairos* teaching, which is linked to my name, forces me to speak.'[274]

Tillich is very offended by the plagiarism of which he feels Hirsch is guilty. He questions whether Hirsch can possibly be unconscious of his debt, or whether political considerations cause him not to acknowledge it.[275] But Tillich is even more concerned that Hirsch has taken concepts which the religious socialists applied towards a revolution of the working class and applies them towards a conservative, middle-class revolution.

Nine years earlier Tillich had sent Hirsch a copy of his book, *Religiöse Lage der Gegenwart*. In that book he describes the breakdown of medieval unity, the role of the demonic and of the boundary, and the search for the 'sustaining substance.' Hirsch had criticized Tillich at the time for trying to be a prophet, but now he has taken over and altered for his own use all of these themes.[276] Hirsch fails to use the word *Kairos*, which characterized Tillich's work, but Tillich feels his constant reference to the 'contemporary moment' and to 'awakening' mean the same thing. Furthermore, his existential-historical method is just what Tillich described in his last lecture in Germany. Tillich feels this places Hirsch close to the young Marx, Kierkegaard, Heidegger and Jaspers, all of whom Tillich drew upon, but to whom Hirsch gives inadequate credit. Hirsch's dynamic concept of 'reality thought,' based upon the 'character of knowledge as bold venture,' and the turn from a 'freefloating arbitrariness' to a concern for community are also claimed by Tillich, as is his proposal for reform of the university.[277]

Tillich protests this borrowing mainly because of the distortion which he feels has occurred. He believes himself between the extremes of Barth, who sees the kingdom of God only in transcendental terms, and Hirsch, who sees the kingdom of God in the present. Tillich insists upon an eschatological, paradoxical view in which the kingdom of God comes near and touches without ever being mistaken for our earthly life. So Tillich's critique of Hirsch is succinct: 'You convert the Kairos teaching, which was intended to be prophetic and eschatological, into a priestly-sacramental consecration of contemporary events.'[278]

Tillich also criticizes a number of specific aspects of Hirsch's work. He asks, 'Is the current event a source of revelation to be placed alongside the Biblical record? It almost appears so by you.'[279] (Tillich admits this problem may also have been inherent in his *Kairos-Lehre*. Though he thinks not, he agrees it did not receive enough attention). Tillich also criticizes Hirsch's scientific approach for ignoring sociological analysis of groups. Many of his judgments would have to be thrown out if he recognized certain common sociological insights, 'And that is easy to account for, because sociaology is one of the sharpest weapons against unrestrained enthusiasm.'[280] For example, if Hirsch would do any comparative analysis with countries outside Germany he would discover that Germany is experiencing a phenomenon of 'late fall' rather than spring.[281] Tillich also charges that Hirsch's emphasis upon the mystical concepts of *Volk* and 'blood bond' make the past 150 years too important in his analysis. A law which changes that often is no law at all. Tillich also notes the irony that Lutherans preached obedience to even the worst forms of government until a state appeared in which the old rulers did not dominate, and then Lutherans recognized the right of revolution: 'Whose unconscious tool were you as you did that and justified it theologically?'[282] Finally, Tillich criticizes Hirsch's endorsement of the *Führer* principle and the totalitarian state. He argues that this leaves no room for personalities to grow, nor, most importantly, for the church. Tillich professes agreement with Hirsch and Barth that many social and cultural functions of the church can be taken over by the state, but he fears that in many subtle, unobtrusive ways a totalitarian state will hem in the church on questions where the new concept of 'Germanness' and Christianity do not match.[283]

The crux of Tillich's attack on Hirsch lies in the issue to what extent the Christian church should support an earthly state. Tillich argued in his prescription for religious socialism for an 'obligation' coupled with a 'reservation.' He feels that although Hirsch allows reservations for an individual, he requires a complete obligation of the institutional church to the state. Hirsch explained in a letter to Tillich that his personal relationship to God allows him to give an unequivocal yes to an historical moment. Tillich replies that to give an unqualified religious and theological yes to an earthly course will lead to 'enthusiasm' rather than 'believing realism.'[284] Tillich then closes his letter, 'with heartfelt greetings, Your Paul.'

Hirsch's response to this letter opens with an angry blast, continues through an extensive explanation and defense, and closes with a tribute to his friendship with Tillich which, considering the circumstances, has traces of humility and poignance. The blast comes first. Hirsch chooses to write his open letter to Wilhelm Stapel for publication. Since Tillich, under cover of a friendly letter, attacked his honesty and honor, Hirsch feels direct discussion has been made impossible.[285] But he does want to defend his honor and his position, so he asks Stapel to publish his response.

Hirsch meets the question of plagiarism by pointing to the common education he shares with Tillich, both in the German idealism of Kant, Fichte and Hegel, and in the critical contemporary 'boundary questions of theories of knowledge and philosophy of religion.'[286] For twenty years Hirsch has been working through the scepticism resulting from Nietzsche and Dilthey, and for ten years he has studied Kierkegaard. Hirsch suggests Tillich might better search for what is really new in his own work rather than accuse Hirsch of plagiarism. Hirsch also feels he has given adequate general credit to others, mainly Heidegger and Jaspers; but he adds that they derived their existentialism from Kierkegaard, and he believes he has worked out his views from Kierkegaard in his own way.[287]

Hirsch then describes the core of his thought as an 'understanding of reality' in which he sees the God of history as decisive. Hirsch comes to this view from his recognition of Fichte's concern with the borders of knowledge. However, the impact of Nietzsche and Dilthey make him recognize the extreme importance of the questions of boundary. His solution is to argue that the mysterious boundary is where we meet God, who creates the meaning of all history. Hirsch credits Barth with at least recognizing this emphasis in his work. Since Barth denies the religious importance of history, it makes his attack on Hirsch consistent. But it is harder to understand why Tillich, who also believes in the God of history, still allies himself with Barth against Hirsch.[288]

Acknowledging the same idealistic philosophy of history and the same recognition of the crisis of 'reality consciousness' resulting in scepticism, Hirsch then has to explain why he and Tillich have gone in different directions. Hirsch feels Tillich lacks his childlike faith in Lutheran 'creation belief . . . which has supported me in every crisis of the spirit.' He also claims a 'bitterness' or 'acerbity,' which binds him to the law of reality and history.[289] Tillich, who has been influenced by Schelling, rejects bonds to a Nomos, and moves naturally and consistently to a position of individualism and internationalism. Hirsch credits Tillich with producing the highest expression of an individualistic ideal.[290] But he still sees the position as a destructive, free-floating individualism, despite the fact that Tillich ties it to Marxism:

I have never understood how Marxist thought could so bewitch Tillich, despite all of the great depth which he had, so that he became blind to the actual, binding, creative center of all earthly-political events.[291]

Hirsch believes he has found a higher and better ideal by firmly rooting himself in his *Volk*. Tillich reached the same starting point, a recognition that every concept is 'wholly and completely . . . bound to history,' that a dialectic of 'truth and history' underlies every philosophical question.[292] But Hirsch allowed that understanding to point him towards the historical significance of the *Volk* and away from the 'free-floating intellectuality and out of the chaos caused by it.'[293] Hirsch's Lutheran understanding of *Zweireichlehre* then allows him to accept an earthly political structure as holy, as part of God's plan, without assuming it is sinless or confusing it with the Kingdom of God.[294] In other words, Hirsch thinks his dialectic of human and divine, of time and eternity, is better than that of the dialectical theologians. He also argues that Christian freedom has to be understood as a freedom in Christ which does not undercut law and duty in our earthly existence.[295] Again the paradoxical *Zweireichlehre* impinges. Finally, Hirsch denies that he sees in the events of 1933 a 'source of revelation' equal to that of the Bible. If he accepted the National Socialist state as a religious utopia, that charge would be just. But once again he argues that his paradoxical, Lutheran *Zweireichlehre* protects him. The Nazi state is simply a desirable state. Since it accepts Christianity and preserves order, it should be accepted and supported by Christians as a tool of God's grace.[296]

Hirsch expresses his keen disappointment at Tillich's reaction to his work, and even his belief that the reaction might have been different:

> I had secretly hoped he would find in my concept of Logos a legitimate contribution to the solution of the problems; and, by virtue of the inseparable connection of this Logos concept with the intellectuality of the German revolution, I could have carried him over into the new German era and thereby have won back for Germany a lively thinker.[297]

In spite of his disappointment, he departs from the anger with which he begins this open letter and closes with a surprisingly friendly statement. He expresses his affirmation that:

> I owe a debt of gratitude to Tillich, and that is why it has pained me to have to carry out this settlement of accounts against a friend from my youth, whom I cannot imagine as absent from my life. I thank him for two things. First, he was the one who in our student years turned me into the stream of idealistic philosophy, at a time when my personal, fruitful stimulus was lacking due to the failures of the Berlin philosophers. With the average Berlin philosopher at that time one learned that the idealists were shameless bunglers whom it did not pay to read. So I had restricted myself to a serious study of Kant. That impetus from Tillich was the beginning of a

captivating, rich, intellectual relationship which continued until the end of the war. It involved a constant, intense opposition — I held to Fichte, he to Schelling; I began my thought from the call to duty, he from the mystical encounter with God; I was tormented by the social question, at that time he rejected it — yet to me (and formerly I thought: to us both), this relationship was a gift. In 1918 when the political break developed between us, a break which I also somehow always found to be accompanied by a religious break, then I was still able to have something from Tillich, and that is the second thing [for which I thank him]. It was now different than it had been. Each went his own way in the intellectual struggles without actual discussion with the other, he quicker and more lustrously, I more ponderously and (through the political will to fight) with more of a clenched fist. But throughout all those years he was to me a unique example of the sort of person who, according to his style and his precept and consistent with his political judgment, endured all the misery and moved in the thought of that crisis-filled time with unprecedented honesty. One cannot have such an example before one without it pushing one farther and deeper into one's own struggles, even if one is in opposition and sometimes even in anger by the third sentence of each treatise.[298]

In analyzing the conflict between these two, the historical judgments made by Tillich are much more attractive. He criticizes Hirsch for the excessive nationalism which now seems so culpable in the support which Hitler received in Germany. But in the philosophical arguments, Tillich's advantage is not nearly so clear. The intensity of Tillich's critique is understandable; Hirsch stood so close to him in his philosophy of history and theology that Tillich felt a special need to distance himself from Hirsch's politics. But whether or not Hirsch should have acknowledged his debt to Tillich, his argument that both developed an existential-historical approach to theology out of the crucible of a common background can hardly be denied.[299] It is also hard to conclude that fine points of theology determined the disparate stances assumed by Tillich and Hirsch. As Hirsch correctly observed, theologically he and Tillich both recognized God's role in history, sharing that position in opposition to Barth. But that obviously did not bring them to a common political view.

Can reason be used to explain the political stances these men took? A close friend and interpreter of Tillich, Rollo May, argues that one of Tillich's chief intellectual contributions to the twentieth century is his concept of 'ecstatic reason,' designed to overcome the crisis of relativism.[300] Ecstatic reason is existential, a rational decision which crosses the border of mystery through a leap of faith. But that appears an exact description of what both Hirsch and Tillich did in taking their respective political stances. Both read history, both saw God acting in history, and both believed in the Christian duty of political commitment. Then Tillich jumped left, believing he had interpreted God correctly, and Hirsch jumped right.

Hirsch also bears a resemblance to two other German theologians who have received much kinder historical treatment than he. Hirsch insists, theologically, on the kind of courage and honesty which can divest the Bible of unnecessary myth and return meaning to its pure core of the Lutheran doctrine of justification by faith.[301] In this position he stands close to Rudolf Bultmann. In spite of the crisis of reason of the twentieth century, he argues,

> It is a mistake when some theologians seek, with the help of the conflicts between reason and the gospel, to smuggle back into our theology and world view the myths and legends which are part of a form of Christian theology that has already died for us.[302]

He defends his sometimes radical exegesis of the New Testament as follows:

> The New Testament . . . is to me the wonder-working book of which I can say, as Luther said of the entire Bible, that it is the Holy Spirit's own book. This is precisely because I always come to it again as an unbiased reader, who examines and judges and does not make himself into a slave.[303]

And he concludes, 'The radical way is the only way by which we can today serve the gospel.'[304] All of this resembles Bultmann's demythologization of the New Testament, but the resemblance led to no political similarity.

It seems ironic to compare Hirsch with Tillich or Bultmann. The irony becomes most complete when the comparison is extended to Dietrich Bonhoeffer. Their two political stances could hardly be more disparate, yet their theological positions bear striking similarities. Bonhoeffer did not have Hirsch's interest nor scope of knowledge in German idealism, nor in the historical-philosophical questions of theories of knowledge. But he did assume an existential stance theologically, and drew, therefore, upon Kierkegaard. He also believed, with Hirsch, that an active political ethic is relevant to Christianity, and he drew the consequences to the point of participating in a plot to kill Hitler. But the most striking similarity with Hirsch emerges in Bonhoeffer's assessment of the modern theological task. While in prison, he wrestled with the role of the church in a 'world come of age.' He proposed to his friend Bethge a book with three parts: 1. a stocktaking of Christianity, 2. the real meaning of the Christian faith, and 3. conclusions. He then expands upon his meaning. Now that man is reaching maturity, i.e. 'come of age,' the concept of God to cover man's embarrassment and insecurity or fill the gaps in his knowledge has become superfluous. One result is that God is no longer meaningful to the masses. The church must learn to explain Christianity as an encounter with Jesus Christ, rather than insist upon acceptance of outworn creeds or concepts such as the omniscience of God.[305]

This is reminiscent of Hirsch's concern with making Christianity understandable to Germans of the twentieth century. It also corresponds to his statement quoted above, 'The radical way is the only way by which we can today serve the gospel.' Both Hirsch and Bonhoeffer demanded intellectual honesty, and both wanted to see a Christianity which would appeal to the healthy and strong in the twentieth century, not just the weak or insecure. Hirsch complains, for example, that he knows no single pastor or theologian who still believes in the fourth-century views of Christology or the Trinity, yet these still are the official dogma of the church.[306] Hirsch fully accepts the scientific-historical tools of the Enlightenment. He knows this will make a new theology necessary:

Because of these consequences it is common in some Protestant circles to consider the Enlightenment a purely destructive force, which must be overcome by theology and the church, which must be, as it were, erased out of their history. It has been, however, until very recently, a special honor and special pride of German Protestant Christianity not to have taken such voices seriously. The fate of Christianity in Western civilization depends on this, that in Protestant Christianity the men do not die out who offer this crisis of reformulation as the path ordained by God to our veracity. In this crisis and with its means, they become bearers of a historical process which will build a new Christian concept of history consistent with the new circumstances and the new understanding.[307]

In other words, Hirsch is describing theology in a world come of age.

Despite the similarities found in Hirsch and Bonhoeffer's theological concerns, their political positions were worlds apart. It would be absurd to suggest otherwise. Although Bonhoeffer was not able to write his proposed book, it is obvious that his theology for a world come of age would not have relied upon the concept of *Volk* nor accepted a totalitarian state. Once again, two men who shared theological ground diverged when it came to politics.

Several scholars have recently interpreted the role of Hirsch in the theological struggles of Germany. Klaus Scholder, for example, describes and thereby condemns Hirsch's position as one of 'political theology':

This drawing of a parallel [to today] overlooks the fact that the enemy at that time was not 'pluralism', but on the contrary a closed group stepping forth with the desire for a radical unification of the church. If the history of this time holds a warning for the Protestant church, then it lies in any event in political enthusiasm, which to be sure found its animated supporters in Protestant theology and the church at that time as today.[308]

The first part of Scholder's statement tells only part of the story. The 'enemy' for the Confessing Church was the *Deutsche Christen*, with their radical desire for unification of the church. But a major enemy for Hirsch and his peers certainly was pluralism, and by focusing with great animosity on that enemy, many Christians readily succumbed to the harsh allure of both the *Deutsche Christen* and the National Socialists. The second part of Scholder's statement suggests that no political stance is theologically acceptable for the church, condemning the behavior of Bonhoeffer, Tillich and perhaps even Barth as well as that of Hirsch. Eberhard Bethge has criticized Scholder's position for its conservative opposition to Christian social and political activity. For example, it would rule out theological concern for the problem of racism in South Africa, hunger in the Third World, or nuclear weapons in the industrialized world, as well as theological support for a Hitler. Bethge would prefer to distinguish between good politics and bad.[309]

Wolfgang Tilgner wrote a study of German theology in 1966, concentrating on the conservative theology of *Volksnomos* and 'orders of creation' of men like Hirsch. In this book, written largely from the Barmen point of view, Tilgner criticizes Hirsch for many of his emphases. Hirsch tends to make *völkisch* unity an absolute value;[310] his view of law, the Nomos of the *Volk*, contains the implicit assumption that this is a second point of revelation in addition to the revelation of the gospel;[311] values of the *Volk* replace Christian values as the most central of values;[312] and implicit in all of the above, Hirsch does not respect the gap between God and man.[313] Tilgner also criticizes Hirsch for accepting a minimal role for the church in the *Volks* state, quoting a comment by Barth from his *Church Dogmatics* of 1959:

> How curious that so educated and shrewd a man as E. Hirsch was able to complete a history of modern Protestant theology and fully overlook this other side of the picture (i.e. the revolutionary awakening of the Christian community in the world), portraying as history a single, consistent withdrawal into an Indian reservation.[314]

But Tilgner relies, ultimately, upon history rather than internal arguments to build his critique of Hirsch's position. He argues that the political theology of the 1930s shows how vital a Christocentric doctrine of revelation, i.e. the position of Barmen, really is.[315] And he also asserts that *experience* shows that Hirsch's view of a *Volks* church did not work, that the state did interfere and make the preaching of the gospel difficult.[316] So Tilgner, armed with the full weight of Barmen theology and writing from a theological perspective, had to turn in the end to history and hindsight: in retrospect we can see that Hirsch was wrong.

A Danish theologian, Jens Schjørring, has written a fine comparative study of Hirsch and Eduard Geismar, cited above. Although acknowledging Hirsch's intelligence and the internal consistency of his thought, Schjørring occasionally criticizes Hirsch on theological grounds. For example, he argues that Hirsch reaches a point in his endorsement of the *Volksnomos* where he fails to remain dialectical.[317] That is, he fails to assert the evil in paradoxical tension with the good in the ethic of the *Volk*. But this criticism suffers from the ambiguity which of necessity surrounds the concept of paradox or dialectic. First of all, Hirsch would never have admitted that he ignored the dialectic. He would have asserted that, while maintaining cognizance of human imperfection, he did not want to be paralyzed into inactivity. So he affirmed the dialectic but also boldly affirmed his faith that the *Volk* ethic coupled with the Christian ethic provides the best possible moral, political basis for the German people.

Thus Schjørring's critique is one of judgment rather than one of substance. Barth, Tillich, Geismar, and even Kierkegaard, all of whom are rooted in paradox and dialectic, all reached a point at which, in spite of paradox, they endorsed a set of values and acted upon them. So did Hirsch. To that extent they are all undialectical. But approbation or criticism of their positions depends finally upon personal, subjective judgment.

An important conclusion towards which this study points is that neither Hirsch's intelligence, his knowledge of history, his insight into theology, his recognition of the crisis of modernity, nor his understanding of Kierkegaardian existentialism protected him from taking a political stance which has been historically condemned. A counterpart to that conclusion is that none of those elements necessarily determined his stance either. Other factors may have been important.

Among those other factors, Hirsch's home, school and vocational environment all encouraged conservative, Lutheran, German nationalism. These were the politics of his father, of the Wingolf *Bund*, and of large elements within the university and the church. Karl Barth, by way of contrast, was Swiss and Reformed in background, rather than German Lutheran. Dietrich Bonhoeffer came from a liberal family with ties to England, and he both lived and traveled abroad extensively, drawing influence from England and the United States as well as Italy and Spain. From his much narrower German nationalist perspective, Hirsch's intelligence and knowledge allowed him to see attacks upon Germany and Christianity within the perspective of a crisis of modernity. The solution which he then proposed was a coherent and reasonable response to a very real problem.

Hirsch's personality, however, probably contributed to both the style and the substance of his political stance. He was a physical weakling who praised strength and courage. His writings are filled with references to valor, heroes, soldiers and bold venture. Much of the courage of which he wrote was the spiritual courage of the existential act; but he also used martial and physical imagery and was strongly influenced by the First World War. When he described his typewriter, that 'feminine apparatus,' as nonetheless an effective weapon of war, the existence of psychological compensation is certainly implied. Hirsch was also demanding, waspish and contentious towards his colleagues, especially as dean of the theological faculty in the thirties. He had few of the easy-going, warm qualities of either Althaus or Kittel.

It is also clear that Hirsch was sensitive to the widespread rumor that he was Jewish. His name implied that possibility, and he was thought to look Jewish. A memorandum circulated by the University of Göttingen in July 1934 verifies that he was both aware of the rumors and anxious to stamp them out:

> In order to counter untruthful rumors, Herr Professor Hirsch of Göttingen has submitted large numbers of personal records regarding his ancestry to the *Rektor*, the University Lecturers' Federation, the University Teachers' Federation of the National Socialist Teachers' League, and the Students' Federation. In the main line of Hirsch they stretch back in authenticated relationship to a thresher and farm manager Hirsch, born in 1585 in Görzig (Anhalt), who is in the eighth generation of forefathers of Professor Hirsch. In the parallel lines the proven relationship of ancestors goes back in all cases at least to the fifth generation of forefathers and to persons born before 1789. One of these ancestors in the fifth generation, Marie Sénéchal was born on 1.1.1746 and baptised on 6.1.1746 in the French-reformed church in Prenzlau. Her parents are Samuel Sénéchal and Jeanne, born Sy. These Sénéchals, as likewise shown by the records, stem from Calais. Marie Sénéchal is therefore quite probably of Huguenot heritage.
>
> Another parallel line in the sixth generation presents perhaps another Huguenot (Maria Dorothea Neffschatas, born 28.1.1750), but this is not yet authenticated. In general it consists of German farmer, sailor, and middle class families. On the basis of these records the *Rektor*, University Lecturers' Federation, University Teachers' Federation, and Students' Federation confirm that Herr Professor Hirsch has demonstrated his Aryan descent to a considerably broad extent, as it might be required by any state or Party office.[318]

Again, the probability of psychological compensation exists. Hirsch's enthusiastic nationalism may have been designed to draw attention away from both his physical disabilities and the suspicion of Jewish forebears. These factors should not be ignored, and they are certainly important. However, it is also worth noting that these factors do not retract from the internal coherence of Hirsch's thought. The value and impact of his ideas are important considerations, whatever the psychological motivation of his ideas.

F. Conclusion

A COMPARISON of Kittel, Althaus and Hirsch reveals a similarity in their political stance. They shared a common attitude towards German nationalism and traditional, conservative, German Christian values. Each of them opposed the development of pluralism in German life, which is to say that each opposed the advent of modernity. The impact of modernity — industrialization, urbanization, mobility, class strife — coupled with the modern attitude of liberalism, which sanctions the rights of the ethnically, culturally and politically diverse, endangered the lifestyle and the political-social environment of Wilhelmine Germany with which Kittel, Althaus and Hirsch felt most comfortable. So each of them envisioned an ideal Germany in which authority, obedience and nationalistic unity would produce community.

Intellectually, these three men assumed different positions. Kittel simply opposed the Enlightenment and did not really wrestle with the difficulties that such a view imposed upon his thought. Althaus accepted the intellectual heritage of the Enlightenment, but with a cautious, mediating approach that ruled out any radical results. Hirsch, on the other hand, enthusiastically welcomed the scientific, rational heritage of the Enlightenment as the self-evident intellectual position for modern man. That is, he endorsed intellectual modernism while opposing political, social and cultural modernism. The resulting tension provided the challenge for Hirsch's lifework.

Three questions must be addressed to the lifework of Emanuel Hirsch. First, was the crisis of modernity real? It was, and it continues to be a point of tension in twentieth-century life. Virtually every contemporary conflict, from racial stress in Britain or America to the imposition of Islam by the revolutionary government in Iran, is rooted in questions similar to those facing Hirsch. How can social unity be maintained when intellectual relativism and socio-cultural pluralism challenge all common values? How can social chaos and disintegration be averted? How can individuals maintain a world view which gives meaning and purpose to life?

Hirsch answered each of the above questions by stressing the binding force of a common cultural identity in Germany, immersed in the historical traditions and continuing meaningfulness of Christianity. This points towards the second overriding question about Hirsch: was his reaction to the crisis of modernity appropriate? Several important issues immediately emerge. He denied the modern push towards egalitarianism and legal equality. He accepted the role of war as a necessary and even healthy force in history. His ideas were susceptible to totalitarian distortion, as confirmed by the worst excesses of the Nazi era, and they manifested a Christianity in which law and order appear to supercede love and grace. Underlying all of these objections is the historical recognition that Hirsch's position placed him in league with National Socialism. So the historical judgment is that his solution to the crisis of modernity is unacceptable.

Finally, can an intelligent person expect to be able to avoid a repetition of Hirsch's error? In an increasingly complex world, the crunch of modernity may manifest itself again with the intensity it reached in Weimar Germany, and it would be nice to be able to learn from Hirsch's mistakes. Perhaps one could insist upon a humanitarian stance in which love or egalitarianism would preclude the most blatant violations of human rights. A strong sense of human rights would certainly have diverted Nazism from committing its worst crimes. But Hirsch would raise at least a twofold protest. First, he disliked the leveling effect of egalitarianism. If people are to be treated equally and valued the same, can the concept or reality of excellence be retained? Hirsch recognized this problem on both a personal level and among nations. He believed that God's differentiated order in life corresponds to reality and encourages true achievement. Secondly, Hirsch would simply argue that dreams of humanitarian love are utopian. It is part of the human order, past, present and future, that some people will starve, some will bleed, some will die, and some will go to war. He had hoped that justice would ensue from his concept of *Volks* state, but he would distrust any world view which relies upon human justice as the vehicle to achieve social good.

Another protection against Hirsch's error might be to emphasize Christian love and grace more than Christian law. In retrospect, the theologians who did so seem to have been less tempted by the National Socialist charms. But this corresponds very closely to the humanitarian position stated above, and again Hirsch would object. First, he argued for a balance between law and gospel in which freedom in Christ is tempered by responsibility in this world. No theologian can get away from this dilemma of good works (ethics), so the question hinges upon the content as much as the stress placed upon law. Secondly, Hirsch would argue that any state based upon the Sermon on the Mount would not survive in the real world. It would be unrealistic to hope to build and preserve a nation based only upon love.

The modern, Western political view would contend that democracy is a protection against the excesses of the Third Reich. The *Führer* principle certainly facilitated Nazi control of German society and the abuses which ensued. But here again Hirsch could raise objections which carry some weight. First, democracy understood as simply the will of the majority need not and often has not protected the rights of minorities. So majority rule cannot be seen as a guarantor against blatant injustice. Secondly, the problems of a crisis situation and the slow pace of democratic action can produce a point of tension. Hirsch, in common with most German conservatives of the Weimar period, saw in democracy only ineffective party strife. And most democratic nations have sacrificed at least some of their principles in time of war. Should insistence upon the purity of democratic forms in a crisis be an unyielding principle?

Finally, a careful study of history is no doubt a prerequisite for an intelligent response to the sort of questions faced by Hirsch. It is only through history, for example, that we have clearly seen which political stances of the 1930s proved ultimately acceptable and which did not. However, the problems are again obvious. Hirsch was nothing if not historically-minded, but the history he studied led him directly to the position he assumed. History, of course, must be seen in broad and narrow focus, in the short and long term. But it is impossible to argue that it ever yields truth or perfect insight.

Despite all the questions raised above, I would draw several conclusions from the study of Emanuel Hirsch. We can best avoid the Nazi error by heavily stressing the values of the liberal, democratic tradition, humanitarianism and justice, and by conscientiously probing history with a view towards its significance for contemporary decision making. But this conclusion is ultimately exactly like that of Hirsch, an existential judgment based upon a leap of faith. Søren Kierkegaard expressed a significant idea in the title of his book about Abraham, *Fear and Trembling*. As Hirsch clearly recognized, a leap of faith allows bold actions, which is good, but it always carries with it the possibility of error. With Hirsch's example before us, we now know more than ever: we must act, but we can only do so in fear and with trembling.

G. Epilogue

IN the last months of the war, and especially after Göttingen fell to American troops on 8 April 1945, thoughts turned to the future of the university and its faculties. On 6 July 1945 Hirsch's name appeared on the first list of Göttingen faculty members to be removed for political reasons; but the British military government soon discovered that he had retired just days before.[319] On 30 May Hirsch had submitted a request for retirement based on medical disability. He had been nearly blind for many years, but he presented testimony to establish a worsening condition so that he could not continue to fill his chair.[320] Apparently the new *Rektor*, Rudolf Smend, had recommended this to Hirsch as the most appropriate way to protect himself from the possibility of worse consequences in a denazification proceeding.[321] Paper work moved quickly and on 19 June Smend met with Major Beatty, British officer in charge of education under the military government. Beatty approved Hirsch's retirement, although for the future 'he withheld removal and appointment decisions for himself.'[322] When Hirsch then appeared on the first list of released faculty anyway, a question arose whether he could still receive his pension (which was only seventy-five per cent of what it would have been if he retired normally as 'emeritus,' but released faculty received no pension at all.) Smend successfully intervened to insure the pension for Hirsch, just as he had earlier insured retention of his university-provided house at 66 Hainholzweg overlooking the beautiful Schiller meadow.[323] In all these matters Hirsch was treated very gently, eased out of the way in a reasonably comfortable manner, though without the honor of a festive retirement or full emeritus status. He thus avoided what would have been an indignity, a disruption to his life and work, and a severe economic loss had he been subjected to the normal denazification procedure.

The disadvantage of the procedure by which Hirsch was removed emerged over the years, however. The absence of honors commensurate with his academic reputation began to wear heavily, both on him and his supporters. And despite virtual blindness, Hirsch at age fifty-seven had clearly not been ready for retirement. He produced a major portion of his scholarly work between 1945 and his death in 1972, and he also gathered a group of followers among the generations of students who passed through the theological faculty at Göttingen in those years.[324]

The first request for improvement in Hirsch's status came from the 'Emergency Association for German Science' in 1949. It requested from the Göttingen curator an assistant for Hirsch in his scientific work, especially in view of his bad eyesight.[325] The curator, Bojunga, replied sharply, noting the political culpability of Hirsch in the years of the Third Reich:

> I am convinced that it was due to his recognition of the hopelessness of further activity at the university, when he on 30 May 1945 requested a disability retirement, immediately after the entry of the Americans, based upon his eye problems of many years standing.[326]

Bojunga also cites the present theological faculty, who blame Hirsch for the political appointment of two theologians, including Birnbaum, who subsequently had to be removed. Furthermore:

> Prof Smend told me recently, as I would like to report to you quite confidentially, that he is quite indignant about the current attitude of Prof Hirsch, which in no way corresponds to the efforts of Prof Smend in overturning the removal of Hirsch's pension in 1945.[327]

In 1952 Birnbaum, now head of the 'Association of University Teachers Displaced from Office' in Göttingen, attempted to intervene for Hirsch. The *Rektor* at that time, the theologian Wolfgang Trillhaas, turned down the intervention but then informed Hirsch. The latter responded that indeed he had nothing to do with the association, and he had rejected the notion of approaching the *Rektor* himself. But that did not mean he felt 'disinterest' in his circumstances.[328] Trillhaas expressed to Hirsch his appreciation for being corrected and his willingness to bring the matter of Hirsch's status to the *Kurator* and the faculty. However, due to the medical basis for Hirsch's retirement, Trillhaas predicted the 'Law for Ending the Denazification' could not be applied to his case. This prediction proved accurate.[329]

In 1954 Birnbaum again initiated an attempt to change Hirsch's status to emeritus.[330] When this new proposal reached the theological faculty, it was accepted because of Hirsch's significance as a theologian and his ongoing work. But the faculty also did not want to directly participate in this request because of its unwillingness to excuse or overlook the fact that Hirsch 'in the days of the so-called "Third Reich", belonged among the most influential representatives of the National Socialist world view in church as well as in university affairs.'[331] In this delicate attempt to approve Hirsch's change to emeritus status while not being willing to push for it, the faculty added one further qualification, which helps to show its lingering hard feelings towards Hirsch: 'During the Weimar Republic, Professor Hirsch succeeded in avoiding taking an oath to the constitution.' The faculty would now approve his emeritus status only on the condition that 'he not be allowed a second time to give expression to his rejection of the democratic system by avoiding the oath of office.'[332] This effort to rehabilitate Hirsch failed, as did a further effort on his behalf by his former colleague and fellow in disrepute, Professor Johannes Hempel.[333] In every case these efforts stumbled on the fact that Hirsch exited the university in 1945 for medical reasons. New legislation dealt only with the rehabilitation of those who had suffered under the military government for political reasons. Hirsch claimed to possess papers which would show the forceful nature of his removal from office, but these papers were never brought to bear on the case.[334]

The legal basis of Hirsch's retirement could only be altered by receipt of a new call to a chair. This loophole allowed for the recovery of medically disabled persons. Hirsch, however, was ineligible due to his age (over sixty-five) by the time this possibility was recognized. He could still have received an honorary professorship, but this is a step the Göttingen theological faculty was simply unwilling to take.[335] An underlying and important factor in all these machinations must be acknowledged — the proud and prickly nature of Hirsch himself. It was widely believed among colleagues that Hirsch never really changed his political beliefs after 1945, and that it was impossible to talk politics with him.[336] This might be hinted at in an incident in 1956. In view of the legal impossibility of changing Hirsch's status, Birnbaum proposed that his name be included in the course schedule with the notation 'in retirement' and that he receive mailings and invitations as if he were emeritus.[337] Rektor Weber wrote to the theological dean for advice, expressing his approval of the idea and his suggestion that they should not be put off by the source of the suggestion (i.e. Birnbaum).[338] Weber subsequently received an affirmative response and passed it on to Hirsch for approval.[339] Hirsch responded sharply and negatively. He accused the university of making only half-hearted efforts to redress his circumstances, also without taking into account his potential contributions regarding the illegal pressures placed on him in 1945. If they had done so and then failed, moderate steps such as these coupled with an open statement distancing the university from the position of the state would have been acceptable to Hirsch. But his lifelong commitment to honesty and full clarity forced him to reject the backhanded and minimal honors now tendered.[340]

7. Emanuel Hirsch, blind, in old age.

The feisty Birnbaum, described by one colleague of that era as a 'little worm' alongside Hirsch, approached his removal under denazification much differently.[341] He visited with Major Beatty and Bishop Marahrens in attempts to secure his position, then he applied for emeritus status, all to no avail. On 17 September 1945 he was released from the faculty.[342] In January Birnbaum tried to have his status changed from 'released' to retired, which would have changed his income from nothing to seventy-five per cent of emeritus retirement pay. His memoirs claim this request was approved by *Rektor,* senate, faculty, curator and military government; but accountants then noted this form of retirement could only be for medical reasons and halted the the process.[343] In 1946 and 1947 Birnbaum went before denazification panels, each of which placed him in category III, i.e. guilty of strong and persistent support of the National Socialist ideology. This prohibited him from both teaching and publishing.[344] When the military government gave way to the Federal Republic in 1948, Birnbaum began a process of three separate trials which ended in 1951 with his rehabilitation.[345]

The next round of conflict was interesting indeed. Birnbaum found that despite his legal exoneration, the theological faculty was unprepared to take him back. Hermann Dörries, dean at the time, told him, 'If you should be forced upon the faculty again, I will lay down my office, and no professor will be prepared to take it up.'[346] The next dean, Zimmerli, repeated the insistence of the faculty, and despite the questionable legal foundation, the faculty successfully avoided having Birnbaum returned to its ranks.[347] The compromise solution was to name Birnbaum professor of the university but without a tie to an individual faculty. He continued on in Göttingen for several years, attempting to give some lectures and to ignore the social ostracism (e.g. people who crossed the street to avoid speaking with him). But he gave up and moved to Munich in 1958, though he kept a legal residence in Göttingen until he was old enough for emeritus retirement in 1961.[348]

On the basis of about four years full time work as a professor, from 1935 until war broke out in 1939, plus partial service from 1939 to 1945, Birnbaum was able to draw his full professor's salary from 1952 until 1961 and his full emeritus salary from 1961 until the present. He does not view this as generous, however, but complains bitterly about the ill treatment he received at the hands of the university and especially the theological faculty after 1945. Never questioning whether his enthusiastic support of the *Deutsche Christen* might have been unwise, and denying the political nature of his appointment, he compares the denazification process in the university *unfavorably* with the Nazi process of cleansing the universities of unwanted elements in 1933 and after, arguing that it affected far more people and was conducted more cruelly. Many of the points Birnbaum makes in his memoirs are worthy of consideration. For example, he argues that Confessing Church history has been too one-sided and laudatory, ignoring much pro-Nazi sentiment within the movement. The process of attempting to cleanse the university of Nazi influences was also clearly very difficult, as he suggests, both in terms of effectiveness and principles. But Birnbaum's arguments are undercut by the one-sided and belligerent tone of his work. He quibbles over minor points, explains all opposition to himself as the fruit of Confessing Church vs. *Deutsche Christen* rivalry, ignores the National Socialist emphasis of his own work, including his role as 'Goering's favorite lecturer,' and finally dismisses all his detractors with the oft-repeated phrase, 'Well, yes, he was a confesser [of the Confessing Church].'[349]

In the final analysis, the process of cleansing the theological faculty at Göttingen seems to have made the best of a difficult situation. It may have been improper to shield Hirsch from the full thrust of responsibility for his role in the Third Reich. It certainly would have earned his removal from the faculty, loss of all income, and a long period of ignominy. Given his age and infirmities, it is almost impossible to imagine him moving out of his home and somehow supporting himself in the first years after 1945 (Birnbaum began to build brick stoves, for example, and to sell black market cuckoo clocks to Americans). If the process did not kill him, it certainly would have reduced or even negated entirely his intellectual contributions after 1945. On the other hand, given the extent of his culpability in the harshness of the Nazi era, it does not seem that the minor indignities and legal obstacles which hampered his last years were overly harsh punishment. Birnbaum too was punished in a manner that was first materially difficult and remained psychologically difficult for him to accept. The question of whether criminal penalties are appropriate in cases such as this is very difficult. Neither Birnbaum nor Hirsch killed Jews. On the other hand, both actively supported the National Socialist regime, sometimes with harsh consequences for those around them. The determination of the theological faculty after 1945 to deny them influence and honor seems in retrospect an appropriate repudiation of their behavior and stance.

It may be that too many faculty were allowed to make the transition of 1945 without having to consider fully the stance they had taken. The case of Otto Weber perhaps most clearly shows the complexity and nuance necessary in any approach to this question. Weber was a loyal Party member and he served as dean of the faculty after Hirsch stepped down in 1939. Yet he emerged relatively unscathed in 1945 and after, subsequently serving even as *Rektor* of the university. Birnbaum bitterly attacked Weber in the process of appealing for Hirsch's vindication:

> One cannot justify this with a special political charge against Hirsch. His successor as dean, Prof Otto Weber, dean from 1939 to 1945, did not show the critical stance of Hirsch nor his boldness of opposition, but he was considered by us as loyal to Party and state . . . but he had — without

saying more — suitable friends, so that after 1945 he was not released for a single hour, and under the *Rektorat* of Smend already sat in the senate![350]

Weber apparently did leap into the Confessing Church-Barthian camp at just the right moment in terms of his career. However, for Birnbaum to place Weber in the same pot as himself and Hirsch illustrates the disregard for discriminating observation which flaws his autobiography. To say Weber did not have Hirsch's talent for opposition is to acknowledge that he did not attack so many people nor do so much injury. Neither was his appointment to Göttingen political, as was Birnbaum's, nor his role such a lightning rod for controversy. Weber's direct culpability was simply much less than either of his two colleagues. Furthermore, his attitude of penitence and his cooperation after 1945 were completely at odds with the intransigence of Hirsch and Birnbaum. When the former *Rektor*, Smend, was shown Birnbaum's charges against Weber, he responded vigorously. According to Smend, Weber remained in his position because he received the approval of the theological faculty, *Rektor*, senate, military government, and the Protestant church, represented by Karl Barth. Smend added that the university could not have opened again without Weber's tremendous contribution, both before and after the collapse, to 'the entire effort of public relief for the student body.'[351] Neither penitence nor cooperative public spirit marked the postwar years of Emanuel Hirsch.

CHAPTER V

Conclusion

THIS study is predicated on the assumption that Germany faced a severe crisis of modernity in the period after the First World War. Within that crisis three well-meaning, intelligent and reputable Protestant theologians — Gerhard Kittel, Paul Althaus and Emanuel Hirsch — chose a political stance which ultimately led them to support Adolf Hitler and National Socialism. Each of these theologians was unique. Kittel, with his knowledge of Judaism and the Talmud, carved an important niche for himself in the world of Nazi scholarship on the Jewish question. In doing so he created a theological foundation for Nazi oppression of the Jews, yet he somehow was able to reconcile this work with his Christian and academic values. Paul Althaus assumed a more moderate political stance. As a leader of Luther scholarship in Germany, he presided over theological and political questions of his day with a mediating style, constantly seeking middle ground and reconciliation of opposing camps. But his choice of middle ground placed him well within the orbit of Nazism, and he welcomed and supported Hitler at least until the late 1930s. Emanuel Hirsch vigorously developed a philosophical-theological world view in which the unity of the German *Volk* within the German community assumed preeminence. This view, based upon a keen insight into intellectual history and an existential leap of faith, made Hirsch a conscious apologist for Nazism within the German state.

Along with their uniqueness in style and stance, these three men shared certain values and concerns which determined their common political attitudes. Each opposed the unsettling impact of political, economic and cultural change in Weimar Germany. Each saw in that change a disintegration of traditional Christian and German values, and each opposed the democratic political system which facilitated that change. These men were nationalists to whom the defeat and humiliation of Germany during and after the First World War was personally painful, and they longed for a rebirth of unity, strength and pride in Germany, based upon the common values of a unified *Volk*. Underlying all of these concerns was the fear that a more radical bolshevik state might replace the already unacceptable Weimar system.

Kittel, Althaus and Hirsch were not isolated or eccentric individuals. Although they spoke their political minds more freely than many of their colleagues, an awareness of their political views helps to explain the political attitudes of many within the university and the church during the period of the Third Reich. Their assumptions, their concerns, and their conclusions represent a position that must have been common to many professors, theologians and pastors in Germany. They were not extremists. Some radicals in both university and church expressed Nazi views in a far less restrained fashion. They can be dismissed as cranks. Some individuals in the university and church courageously opposed Hitler. They are now revered as heroes. But a large middle group in the university and church gravitated to neither extreme. They probably held views resembling those of Kittel, Althaus and Hirsch in many respects. Therefore, these three represent an important segment of the German community under the Third Reich and their appreciation of Hitler helps to explain the general acquiescence to Nazi government within the major institutions of the nation.

This study also speaks to the role of reason in history. Kittel, Althaus and Hirsch were intelligent and conscientious, and they devoted careful thought to their ideal for society. But it did not work. Their conclusions are unacceptable. Reason proved inadequate. The crisis of reason, therefore, appears to be real. Existentialism, the contemporary philosophical tradition which forms the basis for a personally-recognized truth, is shown to be morally neutral. The present need is for historical insight which is more than relative, which can provide reliable guidance to the intelligent student of history. But that need remains unmet.

The role of Christianity in history is also called into question by this study. These three theologians saw themselves and were seen by others as genuine Christians acting upon genuine Christian impulses. Even in retrospect a Christian basis for each of their individual positions can be discerned; Christianity has strains which are both anti-Jewish and anti-modern. In light of the German experience, a Christianity which stresses these strains, in which, for example, the love of Christ cannot be readily perceived, should arouse our suspicion. Kittel, Althaus and Hirsch protested that Christianity need not be sentimental or soft. That emphasis, if valid, hardly represents the Jesus of the Sermon on the Mount. A second warning in the German church experience lies in its failure to distinguish adequately between Christian values and German values, between inherently Christian concerns and inherently patriotic concerns. Finally, there is the question of whether Christianity can face the modern world, the 'world come of age,' without turning for protection to an Adolf Hitler. That is the ironic position in which Kittel, Althaus and Hirsch found themselves, and they were not alone.

This study assumes a crisis of the modern world, a crisis based upon rapid social, economic and cultural change. The modern intellectual tradition contributes to the crisis. It has peered deeply into the abyss, not enough to see the bottom, but enough to suspect there is no bottom. And this crisis is abetted by the democratic tradition, with its defense of personal freedom and pluralism. The catalyst for the crisis of modernity is hard times. Is the non-German world immune to this crisis? Can the experiment with freedom in modern society create a lasting social unity rather than social disintegration? Can it survive hard times?

Hard times are a way of life, of course, for the powerless in society. The world has always contained injustice: rich and poor, rich nations and poor nations. Minorities and the poor have always been put down. And the methods of the rich have often been those of the Nazis, though not usually so blatant. Nineteenth-century Britain abused India to get ahead; nineteenth-century America abused Indians to get ahead. Racism and notions of white, middle class superiority have only just begun to recede in America to give some political meaning to the phrase, 'all men are created equal,' with the additional change that women are sometimes acknowledged now as well. But the social adjustments and the pain produced when the 'haves' really give political freedom to the 'have-nots' are intense. This is true within nations and between nations. For example, will the rich but less populous Western nations ever allow a world government based upon their own democratic principle of one man–one vote? Of course not, at least not willingly. They would lose too much, just as the established classes in Germany lost real privileges and advantages in the political climate of Weimar.

The scenario to fear, then, is one in which a combination of crises makes life difficult: a lost war, economic collapse, shortage of oil, shortage of food. If this is coupled with a meaningful attempt to follow democratic principles, to allow true freedom and give a true politcal voice to the plural groups within society, beware. Then we will hear calls for toughness, for law and order, for national unity. We will be tempted to sacrifice some democratic principles and civil rights for national wellbeing. In short, the crisis will begin to resemble that of Weimar Germany. Will we avoid being the Kittel, Althaus or Hirsch of that time? Will we avoid using our intellect to rationalize a position that protects our comfort and best interests, closing our eyes to the pain created for the different or less fortunate among us? Until we have pondered these questions, we will do well not to condemn Kittel, Althaus and Hirsch too loudly. But, hopefully, our consideration of Kittel, Althaus and Hirsch will encourage us to ponder these questions, to keep searching for a solution to the crisis of modernity, for a fair and just social and political ideal within the modern world.

Notes

CHAPTER I

1. One recent study along these lines is Alan D. Beyerchen, *Scientists under Hitler: Politics ana the Physics Community in the Third Reich* (New Haven, 1977).
2. See Alvin Toffler, *Future Shock* (New York, 1970).
3. For an example of the impact of these changes on one group in Germany, see Fritz K. Ringer, *The Decline of the German Mandarins: The German Academic Community, 1890–1933* (Cambridge, Mass., 1969).
4. See H. Stuart Hughes, *Consciousness and Society: The Reorientation of European Social Thought, 1890–1930* (New York, 1958).
5. See Erich Heller, *The Disinherited Mind,* 4th ed. (New York, 1974). See also F. A. Lee, *The Tragic Philosopher: A Study of Friedrich Nietzsche* (London, 1957, 1972).
6. Werner Heisenberg, *Physics and Beyond; Encounters and Conversations* (London, 1971), p.210.
7. The recent work of Fritz Stern, *Gold and Iron: Bismarck, Bleichröder and the Building of the German Empire* (New York, 1977), sheds interesting light on the changes in society accompanying the growth of capitalism in Germany.
8. Two important books deal with the intellectual reaction to modernity in Germany. Fritz Stern explores the development of cultural pessimism in, *The Politics of Cultural Despair: A Study in the Rise of the Germanic Ideology* (Berkeley, 1961); and George L. Mosse identifies the *völkisch* component in German thought in, *The Crisis of German Ideology; The Intellectual Origins of the Third Reich* (New York, 1964). See also, Klemens von Klemperer, *Germany's New Conservatism; Its History and Dilemma in the Twentieth Century* (Princeton, 1957).
9. This issue is highlighted by an incident at the Western Association of German Studies Meeting at Stanford University in Oct. 1979. During the course of an illustrated lecture on Nazi art, the audience enjoyed a good laugh at the obtuse, philistine tastes of Hitler and his cohort. However, many then acknowledged that a travelling show of Nazi art produced an overwhelmingly positive response at their individual campuses in the United States. See also Walter Laqueur's reference to Liebermann on modern art: *Kunst* (art) comes from *können* (can, to be able to). If it were derived from *wollen* (will, to want to), it would be called *Wulst*. See *Weimar: A Cultural History 1918–1933* (New York, 1974), p.164.
10. See Peter Gay, *Weimar Culture: The Outsider as Insider* (New York, 1968).
11. Among the many books emanating from the First World War, the enormously popular *All Quiet on the Western Front,* by Erich Maria Remarque, is a representative German example. An excellent recent study from the British perspective is by Paul Fussell, *The Great War and Modern Memory* (Oxford, 1975).
12. Albert Schweitzer, *The Quest for the Historical Jesus: A Critical Study of its Progress from Reimarus to Wrede,* Pre-

face by F. C. Burkitt (London, 1945; originally published as *Von Reimarus zu Wrede,* 1906), p.47.

13. *Ibid.,* p.54.
14. *Ibid.,* p.60.
15. *Ibid.,* p.68.
16. *Ibid.,* p.73.
17. See *The Future of Belief* (New York, 1966), by Leslie Dewart, a Catholic work in which the suitability of Greek philosophical categories for Christian theology is rejected.
18. Schweitzer, Op. cit., ch.XI.
19. *Ibid.,* ch.XIX.
20. A new life-of-Jesus research has developed in the last twenty-five years among students of Rudolf Bultmann. See Heinz Zahrnt, *Die Sache mit Gott: Die protestantische Theologie im 20. Jahrhundert* (Munich, 1966), pp.326–81. Hereinafter cited as SG. Zahrnt notes that this new search recognizes that it begins from within the faith and does not hope to establish a historical proof of any sort.
21. William Nicholls gives Schleiermacher this title in his *Systematic and Philosophical Theology* (Harmondsworth, Middlesex, 1969), p.63.
22. Arthur Titius, 'Schleiermachers Grundgedanken über Religion und Christentum in ihrer Bedeutung für die Gegenwart,' a speech delivered at the Kaiser's birthday celebration, 27 Jan. 1913, and published in *Festreden der U. Göttingen, 1911–23* (Göttingen, 1923).
23. Johannes Meyer, *Geschichte der Göttinger theologischen Fakultät* (Göttingen, 1937), p.76.
24. Meyer, p.75.
25. See Nicholls, p.67.
26. Meyer, p.77, notes that the *Landessynode* of Hanover in 1881 passed a resolution requesting church and state authorities to place more confessional moderates on the faculty at Göttingen in order to correct the balance. It was acknowledged that Ritschl was a major concern behind the passing of this resolution.
27. Thomas W. Ogletree, *Christian Faith and History: A Critical Comparison of Ernst Troeltsch and Karl Barth* (New York, 1965).
28. The rating of these three as the primary figures of theology in this century comes from Zahrnt, SG, who holds particular esteem for Tillich.
29. SG, p.28. There is controversy over the extent to which Barth's theology is actually a product of political crisis clothed in theological terms. Barth commented on his great disappointment in finding his theological professors among 93 intellectuals who supported Kaiser Wilhelm II's war policy in 1914, and he added, 'Disconcerted by their ethos, I noticed that I could also not follow their ethics or dogmatics, their biblical exegesis or presentation of history. The theology of the nineteenth century, at least for me, had no more future.' (SG, pp.14–15). Barth also said, 'I neither can nor want to prove that without the world war we would have stood where we now stand. But who can prove that we were led there specifically through the world war?' (SG, p.28). Zahrnt's conclusion is that theological factors were crucial.
30. See SG, p.66. This term is sometimes used indiscriminately. It almost always refers to a theology in which the gap between God and man is important, and it can refer to the method in which God is described through paradox. In this case method is consistent with theology. But 'dialectical method' can also refer to a system of refining theological insights through the process of thesis, antithesis and synthesis, in an evolutionary manner. This method need not correspond to a theology in which the gap between God and man is preeminent. Later Barth largely abandoned the dialectical method while remaining a dialectical theologian.
31. SG, p.21.
32. SG, pp.34, 104–8, 135.
33. The method of analogy does not necessarily lead to objective rationalism. As Helmut Thielicke points out in a critique, Barth's analogy of one baptism, one God and one spirit to support his concept of democracy, might also suggest, 'Ein Volk — ein Reich — ein Führer.' Quoted in SG, p.233.
34. Karl Barth, 'The Christian Understanding of Revelation,' in *Against the Stream: Shorter Post-War Writings, 1946–52,* Ronald Gregor Smith, ed. (London, 1954).
35. Karl Barth, 'The Christian Message and the New Humanism,' in *Against the Stream.*
36. Ogletree, ch.II.

37. *Ibid.,* pp.191–2.
38. It is interesting to note that a romantic such as Schleiermacher anticipated elements in twentieth-century theology, a theology which can certainly be viewed as the logical extension of certain tenets of romanticism.
39. Quoted in Nicholls, op. cit., p.67.
40. *Ibid.,* p.68.
41. *Ibid.,* p.67.
42. Søren Kierkegaard, *Fear and Trembling,* Walter Lowrie, tr, (Princeton, 1941, 1954; first published in 1843).
43. Ogletree, op. cit., ch.II. Note that Overbeck was a friend of Friedrich Nietzsche.
44. Barth, 'The Christian Commitment in the Midst of Religious Change: Documents of a Hungarian Journey,' *Against the Stream.*
45. Barth, 'The Church between East and West,' *Against the Stream.*
46. SG, p.271.
47. I. Cor. 1:23 (Revised Standard Version).
48. Robert M. Grant, *The Bible in the Church: A Short History of Interpretation* (New York, 1958), pp. 156–7.
49. Carl E. Braaten and Roy A. Harrisville, eds., *Kerygma and History: A Symposium on the Theology of Rudolf Bultmann,* selected and translated by Braaten and Harrisville (New York, 1962). Braaten emphasizes the Lutheran character of Bultmann's work in an introductory chapter.
50. SG, p.300.
51. SG, p.296.
52. SG, pp.288–9.
53. Quoted in SG, p.276.
54. SG, pp.279–83.
55. SG, p.314.
56. See Prenter's essay, 'Myth and Gospel,' in Braaten and Harrisville.
57. Roy A. Harrisville, 'Bultmann's Concept of the Transition from Inauthentic to Authentic Existence,' Braaten and Harrisville.
58. SG, pp.334–45.
59. SG, pp.326–7.
60. SG, p.394.
61. Nicholls renders this judgment in his treatment of Tillich, pp.241, 251, 256–8.
62. Quoted in SG, p.384.
63. SG, p.385.
64. SG, pp.418–19.
65. SG, p.413.
66. SG, p.429.
67. Nicholls, p.220.
68. SG, pp.430–1.
69. Nicholls, p.273.
70. SG, p.396.
71. SG, p.397.
72. Dietrich Bonhoeffer, *Christology,* Introduction by Edwin H. Robertson, tr. by John Bowden (London, 1966, 1971). This quote is from Robertson's introduction, p.16.
73. Quoted in SG, p.174.
74. Paul Tillich, 'The Depth of Existence,' in Tillich, *The Shaking of the Foundations* (New York, 1949, 1969), pp. 63–4.
75. SG, p.438.
76. *Ibid.*
77. See Eberhard Bethge's fine biography, *Dietrich Bonhoeffer: Theologian, Christian, Contemporary,* tr. by Eric Mosbacher, et al. (London, 1970; originally published in Munich, 1967).
78. Bonhoeffer, *Christology,* pp.29–32.
79. Dietrich Bonhoeffer, *Ethics* (London, 1955, 1965), p.17.
80. See Theodor Strohm, *Theologie im Schatten politischer Romantik, Eine wissenschaftlich-soziologische Anfrage an die Theologie Friedrich Gogartens* (Munich, 1970).
81. It is ironical that dialectical theologians were often judged conservative in their rejection of liberal theology, and many of the most enthusiastic supporters of Nazism among theologians were in the nineteenth-century liberal theological tradition.
82. See Bethge for details.

CHAPTER II

1. I have pieced together the details of Kittel's life after his arrest from a file of correspondence in the possession of Dr. Herman Preus, retired Professor of Theology at Luther Theological Seminary, St. Paul, Minnesota. Preus studied at Tübingen in 1937–8, and the two men and their families developed a friendship subsequently maintained through correspondence. See also, Leonore Siegele-Wenschkewitz, *Neutestamentliche Wissenschaft vor der Judenfrage: Gerhard Kittels theologische Arbeit im Wandel deutscher Geschichte* (Munich, 1980), p.50.
2. This praise is recalled by Rudolf Kittel

himself in his posthumous retrospective, *Die Universität Leipzig im Jahr der Revolution 1918/19. Rektoratserrinerungen* (Stuttgart, 1930) pp.65–71, 171–3. Despite the self-serving nature of this source, the tone of the book indicates that the elder Kittel valued moderation; his attitude towards the revolutionaries, for example, though far from approving, was free of fanaticism, overblown rhetoric, or even condemnation. Rudolf Kittel's significance as a scholar is confirmed by Hans-Joachim Kraus, *Geschichte der historisch-kritischen Erforschung des Alten Testaments von der Reformation bis zur Gegenwart* (Neukirchen Kreis Moers, 1956).

3. Kittel's book, *Die Oden Salomos. Ueberarbeitet oder einheitlich?* (Leipzig, 1914), was published as vol. 16 of this series. Another book, *Die Probleme des palästinischen Spätjudentums und das Urchristentum* (Stuttgart, 1926), was vol. 37 in the series, now renamed *Beiträge zur Wissenschaft vom Alten und Neuen Testament,* but still edited by Rudolf Kittel.

4. Gerhard Kittel, *Meine Verteidigung* (a manuscript dated June 1945, Tübingen), pp. 1-2. I am greatly indebted to Dr Herman Preus for · access to this document.

5. Kittel edited the first four volumes, published between 1933 and 1942. The entire work has been translated as *Theological Dictionary of the New Testament.*

6. Kittel had membership card no. 3,243,036. His Party file in the Berlin Document Centre contains only one letter, and it is of no significance in explaining his role or commitment to the Party.

7. MV, p.19-20.

8. A letter from Herbert M. J. Loewe to Kittel, 30 Nov. 1933. Photocopies of four letters are in the personality file on Gerhard Kittel at the Weiner Library, London. Neither Loewe's name nor address appear on this correspondence, but I established to my satisfaction his identity as Herbert Loewe, Reader in Rabbinics, Cambridge University. This was subsequently verified for me by his son.

9. Max Weinreich, *Hitler's Professors. The Part of Scholarship in Germany's*

Crimes against the Jewish People (New York, 1946).

10. William Foxwell Albright, *History, Archaeology and Christian Humanism* (New York, 1964), pp.229-40.

11. This obituary and reference to the Porter article are among press clippings in the Kittel personality file, Wiener Library. The *Neue Zürcher Zeitung* obituary appeared on 25 July 1948.

12. Klaus Scholder, *Die Kirche und das Dritte Reiche. Band I: Vorgeschichte und Zeit der Illusionen 1918-1934* (Berlin, 1977).

13. Leonore Siegele-Wenschkewitz, 'Die Evangelisch-theologische Fakultät Tübingen in den Anfangsjahren des Dritten Reichs. II. Gerhard Kittel und die Judenfrage,' *Zeitschrift für Theologie und Kirche,* 4 (1978), p.55.

14. I stress this theme in my article, 'Theologian in the Third Reich: The Case of Gerhard Kittel,' *Journal of Contemporary History,* 12 (1977), pp.595-622.

15. See below, p.58.

16. Siegele-Wenschkewitz, p.80. This statement appears without footnote or substantiation. In response to my inquiry, Siegele-Wenschkewitz indicated she based this conclusion upon conversations with Kittel's son, Eberhard, and the revised version of Kittel's defense statement written in 1946. For my analysis of this statement see pp.42-44.

17. Two years after her article on Kittel, Siegele-Wenschkewitz published a short book, *Neutestamentliche Wissenschaft vor der Judenfrage: Gerhard Kittels theologische Arbeit im Wandel deutscher Geschichte* (Munich, 1980). This presents very useful biographical information about Kittel and a good analysis of Kittel's publications through 1933. The book is flawed, however, in that it serves as a defense against the critique by Martin Rese, 'Antisemitismus und neutestamentliche Forschung, Anmerkungen zu dem Thema "Gerhard Kittel und die Judenfrage,"' *Evangelische Theologie,* 39 (1979), pp. 557-70. In a somewhat emotional reaction to Rese's critique, Siegele-Wenschkewitz stresses the absolute break in Kittel's attitude towards Jews in his work before and after 1933. This is designed to substantiate her earlier

thesis that Kittel's fundamental error was a misassessment of Hitler and National Socialism. Again she fails to take into account Kittel's work between 1933 and 1944. I also believe she distorts Rese's actual arguments in order to more easily attack them. The end result is that an adequate assessment of the complex problem of Gerhard Kittel is not well served. In 1982 Siegele-Wenschkewitz published an excellent article, 'Mitverantwortung und Schuld der Christen am Holocaust,' *Evangelische Theologie,* 42 (1982), pp.171-90. Here she deals with Gerhard Kittel's speech in 1936 at the opening session of Walter Frank's *Reichsinstitut für Geschichte des neuen Deutschlands, Forschungsabteilung Judenfrage.* It is her first attempt to deal with Kittel's work after 1933, and it represents by far her most forthright recognition of the pernicious influence of Kittel's theological work on the Jewish question. Siegele-Wenschkewitz indicated to this author in an interview on 28 September 1982 that the television production 'Holocaust' created a new atmosphere in Germany. She believes the culpability of individuals such as Kittel could then be analyzed more forthrightly. It may also be significant that Siegele-Wenschkewitz produced this final article after her association with the theological faculty at Tübingen University had ended. It should be added that Siegele-Wenschkewitz' work on Kittel, despite what I believe to be weaknesses in emphasis and interpretation, provides access to an important topic long shunned by her colleagues.

18. For a summary of the controversy over Kittel which has developed in recent years, see Robert P. Ericksen, 'Zur Auseinandersetzung mit und um Gerhard Kittels Antisemitismus,' *Evangelische Theologie,* 43 (May/June 1983), pp.250-70.

19. Kittel wrote an expanded and revised version of *Meine Verteidigung* in November/December 1946 (cited below as MV², this manuscript is in the Tübingen University Archive). Here he expands and organizes his material more carefully, but does not significantly change his argument. He does add a general statement of German guilt,

but he admits little or no personal guilt (see pp.42-44).

20. MV, p.1. Note that Kittel refers to himself in the third person throughout this statement.

21. MV, p.5.

22. For example, the *Monatsschrift für Geschichte und Wissenschaft des Judentums* reviewed Kittel's *Jesus und die Juden* (Berlin, 1926) as follows: 'Scarcely anyone working in this area in recent years has become so correct toward Jewry as Kittel.' Kittel also quotes a favorable remark about his book, *Die Probleme des palästinischen Spätjudentums und das Urchristentum* (Stuttgart, 1926), but he gives no source. He also gives no date for the *Monatsschrift* quote above. See below for my argument that these books represent the high point in Kittel's tolerance toward Judaism.

23. MV, p.16. Kittel claims his speech was severely criticized in Nazi quarters for ignoring the Party, so he added references to the Party Program in the published version to prevent false issues from taking precedence over real ones.

24. MV, p.12.

25. MV, p.13.

26. MV, p.14. In support of his claim, Kittel quotes a favorable remark on *Die Judenfrage* from *Der Israelit* (1933, Nr. 4), as well as another favorable passage for which he gives no source.

27. MV, p.15.

28. MV, p.27.

29. This essay is printed in the 2nd and 3rd editions of *Die Judenfrage,* pp.101-13.

30. MV, p.17.

31. MV, p.18.

32. *Ibid.*

33. MV, p.19.

34. See Helmut Heiber's definitive study, *Walter Frank und sein Reichsinstitut für Geschichte des neuen Deutschlands* (Stuttgart, 1966). The same subject is treated with specific regard for the Jewish question in Max Weinreich.

35. Kittel contributed to seven of the nine volumes of the official journal, *Forschungen zur Judenfrage.* Walter Frank, the next highest contributor, had only five articles to his credit.

36. See Heiber, p.421.

37. Gerhard Kittel, 'Die Behandlung des Nichtjuden nach dem Talmud,' *Archiv für Judenfragen,* Heft 1, Group A1

(Berlin, 1943), pp.7-17.

38. This statement, a quotation from the *Völkischer Beobachter,* appears on the back page of *Forschungen zur Judenfrage,* vol. 8, as part of an advertisement for the nine volumes of the journal. It should be noted that the apparent contradiction in this statement was commonplace in Germany under National Socialism. The contradiction was resolved by defining 'truly free research' as research undistorted by the 'errors of perception' outside the Nazi framework of ideas.

39. The Preface in the 2nd and 3rd volumes of *Forschungen zur Judenfrage* confirms Streicher's participation at the corresponding annual conferences. For press reports, see P.C. 1, F6, in the Wiener Library.

40. Max Weinreich, p.98.

41. MV, p.20.

42. MV, p.6.

43. Siegele-Wenschkewitz points out that Kittel is in error with this statement; he actually joined the German Fatherland Party of Tirpitz and Kapp in 1917. See *Neutestamentliche Wissenschaft,* p.79.

44. MV, p.6.

45. These incidents are described in MV, p.7.

46. MV², pp.15, 50. This incident certainly raises questions, both as to how public the street actually was and why Kittel failed to recall this incident in his first defense statement.

47. This letter is in the *Partei Kanzlei* correspondence file, Berlin Document Center.

48. MV, pp.28-31. In MV², pp.13-14, Kittel adds that he was offered the *Rektorat* at Tübingen University in April 1933, i.e. one month before he joined the NSDAP. He cites his refusal of this offer as further proof he did not sell out.

49. MV, p.29-30.

50. MV², p.47-8.

51. MV, p.32.

52. MV, p.28. I judge the contents of the second lecture, 'Die Entstehung des Judentums,' somewhat differently. See below.

53. MV, p.32.

54. MV, pp.28-9. The two distorted articles appeared in *Die Bücherkunde* (1938) and *Schulungsbrief* (1939). The third article was in *Wille und Macht* (1940 or 1941).

55. MV, pp.26-7. The acts of 'resistance' described in this paragraph are related by Kittel on pp.26-7.

56. MV, p.27.

57. *Ibid.*

58. *Ibid.*

59. MV, pp.8-9.

60. For a discussion of this incident, see J. S. Conway, *The Nazi Persecution of the Churches, 1933-1945* (London, 1968).

61. MV, p.11.

62. MV, pp.35-7. The book referred to in no.1 is *Die Probleme des palästinischen Späjudentums und das Urchristentum* (Stuttgart, 1926).

63. MV, p.38.

64. MV, p.33.

65. *Ibid.*

66. This statement raises at least three questions. First, in an earlier passage Kittel claims he restricted himself to his own discipline all the time, not just after 1943. Secondly, his publications and speeches in 1943 and 1944 were some of his most polemical and the farthest removed from his theological roots (see below). Finally, Kittel does not explain why after 1943 God's assignment no longer applied.

67. MV, p.33.

68. MV, pp.33-4.

69. MV, p.33.

70. Weinreich, pp.217-18. The Kittel article referred to is 'Die Behandlung des Nichtjuden nach dem Talmud ,' *Archiv für Judenfragen,* vol. 1, Group A1 (Berlin, 1943), pp.7-17. This journal was itself a Goebbels publication. Weinreich identifies the second article as, 'Jews as Soldiers,' *Deutscher Wochendienst* (10 Nov. 1944).

71. MV, pp.38-40. In MV² Kittel raises thirteen questions, still along these lines. See pp.73-5.

72. MV, p.40.

73. MV², p.1.

74. MV², p.1-2.

75. MV², p.7.

76. MV², p.58.

77. Kittel professes his unwillingness to hide anything (p.76), but I believe he conceals and distorts the full implications of his work between 1933 and 1945. The Christian intentions he posits here are more difficult to detect in his speeches and publications of that period.

78. MV², p.8.
79. MV², p.67.
80. MV², p.40.
81. MV², p.68-9.
82. MV², p.75.
83. MV, p.8.
84. See Siegele-Wenschkewitz, *Neutestamentliche Wissenschaft*, pp.47-9. In 1917 Kittel joined the theological faculty at Leipzig, where his father held a chair in Old Testament and was soon to be *Rektor*.
85. See, for example, Gerhard Kittel, *Jesus und die Juden* (Berlin, 1926). The series was called, *Stimmen aus der deutschen christlichen Studentenbewegung*. For the relation between *völkisch* modes of thought and the neo-conservative reaction, see George L. Mosse, *The Crisis of German Ideology: Intellectual Origins of the Third Reich* (New York, 1964).
86. Rudolf Kittel, *Leipziger Akademische Reden zum Kriegsende* (Leipzig, 1919), pp.1-10, 16-24.
87. Stuttgart, 1930.
88. One incident in Rudolf Kittel's career possibly presaged his son's later entanglement in the Jewish question. Rudolf was called as an expert witness in a trial brought by a German Jewish organization against Theodor Fritsch and his antisemitic book, *Mein Beweismaterial gegen Jahwe*. Kittel later decided to publish his testimony, which appeared as *Judenfeindschaft oder Gotteslästerung* (Leipzig, 1914). The legal case concerned blasphemy, with Fritsch arguing that Jahwe and the God of the modern Jews were not the same. Kittel agreed that the concept of Jahwe had changed over the years, but he added that Fritsch's scholarship was defective. He recommended against criminal punishment, however, arguing that ridicule of Fritsch's position would be a more effective sanction (see p.79). Also on the positive side, Kittel published with this testimony a statement in praise of Jewish efforts in the war (written in October 1914). This public spirit confirmed Jewish commitment to the German community, he wrote. But Kittel also advised Jews that some elements in their Talmud were objectionable, and that this might be an appropriate time for divesting their religious literature of such passages (see pp.88-

9). In the light of Gerhard's later willingness to attack the Jewish faith, this apparent ambiguity in his father's attitude towards Jews may be of significance. It is impossible to know whether the father would have behaved as did the son, if placed in similar circumstances after 1933. The ambiguity of this incident is too complete. The incident may suggest, however, that conservative German Protestants found it difficult to fully accept the autonomy and worth of Judaism.
89. See Fritz Ringer, *The Decline of the German Mandarins: The German Academic Community, 1890-1933* (Cambridge, Mass., 1969), for those factors which prepared German academics in general for an acceptance of the radical right.
90. MV, p.34.
91. It would have spared a great deal of confusion if Christians had read Rosenberg's definition of 'Positive Christianity,' i.e. Christianity cleansed of its Jewish roots. On the other hand, church membership and attendance did increase markedly in the first months of the Hitler regime (see Walter Birnbaum, *Zeuge meiner Zeit: Aussengen zu 1912 bis 1972* [Göttingen, 1973], pp.127-32, for stress on this point). Part of the increase probably resulted from Party attempts to influence the church elections of 1933, but presumably this does not entirely explain the phenomenon.
92. 'Deutsche Wissenschaft und Judenfrage. "Forschungsabteilung Judenfrage" des Reichsinstituts Geschichte des neuen Deutschlands eröffnet,' *Völkischer Beobachter*, 325. Ausgabe, 49. Jahrgang (20 Nov. 1936), Munich edition, p.1.
93. Quoted in Frank's *Vorbemerkung* in *Forschungen zur Judenfrage*, vol. III, 2nd ed. (Hamburg, 1943), p.7.
94. Some confusion centers around this speech. It was delivered by the experimental physicist and disciple of Lenard, Rudolf Tomaschek, with the comment that he was 'representing... Professor Philip Lenard.' The *New York Times* interpreted this to mean that Lenard was unable to attend the conferenece, so his speech was read for him. See 'Reich Science wars on "Jewish Spirit",' *New York Times* (22 Nov.

1936), on file in the Wiener Library, P.C.1, F.8. But the speech was not subsequently published in the first volume of *Forschungen zur Judenfrage,* the only speech of the conference not reproduced. Helmut Heiber sheds some light by noting that Tomaschek delivered the same speech to students in Berlin a month later with notable lack of success. The *Berliner Tageblatt* cautiously reported that such ideas had not yet fully broken through to German students. Perhaps it was then recognized as too questionable to publish (see Heiber, p.421). Whether or not the speech was written by Lenard or Tomaschek is unclear. Alan Beyerchen's study of Lenard, *Scientists under Hitler: Politics and the Physics Community in the Third Reich* (New Haven, 1977), does not touch upon this incident.

95. For press reports, see P.C.1, F.8 in the Wiener Library.

96. See above. The concept of a philosophical difference, as opposed to a merely personal rivalry, between the Frank and Rosenberg organizations is somewhat undercut by the strange career of Wilhelm Grau. He was the first director of Frank's *Forschungsabteilung Judenfrage,* but after a quarrel with Frank he was released and eventually became director of Rosenberg's institute in Frankfurt (Weinreich, p.101). Adding to the confusion is the assertion by Helmut Heiber that Grau represented a religious, Christian approach to antisemitism, an approach supposedly anathema to Rosenberg. Heiber notes that Grau and Kittel were quite close, for both were concerned with 'the saving of the endangered Old Testament.' See Heiber, p.1000.

97. Heiber, pp.463, 626-7, 685, 1000, 1006.

98. Weinreich, p.43.

99. Kittel wrote on 18 March 1940 to Herman Preus, 'Here in the big city we are often homesick for Tübingen and our home there. However, we have here no permanent state, but seek the future.' It is true that Lutherans often use this quotation in difficult circumstances to indicate acceptance of Luther's dictum that the earthly kingdom is to be endured and the heavenly kingdom joyously awaited. But in this case Kittel seems to intend an ironic twist, looking foward to his future in Tübingen as well as in heaven. In any case, the Kittels returned to their home in Tübingen in April 1943.

100. 'Further in the same letter to Preus, Kittel writes, 'Above all the move has been difficult for my wife. But there are certain important tasks here in the small Lutheran diaspora in Austria etc. I was urgently requested to come here especially from the church side. You perhaps know that Austria was once 90 per cent Protestant, and it was only in the Counter-reformation through the Jesuits that it became almost completely Catholic again.' In MV² Kittel addresses directly the charge that his position in Vienna was a reward for services. He claims that he turned down a permanent call to Vienna but agreed to fill the chair on a temporary basis, especially because this would help to thwart the hopes of *Deutsche Christen,* who anticipated filling the chair with one of their own. A letter from Bishop May of Vienna appears to corroborate this claim. See pp.17-18, 70-2.

101. For a description of these events I have relied upon J. R. C. Wright, 'The Political Attitudes of the German Protestant Leadership, November 1918-July 1933,' (a doctoral dissertation, Merton College, Oxford, 1969), pp.331-47. Wright's work has subsequently been published as, *Above Parties: The Political Attitudes of the German Protestant Church Leadership 1918-1933* (Oxford, 1977), and in more substantial form as, *'Ueber den Parteien' Die politische Haltung der evangelischen Kirchenführer 1918-1933* (Göttingen, 1977). See also J. S. Conway, *The Nazi Persecution of the Churches, 1933-45* (London, 1968), pp. 43-4.

102. Ernst Wolf, *Kirche im Widerstand? Protestantische Opposition in der Klammer der Zweireichlehre* (Munich, 1965), pp.16-19. This originated as a speech given 28 March 1965 at the *Katholische Akademie in Bayern* on the theme, 'Gewissen und totalitärer Staat. Ethische Fragen des Widerstandes.'

103. Conway, p.52.

104. Quoted in Wolf, p.102.

105. See I Cor. 9:20-3.

106. MV, p.8.

107. *Ibid.*

108. See Conway, or Ernst Wolf, *Barmen. Kirche zwischen Versuchung und Gnade,* 2nd ed. (Munich, 1970).

109. In 1947 Kittel described his attitude towards Martin Niemöller, a description which indirectly suggests the outlines of his attitude before 1945. In the post-war years Niemöller argued that the church become more politically responsible, e.g. that it oppose the cold war animosities directed towards Russia. In a letter to Preus dated 17 March 1947, Kittle observes, 'Certainly he was very brave in the time of persecution. But it appears that he is not a man for the quiet, ordered and steady building up of the church. One considers him undisciplined and impetuous.' Kittel adds that Niemöller fell too much under the non-Lutheran influence of Barth. The same words almost certainly might have crossed Kittel's lips ten years earlier, this time criticizing the brave U-Boat officer who was too impulsive and undisciplined in his attitude towards the *Führer* and too influenced by Barth. Kittel was so thoroughly respectful of authority that he could only recognize the radical implications of Christian faith after the fact, never in the present. His instincts and his Lutheran orthodoxy could never let him side with rebels.

110. Edward Yarnall Hartshorne, Jr., *The German Universities and National Socialism* (London, 1937), p.16. Beyerchen substantiates this assumption of a heavy toll with his study of the physics community.

111. Kittel's Tübingen colleague in philosophy, Max Wundt, provides a good example. In 'Das Judentum in der Philosophie,' *Forschungen zur Judenfrage,* vol. II (Hamburg, 1937), pp.75-87, Wundt considers three Jews, Philov of Alexandria, Moses Maimonides, and Baruch Spinoza, who were traditionally thought to have been important in the transmission of Greek Platonism to German neo-Platonism. But that did not conform to Nazi ideology. Fortunately, Wundt was able to discover that they were not really significant after all. Along the way, Wundt explains the apparent success of the average Jew in intellectual endeavors. Jewish statelessness forced Jews to adapt to the culture in which they found themselves.

The resulting lack of roots gave them an objectivity through which they could quickly grasp ideas, but only on a superficial level. Wundt insisted they were quite incapable of a depth of understanding. Heiber notes that the University of Tübingen boasted three representatives to the *Forschungsabteilung Judenfrage,* Wundt, Kittel and Karl Georg Kuhn. The Tübingen *Rektor* and the Nazi press exulted in the 'pioneer role of the Neckar city [Tübingen] in the fight of science against Jewry.' Quoted in Heiber, p.453, from the *Tübingen Chronik* (24 January 1939).

112. See my analysis below.

113. Gerhard Kittel, *Die Judenfrage* (Stuttgart, 1933), pp.46, 61-2.

114. Hartshorne notes a book on this topic by Eduard Spranger, *Der Sinn der Voraussetzungslosigkeit in der Geisteswissenschaft* (Berlin, 1929).

115. Hartshorne, pp.105-6.

116. Hans-Joachim Kraus, *Geschichte der historisch-kritischen Erforschung des Alten Testaments von der Reformation bis zur Gegenwart* (Neukirchen Kreis Moers, 1956), p.351.

117. Gerhard Kittel, *Jesus und die Rabbinen* (Berlin, 1914), pp.4-5.

118. *Ibid.,* p.11.

119. The entrance lecture, delivered on 28 Oct. 1926 at the University of Tübingen, was published as *Urchristentum, Spätjudentum, Hellenismus Akademische Antrittsvorlesung* (Stuttgart, 1926).

120. Gerhard Kittel, *Die Probleme des palästinischen Spätjudentums und das Urchristentum* (Stuttgart, 1926), p.88. Hereinafter cited as DP.

121. DP, p.92.

122. DP, pp.89-90. It is ironic that Kittel's Tübingen colleague, Max Wundt, cited this very point in his article mentioned above (footnote 93) to prove the inferiority of Jewish intellectual thought. God proclaimed Jewish dogma, so Jews did not need to think.

123. DP, pp.90, 125.

124. DP, p.125, footnote 3.

125. DP, p.96.

126. DP, pp.90-1.

127. DP, p.95.

128. DP, p.140.

129. Gerhard Kittel, *Jesus und die Juden* (Berlin, 1926), p.4. This passage has attracted much attention. Kittel himself

cites it in MV², p.10, in an effort to show the continuity of his work before and after 1933. Then Martin Rese, apparently having found it in MV², uses it to suggest the possibility of antisemitism in Kittel prior to 1933 (p.564). Finally, Siegele-Wenschkewitz dismisses the significance of the passage and argues an almost total break in Kittel's interpretation of Judaism after 1933. I prefer Siegele-Wenschkewitz' position, but think it too extreme. Certainly Kittel exhibited some insensitivity and prejudice prior to 1933, and this may help explain his later course; but the change in 1933 was dramatic.

130. *Jesus und die Juden*, p.5.
131. Robert Raphael Geis and Hans-Joachim Kraus, eds., *Versuche des Verstehens. Dokumente jüdisch-christlicher Begegnung aus der Jahren 1918-1933* (Munich, 1966), p.185.
132. *Ibid.*, pp.185-6.
133. For an indication of this changed attitude, see *Event*, vol. 12, no.2 (Scarsdale, N.Y., Feb. 1972). This issue, a publication of the American Lutheran Church, centers on the theme, Christian and Jew, and it includes the statement, 'To love a man is to respect his freedom — including his freedom to say "no" to Christ.' See p.19. See also a special issue of *Evangelische Theologie*, vol. 42, no. 2 (March/April 1982), on the theme, 'Juden und Christen.'
134. Gerhard Kittel, 'Judentum und Christentum,' *Religion in Geschichte und Gegenwart*, vol. 3, 2nd ed (Tübingen, 1929), pp.491-4. Siegele-Wenschkewitz quotes extensively from this article, describing it as the 'summation' of twenty years work by Kittel. See *Neutestamentliche Wissenschaft*, pp.71-8. Kittel was one of four scholars asked to prepare the entire article on Judaism found in RGG², vol. 3, pp.469-94. The first three sections were written by the Jewish scholars, Ismar Elbogen and Leo Baeck, and the Old Testament Theologian, Otto Eissfeldt.
135. Gerhard Kittel, *Die religiöse und die kirchliche Lage in Deutschland* (Leipzig, 1921), pp.4-7.
136. *Ibid.*, pp.16-17.
137. *Ibid.*, p.17.
138. *Ibid.*, p.20.

139. Kittel reports that after this speech Archbishop Söderblom came up to tell him that, although the service began in rain and gloom, when Kittel began to speak a ray of sunlight broke over him. Söderblom interpreted this as a sign of God's light returning through Kittel's words.
140. Herbert Loewe to Gerhard Kittel, 11 Aug. 1933, in the personality file on Kittel, Wiener Library.
141. Gerhard Kittel, *Die Judenfrage* (Stuttgart, 1933), p.8. Hereinafter cited as J.
142. J, p.8.
143. J, p.9.
144. J, p.12.
145. J, pp.10-12.
146. J, p.14. This quotation created a minor storm of criticism. In the second and third editions Kittel added the words, 'Furthermore, the whole idea is so absurd, that it is not worth the effort to waste many words in defense: it hardly requires a confirmation of the utterly unchristian nature of such a solution.' Max Weinreich makes a big issue of the original statement, ignoring this addition to the later versions. See Weinreich, p.42. Perhaps he only had access to the first edition.
147. J, pp.14-16.
148. J, p.24.
149. J, p.25.
150. J, p.26.
151. Kittel drew up this list of four alternatives on p.13.
152. J, p.34.
153. J, 2nd ed. (Stuttgart, 1933), p.35.
154. J, 1st ed., p.39.
155. J, pp.45-46.
156. J, p.46.
157. J, pp.46-7.
158. J, p.48.
159. J, p.50. ·
160. J, 2nd ed., p.54.
161. J, 1st ed., pp.57-60.
162. J, p.40.
163. J, pp.61-2.
164. J, p.69.
165. J, pp.36-7, 63-8.
166. J, p.66.
167. MV, pp.14-15. On 2 June 1933, the *Neues Tübinger Tagblatt*, the local National Socialist newspaper, complained that Kittel demanded tolerance for orthodox Jews and special 'guest' privileges for them. The review called his speech a scandal.

168. J, p.39.
169. J, 2nd ed., p.52. These quotations are exactly the same in the 3rd ed. (Stuttgart, 1934). The pagination in these two editions is the same throughout.
170. In a footnote to the 2nd edition, Kittel explains his more cautious statement about extermination (quoted in a footnote 127 above) as prompted by a colleague's review in the *Neue Zürcher Zeitung* (1 July 1933), which he quotes: 'Kittel rejects the pogrom. "To kill all Jews does not mean to master the situation." No, truly it does not. One does not need a professor of theology in order to establish that. But is it possible that a German writes this sentence without adding that to kill all the Jews would also be a little bit inhuman ... There are things which a person does not do because of his own determination. And I believe a German, member of the *Volk* to which we ascribe all nobility, cultivation, sincerity, graciousness, greatness and humanity, should be incapable of writing in this way. That Kittel is not incapable is no honor to him.' In the same footnote but in the 3rd edition, Kittel mentions a sentence by 'Benammi' in the *Jewish Chronicle* (London, 11 Aug. 1933): 'Hitler's revolution has been termed "the meanest revolution in history." Professor Kittel's book is the meanest handling of the Jewish question.' Kittel merely indicates his pride at being compared to Hitler: 'B. can hardly imagine what superb and distinguished praise this comparison is to a German in the year 1933, who is conscious of his *Volk* and of his devotion to his great *Führer*.'' See J, 3rd ed., footnote to p.14.
171. *Theologische Blätter*, 12. Jahrgang, 1933, no. 8, pp.148-50. This letter is reprinted in *Versuche des Verstehens*, pp.166-70. Jewish papers, e.g. the *Jüdische Rundschau* (No. 72) and *Israelitisches Familienblatt* (28 Sept. 1933), published parts of Buber's open letter and clearly supported him, though it should be noted that the *Israelitisches Familienblatt* also recommended that Kittel be read, for 'also many words of honest appreciation stand there for us.' For press coverage of this controversy, see the Kittel personality file, Wiener Library.
172. J, 2nd ed., p.87.

173. J, p.96.
174. J, pp.88-90.
175. J, p.90.
176. Kittel supports this mystical 'difference' idea with two references. The granddaughter of Franz Delitsch, a third-generation Jewish Christian who studied Hebrew together with Kittel, said when she read Hebrew, 'then generations wake up inside of me' (J, p.92). Secondly, Jakob Wassermann wrote *Alexander in Babylon* without ever having traveled there, but a well-traveled reader assumed he must have lived in the Near East a long time to have described the landscape so well. Wassermann added that the German landscape had always seemed foreign to him, though he grew up in it (J, 3rd ed., footnote 53).
177. This letter to Loewe is in the Kittel personality file, Wiener Library.
178. *Ibid.*
179. Richard Guttridge recently produced an important book, *The German Evangelical Church and the Jews, 1879-1950* (London, 1976). As a former student and friend of Kittel, he is somewhat kinder to Kittel than I am. He places *Die Judenfrage* in the context of the conflict over the Aryan Paragraph in the church (a point stressed also by Siegele-Wenschkewitz) and writes, '*Die Judenfrage*, whatever else it may have been, was a sincere and courageously independent contribution to the argument.' Gutteridge then uses words like 'unhappily' and 'regrettably' in reference to the most insensitive parts of the book, e.g. 'Regrettably, this sensitive and erudite scholar made considerable use of the jargon of current anti-semitism without embracing the vulgar racial standpoint of which he was in fact a formidable opponent, joining in the chorus of racial hatred or subscribing to the Nazi doctrine of the inherent inferiority of the Jewish character.' See pp.111-14 for Gutteridge's treatment of Kittel. I am indebted to Gutteridge for his stress on the good qualities of Kittel. However, I think a balanced account of Kittel must also stress his writings after 1933.
180. Gerhard Kittel, 'Die Entstehung des Judentums und die Entstehung der Judenfrage,' *Forschungen zur Judenfrage,* vol. 1 (Hamburg, 1936), pp.47-8.

Leonore Siegele-Wenschkewitz analyzes this speech in her most recent article on Kittel, 'Mitverantwortung und Schuld der Christen am Holocaust,' *Evangelische Theologie,* 42 (March/April 1982), pp.171-90. It is the only time she has gone beyond 1933 in her analysis, and it is the only time she has dealt forthrightly with Kittel's shared responsibility. Although the work is brief (and only about half the article is devoted to Kittel), I consider it her best contribution to an accurate interpretation of Kittel.

181. *Ibid.,* pp.48-50.
182. *Ibid.,* pp.51-6.
183. *Ibid.,* pp.56-8.
184. *Ibid.,* pp.61-2.
185. *Ibid.,* p.63.
186. Gerhard Kittel, 'Das Konnubium mit den Nicht-Juden im antiken Judentum,' *Forschungen zur Judenfrage,* vol. 2 (Hamburg, 1937), pp.30-62.
187. *Ibid.,* p.62.
188. *Ibid.,* p.30.
189. Gerhard Kittel, 'Die Abstammung der Mutter des Origenes. Die Geschichte eines genealogischen Irrtums,' *Forschungen zur Judenfrage,* vol. III, 2nd ed. (Hamburg, 1943), p.247.
190. Gerhard Kittel, 'Die ältesten jüdischen Bilder. Eine Aufgabe für die wissenschaftliche Gemeinschaftsarbeit,' *Forschungen zur Judenfrage,* vol. IV (Hamburg, 1940), pp.237-49.
191. Gerhard Kittel, 'Die ältesten Judenkarikaturen. Die "Trierer Terrakotten",' *Forschungen zur Judenfrage,* vol. IV (Hamburg, 1940), pp.254-8.
192. *Ibid.,* pp.258-9.
193. *Ibid,* p.259. In MV² Kittel actually singles out his work on these Jewish portraits and caricatures as an instance in which he was able to bring his Christian perspective into the field of anthropology. See below, note 201.
194. Eugen Fischer and Gerhard Kittel, 'Das antike Weltjudentum. Tatsachen, Texte, Bilder,' *Forschungen zur Judenfrage,* vol. 7 (Hamburg, 1943), pp.10-11.
195. *Ibid.,* pp.15-92. Topic headings in this section include, 'Racial Purity and Racial Mixture,' 'The Assimilationist Jew,' 'The Business Jew,' 'Actual and Falsified Privileges,' and 'The Enemy of Humanity,' among others.
196. See DP, p.95.

197. Fischer and Kittel, p.113.
198. *Ibid.,* p.160.
199. *Ibid.,* pp.167-219. Albright focuses his attack on Kittel on this book, condemning it as unscientific and dismissing the Trier figures as obvious forgeries. See pp.239-40.
200. Gerhard Kittel, 'Die Ausbreitung des Judentums bis zum Beginn des Mittelalters,' *Forschungen zur Judenfrage,* vol. 5 (Hamburg, 1941), pp.290-310. Heiber reports that Kittel received his first payment for this commissioned work in 1938, but that he never got beyond a brief sketch of the intended project. See p.463.
201. The discrepancy between Kittel's work in *Forschungen zur Judenfrage* and his self-serving defense in MV² seems especially acute. For example, he writes of his work on the Trier caricatures, 'There was a question whether it was at all possible to offer to anthropologists and archaeologists exact, historically tangible material... The NS propaganda began to take possession of the Trier pieces and publicize them in the sense of the *Stürmer* caricatures, e.g. in the *Völkischer Beobachter.* Kittel performed the singular service of pulling the rug out from under this unworthy and ridiculous practice... Thereby Kittel removed the Trier pieces from the isolation in which they appeared to stand up until then, and for the first time he brought them under serious scientific discussion.' MV², pp.36-7.
202. Gerhard Kittel, *Die historischen Voraussetzungen der Jüdischen Rassenmischung* (Hamburg, 1939), pp.40-1.
203. *Ibid.,* p.43.
204. See Weinreich, pp.215-16.
205. See MV, p.27. Kittel received this news from his son in early 1943, but he may have written his article before that.
206. Gerhard Kittel, 'Die Behandlung des Nichtjuden nach dem Talmud,' *Archiv für Judenfragen,* vol. 1, Group A1 (Berlin, 1943), p.7.
207. *Ibid.,* p.11. The reference is to Mishna, Sanh. 9:2.
208. *Ibid.,* pp.15-16.
209. MV, pp. 28-9.
210. Gerhard Kittel, 'Die Entstehung des Judentums' (a lecture delivered at the University of Vienna, 22 March 1943), p.5. I found a copy of this lecture at the theological library, University of

Tübingen.
211. *Ibid.*, pp.2-3.
212. *Ibid.*, pp.8-9.
213. *Ibid.*, pp.13-14.
214. MV, p.27. See above.
215. How the Jews could manage to take over the world, with a population base so racially decomposed it would destroy any other *Volk,* is a contradiction Kittel and his antisemitic colleagues never adequately resolved.
216. Gerhard Kittel, 'Das Rassenproblem der Spätantike und das Frühchristentum' (a lecture, University of Vienna, 15 June 1944), pp.1, 4-5. I saw this lecture in the theological library, University of Tübingen.
217. See Gerhard Kittel, *Dürfen wir dem Neuen Testament trauen? Die Geschichte des Neuen Testamentes* (Stuttgart, 1939), and *Dichter, Bibel und Bibelrevision* (Leipzig, 1939).
218. Gerhard Kittel, 'Adolf Schlatter, Gedankenrede,' *Beiträge zur Förderung christlicher Theologie,* 40. Band, 1. Heft (1939), pp.16-30.
219. William Foxwell Albright, *History, Archaeology and Christian Humanism* (New York, 1964), p.230.
220. *Ibid.*, p.229.
221. William Foxwell Albright, 'The War in Europe and the Future of Biblical Studies,' in Harold R. Willoughby, ed., *The Study of the Bible Today and Tomorrow* (Chicago, 1947), p.165.
222. Albright, *History,* pp.50-61.
223. This is quoted from one of three testimonials which Kittel included in a letter to Herman Preus, 10 Nov. 1946.
224. This statement by Walter Rey of 27 Dec. 1946, is one of several quoted by the Swiss Professor Albert Debrunner in a document he prepared to defend Kittel, 'Professor Gerhard Kittel und die Judenfrage.' Preus received a copy of this document in 1947. See Debrunner, p.5.
225. Quoted by Debrunner, p.8.
226. Quoted by Debrunner, p.3.
227. Quoted by Debrunner, p.4.
228. Wilhelm Dittman, an 'Erklärung' written 13 Feb. 1947. This document is in the Preus file.
229. This quotation is from a group of ten statements circulated on Kittel's behalf and in the possession of Preus. Debrunner also quotes from Frl. Tugenhat's statement, but at less length.
230. Gutteridge, fn. 67, p.145.
231. Leonore Siegele-Wenschkewitz to this author, 7 Aug. 1979. See also Siegele-Wenschkewitz, 'Mitverantwortung und Schuld der Christen am Holocaust,' *Evangelische Theologie,* 42 (1982), 171-90, for a continuation of this theme.
232. See Debrunner, pp.3-5.
233. In an interview on 28 Sept. 1982, Siegele-Wenschkewitz agreed with this interpretation and also speculated that, if he had lived, he would have ultimately worked his way back into a place of honor in the eyes of his colleagues.
234. Kittel followed in his father's career, published in a series edited by his father, and received an appointment to his father's university (see above, p.28), but he possibly never achieved the stature of his father. This is a view expressed to this author by more than one theologian in Germany, sometimes with the additional suggestion that the younger Kittel's ambition was spurred by the comparison.
235. After the first years of the Third Reich, more theological students sympathized with the Confessing Church than the *Deutsch Christen.* During the war years this was particularly true.
236. Siegele-Wenschkewitz, *Neutestamentliche Wissenschaft,* p.31.
237. We can probably assume that Kittel opposed genocide; the alternative is almost impossible to imagine. His shock and generalized sense of guilt expressed in 1946 must have been a genuine reaction to the full scope of the 'final solution' as news emerged. But there is no evidence to support this conclusion beyond Kittel's own testimony and that of his children. (See MV², p.1 and Siegele-Wenschkewitz, *Neutestamentliche Wissenschaft, p.110,* note 104). Since Kittel admits knowing of Jewish murders by early 1943, one wishes he would have attacked Jews less harshly and endorsed National Socialism less warmly afterwards.
238. A letter from Elisabeth Kittel to N. M. MacLeod, 4 June 1946. MacLeod sent a copy of this letter on to Preus at Frau Kittel's request.
239. These men included Roger F. C. Nikel, E. T. Bachmann, Norman MacLeod, Jr., and F. Helleger.

240. Kittel to Preus, 17 March 1947.
241. The letters of endorsement came from Arthur D. Nock and Henry J. Cadbury, both of Harvard, and Ernest C. Colwell, President of the University of Chicago. Carl H. Kraeling of Yale and Morton S. Enslin of Crozer Theological Seminary declined.
242. Kittel to Preus, 23 Nov. 1947 and 13 Feb. 1948.
243. Kittel to Preus, 17 March 1947.
244. Kittel to Preus, 2 Nov. 1946 and 10 Nov. 1946.
245. Kittel to Preus, 10 May 1947.
246. Frau Kittel to Mrs. Preus, 31 July 1947.
247. Theo Preiss to C. H. Dodd, 12 Oct. 1945.
248. Kittel to Preus, 10 Nov. 1946. See also Debrunner, p.4.
249. Preiss to Dodd, 12 Oct. 1945.
250. Kittel to Preus, 13 Feb. 1948.
251. *Ibid.*
252. See Siegele-Wenschkewitz, *Neutestamentliche Wissenschaft*, p.50, for a brief account of Kittel's imprisonment and death.

CHAPTER III

1. *Kürschners Deutscher Gelehrten-Kalendar auf das jahr 1954*, 8th ed. (Berlin, 1954).
2. Franz Lau, ed., *Festgabe für Paul Althaus* (Berlin, 1958), p.viii.
3. Althaus' bibliography through 1957, compiled by Wenzel Lhoff, is found in Walter Künneth and Wilfried Joest, eds., *Dank an Paul Althaus. Eine Festgabe zum 70. Geburtstag* (Gütersloh, 1958), pp.245-72. It lists publications on an annual basis beginning in 1911, and shows more than a dozen articles and books per year in some of the later years. Hans Grass provides a bibliography for the years 1958-66 in 'Die Theologie von Paul Althaus,' *Neue Zeitschrift für Systematische Theologie*, 8 (1966), pp.237-41.
4. Bishop Wurm's comment on the election, dated 30 May 1933, is quoted in Gerhard Schäfer, *Die Evangelische Landeskirche in Württemberg und der Nationalsozialismus*, vol. 2 (Stuttgart, 1972), p.107.
5. See, for example. the comments of his colleague, Wolfgang Trillhaas, in *Aufgehobene Vergangenheit. Aus meinem Leben* (Göttingen, 1976), pp.85-6. Trillhaas criticizes Althaus' theology as lacking in philosophical rigor or understanding, in comparison to Hirsch, for example. But Trillhaas

goes on to stress his full lecture halls and confident success. This corresponds to much other testimony and seems to be a general opinion.
6. See Wolfgang Tilgner, *Volksnomostheologie und Schöpfungsglaube. Ein Beitrag zur Geschichte des Kirchenkampfes. Arbeiten zur Geschichte des Kirchenkampfes*, vol. 16 (Göttingen, 1966), p.180. For an example of Althaus' conservative Lutheran principles, see Paul Althaus, 'Um die lutherische Kirche Deutschlands!', *Allgemeine Evangelische-Lutherische Kirchen-Zeitung*, vol. 67, no. 37 (14 May 1934), pp.868-77.
7. Emanuel Hirsch, *Die Auferstehungsgeschichten und der christliche Glaube* (Tübingen, 1940).
8. Paul Althaus, 'Die Wahrheit des kirchlichen Osterglaubens. Einspruch gegen Emanuel Hirsch,' *Beiträge zur Förderung christlicher Theologie*, vol. 49, No. 2, p.5.
9. *Ibid.*, pp.16-20.
10. *Ibid.*, p.23.
11. *Ibid.*, pp.26-30, 39-40.
12. *Ibid.*, p.80. Althaus refused to let this issue die. He even took the occasion of a *Festschrift* honoring Hirsch's seventy-fifth birthday to redirect his attack. See Paul Althaus, 'Christologisches. Fragen an Emanuel Hirsch,' in Hayo Gerdes, ed., *Wahrheit und Glaube. Festschrift an Emanuel Hirsch* (Itzehoe, 1963).
13. See Chapter I.
14. Paul Althaus, *The So-Called Kerygma and the Historical Jesus*, David Cairns, tr. (Edinburgh, 1959), p.17. First published as, *Das sogennante Kerygma und der historische Jesus; Zur Kritik der heutigen Kerygma-Theologie* (Gütersloh, 1958).
15. *Ibid.*, p.89.
16. Paul Althaus, 'Zum Gedächtnis der abgerufenen Herausgeber der Beiträge', *Beiträge zur Förderung christlicher Theologie*, vol. 40, no. 1 (1938), p.14. In another article in the same issue Althaus criticizes *Biblizismus* for giving too much authority to the Bible in relation to the Holy Spirit and history. See 'Adolf Schlatters Gabe an die systematische Theologie,' pp.37-8.
17. Paul Althaus, *Die deutsche Stunde der Kirche*, 3rd ed. (Göttingen, 1934), pp.55-60. The nature of Althaus' position in Lodz is unclear, but he probably served the civilian population. Although Lodz is in Poland, the middle and upper classes in this city were largely German, and the German language was widely used. German forces occupied the city during the war, includ-

ing the period during which Althaus
was there.
18. *Ibid.*, p.18.
19. Paul Althaus, *Obrigkeit und Führertum* (Gütersloh, 1936), p.51.
20. *Ibid.*, p.52.
21. Julius Leutheuser and Erich Fascher, *Ein theologisches Missverständnis. Unsere Antwort an Paul Althaus,* 2nd ed. (Weimer, n.d.), p.7.
22. Paul Althaus, *Kirche und Volkstum. Der völkische Wille im Lichte des Evangeliums* (Gütersloh, 1928), pp.5-12.
23. *Ibid.*, p.24.
24. This view was expressed, for example, by Hermann Dörries, Emeritus Professor of Church History at Göttingen, in an interview on 14 Oct. 1972.
25. *Die deutsche Stunde der Kirche,* p.5.
26. *Ibid.*
27. *Ibid.*, p.12. This passage is from Acts 17:23.
28. *Ibid.*, p.19.
29. Paul Althaus, *Kirche und Staat nach lutherische Lehre* (Leipzig, 1935), p.29.
30. See Ernst Wolf, *Barmen. Kirche zwischen Versuchung und Gnade,* 2nd ed. (Munich, 1970). See also Robert P. Ericksen, 'The Barmen Synod and its Declaration: A Historical Synopsis,' in Hubert G. Locke, ed. *The Church Confronts the Nazis Barmen, Then and Now,* (New York, 1984).
31. This document took its name from a theological statement of 1524. See Wolf, p.99. Four of the eight signators were from Ansbach or its environs. Hence they named themselves the 'Ansbacher Circle' and borrowed the centuries-old title for their statement. I found references to this group in the Paul Althaus Papers, hereinafter cited as PAP. These papers were graciously shown to me by Althaus' son, Pastor Gerhard Althaus.
32. Gerhard Niemöller, *Die erste Bekenntnissynode der Deutschen Evangelischen Kirche zu Barmen,* vol. 1 (Göttingen, 1959), p.143.
33. See *Evanglieum im Dritten Reich,* no. 25 (1 July 1934). The entire article is reprinted in Niemöller, p.143. The layout of it includes a centrally-placed poem by Baldur von Schirach, the Nazi youth leader, entitled, 'Christus.'
39. See Niemöller, p.142. The entire *Ansbacher Ratschlag* is reprinted here.
35. *Ibid.*, p.145.
36. *Ibid.*
37. *Ibid.*, p.146.
38. See *Junge Kirche,* 18 (22.9.34). Reference to this article appears in Niemöller, p.151.
39. Asmussen's article is quoted in full in

Niemöller, p.149.
40. Der Dekan des Ev. Luth. Kirchenbezirks München 1, to Paul Althaus, 12.6.34, in PAP. Please note that document dates follow the European form, day-month-year.
41. Dr. Schweitzer, Wustermarck, to Paul Althaus, 29.6.34 and 5.7.34, in PAP.
42. Heinrich Benckert, Schönow (Neumarck), to Paul Althaus, 3.7.34, in PAP.
43. Niemöller, p.149.
44. For example, Schweitzer to Althaus, 5.7.34, in PAP.
45. Paul Althaus to Pastor Henn, 11.6..64, in PAP. Note that while Althaus tries to establish his distance from the *Ansbacher Ratschlag,* he does not claim to have withdrawn his signature.
46. Paul Althaus, 'Gedanken zur "Theologischen Erklärung" der Barmer Erkenntnissynode,' *Korrespondenzblatt für die evangelisch-lutherischen Geistlichen in Bayern,* 28 (9.7.34). This statement is discussed in Niemöller, pp.168-70.
47. *Ibid.*, p.169.
48. See Wolf.
49. Niemöller, pp.169-70.
50. Quoted in Wolf, p.39.
51. *Ibid.*
52. *Ibid.*, pp.39-40.
53. Julius Leutheuser, *Der Heiland in der Geschichte der Deutschen, oder Der Nationalsozialismus, vom Evangelium aus gesehen* (Weimar, 1933), p.5.
54. *Ibid.*, pp.10-15.
55. Julius Leutheuser, *Die deutsche Christusgemeinde und ihre Gegner. Eine Antwort an Herrn Pfarrer Ernst Otto und die lutherische Bekenntnisgemeinschaft in Thüringen* (Weimar, n.d.), pp.18-19. Note that the arguments show Leutheuser's debt to liberal theology. He reinterprets Scripture freely to make it relevant to the present situation.
56. Siegfried Leffler, *Christus im Dritten Reich der Deutschen. Wesen, Weg und Ziel der Kirchenbewegung 'Deutsche Christen'* (Weimar, n.d., foreword signed in 1935), pp.13-18.
57. *Ibid.*, pp.19-23.
58. *Ibid.*, pp.24-5.
59. *Ibid.*, p.75.
60. *Ibid.*, p.34.
61. *Ibid.*, p.47.
62. *Ibid.*, p.103.
63. *Die deutsche Stunde der Kirche,* p.8.
64. Paul Althaus, *Christus und die deutsche Seele* (Gütersloh, 1934), p.5.
65. *Ibid.*, pp.7-16.
66. *Ibid.*, pp.22-3.
67. *Ibid.*, pp.24-6.
68. *Ibid.*, pp.27-9.

69. For Althaus' critique of Hauer, see Paul Althaus, 'Die Frage nach der Schuld im Deutschglauben. Zur Auseinandersetzung mit Wilhelm Hauer,' *Allgmeine Evangelisch-Lutherische Kirchenzeitung*, vol. 68, no. 20 (17 May 1935), pp.458-66.
70. *Christus . . .*, pp.30, 33.
71. Paul Althaus, *Politisches Christentum. Ein Wort über die Thüringer 'Deutscher Christen'* (Leipzig, 1935), p.2. Hereinafter cited as PC, this work was published as vol. 5 of *Theologie Militans*.
72. PC, p.6. Quoted from Julius Leutheuser, *Die deutsche Christusgemeinde*, 3rd ed. (Weimar, 1935), p.4.
73. PC, pp.7-8.
74. PC, p.9.
75. PC, p.12.
76. PC, p.9.
77. PC, p.14.
78. PC, pp.14-16.
79. PC, p.19.
80. PC, p.22.
81. PC, pp.27-31.
82. Julius Leutheuser and Erich Fascher, *Ein theologisches Missverständnis. Unsere Antwort an Paul Althaus*, 2nd ed. (Weimar, n.d.), pp.3-5.
83. *Ibid.*, pp.5-6.
84. *Ibid.*, p.10.
85. *Ibid.*, pp.11-13.
86. *Ibid.*, pp.22-8.
87. *Ibid.*, p.37.
88. Bethge outlined these events in a lecture on the *Kirchenkampf,* 24 July 1979, at the Vancouver School of Theology, Vancouver, B.C.
89. Paul Althaus, 'Kirche, Volk und Staat,' in Eugen Gerstenmeier, ed., *Kirche, Volk und Staat* (Berlin, 1937), p.29.
90. *Ibid.*, p.30.
91. *Ibid.*
92. *Ibid.*, p.31.
93. *Ibid.*, p.24.
94. Paul Althaus, 'Christentum, Krieg und Frieden,' in Eugen Gerstenmeier, ed., *Kirche, Volk und Staat* (Berlin, 1937), pp.176-9.
95. *Ibid.*, pp.179-82.
96. Paul Althaus, *Verantwortung und Schuld der Kirche* (Berlin, 1937), p.11.
97. *Ibid.*, p.13.
98. *Ibid.*, p.14.
99. *Ibid.*
100. See *ibid.*, p.3.
101. Paul Althaus to Bishop Marahrens, 15.9.33, in *Landeskirchliches Archiv* Hanover, L2, 4a, Bd. 1.
102. *Ibid.* In an interview of 19.5.73, Klaus Scholder told me of similar correspondence between Althaus and Hirsch, in which the former expresses his disillusionment but also his unwillingness to break ranks publicly with Hirsch or

with the National Socialist movement. Scholder also quotes Althaus' advice to Bishop Meiser in the *Reichs* bishop election of 1933: 'I see no other way than this: to stand for Bodelschwingh.' See Klaus Scholder, *Die Kirche und das Dritte Reiche. Band I: Vorgeschichte und Zeit der Illusionen 1918-1934* (Berlin, 1977), p.440.
103. Bodelschwingh wrote to express his thanks for Althaus' 'faithful participation in the recent struggle.' See F. v. Bodelschwingh to Paul Althaus, 12.7.33, in PAP.
104. Interview with Pastor Gerhard Althaus, 30.9.82.
105. See *Staatskommissar für das Gesundheitswesen, Staatsministerium des Innern,* to Paul Althaus, 4.8.33. This letter forbids Althaus to write or speak on subjects dealing with 'racial hygiene.' Paul Althaus replied in a 3-page letter requesting reconsideration of the ban in light of his professional concern as a systematic theologian with questions of Christian ethics. See Paul Althaus to *Staatskommissar . . .* Dr. Schultze, München, 9.8.33. Both letters are in PAP.
106. Interview with Gerhard Althaus, 30.9.82.
107. Paul Althaus, 'Adolf Schlatter's Gabe an die systematische Theologie,' *Beiträge zur Förderung christlicher Theologie*, vol. 40, no. 1 (1938), p.32.
108. *Ibid.*, p.33. Also note Wolfgang Tilgner's suggestion that Althaus tried to build a Lutheran alternative to Roman Catholic natural theology. See Tilgner, pp.179-80.
109. See, for example, *Die deutsche Stunde der Kirche*, pp.10, 14.
110. After the war Althaus published a two-volume textbook on dogmatics, *Die christliche Wahrheit. Lehrbuch der Dogmatik* (Gütersloh, 1947, 1948). A second edition of both volumes appeared in 1949, and a third in 1952. Pastor Enno Haase, who studied theology at Göttingen from 1946 to 1950, remembers studying *Ur-Offenbarung* from this text, and he describes it as the only text on dogmatics available at the time. Interview with Pastor Haase, Duderstadt, 25.8.82.
111. Grass, p.236.
112. *Ibid.*
113. As reprinted in Niemöller, pp.144-45.
114. See 'Gedanken zur "Theologischen Erklärung" der Barmer Bekenntnissynode,' as reprinted in Niemöller, p.169.
115. *Ibid.*
116. Paul Althaus, *Theologie der Ordnungen* (Gütersloh, 1934), p.7. Hereinafter

cited as TO.
117. TO, p.23.
118. TO, p.9.
119. TO, pp.13-14.
120. TO, p.17.
121. TO, p.15.
122. TO, pp.26-30.
123. TO, p.39.
124. Paul Althaus, *Völker vor und nach Christus* (Leipzig, 1937), p.4. Hereinafter cited as VC.
125. Quoted in Tilgner, p.181.
126. VC, pp.3-5. This lecture was presented at the University of Leipzig, 28 May 1937, and published as no. 14 in *Theologie Militans,* a series in which Althaus served as an editor.
127. VC, p.6.
128. VC, p.7.
129. VC, pp.8, 10-11.
130. VC, p.8.
131. VC, pp.13, 19.
132. Paul Althaus, 'Luthers Lehre von den beiden Reichen im Feuer der Kritik,' in *Um die Wahrheit des Evangeliums. Aufsätze und Vorträge* (Stuttgart, 1962), pp.265-71.
133. Althaus expressed this concern as early as 1916 (see *Die deutsche Stunde der Kirche,* pp.55-60). It also was the main theme of his speech in 1927 before the Second Evangelical Church Conference at Königsberg.
134. Paul Althaus, *Obrigkeit und Führertum* (Gütersloh, 1936), p.51. Herinafter cited as OF.
135. *Die deutsche Stunde der Kirche,* p.7.
136. *Kirche und Staat nach lutherische Lehre,* pp.5, 7-8.
137. *Ibid.,* p.8.
138. OF, p.5.
139. OF, pp.18-22.
140. OF, p.42. This quote is from G. May.
141. OF, p.54.
142. *Kirche und Staat nach lutherische Lehre,* pp.9-10.
143. OF, p.47.
144. OF, pp.48-9.
145. OF, p.50.
146. 'Kirche, Volk und Staat,' p.18.
147. *Ibid.,* p.19.
148. *Kirche und Volkstum,* p.34.
149. See, for example, VC, p.13.
150. 'Kirche, Volk und Staat,' p.25.
151. *Die deutsche Stunde der Kirche,* pp.51-3.
152. See *Theologische Blätter,* vol. 12, no. 10 (Oct. 1933), pp.289-94.
153. See *ibid.,* pp.294-6.
154. Paul Althaus and Werner Elert, 'Theologische Gutachten über die Zulassung von Christen jüdischer Herkunft zu den Aemtern der deutschen evangelischen Kirche,' *Theologische Blätter,* vol. 12, no. 11 (Nov. 1933),

pp.321-3.
155. *Ibid.,* p.323.
156. *Ibid.,* p.324.
157. Interview with Gerhard Althaus, 30.9.82.
158. Remembered in Wolfgang Trillhaas, *Aufgehobene Vergangenheit. Aus meinem Leben* (Göttingen, 1976), p.190.
159. See Paul Althaus to Dr. Hans Meinzolt, 22.9.47, in PAP. Althaus mentions that his daughter was institutionalized for 'mental illness'. From other evidence I believe she was brain damaged from birth and it had become too difficult for the family to care for her.
160. Trillhaas, p.202.
161. Paul Althaus, *Der Trost Gottes; Predigten in schwerer Zeit* (Gütersloh, 1946). This sermon, 'Die gewaltige Hand Gottes,' was preached 22.4.45. See pp.222-9.
162. '76 Entlassungen an der Erlanger Universität,' *Die Neue Zeitung* (3.2.47), p.3.
163. Dr. Hans Meinzolt to Paul Althaus, 21.8.46, in PAP.
164. *Ibid.*
165. '76 Entlassungen an der Erlanger Universität.'
166. *Ibid.*
167. Helmut Thielicke to Paul Althaus, 8.11.46, in PAP.
168. A former student to Paul Althaus, 30.11.46, in PAP.
169. Dekan Prof. Dr. Künneth, Bezirkssynode in Erlangen, 9.2.47. This message was printed by the church with the heading, 'Not intended for the public!' I found it in PAP.
170. Paul Althaus to Hans Meinzolt, 22.9.47, in PAP.
171. Helmut Thielicke, 28.3.47, in PAP.
172. Karl Heine, 10.5.47, in PAP.
173. 'Der öffentlicher Kläger bei der Spruchkammer, Stadtkreis Erlangen. Aktenzeichen 2530/47 Dr. Th/Hg. TS-Nr. 3881,' 30.12.47, in PAP.
174. Military Government Liaison and Security Office, Erlangen, 17.2.48, in PAP.
175. Althaus, *Der Trost Gottes,* pp.13-14.
176. *Ibid.,* pp.41, 44.
177. *Ibid.,* p.110.
178. *Ibid.,* p.144.
179. *Ibid.,* p.150.
180. *Ibid.,* p.224.
181. *Ibid.*
182. *Ibid.,* pp.226-9.
183. *Ibid.,* p.234.
184. *Ibid.,* p.235.
185. *Ibid.,* p.246.
186. *Ibid.,* p.282.
187. *Ibid.,* p.297.
188. This is part of a statement under the

heading, *Die Arbeiten der Erlanger* (no date) in PAP. Approximately ten pages of material appear to be the working papers of Althaus' defense statement.

189. 'Luthers Lehre von den beiden Reichen im Feuer der Kritik,' *Jahrbuch der Luthergesellschaft,* vol. 24 (1957), pp. 40-68. This was reprinted in Paul Althaus, *Um dei Wahrheit des Evangeliums. Aufsätze und Vorträge* (Stuttgart, 1962), pp.263-92.

190. Paul Althaus, *Um die Wahrheit...,* p.284.

191. *Ibid.,* p.289.

192. *Kirche und Volkstum,* p.34.

193. Interview with R. T. C. Gutteridge, 3.6.74. See also Gutteridge's book, *The German Evangelical Church and the Jews, 1879-1950* (London, 1976).

194. See Niemöller, p.218.

CHAPTER IV

1. See Jens Holger Schjørring, *Theologische Gewissensethik und politische Wirklichkeit: Das Beispiel Eduard Geismars und Emanuel Hirschs* (Göttingen, 1979), p.53. Hereinafter cited as TG. Hirsch maintains that in those years Holl was sharper and more radical in his historical and theological analysis than was Harnack. In a letter of 13 March 1923 to Eduard Geismar, Hirsch adds, 'It has been one of the greatest gifts from God in my life that as a young fox [a German university term for a neophyte or beginner] my path to my first course of lectures led me to the first course of lectures given by Holl as a young professor at Berlin University.' Quoted in TG, p.53, n. 3.

2. Holl wrote to Adolf Schlatter on 5 May 1917, 'I have the desire to bring these researches on Luther to a positive end and I believe I will also be performing thereby a war work.' Quoted in TG, P.59, n.17. Both Holl and Hirsch sought to overturn the conclusion of Ernst Troeltsch that Luther's ethic was a product of the Middle Ages without relevance for modern Germans.

3. See Emanuel Hirsch, *Christliche Freiheit und politische Bindung. Ein Brief an Dr. Stapel und anderes* (Hamburg, 1935), pp.46-7, for a comment on his friendship and debt to Tillich. This work is hereinafter cited as CF. The very close friendship between Hirsch and Tillich in those early years is also described in Wilhelm and Marion Pauck, *Paul Tillich; His Life and Thought, vol. I: Life* (New York, 1976), pp.30-6.

4. Emanuel Hirsch, *Fichtes Religionsphilosophie im Rahmen der philosophischen Gesamtentwicklung Fichtes* (Göttingen, 1914). A *Habilitationsschrift,* or inaugural dissertation, is a postdoctoral dissertation required of anyone aspiring to teach at a German university.

5. Hirsch later recounted that he and his generation became interested in Kierkegaard before 1914. See Emanuel Hirsch, *Die gegenwärtige geistige Lage im Spiegel philosophischer und theologischer Besinnung* (Göttingen, 1934), p.85. But he seems to have begun to read Kierkegaard in earnest only after the war. Compare TG, p.145.

6. Karl Barth wrote to Geismar on 12.12.21, 'For I am unfortunately not as industrious and clever as my neighbor, Hirsch, who learned Danish in an instant and can step forth as a translator.' Quoted in TG, p.122, n. 8. Wolfgang Trillhaas reports the possibly apocryphal story that Hirsch made use of a feverish illness of several weeks duration to learn Danish. See 'Repräsentant und Aussenseiter einer Generation; Nach dem Tode von Emanuel Hirsch,' *Evangelische Kommentare. Monatsschrift zum Zeitgeschehen in Kirche und Gesellschaft,* 5 (1972), p.602.

7. See, for example, Walter Lowrie's references to Hirsch in the introduction to his translation of Søren Kierkegaard, *Fear and Trembling, and The Sickness unto Death* (Princeton, 1954), pp.17-19.

8. See *Kürschners deutscher Gelehrten-Kalender auf das Jahr 1970* (Berlin, 1970). See also the biographical notes on Hirsch in *Chronik der Georg-August-Universität zu Göttingen für das Rechnungsjahr 1913-1930,* p.17. Finally, some biographical information is found in the foreword to Hans-Walter Schütte, ed., *Bibliographie Emanuel Hirsch* (Berlin, 1972), p.7.

9. This interpretation was first given to me by Götz Harbsmeier in an interview on 13.10.72. Harbsmeier was a student in the theological faculty at Göttingen from 1930 to 1935 and subsequently served on the faculty there. An interview with two other colleagues of Hirsch, Professors Hermann Dörries and Joachim Jeremias, on 14.10.72, confirmed this explanation of Hirsch's forced retirement. It is worth noting that Hirsch was reputedly an excellent teacher. Harbsmeier noted his ability to relate the ideas of nineteenth-century philosophers and theologians and make them come alive for students. Furthermore, he remembered at least one occasion when students held a torch-

light parade to celebrate Hirsch's decision to turn down an appointment elsewhere. For confirmation, see 'Fackelzug der Studentenschaft für Prof. Dr. Hirsch,' *Göttinger Tageblatt*, 18.2.31.
10. Hirsch even wrote some relatively unsuccessful novels in his retirement, apparently with a view of gaining income. One example is *Rückkehr ins Leben* (Hamburg, 1952), a romantic adventure about Huguenots living in Germany after fleeing France. This theme draws at least indirectly on Hirsch's own family background.
11. Wolfgang Trillhaas, 'Repräsentant und Aussenseiter einer Generation; Nach dem Tode von Emanuel Hirsch,' *Evangelische Kommentare. Monatsscrift zum Zeitgeschehen in Kirche und Gesellschaft*, 5 (1972), p.602. Trillhaas is also considering the professional style of Hirsch in this assessment, and, no doubt, the fact that Tillich and Barth had preceded him in death. For a list of Hirsch's work, see Schütte's bibliography. For his *Festschrift*, see Hayo Gerdes, ed., *Wahrheit und Glaube. Festschrift für Emanuel Hirsch zu seinem 75. Geburtstag* (Itzehoe, 1963).
12. This view was expressed, for example, by Leszek Kolakowski on 9.10.78 at the International Scholars Symposium, 'Western Society after the holocaust,' in Seattle, Washington.
13. Interviews with Harbsmeier, Dörries and Jeremias confirm that Hirsch's politics appeared unchanged after 1945.
14. Schjørring notes that Hirsch was not alone in this view. It was shared by the Berlin theologians, Seeberg, Harnack, Troeltsch and Holl. See TG, p.56, n. 10
15. Quoted in TG, p.58.
16. Quoted in TG, p.57.
17. *Ibid*.
18. This is not surprising in light of Fritz Fischer's work, *Germany's Aims in the First World War* (New York, 1967). Schjørring also notes that Holl shared this annexationist view. See TG, p.62, n. 23.
19. Quoted in TG, p.64.
20. *Ibid*.
21. This is clear in all his subsequent work. He developed a social concern, as he later reported in *Die gegenwärtige geistige Lage*, pp.111-12, but he never accepted socialist answers. Schjørring calls it typical that his main social concern after 1918 was for the plight of soldiers returning from the front. See TG, p.63.
22. Hirsch described these circumstances in the journal of the theological seminary.

I am indebted to Professor Walther Zimmerli, interviewed 29.10.82, for telling me of this entry.
23. Helmut Heiber, *Walter Frank und sein Reichsinstitut für Geschichte des neuen Deutschlands* (Stuttgart, 1966), p.1183.
24. See CF, p.5. Compare this to Holl's use of similar imagery in TG, p.59, n. 17.
25. Emanuel Hirsch, *Deutschlands Schicksal*, 2nd ed. (Göttingen, 1922), p.1. The first edition of this work appeared in 1920, and a third edition was published in 1925. All citations, hereinafter noted as DS, are from the second edition.
26. DS, p.1.
27. DS, p.5.
28. *Ibid*.
29. DS, pp.7-8.
30. DS, p.8.
31. DS, pp.10-11.
32. DS, pp.11-4.
33. DS, p.14.
34. DS, p.15.
35. DS, p.17.
36. DS, pp.18-20. It is interesting to note the complementary reasoning of Hirsch with Werner Heisenberg, as quoted above, p.3.
37. DS, p.20.
38. DS, p.21.
39. DS, p.22.
40. DS, p.25.
41. DS, p.29.
42. DS, p.31.
43. DS, p.32.
44. DS, p.33.
45. DS, p.34.
46. DS, pp.34-5.
47. DS, p.36.
48. DS, pp.36-45.
49. DS, p.48.
50. DS, p.49.
51. DS, p.55.
52. DS, pp.56-7.
53. DS, p.58.
54. DS, pp.59-62.
55. DS, p.67.
56. DS, p.70.
57. DS, p.75.
58. DS, p.78.
59. DS, p.84.
60. DS, p.87.
61. DS, p.90.
62. *Ibid*.
63. DS, pp.91-3.
64. DS, pp.93, 95.
65. DS, pp.96-101.
66. DS, pp.105-6.
67. DS, p.108.
68. DS, p.109. This statement recalls Hirsch's sermon of 13 Sept. 1914, see above. Hirsch again seems to have Genesis 32 in mind.
69. DS, p.110.

70. DS, pp.118-9.
71. DS, p.122.
72. DS, pp.130-2, 134-5.
73. DS, pp.136-7.
74. DS, pp.139-41.
75. DS, pp.142-3.
76. DS, p.142.
77. DS, p.144.
78. DS, p.145.
79. DS, pp.147-8.
80. DS, pp.149-51.
81. DS, pp.149-50.
82. DS, p.153.
83. *Ibid.*
84. DS, p.155.
85. DS, p.157. In the early 1920s Barth and Hirsch were colleagues and very consciously rivals on the theological faculty at Göttingen. Wolfgang Trillhaas describes this rivalry and suggests that Hirsch was Barth's only intellectual peer at Göttingen in those years. See *Aufgehobene Vergangenheit. Aus meinem Leben* (Göttingen, 1976), pp.88, 97-8.
86. DS, p.159.
87. DS, p.161.
88. Quoted in DS, p.162.
89. DS, p.163.
90. DS, pp.164-5.
91. DS, p.166.
92. TG, pp. 129. 138.
93. One occasion on which Hirsch may have passed into the extremist camp during these years was after the murder of Walther Rathenau. Schjørring cites a letter from Barth to E. Thurneysen to suggest that Hirsch approved the murder. See TG, p.131.
94. TG, pp 138-9.
95. TG, p.137.
96. Quoted in TG, p.165.
97. *Ibid.*
98 Quoted in TG, p.166.
99. This letter of 4 July 1932 is quoted in TG, p.167, n. 31. It is interesting to note Hirsch told Geismar his anti-ecumenical statement was not directed against Denmark, but against England, France and the United States for their position on the Versailles Treaty.
100. Quoted in TG, pp.167-8.
101. Quoted in TG, p.168.
102. Jonathan R. C. Wright, '*Ueber den Parteien.' Die politische Haltung der evangelischen Kirchenführer 1918-1933* (Göttingen, 1977), p.117.
103. *Ibid.*, p.118.
104. *Ibid.*
105. For background on this incident, see Ernst Bizer, 'Der Fall Dehn,' in Wilhelm Schneemelcher, ed., *Festschrift für Günther Dehn* (Neukirchen, 1957), pp.239-61. See also Günther Dehn, *Kirche und Völkerver-*

söhnung. Dokumente zum Halleschen Universitätskonflikt (Berlin, 1931).
106. Wright, p.173.
107. This book, *Kirche und Völkersöhnung. Dokumente zum Halleschen Universitätskonflikt,* is quoted in TG, p.171.
108. TG, pp.171-2.
109. TG, p.173.
110. Dehn himself accepted a one-year leave for study and travel which was forced upon him. During this year the faculty declared itself against his return, and under the civil service law of 1933 he was released. See TG, p.172.
111. Letter from Hirsch to Geismar, 24 Oct. 1931, quoted in TG, p.152.
112. *Göttinger Tageblatt,* 9/10.4.32, 'Ich werde Hitler wählen!' This letter from Hirsch, signed 8.4.32, was obviously intended to encourage votes for Hitler.
113. Emanuel Hirsch, *Das kirchliche Wollen der Deutschen Christen* (Berlin, 1933), p.7. Hereinafter cited as KW.
114. Letter from Hirsch to Bishop Marahrens, 15 April 1933, quoted in TG. p.179.
115. KW, pp.14-15.
116. KW, p.27.
117. KW, pp.14-5.
118. KW, p.28.
119. KW, p.22.
120. KW, p.24.
121. See Wright's description of these events, pp.197-230. Hirsch described his role in those controversial days in an article, 'Zur Geschichte des Streits um den Reichsbischof,' which first appeared in *Der Reichsbote,* no. 130 (7 June 1933), and later in KW, pp.29-31. Hirsch gave a *Deutsche Christen* cast to these events. The only factual error he seems to have made is his failure to note that Müller was nominated for *Reichs* bishop by an East Prussian group of *Deutsche Christen* before the Young Reformation Movement put forward Bodelschwingh. Hirsch makes a big point of his contention that the Young Reformers moved first.
122. This article, 'Volk, Staat, Kirche,' appeared in *Evangelisches Deutschland* (4 June 1933), pp.204 ff, and it was reprinted in KW, pp.25-7.
123. KW, p.30.
124. 'Nationalsozialismus und Kirche. Um die Berufung des evangelischen Reichsbischofs,' *Völkischer Beobachter,* vol 26, no. 148-9 (28/29 May 1933). This article appeared in KW, pp.23-4.
125. KW, pp.27-8.
126. Emanuel Hirsch, 'Theologisches Gutachten in der Nichtarierfrage,' *Deutsche Theologie,* 5 (May 1934),

pp.182-4.
127. *Ibid.,* pp.191-2. Hirsch's wife may have been more vigorously antisemitic than he. An eyewitness describes an incident during a women's meeting at St. Albani Church in about 1934. After a woman guest speaker had spoken sensitively on the subject of National Socialism and Judaism, 'the wife of the theologian, Hirsch, stood up and said, did we know that the lecturer had given birth to a bastard.' Frau Hirsch then described her as having been married to a Jew. The woman making this report claims that she later confronted Frau Hirsch to express shock at her rudeness, and that they never spoke to each other again. See Ulrich Popplow, 'Die Machtergreifung in Augenzeugenberichten: Göttingen 1932-1935,' *Göttinger Jahrbuch 1977* (Göttingen, 1977), p.166.
128. Emanuel Hirsch, *Die gegenwärtige geistige Lage im Spiegel philosophischer und theologischer Besinnung* (Göttingen, 1934), p.1. Hereinafter cited as GG.
129. GG, p.1.
130. GG, Introduction.
131. In his preface Hirsch directs this book towards those students who through the SA and the Nazi movement have protected the rest of the nation from Bolshevism. He also intends the book for pastors. Finally, he directs it to foreigners, to show them how a Christian in Germany understands the events of 1933. GG. p.3.
132. GG, pp.7-9.
133. GG, p.12.
134. GG, p.13.
135. GG, pp.14-5.
136. GG, p.15.
137. GG, p.16.
138. GG, p.27.
139. *Ibid.*
140. Hirsch apologizes for resorting to Greek rather than German terminology, but maintains that he restricts himself to the German language more than most writers. This was naturally a concern of German nationalists, dating back to Ernst Moritz Arndt and Father Jahn. GG, pp.3, 5.
141. GG, pp.28, 33.
142. GG, pp.29-30.
143. GG, p.37.
144. GG, pp.34-5.
145. GG, pp.39-40.
146. GG, p.41.
147. GG, p.44.
148. *Ibid.*
149. GG, pp.23-4.
150. GG, p.24.
151. *Ibid.*
152. GG, p.48.

153. GG, pp.52-4.
154. GG, pp.57-8.
155. *Ibid.*
156. These suggestions are discussed in GG, pp.62-5.
157. GG, p.67.
158. GG, p.74.
159. GG, p.77.
160. GG, p.82.
161. Although Schjørring traces Hirsch's reading of Kierkegaard to 1920, Hirsch maintains his interest was aroused in his student years. See GG, p.85.
162. GG, p.97.
163. GG, p.98.
164. GG, p.100.
165. GG, p.105.
166. GG, p.108.
167. GG, pp.111-2.
168. GG, p.114.
169. GG, p.116.
170. GG, p.117.
171. GG, pp.116-7.
172. GG, pp.118-9.
173. GG, p.126.
174. GG, p.127.
175. GG, p.128.
176. GG, p.133.
177. GG, pp.139-40. Hirsch does not name Barth in this reproach, but Barth is clearly the object of his concern.
178. GG, p.145.
179. GG, p.144.
180. GG, pp.147-9.
181. GG, p.151.
182. *Ibid.*
183. GG, p.153.
184. Heim's position is described in GG, pp.154-6. Hirsch's response first appeared in *Glaube und Volk,* vol. 1, no. 5 (15 May 1932), pp.65-71.
185. GG, p.160.
186. GG, pp.161-2.
187. GG, p.164.
188. Emanuel Hirsch, *Der Weg der Theologie* (Stuttgart, 1937), p.21.
189. *Ibid.,* pp.23-5.
190. Emanuel Hirsch, *Das Wesen des Christentums* (Weimar, 1939), p.vi. Hereinafter cited as WC.
191. WC, p.57.
192. WC, pp.57-8.
193. WC, p.158.
194. Although both passages may support Hirsch, the first could also be interpreted as highlighting the divine-human paradox of Jesus, and the second could be ascribed to the crowds' ignorance of the true origins of Jesus.
195. This argument is developed in an appendix, WC, pp.158-65.
196. WC, p.8.
197. WC, pp.87-91.
198. WC, pp.138-41.
199. WC, p.145.

200. WC, p.155.
201. Berlin Document Center, *Partei Kanzlei Korrespondenz* file.
202. Berlin Document Center, *NS Lehrerbund* file.
203. The history of Marahrens and the Hanoverian church can be found in Eberhard Klügel, *Die Lutherische Landeskirche Hannovers und ihr Bischof 1933-1945* (Berlin, 1964).
204. See above, p.144-5.
205. Marahrens to Paul Althaus, 19.5.33. I saw this letter in the Paul Althaus Papers.
206. Interview with Prof. Hermann Dörries, 14.10.72.
207. This account was given to me by Prof. Walther Zimmerli in an interview on 29.10.82, and confirmed by Prof. Wolfgang Trillhaas in an interview on 2.11.82.
208. This information appears in the personal file on Hirsch in the Göttingen University Archive. This file will be cited as PFH with the appropriate entry number, in this case, PFH 3. The significance of Hirsch's position with the NS Lecturers' Federation was suggested to me by Prof. Trillhaas.
209. D. Adolf Wischmann to Prof. Wolfgang Trillhaas, 18.3.82. This letter was kindly shown to me by Prof. Trillhaas.
210. Hirsch to *Kirchenrat* Mattiat, *Ministerium für Wissenschaft, Kunst und Volksbildung,* 14.12.34. This letter is in the records of the theological faculty in the Göttingen University Archive. These records will be cited TF, with the appropriate file number, in this case, TF 140.
211. *Minister für Wissenschaft* to *Rektoren,* 10.1.35, in TF 140.
212. Rust to Curators, 28.2.35, in TF 140.
213. Stange, Meyer, Bauer, Dörries, von Campenhausen and Hoffmann to *Minister für Wissenschaft,* 12.3.35. Hirsch to *Minister für Wissenschaft,* both in TF 140.
214. This report came from a longtime member of the theological faculty. Although I cannot verify its accuracy, I believe it consistent with the personalities of the two men.
215. Walter Birnbaum, *Zeuge Meiner Zeit. Aussagen zu 1912 bis 1972* (Göttingen, 1973), p.139.
216. *Ibid.,* pp.156-9.
217. *Ibid.,* pp.190-1.
218. *Ibid.,* p.194.
219. Wolfgang Schroeder to Pastor Klügel, 25.7.35, in the *Landeskirchlichesarchiv* Hannover, hereinafter cited LKA, file S1 HII 133a.
220. *Ibid.*
221. Rust to deans, 6.6.35, in TF 140.

222. Hirsch to Rust, 17.6.35, in TF 140. Hirsch wrote also to Mattiat in the ministry on 13.6.35. In this letter he reported on Bishop Marahrens' support of the Confessing Church, including endorsement of the Augsburg Synod with its advocacy of *Ersatz* instruction for Confessing Church students.
223. Rust to Evangelical Theological Faculties, 4.7.35, in TF 140.
224. Hirsch to *Stiftsinspektor,* 6.11.35, in TF 140.
225. *Präsident* Schnelle to Hirsch, 23.11.35, and Hirsch to Schnelle, 3.12.35, in TF 140.
226. Birnbaum prepared two statements, both dated 22.11.35, both in TF 140.
227. 'Urteil des Dekans der Theologischen Fakultät über das zweckmässig einzuschlagende Verfahrens,' sent to Mattiat on 22.11.35, in TF 140.
228. In a later letter to Mattiat, 26.11.35, Hirsch wrote, 'For God's sake, there should not be martyrs created.' In TF 140.
229. *Reichsminister für Wissenschaft, Erziehung und Volksbildung* to Curator, 14.12.35, in TF 140.
230. Hirsch to *Reichsminister,* 23.12.35, in TF 140.
231. Hirsch to Hoffmann, 23.12.35, in TF 140. Records in Hanover indicate that Hoffmann indeed filled this role for the Confessing Church, upon the suggestion of Dörries. See 'Ersatz för die Birnbaumschen Seminare,' in LKA, S1 HII 133a.
232. Hoffmann to Hirsch, 1.1.36, in TF 140.
233. Hirsch to *Reichminister,* 'confidential,' 3.1.36, in TF 140.
234. *Minister für Wissenschaft* to University Curators, 15.1.36, in TF 140.
235. Hirsch to Curator, 21.2.36, in TF 140.
236. Hirsch to *Dozent* Dr. Freiherr von Campenhausen, 25.2.36, in TF 140.
237. Von Campenhausen to Hirsch, 29.2.36, in TF 140.
238. Hirsch to von Campenhausen, 3.3.36, in TF 140.
239. See Klügel, pp.326-7.
240. Hirsch to Minister, 13.11.36, in TF 140.
241. Minister to deans, 17.11.36, in TF 140.
242. Hirsch to *Stadtsuperintendant* Dr. Lueder, 24.11.36, and Hirsch to Minister, 24.3.37, in TF 140.
243. Minister (*im Auftrag* Mattiat) to LKA Hanover, 16.4.37, in TF 140.
244. Heinz Rettberg to Minister, 16.2.37, in TF 140.
245. Hirsch to Minister, 19.2.37, Minister to Hirsch, 22.3.37, in TF 140.
246. One article, 'Die Lage der Theologie,' appeared in *Deutsche Theologie* and was criticized in 'Der Rat der

Evangelisch-Lutherischen Kirche Deutschlands, An die Bekenntnisgemeinschaft der evang. Luth. Landeskirche Hannovers,' 8.9.36, a document signed Stoll, in LKA, S1 HII 132. The second work, *Das Alte Testament und die Predigt des Evangeliums,* is criticized in 'Zu der im Erlass des Herrn Reichsministers für die kirchlichen Angelegenheiten... vom 16. Mai 1938,' p.3, in LKA, S1 HII 133. This is a draft of a statement in opposition to the ministerial decree.
247. Evidence for this is in LKA, S1 HII 133a, e.g. *Minister für kirchliche Angelegenheiten* to *Landeskirche* Hanover, 15.8.38.
248. Hirsch to members of the theological faculty, 15.5.37, in TF 140.
249. Hirsch to Curator, 14.8.37, in TF 140.
250. Hirsch to *Rektor,* 26.19.37, in TF 140.
251. Reference to this decree is in LKA S1 HII 133 and 133a.
252. These petitions are in LKA Sl HII 133.
253. 'Denkschrift: Die Zukunft der theologischen Prüfungen' (June 1938), p.2, in LKA S1 HII 133a.
254. *Ibid.,* p.3.
255. *Ibid.,* p.4.
256. Marahrens, *Tagebuch* Nr. 2490, 16 June 1938, in LKA S1 HII 133a.
257. *Reichminister für die kirchlichen Angelegenheiten* to *Kirchenregierung der Evangelisch-Lutherischen Landeskirche Hannover,* 15.8.38, in LKA S1 HII 133a.
258. *Ibid.*
259. Hirsch to students of theology, 16.8.38, in LKA S1 HII 133a.
260. *Oberlandeskirchenrat* Stalmann to Marahrens, 27.8.38, in LKA S1 HII 133a. Stalmann's name does not appear on this letter, but a subsequent letter in this file from Stalmann to *Oberlandeskirchenrat* Meyer suggests both in typescript and content that Stalmann must have been the emissary and thus the author of the letter to Marahrens.
261. 'Erwägungen zum Schreiben von 27.8,' initialed by Marahrens, in LKA S1 HII 133a. This is a reaction to Stalmann's report of his meeting with Hirsch.
262. I infer this on the basis of a letter from Stalmann to Meyer, 9.9.38, in which Stalmann explains that he is arranging for the fall examinations. He regrets to inform Meyer that he will be examining with Birnbaum, but no outspoken Confessing Church students will have to do so. See LKA S1 HII 133a.
263. Birnbaum, pp.232-3.
264. Interview with Harbsmeier.
265. Jeremias and Dörries confirm Hirsch's political intransigence after 1945. Prof. Roy Harrisville of Luther Theological

Seminary, St. Paul, Minn., reports hearing the latter rumor while visiting in Germany.
266. John Gardner, founder of the liberal American organization, Common Cause, charged in a speech at Stanford University in the fall of 1979 that America is suffering from too much pluralism today: 'A society in which pluralism is not undergirded by some shared values cannot survive. Pluralism that reflects no commitments to the common good is pluralism gone berserk.' See, 'American Society OD'ing on Pluralism-Gardner', *Campus Report,* vol. 12, no. 4 (10 Oct. 1979), p.11. (This is a Stanford University faculty and staff publication). Recent political concern in Britain over immigration policy is another example of the contemporary fear of pluralism and its impact.
267. See Karl Barth, *The German Church Struggle. Tribulation and Promise* (London, 1938).
268. See Hirsch's arguments in *Deutsches Volkstum und evangelischer Glaube* (Hamburg, 1934). Hirsch's specific response to Barth is found in KW, pp.5-17.
269. See Karl Barth, 'The Christian Commitment in the Midst of Religious Change: Documents of a Hungarian Journey,' in *Against the Stream: Shorter Post-War Writings, 1946-52,* Ronald Gregor Smith, ed. (London, 1954).
270. Wilhelm and Marion Pauck, *Paul Tillich; His Life and Thought. Vol. I: Life* (New York, 1976), p.30.
271. *Ibid.,* pp.35-6.
272. *Ibid.,* p.36.
273. Paul Tillich, 'Die Theologie des Kairos und die gegenwärtige geistige Lage. Offener Brief an Emanuel Hirsch, Göttingen, von Paul Tillich, z. Zt. New York,' *Theologische Blätter,* vol. 13, no. 11 (Nov. 1934), p.305. Hereinafter cited as TK.
274. TK, p.306.
275. TK, p.307.
276. TK, p.308.
277. TK, pp.309-10.
278. TK, p.312.
279. TK, p.318.
280. TK, p.319.
281. TK, p.320.
282. TK, p.323.
283. TK, p.326.
284. TK, p.328.
285. Emanuel Hirsch, *Christlich Freiheit und politische Bindung. Ein Brief an Dr. Stapel und anderes* (Hamburg, 1935), p.7. Hereinafter cited as CF.
286. CF, pp.13-14.
287. CF, pp.14, 16.

288. CF, pp.17, 19.
289. CF, p.20.
290. CF, p.28.
291. CF, p.26.
292. CF, p.25.
293. CF, p.29.
294. CF, pp.39-41.
295. CF, p.38.
296. CF, pp.42, 45.
297. CF, p.26.
298. CF, pp.46-7.
299. In addition to their common existential-historical approach to theology, Hirsch and Tillich often mirrored each other in specifics as well. For example, in *Das Wesen des Christentums* Hirsch describes the term God as the name we have for the secret or depth of life, an approach similar to Tillich's 'Ground of all Being.'
300. See Rollo May, *Paulus. Reminiscences of a Friendship* (New York, 1973). This view was also expressed by May in a lecture at Tacoma, Wa., 12 Feb. 1975, and in a subsequent conversation with this writer.
301. For Hirsch's view of the importance of *Rechtfertigungslehre*, see WC, pp. 47-8.
302. Emanuel Hirsch, *Der Weg der Theologie* (Stuttgart, 1937), p.39.
303. *Ibid.*, p.40.
304. *Ibid.* See Chapter III for a description of Hirsch's interpretation of the Easter story.
305. Dietrich Bonhoeffer, *Letters and Papers from Prison* (London, 1953, 1959), pp.163-6.
306. *Der Weg der Theologie*, pp.40-2.
307. WC. p.133.
308. Scholder, pp.viii-ix.
309. Interview with Eberhard Bethge, 25 July 1979.
310. Wolfgang Tilgner, *Volksnomostheologie und Schöpfungsglaube. Ein Beitrag zur Geschichte des Kirchenkampfes* (Göttingen, 1966), p.142. This is vol. 16 of the series, *Arbeiten zur Geschichte des Kirchenkampfes*.
311. *Ibid.*, p.151.
312. *Ibid.*, p.15.
313. *Ibid.*, p.155.
314. This quote from Barth's *Kirchliche Dogmatik*, vol. 4, p.20, is found in Tilgner, p.157, n. 3.
315. Tilgner, p.200.
316. *Ibid.*, p.156.
317. Schjørring, p.134.
318. I am thankful for the assistance of Klaus Scholder of Tübingen University in sending me a photocopy of this document, dated 9 July 1934.
319. PFH 179 in the Göttingen University Archive.

320. Hirsch to *Rektor* (Smend), 30.5.45, in TF 17, Göttingen University Archive.
321. This view was expressed in interviews with Professors Dörries 14.10.72), Jeremias (14.10.72), Harbsmeier (13.10.72) and Trillhaas (2.11.82). It also appears in a letter, Curator to Dr. Zierold, 11.10.49, in PFH 184.
322. *Rektor* to Curator, 25.6.45, in TF 17.
323. *Rektor* to Curator, 13.6.45, in PFH 172.
324. This activity is reported, for example, by Trillhaas, *Aufgehobene Vergangenheit*, p.218.
325. Dr. Zierold, *Geschäftsfürende Vizepräsident der Notgemeinschaft der deutschen Wissenschaft*, to Curator (Bojunga), 7.10.49, in PFH 183.
326. Curator to Zierold, 11.10.49, in PFH 184.
327. *Ibid.*
328. Hirsch to *Rektor*, 12.2.52, in PFH 186.
329. *Rektor* (Trillhaas) to Hirsch, 14.2.52, in PFH 185.
330. Birnbaum to *Oberbürgermeister* Abg. Föge, 26.9.54, in PFH 188-9.
331. Theological dean to *Rektor*, 29.2.56, in TF 17.
332. *Ibid.*
333. Prof. Hempel to dean, 13.2.59, and to Curator, 2.5.59, in PFH 219, 222.
334. Hempel to dean, 13.2.59, in PFH 219.
335. *Rektor* to dean, 9.10.56, in TF 17. Also, *Niedersächsische Kirchenminister* to Curator, 6.2.57, in PFH 202.
336. Interviews with Harbsmeier, Dörries, Jeremias and Trillhaas.
337. Birnbaum to *Rektor*, 12.11.56, in PFH 196.
338. *Rektor* to dean, 19.11.56, in PFH 197.
339. *Rektor* to Hirsch, 8.12.56, in PFH 199.
340. Hirsch to *Rektor*, 12.12.56, in PFH 200.
341. For Birnbaum's account of his denazification and his struggle to overcome it, see pp.242-78. Archival records are in LKA S1 HII 133 and 133a.
342. Birnbaum, pp.242-51.
343. *Ibid.*, p.253.
344. *Ibid.*, pp.255-7.
345. *Ibid.*, pp.262-8.
346. Quoted in Birnbaum, p.269.
347. According to Birnbaum, the legal faculty even protested the illegal nature of the theological faculty's stand. See p.272.
348. Birnbaum, p.289.
349. See, for example, p.246.
350. Birnbaum to *Oberbürgermeister* Abg. Föge, 26.9.54, in PFH 189.
351. Prof. R. Smend to Curator, 23.4.58, in PFH 207. This positive view of Weber is corroborated by Zimmerli in an interview, 29.10.82.

Bibliography

The following is a selected bibliography of materials useful to this study. A complete bibliography of the works of Paul Althaus for the years 1911-1958 can be found in Walter Künneth and Wilfried Joest, eds., *Dank an Paul Althaus. Eine Festgabe zum 70. Geburtstag* (Gütersloh, 1958). Publications from 1958-1966 are listed in Hans Grass, 'Die Theologie von Paul Althaus', *Neue Zeitschrift für Systematische Theologie,* 8 (1966). A complete bibliography of the works of Emanuel Hirsch can be found in Hans-Walter Schütte, ed., *Bibliographie Emanuel Hirsch* (Berlin, 1972).

UNPUBLISHED MATERIAL

Böbel, Friedrich. 'Menschliche und christliche Wahrheit bei Emanuel Hirsch,' Erlangen Diss., 1961.

Debrunner, Albert. 'Professor Gerhard Kittel und die Judenfrage,' a document prepared in Kittel's defense. Herman Preus received a copy of this document in 1947.

Dittmann, Wilhelm. *Erklärung,* written 13 Feb. 1947 in Kittel's defense. A copy of this document is in the possession of Herman Preus.

Göttingen University Archive. This archive contains the *Akten* of the theological faculty and the *Personalakten* for Emanuel Hirsch.

Jacobs, Manfred. 'Vom Liberalismus zur Dialektischen Theologie,' *Habilitationsschrift*, Hamburg, 1966.

Kelly, Reece C. 'National Socialism and German University Teachers; The NSDAP's efforts to Create a National Socialist Professoriate and Scholarship,' University of Washington Diss., 1973.

Kittel, Gerhard-Herbert Loewe correspondence. This is in the possession of Loewe's son, Raphael, and photocopies are in the Wiener Library.

Kittel, Gerhard-Herman Preus correspondence. This is in the possession of Herman Preus.

Kittel, Gerhard. 'Die Enstehung des Judentums,' a lecture delivered at the University of Vienna, 22 March 1943, now in the theological library, Tübingen University.

—— 'Die Judenfrage in Neuen Testament,' a manuscript dated 1944-45, now in the possession of Herman Preus.

—— 'Meine Verteidigung.' A copy of this manuscript, dated June 1945, is in the possession of Herman Preus.

—— 'Meine Verteidigung,' a revised and expanded version dated November/December 1946. A copy of this manuscript is in the Tubingen University Archive.

—— 'Das Rassenproblem der Spätantike und das Frühchristentum,' a lecture delivered at the University of Vienna, 15 June 1944, now in the theological library, Tübingen University.

Kittel Personality File, Wiener Library.

Landeskirchlichesarchiv Hanover. This church archive contains the following files of particular interest: 'Streit über Prof. Emanuel Hirsch,' S1 HII 132; 'Streit über Prof. Birnbaum,' S1 HII 133; 'Universität Göttingen, Prof. Birnbaum gegen Prof. Dorries, 1954,' S1 HII 133a.

NS *Lehrerbund* File, Berlin Document Center.
Partei Kanzlei Korrespondenz, Berlin Document Center.
Paul Althaus Papers. This file is in the possession of Gerhard Althaus.
Schwartz, George M. 'Political Attitudes in the German Universities during the Reign of William II,' Oxford Diss., 1961.
Schweer, Wennemar. 'Die theologische Ethik des Politischen bei Emanuel Hirsch,' Heidelberg Diss., 1969.
Trillhaas, Wolfgang-Emanuel Hirsch correspondence. This file is in the possession of Wolfgang Trillhaas.
Wright, J. R. C. 'The Political Attitudes of the German Protestant Leadership, November 1918-July 1933,' Oxford Diss., 1969. This dissertation has subsequently been published in revised versions in English and German.

PUBLISHED MATERIAL

Articles

Albright, William Foxwell. 'The War in Europe and the Future of Biblical Studies,' Harold R. Willoughby, ed., *The Study of the Bible Today and Tomorrow,* Chicago, 1947.
Althaus, Paul. 'Adolf Schlatters Gabe an die systematische Theologie,' *Beiträge zur Förderung christlicher Theologie (Beiträge),* 40, 1 (1938).
—— 'Christentum, Krieg und Frieden,' Eugen Gerstenmeier, ed., *Kirche, Volk und Staat,* Berlin, 1937.
—— 'Christologisches. Fragen an Emanuel Hirsch,' Hayo Gerdes, ed., *Wahrheit und Glaube. Festschrift an Emanuel Hirsch,* Itzehoe, 1963.
—— 'Der Schöpfungsgedanke bei Luther,' *Bayerische Akademie der Wissenschaften Sitzungsberichte,* 7 (1959).
—— 'Die Frage nach der Schuld im Deutschglauben. Zur Auseinandersetzung mit Wilhelm Hauer,' *Allgemeine Evangelisch-Lutherische Kirschenzeitung (AELKZ),* 68, 20 (17 May 1935).
—— 'Die Wahrheit des kirschlichen Osterglaubens. Einspruch gegen Emanuel Hirsch,' *Beiträge,* 49, 2.
—— 'Gedanken zur "Theologischen Erklärung" der Barmer Erkenntnissynode,' *Korrespondenzblatt für die evangelischlutherischen Geistlichen in Bayern,* 28 (July 1934).
—— 'Kirche, Volk und Staat,' in Gerstenmeier, ed.
—— 'Luthers Lehre von den beiden Reichen im Feuer der Kritik,' in Paul Althaus, *Um die Wahrheit des Evangeliums. Aufsätze und Vorträge,* Stuttgart, 1962.
—— 'Toleranz und Intoleranz des Glaubens,' AELKZ, 66, 44 (3 Nov. 1933).
—— 'Um die lutherische Kirche Deutschlands,' AELKZ, 67, 37 (14 May 1934).
—— 'Zum Gedächtnis der abgerufene Herausgeber der Beiträge,' *Beiträge,* 40, 1 (1938).
Althaus, Paul, and Werner Elert. 'Theologisches Gutachten über die Zulassung von Christen jüdischer Herkunft zu den Aemtern der deutschen evangelischen Kirche,' *Theologische Blätter,* 12, 11 (Nov. 1933).
—— and Emanuel Hirsch. 'Erklärung zur Hamburger Tagung der Weltfriedenschristen,' *Deutsches Volkstum* (1931).
Baethge, Martin, et al., eds. 'Georgia Augusta — Universität im Dritten Reich,' *Politikon: Göttinger Studentenzeitschrift für Niedersachsen,* 9 (1965). This issue of the Göttingen student newspaper is devoted to the subject of the university's experience in the Nazi era.
Bentley, James. 'British and German High Churchmen in the Struggle against Hitler,' *Journal of Ecclesiastical History,* 23, 3 (July 1972).
Bethge, Eberhard. 'Troubled Self-interpretation and Uncertain Reception in the Church Struggle,' in Franklin H. Littell and Hubert G. Locke, eds., *The German Church Struggle and the Holocaust,* Detroit, 1974.
Conway, John. 'Friedrich Siegmund-Schultze (1885-1969),' *Evangelische Theologie,* 43, 3 (1983).
Ericksen, Robert P. 'The Barmen Synod and its Declaration: An Historical Synopsis,' Hubert G. Locke, ed., *The Church Confronts the Nazis: Barmen Then and Now,* New York, 1984.
—— 'Theologian in the Third Reich: The Case of Gerhard Kittel,' *Journal of Contemporary*

History, 12 (1977).
—— 'Zur Auseinandersetzung mit und um Gerhard Kittels Antisemitismus,' *Evangelische Theologie*, 43, 3 (1983).
Fischer, Fritz. 'Der deutsche Protestantismus und die Politik in 19. Jahrhundert,' *Historische Zeitschrift*, 171 (1951).
Grass, Hans. 'Die Theologie von Paul Althaus,' *Neue Zeitschrift für Systematische Theologie*, 8 (1966).
Hirsch, Emanuel. 'Antwort an Rudolf Bultmann,' *Zeitschrift für systematische Theologie*, 4 (1926).
—— 'Antwort von E. Hirsch an den Herausgeber,' *Deutsches Volkstum* (1932).
—— 'Arier und Nichtarier in der deutschen evangelischen Kirche,' *Kirche und Volkstum in Niedersachsen*, 1 (1933).
—— 'Brief an einen Schüler im Pfarramt über Evangelium und Politik,' *Glaube und Volk*, 2 (1933).
—— 'Bultmanns Jesus,' *Zeitwende*, 2 (1926).
—— 'Das Amt der Verkündigung,' *Deutsche Theology* DT, 7 (July 1934).
—— 'Das Ewige und das Zeitliche,' *Glaube und Volk*, 1 (1932).
—— 'Das Verhältnis des Schriftstellers zur Sprache,' *Deutsches Volkstum* 1935.
—— 'Der Schriftsteller und die Zeit. Zu Hans Grimms Bekenntnisbuch,' *Zeitwende*, 7 (1931).
—— 'Der Tod Jesu,' DT, 4/5 (April/May 1935).
—— 'Deutsche Zukunft,' *Wingolf-Blätter*, 47 (1917).
—— 'Die Bergpredigt,' *Deutsches Volkstum* (1938).
—— 'Die Einheit der Kirche,' *Zeitschrift für systematische Theologie*, 3 (1925).
—— 'Die Kirsche des Sowohl-als-auch,' *Deutsches Volkstum* (1938).
—— 'Die Lage der Theologie,' DT, 2/3 (Feb./Mar. 1936).
—— 'Die notwendige Vertiefung des Nationalstaatsgedankens,' *Eiserne Blätter* (1921).
—— 'Die Vollmacht des Reichskirchenausschusses und der evangelischlutherische Christ,' *Deutsche evangelische Erziehung. Zeitschrift für den evangelischen Unterricht*, 47 (1936).
—— 'Dr. Macfarland, die Deutschen und das Ökumenische,' *Deutsches Volkstum* (1934).
—— 'Eine Meditation Kierkegaards,' DT, 11/12 (Nov./Dec. 1934).
—— 'Etwas von der christlichen Stellung zum Alten Testament,' *Glaube und Volk*, 1 (1932).
—— 'Evangelische Kirche und Völkerverständigung,' *Theologische Blätter*, 10 (1930).
—— 'Jesus und das Alte Testament,' *Deutsches Volkstum* (1937).
—— 'Luthers Berufung,' *Deutsche Theologie*, 1 (1934).
—— 'Luthers Gedanken über Staat und Krieg,' *Wingolf-Blätter (Zeitschrift des Wingolf-Bundes)*, 46 (1917).
—— 'Meine Stellung zur Kirchenwahl,' *Kommende Kirche*, (25 April 1937).
—— 'Meine theologischen Anfänge,' *Freies Christentum*, 3 (1951).
—— 'Meine Wendejahre (1916-21),' *Freies Christentum*, 3 (1951).
—— 'Mein Weg in die Wissenschaft,' *Freies Christentum*, 3 (1951).
—— 'Nachruf auf Oxford,' *Deutsches Volkstum* (1937).
—— 'Nationalsozialismus und Kirche. Um die Berufung des evangelischen Reichsbischofs,' *Völkischer Beobachter*, 26, 148-149 (28-29 May 1933).
—— 'Nation, Staat und Christentum. 30 Thesen,' *Mitteilungen zur Förderung einer deutschen christlichen Studentenbewegung* (1923).
—— 'Offener Brief an Karl Barth,' *Deutsches Volkstum* (1932).
—— 'Oxford 1937 und Herr Oldham,' *Deutsches Volkstum* (1937).
—— 'Staat und Kirche im Kalvinismus,' *Deutsches Volkstum* (1936).
—— 'Theologisches Gutachten in der Nichtarierfrage,' DT, 5 (May 1934).
—— 'Unsere Frage an Gott,' *Evangelische Wahrheit*, 5 (1914).
—— 'Volk, Staat, Kirche,' *Evangelisches Deutschland* (4 June 1933).
—— 'Vom verborgenen Souverän,' *Glaube und Volk*, 2 (1933).
—— 'Weltanschauung, Glaube und Heimat,' *Deutsches Volkstum* (1936).
—— 'Wissenschaftliche Tarnung. Zu den Studien zum Mythus des XX. Jahrhunderts,' *Deutsches Volkstum* (1935).
—— 'Zum halleschen Universitätskonflikt,' *Die Wartburg*, 31 (1932).
—— 'Zum Problem der Ethik. Erwiderung an Friedrich Gogarten,' *Zwischen den Zeiten*, 3 (1923).

—— 'Zum Verständnis von Kierkegaards Verlobungszeit,' *Zeitschrift für systematische Theologie*, 5 (1927).

—— 'Zur Grundlegung der Ethik. Eine Auseinandersetzung mit Albert Schweitzer,' *Die Tat*, 16 (1924).

Kittel, Gerhard. 'Adolf Schlatter, Gedankenrede,' *Beiträge zur Förderung christlicher Theologie*, 40, 1 (1939).

—— 'Das Konnubium mit Nicht-Juden im antiken Judentum,' *Forschungen zur Juderfrage* (FrJ), 2 (Hamburg, 1937).

—— 'Das Menschenschätzgesetz,' *Deutsche Theologie*, 8 (Aug. 1934).

—— 'Die Abstammung der Mutter des Origenes. Die Geschichte eines genealogischen Irrtums,' FzJ, 3, 2nd ed. (Hamburg, 1943).

—— 'Die ältesten Judenkarikaturen. Die "Trierer Terrakotten",' FzJ, 4 (Hamburg, 1940).

—— 'Die ältesten jüdischen Bilder,' FzJ, 4 (Hamburg, 1940).

—— 'Die Auferstehung Jesu,' *Deutsche Theologie*, 4/5 (April/May 1937).

—— 'Die Ausbreitung des Judentums bis zum Beginn des Mittelalters. Karten Beilage: Die Ausbreitung des Judentums bis zum Beginn des Mittelalters,' FzJ, 5 (Hamburg, 1941).

—— 'Die Behandlung des Nichtjuden nach dem Talmud,' *Archiv für Judenfrage*, 1, A1 (Berlin, 1943).

—— 'Die Entstehung des Judentums und die Entstehung der Judenfrage,' FzJ, 1 (Hamburg, 1936).

—— 'Die Glaubenswürdigkeit der Geschichte Jesus,' *Deutsche Theologie*, 2 (Feb. 1934).

—— 'Gedanken eines evangelischen Nationalsozialisten zum 19. Aug. 1934,' AELKZ, 67, 35 (31 Aug. 1934).

—— 'Judentum und Christentum,' *Religion in Geschichte und Gegenwart*, 3, 2nd ed., (Tubingen, 1929).

—— 'NT Gedanken zur Judenfrage,' AELKZ, 66, 39 (1933).

—— 'Vom Echo eines "theologischen Briefwechsels",' *Deutsche Theologie*, 4/5 (April/May 1935).

—— and Eugen Fischer. 'Das antike Weltjudentum. Tatsachen, Texte, Bilder,' FzJ, 7 (Hamburg, 1943). This entire volume is devoted to the work by Kittel and Fischer.

Knitter, Paul. 'Die Uroffenbarungslehre von Paul Althaus — Anknüpfungspunkt für den Nationalsozialismus?', *Evangelische Theologie*, 33, 2 (1973).

Kunkel, Wolfgang. 'Der Professor im Dritten Reich,' *Die deutsche Universität im Dritten Reich*, Munich, 1966.

Lohff, Wenzel. 'Paul Althaus,' in H. J. Schultz, ed., *Tendenzen der Theologie im 20. Jahrhundert. Eine Geschichte in Porträts*, Berlin, 1966.

Mann, Golo. 'The German Intellectuals,' *Encounter*, 4 (June 1955).

Popplow, Ulrich. 'Die Machtergreifung in Augenzeugenberichten: Göttingen 1932-1935, *Göttinger Jahrbuch 1977*, Göttingen, 1977.

—— 'Göttingen 1932-1935. Ein Nachtrag zum Aufsatz "Die Machtergreifung in Augenzeugenberichten",' *Göttinger Jahrbuch 1979*, Göttingen, 1979.

Porter, J. R. 'The Case of Gerhard Kittel,' *Theology*, 50 (Nov. 1947).

Rese, Martin. 'Antisemitismus und neutestamentliche Forschung, Anmerkungen zu dem Theme "Gerhard Kittel und die Judenfrage",' *Evangelische Theologie*, 30 (1979).

Scholder, Klaus. 'Die Kapitulation der evangelischen Kirche vor dem nationalsozialistischen Staat,' *Zeitschrift für Kirschengeschichte*, 2 (Stuttgart, 1970).

—— 'Die Kirchen im Dritten Reich,' *Beilage zur Wochenzeitung das Parlament*, 15, 71 (10 April 1971).

Seier, Hellmut. 'Der Rektor als Führer,' *Vierteljahresheft für Zeitgeschichte*, 12, 2 (April 1964).

Siegele-Wenschkewitz, Leonore. 'Die Evangelisch-theologische Fakultät Tübingen in den Anfangsjahren des Dritten Reichs. I. Karl Fezer und die Deutschen Christen.' The reprint of this article contains no information about its publication, but it may have been published in *Zeitschrift für Theologie und Kirche*.

—— 'Die Evangelisch-theologische Fakultät Tübingen in den Anfangsjahren des Dritten Reichs. II. Gerhard Kittel und die Judenfrage,' *Zeitschrift für Theologie und Kirche*, 4 (Tübingen, 1978).

—— 'Mitverantwortung und Schuld der Christen am Holocaust,' *Evangelische Theologie*, 42 (1982).

Sontheimer, Kurt. 'Anti-Democratic Thought in the Weimar Republic,' Theodor Eschenburg, et al., *The Path to Dictatorship, 1918-1933*, John Conway, tr., Garden City, N.Y., 1966.
Tillich, Paul. 'Die Theologie des Kairos und die gegenwärtige geistige Lage. Offener Brief an Emanuel Hirsch, Göttingen, von Paul Tillich, z. Zt. New York,' *Theologische Blätter*, 13, 11 (Nov. 1934).
Titius, Arthur. 'Schleiermachers Grundgedanken über Religion und Christentum in ihrer Bedeutung für die Gegenwart,' *Festreden der U. Göttingen 1911-1923*, Göttingen, 1923.
Trillhaas, Wolfgang. 'Repräsentant und Aussenseiter einer Generation. Nach dem Tode von Emanuel Hirsch,' *Evangelische Kommentare: Monatsschrift zum Zeitgeschehens in Kirche und Gesellschaft*, 5 (1972).
Wundt, Max. 'Das Judentum in der Philosophie,' *Forschungen zur Judenfrage*, 2 (Hamburg, 1937).

BOOKS

Adams, Uwe Dietrich. *Hochschule und Nationalsozialismus: Die Universität Tübingen im Dritten Reich*, Tübingen, 1977.
Albright, William Foxwell. *History, Archaeology and Christian Humanism*, New York, 1964.
Allen, William Sheridan. *The Nazi Seizure of Power: The Experience of a Single German Town, 1930-1935*, Chicago, 1965.
Althaus, Paul. *Christus und die deutsche Seele*, Gütersloh, 1934.
—— *Das sogennante Kerygma und der historische Jesus; Zur Kritik heutigen Kerygma Theologie*, Gütersloh, 1958.
—— *Der Trost Gottes: Predigten in schwerer Zeit*, Gütersloh, 1946.
—— *Die christliche Wahrheit. Lehrbuch der Dogmatik*, 3rd ed., Gütersloh, 1952.
—— *Die deutsche Stunde der Kirche*, 3rd ed., Göttingen, 1934.
—— *Kirche und Staat nach lutherische Lehre*, Leipzig, 1935.
—— *Kirche und Volkstum. Der völkische Wille im Lichte des Evangeliums*, Gütersloh, 1928.
—— *Obrigkeit und Führertum*, Gütersloh, 1936.
—— *Politisches Christentum. Ein Wort über die Thüringer 'Deutscher Christen,'* Leipzig, 1935.
—— *Religiöser Sozialismus. Grundfragen der christlichen Sozialethik*, Gütersloh, 1921.
—— *Staatsgedanke und Reich Gottes*, Langensalza, 1923.
—— *Theologie der Ordnungen*, Gütersloh, 1934.
—— *Um die Wahrheit des Evangeliums. Aufsätze und Vorträge*, Stuttgart, 1962.
—— *Verantwortung und Schuld der Kirche*, Berlin, 1937.
—— *Völker vor und nach Christus*, Leipzig, 1937.
Angress, Werner T. *Stillborn Revolution: The Communist Bid for Power in Germany, 1921-1923*, Princeton, 1963.
Baier, Helmut. *Die Deutschen Christen Bayerns im Rahmen des bayerischen Kirchenkampfes*, Nuremberg, 1968.
Barth, Karl. *Against the Stream: Shorter Post-War Writings, 1946-52*, London, 1954.
—— *A Letter to Great Britain from Switzerland*, London, 1941.
—— *Church and State*, London, 1939.
—— *Church Dogmatics*, 14 vols., N.Y., 1955.
—— *Eine Schweizer Stimme, 1938-1945*, Zürich, 1945.
—— *Evangelium und Gesetz*, Munich, 1935.
—— *How I changed my Mind*, Richmond, Va., 1966.
—— *Karl Barth-Eduard Thurneysen Briefwechsel*, 2 vols., Zürich, 1973-74.
—— *Karl Barth-Rudolf Bultmann Briefwechsel 1922-1966*, Zürich, 1971.
—— *The Church and the Political Problem of Today*, N.Y., 1939.
—— *The Church and the War*, N.Y., 1944.
—— *The Epistle to the Romans*, 8th ed., London, 1950.
—— *The Germans and Ourselves*, London, 1945.
—— *The Word of God and the Word of Man*, London, 1935.
—— *Theological Existence Today*, London, 1933.
—— and Johannes Hamel. *How to Serve God in a Marxist Land*, N.Y., 1959.
Baumgärtel, Friedrich. *Wider der Kirchenkampflegenden*, 1959.
Beckmann, Joachim. *Evangelische Kirche im Dritten Reich*, 1948.

Bentley, James. *Between Marx and Christ: The Dialogue in German-Speaking Europe*, 1870-1970, London, 1982.

Beste, Niklot. *Der Kirchenkampf in Mecklenburg 1933-1945*, Göttingen, 1975.

Bethge, Eberhard. *Dietrich Bonhoeffer: Theologian, Christian, Contemporary*, London, 1970.

Beyerchen, Alan D. *Scientists under Hitler: Politics and the Physics Community in the Third Reich*, New Haven, 1977.

Bielfeldt, Johann. *Der Kirchenkampf in Schleswig-Holstein 1933-45*, Göttingen, 1964.

Birnbaum, Walter. *Zeuge meiner Zeit: Aussagen zu 1912 bis 1972*, Göttingen, 1973.

Bloch, Ernst. *Man on his own; Essays in the Philosophy of Religion*, N.Y., 1970.

Bluchheim, Hans. *Glaubenskrise im Dritten Reich*, Stuttgart, 1953.

Bonhoeffer, Dietrich. *Christology*, London, 1971.

—— *The Cost of Discipleship*, N.Y., 1960.

—— *Ethics*, London, 1965.

—— *Letters and Papers from Prison*, London, 1959.

—— *Life Together*, N.Y., 1954.

—— *Gesammelte Schriften*, 6 vols., Munich, 1958.

Bosanquet, Mary. *The Life and Death of Dietrich Bonhoeffer*, N.Y., 1969.

Braaten, Carl E. and Roy A. Harrisville, eds. *Kerygma and History: A Symposium on the Theology of Rudolf Bultmann*, N.Y., 1962.

Bracher, Karl Dietrich. *Die Auflösung der Weimarer Republik. Eine Studie zur Problem des Machtverfalls in der Demokratie*, 4th ed., Villingen, 1964.

—— *Die deutsche Diktatur; Entstehung, Struktur, Folgen des Nationalsozialismus*, Köln, 1969.

—— Wolfgang Sauer and Gerhard Schultz. *Die nationalsozialistische Machtergreifung. Studien zur Errichtung des totalitären Herrschaftssystems in Deutschland 1933-1934*, 2nd ed., Köln, 1962.

Brakelmann, Günter. *Der deutsche Protestantismus im Epochenjahr 1917*, Witten, 1974.

Bredendiek, Walter. *Irrwege und Warnlichter; Anmerkungen zur Kirchengeschichte der neueren Zeit*, Hamburg, 1966.

—— *Zwischen Revolution und Restauration. Zur Entwicklung im deutschen Protestantismus während der Novemberrevolution und in der Weimarer Republik*, 1969.

Broszat, Martin. *German National Socialism 1919-1945*, Santa Barbara, 1966.

Buber, Martin. *Briefwechsel aus sieben Jahrzehnten*, vol. 3, 1938-1965, Heidelberg, 1975.

Bultmann, Rudolf. *Essays, Philosophical and Theological*, London, 1955.

—— *Das Evangelium des Johannes; erklärt*, 15th ed., Göttingen, 1957.

—— *Theology of the New Testament*, 2 vols., N.Y., 1951.

—— *This World and Beyond, Marburg Sermons*, N.Y., 1960.

—— and Karl Jaspers. *Die Frage der Entmythologisierung*, Munich, 1954.

Busch, Alexander. *Die Geschichte des Privatdozenten: Eine soziologische Studie zur grossbetrieblichen Entwicklung der deutschen Universitäten*, Stuttgart, 1959.

Busch, Eberhard. *Karl Barth: His Life from Letters and Autobiographical Texts*, Philadelophia, 1976.

Chronik der Georg-August-Universität zu Göttingen für das Rechnungsjahr 1913, Göttingen, 1914.

Cochrane, Arthur C. *The Church's Confession under Hitler*, Philadelphia, 1962, 2nd ed., 1976.

Conway, John S. *The Nazi Persecution of the Churches, 1933-1945*, London, 1968.

Davidson, Clarissa Stuart. *God's Man. The Story of Pastor Niemöller*, N.Y., 1959.

Deak, Istvan. *Weimar Germany's Left-wing Intellectuals. A Political History of the Weltbühne and its Circle*, Berkeley, 1968.

Dehn, Günther. *Kirche und Völkerversöhnung. Dokumente zum Halleschen Universitätskonflikt*, Berlin, 1931.

Dewart, Leslie. *The Future of Belief: Theism in a World Come of Age*, N.Y., 1966.

Diehn, Otto. *Bibliographie zur Geschichte des Kirchenkampfes 1933-1945*, Göttingen, 1966.

Dipper, Theodor. *Die evangelische Bekenntnisgemeinschaft in Württemberg 1933-1945*, Göttingen, 1966.

Ehrenberg, Hans P. *Autobiography of a German Pastor*, London, 1943.

Ehrenforth, Gerhard. *Die schlesische Kirche im Kirchenkampf 1932-1945*, Göttingen, 1968.

Eschenburg, Theodor, et al. *The Path to Dictatorship*, 1918-1933, John Conway, tr., Garden City, N.Y., 1966.

Festreden der Universität Göttingen 1911-1923, Göttingen, 1923.

Fischer, Fritz. *Germany's Aims in the First World War,* Introduction by Hajo Holborn and James Joll, New York, 1967.

—— *War of Illusions: German Policies from 1911-1914,* N.Y., 1975.

—— *World Power or Decline: The Controversy over Germany's Aims in the First World War,* N.Y., 1974.

Fischer, Joachim. *Die sächsische Landeskirche im Kirchenkampf 1933-1937,* Göttingen, 1972.

FitzGibbon, Constantine. *Denazification,* London, 1969.

Gallin, Mary Alice. *German Resistance to Hitler: Ethical and Religious Factors,* Washington, 1961.

Gay, Peter. *Weimar Culture: The Outsider as Insider,* N.Y., 1968.

Geis, Robert Raphael, and Hans-Joachim Kraus, eds. *Versuche des Verstehens. Dokumente jüdisch-christlicher Begegnung aus den Jahren 1918-1933,* Munich, 1966.

Gerdes, Hayo, ed. *Wahrheit und Glaube. Festschrift für Emanuel Hirsch zu seinem 75. Geburtstag,* Itzehoe, 1963.

Gerlach, Angelika. *Die Kirche vor der Eidesfrage,* Göttingen, 1967.

Gerstenmeier, Eugen, ed. *Kirche, Volk und Staat. Stimmen aus der Deutschen Evangelischen Kirche zur Oxforder Weltkirchenkonferenz,* Berlin, 1937.

Glock, Charles Y., and Rodney Stark. *Christian Beliefs and anti-Semitism,* N.Y., 1966.

Grant, Robert M. *The Bible in the Church; A Short History of Interpretation,* N.Y., 1958.

Gürtler, Paul. *Nationalsozialismus und Evangelische Kirche im Warthegau,* Göttingen, 1958.

Gutteridge, Richard. *The German Evangelical Church and the Jews, 1879-1958,* London, 1976.

Harnack, Adolf von. *What is Christianity?,* London, 1957.

Hartshorne, E. Y., Jr. *The German Universities and National Socialism,* London, 1937.

—— *German Youth and the Nazi Dream of Victory,* London, 1941.

Heiber, Helmut. *Walter Frank und sein Reichsinstitut für Geschichte des neuen Deutschlands,* Stuttgart, 1966.

Heinonen, Reijo E. *Anpassung und Identität. Theologie und Kirchenpolitik der Bremer Deutsche Christen 1933-1945,* Göttingen, 1978.

Helmreich, Ernst C. *The German Churches under Hitler: Background, Struggle and Epilogue,* Detroit, 1979.

Hermelink, Heinrich. *Kirche im Kampf. Dokumente des Widerstands und des Aufbaus in der Evangelischen Kirche Deutschlands von 1933 bis 1945,* Tübingen, 1950.

Hirsch, Emanuel. *Betrachtungen zu Wort und Geschichte Jesu,* Berlin, 1969.

—— *Christentum und Geschichte in Fichtes Philosphie,* Tübingen, 1920.

—— *Christliche Freiheit und politische Bindung. Ein Brief an Dr. Stapel und anderes,* Hamburg, 1935.

—— *Das Alte Testament und die Predigt des Evangeliums,* Tübingen, 1936.

—— *Das Evangelium. Predigten,* Gütersloh, 1929.

—— *Das kirchliche Wollen der Deutschen Christen,* Berlin, 1933.

—— *Das Wesen des Christentums,* Weimar, 1939.

—— *Das Wesen des reformatorischen Christentums,* Berlin, 1963.

—— *Der Offenbarungsglaube,* Bordesholm, 1934.

—— *Der Pazifismus,* Mühlhausen, 1918.

—— *Der Sinn des Gebets,* Göttingen, 1921.

—— *Der Weg der Theologie,* Stuttgart, 1937.

—— *Der Weg des Glaubens,* Bordesholm, 1934.

—— *Der Wille des Herrn. Predigten,* Gütersh, 1925.

—— *Deutsches Volkstum und evangelischer Glaube,* Hamburg, 1934.

—— *Deutschlands Schicksal. Staat, Volk und Menschheit im Lichte einer ethischen Geschichtsansicht,* 3rd ed., Göttingen, 1925.

—— *Die Auferstehungsgeschichten und der christliche Glaube,* Tübingen, 1940.

—— *Die gegenwärtige geistige Lage im Spiegel philosophischer und theologischer Besinnung. Akademische Vorlesungen zum Verständnis des deutschen Jahres 1933,* Göttingen, 1934.

—— *Die idealistische Philosophie und das Christentum. Gesammelte Aufsätze,* Gütersloh, 1926.

—— *Die Liebe zum Vaterlande,* Langensalza, 1924.

—— *Die Reich-Gottes-Begriffe des neueren europäischen Denkens. Ein Versuch zur Geschichte der Staats- und Gesellschaftsphilosophie,* Göttingen, 1921.

—— *Die Theologie des Andreas Osiander und ihre geschichtlichen Voraussetzungen*, Göttingen, 1919.

—— *Ethos und Evangelium*, Berlin, 1966.

—— *Fichtes Religionsphilosophie im Rahmen der philosophischen Gesamtentwicklung Fichtes*, Göttingen, 1914.

—— *Fichtes, Schleiermachers und Hegels Verhältnis zur Reformation*, Göttingen, 1930.

—— *Frühgeschichte des Evangeliums. Erstes Buch: Das Werden des Markusevangeliums. Zweites Buch: Die Vorlagen des Lukas and das Sondergut des Matthäus*, Tübingen, 1941.

—— *Geschichte der neuern evangelischen Theologie im Zusammenhang mit den allgemeinen Bewegungen des europäischen Denkens*, 5 vols., Gütersloh, 1949-54.

—— *Hauptfragen christlicher Religionsphilosphie*, Berlin, 1963.

—— *Jesus Christus der Herr. Theologische Vorlesungen*, Göttingen, 1926.

—— *Karl Barth. Das Ende einer theologischen Existenz. Brief an einen ausländischen Freund*, Göttingen, 1940.

—— *Kirkegaard-Studien*, 2 vols., Gütersloh, 1933.

—— *Leitfaden zur christlichen Lehre*, Tübingen, 1938.

—— *Luthers Gottesanschauung*, Göttingen, 1918.

—— *Lutherstudien*, 2 vols., Gütersloh, 1954.

—— *Predigerfibel*, Berlin, 1964.

—— *Rückkehr ins Leben*, Hamburg, 1952.

—— *Schleiermachers Christusglaube, Drei Studien*, Gütersloh, 1968.

—— *Schöpfung und Sünde in der natürlich-geschichtlichen Wirklichkeit des einzelnen Menschen. Versuch einer Grundlegung christlicher Lebensweisung*, Tübingen, 1931.

—— tr. *Søren Kirkegaard. Gesammelte Werke*, Düsseldorf, 1956-66.

—— *Staat und Kirche im 19. und 20. Jahrhundert*, Göttingen, 1929.

—— *Studium zum vierten Evangelium*, Tübingen, 1936.

—— *Wege zu Kierkegaard*, Berlin, 1968.

—— *Weltbewusstsein und Glaubensgeheimnis*, Berlin, 1967.

—— *Zweifel und Glaube*, Frankfurt am Main, 1937.

—— *Zwiesprache auf dem Wege zu ott*, Düsseldorf, 1960.

Heisenberg, Werner. *Physics and Beyond; Encounters and Conversations*, London, 1971.

Heller, Erich. *The Disinherited Mind*, 4th ed., N.Y., 1974.

Hochhuth, Rolf. *The Deputy*, N.Y., 1964.

Hoffmann, Peter. *The History of the German Resistance, 1933-1945*, Cambridge, Mass., 1977.

Hornig, Ernst. *Die Bekennende Kirche in Schlesien 1933-1945*, Göttingen, 1977.

Hug, Herbert. *Das Volk Gottes. Der Kirche Bekenntnis zur Judenfrage*, Zürich, 1942.

Hughes, H. Stuart. *Consciousness and Society: The Reorientation of European Social Thought, 1890-1930*, New York, 1958.

Hunsinger, George, ed. *Karth Barth and Radical Politics*, Philadelphia, 1976.

I was in Prison: Letters from German Pastors, London, 1938.

Jacobsen, Hans Adolf and Erich Zimmermann, eds. *Germans against Hitler, July 20, 1944*, 4th ed., Bonn, 1964.

Jarausch, Konrad. *Students, Society and Politics in Imperial Germany: The Rise of Academic Illiberalism*, Princeton, 1982.

Joll, James. *Three Intellectuals in Politics*, London, 1960.

Kater, Horst. *Die Deutsche Evangelische Kirche in den Jahren 1933 und 1934*, Göttingen, 1970.

Kershaw, Ian. *Popular Opinion and Political Dissent in the Third Reich*, Oxford, 1983.

Klemperer, Klemens von. *Germany's New Conservatism: Its history and Dilemma in the Twentieth Century*, N.Y., 1957.

Kierkegaard, Søren. *Fear and Trembling*, Princeton, 1954.

Kittel, Gerhard. *Christus und Imperator. Das Urteil der ersten Christenheit über den Staat*, Stuttgart, 1939.

—— *Dichter, Bibel und Bibelrevision*, Leipzig, n.d. (about 1939).

—— *Die historischen Voraussetzungen der jüdischen Rassenmischung*, Hamburg, 1939.

—— *Die Judenfrage*, 3rd ed., Stugart, 1934.

—— *Die Oden Salomos. Ueberarbeitet oder einheitlich?*, Leipzig, 1914.

—— *Die Probleme des palästinischen Spätjudentums und das Urchristentum*, Stuttgart, 1926.

—— *Die religiöse und die kirchliche Lage in Deutschland*, Leipzig, 1921.
—— *Dürfen wir dem Neuen Testament trauen? Die Geschichte des Neuen Testamentes*, Stuttgart, 1939.
—— *Jesus und die Juden*, Berlin, 1926.
—— *Jesus und die Rabbinen*, Berlin, 1914.
—— *Urchristentum, Spätjudentum, Hellenismus. Akademische Antrittsvorlesung, Gehalten am 28. Oktober 1926 von G. Kittel*, Stuttgart, 1926.
—— and Karl Barth. *Ein theologischer Briefwechsel*, Stuttgart, 1934.
Kittel, Rudolf. *Judenfeindschaft oder Gotteslästerung*, Leipzig, 1914.
—— *Leipziger akademische Reden zum Kriegsende*, Leipzig, 1919.
—— *Die Universität Leipzig im Jahr der Revolution 1918-19. Rektoratserinnerungen*, Stuttgart, 1930.
Klotz, Leopold, ed. *Die Kirche und das Dritte Reich: Fragen und Forderungen deutschen Theologen*, 2 vols., Gotha, 1932.
Klügel, Eberhard. *Die lutherische Landeskirche Hannovers und ihr Bischof 1933-45*, Berlin, 1964.
Kraus, Hans-Joachim. *Geschichte der historisch-kritischen Erforschung des Alten Testaments von der Reformation bis zur Gegenwart*, Neukirchen Kreis Moers, 1956.
Kupisch, Karl. *Quellen zur Geschichte des deutschen Protestantismus, 1871-1945*, Göttingen, 1960.
—— *Zwischen Idealismus und Massendemokratie; eine Geschichte der evangelischen Kirche in Deutschland von 1815-1945*, Berlin, 1955.
Kürschners Deutscher Gelehrten-Kalender auf das Jahr 1926; 1954; 1970, Berlin, 1926, 1954, 1970.
Laqueur, Walter, and George L. Mosse, eds., *Literature and Politics in the Twentieth Century*, N.Y., 1967.
Laqueur, Walter. *Weimar: A Cultural History 1918-1933*, N.Y., 1974.
Lau, Franz, ed. *Festgabe für Paul Althaus*, Berlin, 1958.
Lea, F. A. *The Tragic Philosopher: A Study of Friedrich Nietzsche*, London, 1957, 1972.
Leber, Annedore, ed. *Conscience in Revolt: Sixty-four Stories of Resistance in Germany, 1933-1945*, London, 1957.
Lebovics, Herman. *Social Conservatism and the Middle Classes in Germany, 1914-1933*, Princeton, 1969.
Leffler, Siegfried. *Christus im Dritten Reich der Deutschen. Wesen, Weg und Ziel der Kirchenbewegung 'Deutsche Christen'*, Weimar, n.d.
Leutheuser, Julius. *Der Heiland in der Geschichte der Deutschen, oder, Der Nationalsozialismus, vom Evangelium aus gesehen*, Weimar, 1933.
—— *Die deutsche Christusgemeinde und ihre Gegner, Eine Antwort an Herrn Pfarrer Ernst Otto und die lutherische Bekenntnisgemeinschaft in Thüringen*, Weimar, n.d.
—— and Erich Fascher. *Ein theologisches Missverständnis. Unsere Antwort an Paul Althaus*, 2nd ed., Weimar, n.d.
Lewy, Guenter. *The Catholic Church and Nazi Germany*, N.Y., 1964.
Littell, Franklin H. *The Crucifixion of the Jews*, New York, 1974.
—— *The German Phoenix; Men and Movements in the Church in Germany*, Garden City, N.Y., 1960.
—— and Hubert Locke, eds., *The German Church Struggle and the Holocaust*, Detroit, 1974.
Locke, Hubert G. *The Church Confronts the Nazis: Barmen Then and Now*, New York, 1984.
Loewenich, Walther von. *Erlebte Theologie: Begegnungen, Erfahrungen, Erwägungen*, Munich, 1979.
Long, Eugene Thomas. *Jaspers and Bultmann: A Dialogue between Philosophy and Theology in the Existential Tradition*, Durham, N.C., 1968.
Löwith, Karl. *Kierkegaard und Nietzsche, oder theologische und philosophische Ueberwindung des Nihilismus*, Frankfurt am Main, 1933.
Luther, Christian. *Das kirchliche Notrecht, seine Theorie und seine Anwendung im Kirchenkampf, 1933-37*, Göttingen, 1969.
Mann, Thomas. *Betrachtungen eines Unpolitischen*, Berlin, 1929.
—— *Nietzsche's Philosophy in the Light of Contemporary Events*, Washington, 1947.
Mannheim, Karl. *Ideology and Utopia: an Introduction to the Sociology of Knowledge*, N.Y.,

1936.
Marty, Martin E., ed. *The Place of Bonhoeffer: Problems and Possibilities in his Thought*, N.Y., 1962.
Masur, Gerhard. *Prophets of Yesterday: Studies in European Culture, 1890-1914*, New York, 1961.
May, Rollo. *Paulus. Reminiscences of a Friendship*, New York, 1973.
Mehnert, Gottfried. *Evangelische Kirche und Politik 1917-1919. Die politische Strömungen im deutschen Protestantismus von der Julikrise 1917 bis zum Herbst 1919*, Düsseldorf, 1959.
Meier, Kurt. *Die Deutsche Christen*, 3rd ed., Göttingen, 1968.
—— *Kirche und Judentum*, Göttingen, 1968.
Merkl, Peter H. *Political Violence under the Swastika: 581 Early Nazis*, Princeton, 1975.
Meyer, Johannes. *Geschichte der Göttinger theologischen Fakultät*, Göttingen, 1937.
Moltke, Count Helmuth James von. *A German of the Resistance: The Last Letters of Count Helmuth James von Moltke*, London, 1946.
Mosse, George L. *The Crisis of German Ideology; Intellectual Origins of the Third Reich*, N.Y., 1964.
—— *Germans and Jews: the Right, the Left, and the Search for a 'Third Force' in pre-Nazi Germany*, N.Y., 1970.
—— *Toward the Final Solution; A History of European Racism*, N.Y., 1978.
—— *The Nationalization of the Masses; Political Symbolism and mass movements in Germany from the Napoleonic Wars through the Third Reich*, N.Y., 1975.
—— ed. *Nazi Culture: Intellectual, Cultural and Social Life in the Third Reich*, N.Y., 1966.
—— and Walter Laqueur, eds., *Historians in Politics*, London, 1974.
Müller, Hans. *Katholische Kirche und Nationalsozialismus*, Munich, 1963.
Neuhäusler, Johann. *Kreuz und Hakenkreuz; der Kampf des Nationalsozialismus gegen die katholische Kirche und der kirchliche Widerstand*, Munich, 1946.
Neumann, Peter. *Die Jungreformatorische Bewegung*, Göttingen, 1971.
Nicholls, William. *Systematic and Philosophical Theology*, Harmondsworth, Middlesex, 1969.
Niemöller, Gerhard. *Die erste Bekenntnissynode der Deutschen Evangelischen Kirche zu Barmen. I. Geschichte, Kritik und Bedeutung der Synode und ihrer Theologischen Erklärung. II. Text, Dokumente, Berichte*, Göttingen, 1959.
—— *Die Bekenntnissynode zu Halle, 1937*, Göttingen, 1963.
Niemöller, Martin. *'God is my Führer', being the last twenty-eight Sermons by Martin Niemöller . . . with a Preface by Thomas Mann*, N.Y., 1941.
Niemöller, Wilhelm. *Kampf und Zeugnis der Bekennende Kirche*, 1948.
—— *Kirchenkampf im Dritten Reich*, 1946.
—— *Wort und Tat im Kirchenkampf; Beiträge zur neuesten Kirchengeschichte*, Munich, 1969.
—— and Günther Harder, eds. *Die Stunde der Versuchung: Gemeinden im Kirchenkampf 1933-1945, Selbstzeugniss*, Munich, 1963.
Noakes, Jeremy. *The Nazi Party in Lower Saxony 1921-1933*, Oxford, 1971.
Oden, Thomas C. *Radical Obedience. The Ethics of Rudolf Bultmann*, Philadelphia, 1964.
Ogletree, Thomas W. *Christian Faith and History; A Critical Comparison of Ernst Troeltsch and Karl Barth*, N.Y., 1965.
Pertiet, Martin. *Das Ringen um Wesen und Auftrag der Kirche in der nationalsozialistischen Zeit*, Göttingen, 1968.
Pressel, Wilhelm. *Die Kriegspredigt 1914-1918 in der evangelischen Kirche Deutschlands*, Göttingen, 1967.
Rauschning, Hermann. *The Revolution of Nihilism; Warning to the West*, New York, 1939.
Reich, Wilhelm. *The Mass Psychology of Fascism*, N.Y., 1970.
Reimers, Karl F. *Lübeck im Kirchenkampf des Dritten Reiches*, Göttingen, 1965.
Ringer, Fritz K. *The Decline of the German Mandarins: The German Academic Community, 1890-1933*, Cambridge, Mass., 1969.
Robertson, E. H. *Christians against Hitler*, London, 1963.
Rubenstein, Richard L. *The Cunning of History: The Holocaust and the American Future*, N.Y., 1978.
Schäfer, Gerhard. *Die Evangelische Landeskirche in Württemberg und der Nationalsozialismus. Eine Dokumentation zum Kirchenkampf*, Stuttgart, 1972.
Schjørring, Jens Holger. *Theologische Gewissensethik und politische Wirlichkeit; Das Beispiel*

Eduard Geismars und Emanuel Hirschs, Göttingen, 1979.
Schmidt, Kurt Dietrich, ed. *Die Bekenntnisse und grundsätzlichen Äusserungen zur Kirchenfrage 1933,* Göttingen, 1934.
Schneemelcher, Wilhelm, ed. *Festschrift für Günther Dehn,* Neukirchen, 1957.
Schneider-Flume, Gunda. *Die politische Theologie Emanuel Hirschs 1918-1933,* Frankfurt am Main, 1971.
Schoenbaum, David. *Hitler's Social Revolution; Class and Status in Nazi Germany, 1933-1939,* Garden City, N.Y., 1966.
Scholder, Klaus. *Die Kirchen und das Dritte Reich. Bd. 1: Vorgeschichte und Zeit der Illusionen 1918-1934,* Stuttgart, 1977.
Schorske, Carl E. *Fin-de-siècle Vienna: Politics and Culture,* N.Y., 1979.
Schultz, H. G., ed. *Tendenzen der Theologie im 20. Jahrhundert. Eine Geschichte in Porträts,* Stuttgart, 1966.
Schütte, Hans-Walter, ed. *Bibliographie Emanuel Hirsch,* Berlin, 1972.
Schwabe, Klaus. *Wissenschaft und Kriegsmoral. Die deutschen Hochschullehrer und die politischen Grundfragen des Ersten Weltkrieges,* Göttingen, 1969.
Schweitzer, Albert. *The Quest for the Historical Jesus: A Critical Study of its Progress from Reimarus to Wrede,* London, 1945.
Shanahan, William O. *German Protestants Face the Social Question. Vol. 1, The Conservative Phase, 1815-1871,* Notre Dame, Ind., 1954.
Siegele-Wenschkewitz, Leonore. *Nationalsozialismus und Kirchen. Religionspolitik von Partei und Staat bis 1935,* Düsseldorf, 1974.
—— *Neutestamentliche Wissenschaft vor der Judenfrage: Gerhard Kittels theologische Arbeit im Wandel deutscher Geschichte,* Munich, 1980.
Sonne, Hans Joachim. *Die politische Theologie der Deutsche Christen,* Göttingen, 1975.
Stern, Fritz. *The Failure of Illiberalism. Essays on the Political Culture of Modern Germany,* N.Y., 1972.
—— *The Politics of Cultural Despair: A Study in the Rise of the Germanic Ideology,* Berkeley, 1961.
—— *Gold and Iron: Bismarck, Bleichröder and the Building of the German Empire,* N.Y., 1977.
Strohm, Theodor. *Theologie im Schatten politischer Romantik. Eine wissenschaftlich-soziologische Anfrage an die Theologie Friedrich Gogartens,* Munich, 1970.
Tent, James F. *Mission on the Rhine: Reeducation and De-Nazification in American-Occupied Germany,* Chicago, 1983.
Thierfelder, Jörg. *Das kirchliche Einigungswerk des württembergischen Landesbischofs Theophil Wurm,* Göttingen, 1976.
Tilgner, Wolfgang. *Volksnomostheologie und Schöpfungsglaube. Ein Beitrag zur Geschichte des Kirchenkampfes,* Göttingen, 1966.
Tillich, Elizabeth. *From Place to Place: Travels with Paul Tillich, Travels without Paul Tillich,* N.Y., 1976.
Tillich, Paul. *The Courage to be,* New Haven, 1952.
—— *Gesammelte Werke,* 14 vols., Stuttgart, 1959.
—— *My Search for Absolutes,* N.Y., 1967.
—— *Morality and Beyond,* N.Y., 1963.
—— *On the Boundary; an Autobiographical Sketch,* N.Y., 1966.
—— *Die religiöse Lage der Gegenwart,* Berlin, 1926.
—— *The Shaking of the Foundations,* N.Y., 1948.
—— *Systematic Theology,* 3 vols., Chicago, 1951-63.
Töpner, Kurt. *Gelehrte Politiker und politisierende Gelehrte: Die Revolution von 1918 im Urteil deutscher Hochschullehrer,* Göttingen, 1970.
Trillhaas, Wolfgang. *Aufgehobene Vergangenheit. Aus meinem Leben,* Göttingen, 1976.
Vorländer, Herwart. *Kirchenkampf in Elberfeld 1933-45,* Göttingen, 1968.
Weinreich, Max. *Hitler's Professors. The Part of Scholarship in Germany's Crimes against the Jewish People,* N.Y., 1946.
Wilhelm, Peter. *Die Synagogengemeinde Göttingen, Rosdorf und Geismar 1850-1942,* Göttingen, 1978.
Willhelmi, Heinrich. *Die Hamburger Kirche in der Nationalsozialistischen Zeit, 1933-1945,* Göttingen, 1968.

Wilson, Edmund. *Axel's Castle: A Study in the Imaginative Literature of 1870-1930,* London, 1954.
Wolf, Ernst. *Barmen. Kirche zwischen Versuchung und Gnade. Zweite, mit einem Nachwort und einem Personenregister erweiterte Auflage,* Munich, 1970.
—— *Kirche im Widerstand? Protestantische Opposition in der Klammer der Zweireichlehre,* Munich, 1965.
Wright, J. R. C. *Above Parties: The Political Attitudes of the German Protestant Church Leadership 1918-1933,* Oxford, 1977.
—— *'Ueber den Parteien'. Die politische Haltung der evangelischen Kirchenführer 1918-1933,* Göttingen, 1977.
Wurm, Theophil. *Christus, Christentum, Kirche. Ein Wort zu den kirchlichen Wahlen,* Stuttgart, 1937.
—— *Erinnerungen aus meinem Leben,* Stuttgart, 1953.
Zabel, James C. *Nazism and the Pastors,* Missoula, Mt., 1976.
Zahn, Gordon C. *German Catholics and Hitler's Wars; a Study in Social Control,* N.Y., 1962.
—— *In Solitary Witness: The Life and Death of Franz Jägerstätter,* New York, 1964.
Zahrnt, Heinz. *Die Sache mit Gott. Die protestantische Theologie im 20. Jahrhundert,* Munich, 1966.
Zillessen, Horst, ed. *Volk-Nation-Vaterland. Der deutsche Protestantismus und der Nationalismus,* 2nd ed., Göttingen, 1970.
Zipfel, Friedrich. *Der Kirchenkampf in Deutschland 1933-1945. Religionsverfolgung und Selbstbehauptung der Kirchen in der nationalsozialistischen Zeit,* Berlin, 1965.
Zoellner, Wilhelm. *Die ökumenische Arbeit des Deutschen Evangelischen Kirchenausschusses und die Kriegsschuldfrage,* Berlin, 1931.

Index

Abraham, 17, 191
Academic freedom, 49, 110, 145, 168
Albright, William Foxwell, 29, 70, 73, 75
'All-encompassing debate about everything,' 151, 163
Althaus, Frau, 98
Althaus, Gerhard, 97-8
Althaus, Paul, 1, 5, 6, 24, 25, 26, 27, 30, 41, 79-119; political stance, 83-98; speech on *Volkstum* to Second Evangelical Church Conference, Koenigsberg, 84-5; relation to *Ansbacher Ratschlag*, 87-9; relation to *Deutsche Christen*, 88-94; hints at disillusionment with National Socialism, 97-8; theological stance, 98-109; doctrine of *Ur-offenbarung*, 99-100; doctrine of 'orders of creation,' 100-2; theology of *Volk*, 102-4; *Zweireichlehre* (doctrine of two kingdoms), 104-7; relation to Jewish question, 107-9; post-1945 experience, 109-15; denazification, 110-12; sense of guilt, 112-15; comparisons with Hirsch, 120, 121, 177, 188-9; friendship with Hirsch, 142, 147; opposition to ecumenism, 143-4; approached by Bishop Marahrens about Hirsch, 167; comparisons with Hirsch and Kittel, 198-200
America, 18, 28, 76, 134, 177, 187, 200
American postwar occupation, 77, 102-12, 114
Amos, 129
Amsterdam, 28
Anglican Church, The, 165
Anhalt, 188
Annexationist policies, First World War, 125
Ansbacher Ratschlag, 87-9, 100, 115
Anti-Jüdische Aktion (a Goebbels organization), 34, 67
Antisemitism, with relation to Kittel, 31-4, 37, 40-1, 43-4, 46, 50, 56-7, 60, 74-6; with relation to Althaus, 84, 95, 115; with relation to Hirsch, 149, 188

Archiv für Judenfragen (a Gobbels publication), 34, 67
Arndt, Ernst Moritz, 91, 93, 106, 139
Aryan, 46, 48, 49, 73, 162
Aryan Paragraph, 48, 108-9, 149
Asmussen, Hans, 87-8
Assimilation, 32-3, 55-6, 64-6, 76
Association of University Teachers Displaced from Office, 192
Athens, 135

Bach, J. S., 162
Baden, 121
Bahrdt, Karl, 7
Balingen Internment Camp, 77
Barmen, the Barmen Declaration, 48, 86-9, 98-100, 104, 177, 186
Barth, Karl, significance for modern theology, 12, 14-18, 20, 21, 23-6, 28, 123; role in Church Struggle, 43, 48, 49, 86, 98, 99, 197; relationship with Hirsch, 127, 139, 145, 149, 158, 160, 167-8, 177-81, 183, 187
Barthians, 93, 98-9, 115, 162, 197
Basel, 21, 177
Bauer, Bruno, 8, 10
Baumgaertel, Friedrich, 167
Bavaria, 88, 97
Bavarian church synod, 85
Bavarian cultural ministry, 110
Bavarian *Landeskirche*, 169, 175
Beatty, Major (education officer during British occupation), 191, 195
Beiträge zur Förderung christlicher Theologie, 83
Beiträge zur Wissenschaft vom Alten Testament, 28
Bekennende Kirsche, see Confessing Church
Belgium, 176
Benckert, Heinrich, 88
Berlin, 36, 45, 66, 121
Berlin Document Center, 35, 166